The
Psychoanalytic
Study
of the Child

VOLUME TWENTY-EIGHT

The Psychoanalytic Study of the Child

VOLUME TWENTY-EIGHT

New Haven and London
Yale University Press
1973

MT

11/9/04

CONTENTS

CONTRIBUTIONS TO PSYCHOANALYTIC THEORY

APPLICATIONS OF PSYCHOANALYSIS

IN MEMORIAM

Bertram D. Lewin
(1896–1971)

The Renaissance Cosmopolite
With Tongue in Cheek

LAWRENCE S. KUBIE, M.D., D.SC.

NO ANALYST CAN BE UNAWARE OF THE FACT THAT TO UNDERSTAND
how the neurotic process develops requires an intimate comparison
of its history in many and diverse individuals. Surely the same thing
is true of the creative process. Creativity depends upon freedom
from neurotic restrictions: freedom for the intake and imprintings of
bits of information not only conscious but especially preconscious;
freedom for their representation, and also for the swift preconscious
ordering, coding, and processing of all such data; freedom for the
quick retrieval of samples of this swift stream, however weighted;
freedom again for the representation of these samples by conscious
symbols and for the rumination, reality testing, and symbolic
communication of that which is retrieved and represented. This is
how we think and create. All of these components enter into the
movement of the human spirit toward creativity—and Bert Lewin
possessed each of these to a unique degree.

Any distortion of any one of these ingredients of the creative
process or of their interdependent relationships plays a role in the

Senior Associate in Research and Training, The Sheppard and Enoch Pratt
Hospital; Clinical Professor in Psychiatry, University of Maryland School of
Medicine.

I

neurotic process. Consequently, if we are to understand how this moves toward creativity in some people and toward neurosis in others, we must study the individual lives of those who are creative as intimately as we study the lives of patients. Furthermore, if biographical writing is ever to make any contribution to human wisdom, it must include data on this level, and not limit itself to dancing a stereotyped and prettified minuet around superficial facts.

Unhappily, this traps us in difficult problems; because even if such studies are not published until after a man's death, they must continue to respect his right to privacy and that of his family as well. This problem has plagued me in my brief biographical studies of Dr. Edward Glover, Sir Gordon Holmes, Dr. Stanley Cobb, and several writers. To write meaningful biography is far from simple.

In this biographical sketch of my well-loved friend, Bertram D. Lewin, I have tried to relate some of the facts of his adult years to some of those of his early life, which I have been able to learn from his family and from his earliest friendships, as I searched for hints as to what made him a precocious child, a prodigy in many fields, and also what protected his prodigious creativity throughout his life. Primarily, I want to give a verbal picture of Bert, the creative, versatile, lovable, loving, and, above all, unpretentious adult.

No one remains throughout life equally creative in every field of interest. As with everyone else, Bert's creativity and his self-critique varied. This too is an important aspect of the general problem; i.e., why creativity persists in some areas more than in others and in some people more than others. I do not pretend that I can answer many of these questions, much less all of them. The most that I can do is to ask them and then to give some hints in a few directions. Yet any biography that is so formal and so conventionally restricted as not to touch on any of them is a mere chronology and not a true biography of the human spirit. No one would have had less patience with such an empty exercise than Bertram David Lewin himself.

Bert was uniquely gifted in many ways—indeed, in so many that one could devote much of this verbal portrait merely to a description of his uniqueness. This starts with his background, which was as original as he was; and we can sense its influence throughout his development. Unfortunately, we do not know enough precise details about any phase of it (not even the exact sequence of all events) to be sure of their interdependent relationships. Perhaps, therefore, it will be safest and most helpful just to sketch briefly what I have been able to gather about his early history and then to paint a picture of the man as I knew him in medical school and thereafter; i.e., from 1917, through 54 years of friendship, until his death on January 8, 1971.

I

In 1892 Bert Lewin's father, Samuel Lewin, married Justine Levy in Victoria, Texas, where Bert was born in November, 1896. About 3 years later they moved to San Antonio, Texas, where Bert lived throughout his elementary and high school years.

In 1922, when Bert was between 25 and 26, his father died. His mother died 20 years later in 1941, when Bert was about 45. While he himself was still a baby, two brothers, one older and one younger, died in their infancies. (The older may have died before Bert was born.) In fact, not many of his early family are left. One cousin is a librarian in Israel; another Israeli works for the U.N. in Rome. Others have visited or lived in various parts of our country, including Topeka, the South in general, and on Long Island, N.Y.

Bert referred to his childhood only rarely; but in *Dreams and the Uses of Regression*, he records a dream in which a strain on his upper body and left arm evoked memories of the steeply inclined streets and the lively horse-and-buggy traffic of his hometown. He had fallen asleep while reading, and while asleep was attempting to hold the book up with his left arm, at the angle of the dreamed street. The tension in the left arm with which he was bracing himself appeared in the dream as a somatic carry-over from his memories of those early years.

There are endless examples of his precocity. In primary school Bert "skipped" two full years to the 8th grade. The teacher (who was also the principal) went out of her way to caution the other students not to be sensitive about his presence in their class, merely because he was 2 to 4 years younger than the rest of them. The class respected her wishes and welcomed Bert as one of themselves. In this warm atmosphere, as a further demonstration of his precocity, Bert went on to win the highest marks in the class.

His interest in science began early in high school. To the pride of the teacher, Bert and two other high school students were able to produce metallic sodium, something which had never before been done in that school laboratory.

During his college years in Texas Bert's roommate was Dr. Daniel Stiefel (now in Detroit). They lived on the same floor with Herbert Davis (now an attorney in San Antonio) and Dr. Sidney R. Kaliski (now semiretired but still practicing pediatrics in San Antonio). To all three of these men, and to some others, besides, I am indebted for the scanty details of Bert's early years.

Bert's parents were deeply German in their roots; and his mother traveled back to Germany frequently both before and after his father's death, often taking Bert with her. The family probably had entered America via Mexico, a country which continued to play an active role in the lives of Bert and his family. These varied influences on his development were evident in every aspect of his personality.

His father's commercial life was built around the wholesale dry-goods industry of Texas and the Mexican economy. This business necessitated many trips into Mexico, on which Bert sometimes accompanied him. In fact, his father sold many things to the Mexicans, including uniforms for the army of Pancho Villa. The only items of clothing of which he had enough in stock to clothe that whole rebellious army were green-striped pajamas. Consequently, these became their standard uniform. Those of us who remember newspaper photographs of Pancho Villa and his army during General Pershing's pursuit of him in the years before World War I will remember those pajamas. When we see them now in ancient photographs of that period, we should drink a smiling toast to the memory of Bert's forebears.

These trips into Mexico and the trips to Germany added to his early firsthand knowledge of the several cultures which made up the Texan communities of those days—the Texas frontiersman; the German communities of central Texas; the Mexican communities in San Antonio and in Mexico itself; and the Indian and Negro cultural heritages as well. All of these became part of him.

After his father's death the only adult male left in the home was his mother's brother; a lovable, relaxed, eccentric small-town salesman. At an early age this uncle taught Bert many things, but especially to smoke and to drink beer and to sing popular and sometimes mildly bawdy Mexican songs. Indeed, this uncle's benign and indulgent temperament can be recognized in many of Bert's later traits.

His mother is variously described as petite (or at least small in stature), vivacious, eccentric, constantly exhorting the chauffeur not to drive 80 mph; yet when he slowed down, she would egg him on to drive more rapidly over the open Texas roads of that period. In short, she was an anxious nagger, self-centered and spoiled, a lover of what today would be called "brinksmanship," and with a particular interest in diamonds.

I have mentioned the early deaths in infancy of Bert's older and younger brothers. This left on him a lasting impression of the vulnerability of early childhood. In later years he often referred to this as something which had first become clear to him in his training analysis in Berlin in the mid-20s: and he believed that this had played a role in the subsequent development of his interest in medicine. These two infant brothers also played a special role in our own personal relationship especially at its inception, although we did not recognize this until many years later. After all, I too was both older and younger (i.e., a few months older than Bert chronologically, but one year behind him in medical school).

Young though Bert was, while still in college he was selected by the president of the university as the outstanding student on the campus, and was chosen to accompany Henry Ford on his "Peace Ship" to Europe during World War I. Two reasons are given for his not going; one was that Ford would not take him because he was Jewish; the other was that his father forbade his participating in this enterprise because he was barely 18 at the time.

Inevitably, his precocity meant that he was always associated in school and college and medical school and hospital not with his age peers but with a group of older fellow students. This had something to do with his developing certain youthful and almost bashful mannerisms, which persisted in some degree throughout his life.

Those who have a clear visual image of Bert's physical presence know that physical coordination was not his forte; not in swimming, sailing, or even dancing. True, he loved the rhythm of the dance as he loved music. Home-grown music played an important role in his early years: ukuleles out of cigar boxes, the mandolin and guitar and ultimately a bass horn, with which the neighbors became all too familiar. But he never cared very much for carefully coordinated movements, largely because they interfered with speech. In fact, as he hitched and shuffled around a dance floor, he never stopped talking long enough to give serious attention to his feet or what they were doing.

The special quality of his shared intellectual excitement and inquiry had first become manifest during his college years in the University of Texas, where it created bonds between Bert and several members of the faculty. When Bert approached Frederick Prokosch for advice about courses in German, quite naturally and without giving it two thoughts, Bert started to speak to Prokosch in the excellent colloquial and idiomatic German with which he had become fluent during his European trips. Because of this, Prokosch took it for granted that Bert also possessed an extensive knowledge of German literature, which in fact Bert gained only in later years. Consequently, when Prokosch asked him, "Was haben Sie gelesen?" Bert was so nonplussed that he was unable to answer; whereupon Prokosch assumed that he had read "everything." Bert stood there frozen, while Prokosch listed Goethe, Heine, Lessing, etc., assuming erroneously that Bert had read all of these and more besides, and ended up by placing Bert, still a freshman, in a senior honors reading course. Unprepared though he was, Bert worked so hard at this that in the end he came through with high honors.

From 1916 to 1920 came his years at the medical school of Johns Hopkins University, followed by 3 years in the Henry Phipps Psychiatric Clinic under Adolf Meyer. In 1923 he went to New York City to the Department of Neuropathology of the New York State Psychiatric Institute (then on Wards Island) where he worked under the late Dr. Charles P. Dunlop. He was fascinated by Dunlop's wonderful skepticism about the excessive claims which were made by Mott, Hunt, and many of the other leading neuropathologists of those times.

II

Let me turn back here to our own first meetings. These had occurred under the tragic shadow of the flu epidemic of 1918. Many nurses and orderlies, faculty members, and medical students were sick and dying; others left. Finally, the medical school itself had to close. My own introduction to the realities of medicine came during those long weeks when I worked as a night orderly on one of the flu wards at Hopkins. There for the first time I saw death close at hand. One who nearly died twice, yet survived, was Bert Lewin; and that is where our friendship began. For as Bert began to convalesce, his irrepressible humor, gaiety, and warmth came through the weakness and diminished the tragic impact on me of these confrontations with illness and death, from which Bert had just escaped.

As I have pointed out, we would have been classmates in medical school had it not been for the fact that I had taken an extra year to do some graduate work in chemistry and physics before starting medical school. Even a difference of only one year makes an enormous difference in the lives of two medical students; because our days were so tightly scheduled that one could hardly see anyone who was not on the same treadmill. However, as we moved along through medical school and then into the hospital, work schedules became more flexible and allowed some time for companionship. This became especially true when we found ourselves together in the Henry Phipps Psychiatric Clinic of the Johns Hopkins Hospital; Bert as a second year assistant resident and myself as a lowly first year intern.[1]

In later years we often wondered how even then our friendship

---

[1] At some point in his years at the Henry Phipps Psychiatric Clinic he developed a desire to study some of the French psychiatrists, particularly Janet, for comparison with Meyer and others. As a house officer he once requested a leave of absence to go to France to pursue this study; but when the hierarchy rather officiously asked why he wanted to go, he said with a characteristic little shrug, "Oh, just to pick violets on the Bois de Boulogne."

had had a chance to ripen when our diurnal rhythms diverged so sharply. Bert, the night owl, was always up late, growing sharper, more articulate and gayer as the hours wore on—then sleeping until he had to be pried out of bed forcibly to get him up in time for morning rounds. My rhythm was the reverse. Yet in spite of this we became friends, with a growmg sense of devoted respect for the many challenging differences in our temperaments, and in our areas of inner freedom and of inhibition. In the course of time we were able to discuss all of this in a freely exploratory spirit of puzzlement.

At this point my memories skip from our years together in medical school and hospital to Bert's last summer in Baltimore before he left for New York. This was a hot summer as only Baltimore summers can be hot. My small family and I had moved into a house near the hospital where, after I had finished on the wards, I would spend many hot evening hours on the top shelf of a ladder, painting the ceiling and the upper walls. And when I climbed down, there Bert would be sitting in an unpainted corner of the floor, a guitar in his arms with a contraption over his shoulders and head which held a harmonica to his lips. While I had painted he had become a one-man band: blowing the harmonica and playing the guitar and singing bawdy Texas songs from his childhood, while we drank together one of the strange concoctions of those prohibition years. Usually this consisted of homemade gin, brewed in the bathtub from oil of juniper and laboratory alcohol and poured over lemon ice from Leo's, the nearby soda shop. That was the standard Hopkins beverage for those hot nights and helped to ease the heat of Baltimore in the months before Bert left for New York.

A few years after he moved from Baltimore to New York City he married Alice Benjamin of New York City on February 5, 1926. Alice was a sister of our recently deceased friend and colleague, Dr. John Benjamin. She shared with Bert not only his interest in literature and music, but also his technical interests; and her death on October 16, 1961 left a gap in his life. This happened at about the time when the survey of psychoanalytic education (see below) came to an end. Bert decided not to return to practice, but moved to the farm in Pipersville, Pa., which he and Alice had owned for many years and where they had many friendships in the country-side both among the local folk and among the writers and artists from New York. Thereafter for the rest of his life he used the farm as his base except for his annual winter journey to Pittsburgh to teach. He transplanted his entire library to the farm and shielded it even from country dirt by hanging long sheets of thin plastic in front of it from ceiling to floor. This left the books visible and accessible yet protected.

Here his children and grandchildren would visit him and sense his enormous joy in the country and in nature. Thus in several ways Bert shared the interests of our old friend and colleague, Smith Ely Jelliffe, whom Bert had looked upon with affection and special interest. Both were bibliophiles, historians, botanists, horticulturists, and natural pharmacologists. All of this came to light in Bert in those years on the farm which he had always loved, but had not been able to enjoy for some years before Alice's death, because of her prolonged illness.

III

It is hard to list, much less to illustrate, all of his gifts: his wit and his lusty humor, his aptitudes for languages, music, mathematics, history, and biography; but above all else, the extraordinary relaxation with which he approached all human problems. In our days at the Phipps the famous head nurse was named Bernadette Mullins. She would sit in on our lectures to the nurses, most particularly of course our lectures on sex—about which, incidentally, most of us knew very little. I can well remember her teasing us by imitating and taking us off; how most of us talked as though we were walking on eggs, and as though there was nobody in the room with us. We talked to the walls, windows, and ceilings. Not so Bert. In Bernadette's version, he was so relaxed that as Miss Mullins said he could have been talking about anything or nothing at all, chuckling as he spoke, half teasingly, half seriously. Sometimes, in his early years, this light touch and this easy, relaxed approach miscarried; as when he offended a patient by speaking of one of his pieces of sculpture as "cute," not meaning this in a derogatory sense.

He carried his remarkable erudition so lightly that many people never realized the depth and breadth of his knowledge. As a minor example, a friend had written an excellent pamphlet on bringing up children, which had been translated into many languages. In Bert's presence the author spoke of one of these as "Arabic." "Not at all," said Bert, "it wasn't Arabic, it was Urdu." This friend could not believe that he was right until she had looked it up and confirmed it.

That same wide-ranging command played into his fun with music and with words. He could recite many wonderful old ditties, such as the English–Hebrew–German–Yiddish poem about the immigrant, called "Die Schönste Lengwisch"; or the story of "Frau Wirtin's dog" which died of urinary retention. And the same relaxed quality expressed itself in his sophisticated tolerance for differences of all kinds, and in his ability to establish rapport with rabbis, priests, bankers, and blue-collar workers, hoydens and suburban dowagers—anybody. All were within range of his humorous, loving, and air-light acceptance. We must add that sometimes this lightness affected and even afflicted his own feelings for himself and for his own enormous gifts.

For his gifts were truly great. Many people have photographic memories. Others have phonographic memories. Bert was one of the few who had both, as showed in his feeling for paintings, etchings, sculpture, for music and for the sounds of words. Everything registered in him. Like the late Harold Laski, even with his eyes closed Bert could find anything in his enormous library without any filing system, finding a book just because he knew where he would be likely to have placed it on his shelves. Then he would riffle through the book and on the left lower side of some page down toward the bottom he would locate the precise quotation he was after; and this without looking up the pagination or even the chapter. He just knew where to look and where to find. This was no mere trick. In retrieving bits of data out of the incessant, swift, and tumultuous stream of preconscious material that poured through his mind, he showed this same capacity to find, to sample, and then to represent the samples by visual and verbal symbols. In this respect, his mind was like a computer. And all of this came to him so easily and naturally that he took it for granted, even depreciating it with a shrug as he depreciated so many of his gifts, never quite realizing the uniqueness of the facility with which his mind worked. Elsewhere I have said of him that he probably had the best-stocked and the most erudite mind that I personally have ever known; and that he carried this more lightly and gaily than I have ever known anyone else to carry so much erudition.

I have also said that this applied not only to thoughts, ideas, words, colors, forms, and shapes, but also to sounds and their relationships to music, to poetry and to mathematics. It made it possible for him to pick up idiomatic language with accuracy almost automatically and without apparent effort: whether this was the stiff formality of adult schooled language, or colloquial slang and the language of the nursery and kindergarten. He could write poetry, both serious and humorous in several foreign tongues; and he could enjoy poetry whether light or serious in those foreign tongues as well. These gifts made vital and close bonds between him and his son, David, who is both a musician and a mathematician, with his son-in-law, Kessel Schwartz, who is a master of the Spanish language and Spanish literature, and with his gifted daughter, Barbara.

When David was a student at Harvard, Bert studied with David some of the recent developments in the graduate courses in mathematics. About this David writes that Bert asked him to go over some of this with him as David was learning it; and that David ended up conducting an informal cram seminar in these new developments. At the same time Bert read with absorbed interest David's notes from a course on the novel, which had been given by Thornton Wilder.

It was remarkable to observe how every informed mind who crossed his path in school and college and later years, whether in person or in a book, left in him a vital, living imprint. There are those hard-working, industrious, leaden-footed students who acquire data only as a stamp collector collects old stamps; not for use. Bert was never one of these. For him everything that entered into his mind became part of a ferment of gay, interested, amusing, and creative activity. Thus he continued to show through the years the influence of all of his earlier associations: whether this was his permissive maternal uncle, the salesman; Stark Young, the critic;

Prokosch, the linguist; Hartman, the geneticist; Sidney Kaliski, later a pediatrician; John Boles, the actor; or Beauford Jester, later the governor of Texas. Furthermore, among Bert's particular friends from his school and college years was the Texan, Maury Maverick, who later became a well-known politician, and who maintained a close and gay friendship with Bert as long as he lived. This is the Texas family from whom the term "maverick" as applied to cattle was derived; and the vital and spontaneous maverick in Bert had some of its roots in this friendly identification, as well as his interest in liberal politics.

Bert ended up with a command of German, French, Spanish, and some Portuguese. To this he later added Swedish and Russian because of his love for Chekhov, Gogol, Pushkin, and Turgenev, and his dissatisfaction with existing translations into English, French, and German (a dissatisfaction which was confirmed by his Russian-speaking friends). He was well started on Chinese and Japanese when other interests and activities and the move from Baltimore to New York made him curtail these particular pursuits. Here we encounter something else which is puzzling. Most of us soon forget what we have learned but do not use. Not so Bert. Everything he had ever known seemed to remain forever available for prompt retrieval, and this despite long periods of disuse.

Perhaps the essence of Bert was his total lack of false reverence. He never bent "the pregnant hinges of the knee" to anyone. The same tendency which led him to take his own gifts for granted, and even to undervalue them, protected him from overvaluing the pretensions of others. Indeed, that with which he probably had the least patience was pretentiousness. I think of the delightful story of Bert being reprimanded by a slightly older member of the hospital hierarchy for not treating a rather pompous European visitor with more respect. Bert responded with wide-eyed and honest amazement, "Why, I just treated him like an equal. I thought he would like it."

Dr. George Boas tells another story which is an example of Bert's humorous rejection of pretentiousness. A woman who set great store by family position and possessions spoke at length of a silver punch bowl which had come down to her through her family from George Washington. She ended by saying, "I would not take a million dollars for it." Bert, dead-pan but with a twinkle said, "I know just how you feel. I know an old man in the Bronx who has a pair of garters that belonged to Moses and he said he would not take two million dollars for them."

During the horrors of the Hitler years, Bert worked hard with a team of colleagues in New York City to secure affidavits which would make it possible to bring many German and Austrian analysts to the United States. His thorough background in German culture made this project a matter of personal as well as humane and professional importance to him. Indeed, so bitterly did he feel about Hitler's total destruction of everything that had been finest in German culture that in all the years since World War II he could never bring himself to visit not only Germany and Austria but any part of Europe. During the war years he did a great deal of work for the U.S. war effort, such as analytic studies of Hitler's writings and speeches, interviews with prisoners of war at Halloran Hospital, etc. Little, if anything, was said of this at the time; but in the long run he made a considerable quiet contribution to our understanding of the forces with which we were contending.

There are those who thought that Bert was cynical, or that he did not value people highly, when in fact he really paid them the highest possible tribute by recognizing their values without exaggerating them. Indeed, no one could have doubted his loving warmth who had ever felt or witnessed his simple, unpretentious, immediate, all-embracing hospitality even to strangers, especially in the wonderful and unforgettable clutter of the old Pennsylvania fieldstone farmhouse in Pipersville. And through all of this the same strain of delightful humor always ran. Witness our visit in 1926 to the Magnus Hirschfeld Museum für Sexual-Wissenchaft in Berlin. The museum had a gallery of portraits of an enormous number of more or less distinguished people, all presumably homosexual. As we left Bert shrugged his shoulders, shook his head, and said, "You know, homosexuals are just like us Jews! Claim all the famous people."

Because things came to him with such extraordinary ease, he had little patience with the word "industrious" (*fleissig*). I remember our visit to the home of his doctor relative in Berlin where we listened to the fiddling of a daughter of whom all were very fond, Bert among them. She was struggling desperately to master the violin. Later after we had listened respectfully to her feeble performance, Bert turned to me and whispered, "They do not say what a good musician she is. They say how *fleissig* she is." Perhaps if Bert had ever felt an inner need to become a performer of any kind (whether in music or art, photography or anything else), he might have discovered why in the lives of many of us to be *fleissig* plays such an important and painful role.

Yet do not conclude from this that Bert himself was lacking in industry. It was just that in the areas in which he cared to be active the flow from thought to action and expression was so effortless that he could not imagine that anyone would have to sweat and labor over it. In a sense, this is true of all prodigies; and Bert was in the deepest sense a prodigy; yet unlike most prodigies he was also a magnificent teacher. This is a rare combination. Just because the prodigy himself rarely has had to struggle to learn, only rarely is he a great teacher. This is why the greatest virtuosi are almost never the greatest teachers and the greatest teachers are never the greatest virtuosi, whether of violin, tennis, or languages.

In part Bert was an exception to this rule. He was a superb example of tolerance and an exponent and teacher of tolerance. Perhaps it was his facility in learning which made it easy for him to tolerate views with which he did not agree. Such differences did not threaten him. For this reason he seemed to some to lack the unsparingly critical attitude which these others felt that *important* issues should command. But "important" was another word that did not often enter into the vocabulary of Bert's value systems. He would accept almost with nonchalance and an amused laugh bits of theory, both in analysis and in other fields, which he knew made little sense. This did not bother him. Ideas were to play with, to take apart and reassemble and re-explore in the process of testing their validity and workability. It was fun to fit the pieces together; and this he could do with superb skill and ease. He had less need to condemn differences than anyone I have ever known. And he could always listen and listen and listen, something so many of us find hard to do. These were some of the traits that made him a superb analyst not only of individuals but also of the psychoanalytic institutes he studied.

As a further consequence, with ease, clarity, economy, and color, in English and in other tongues, he could write poetry, which at the same time was both humorous and serious. In his poetry, humor and solemnity blended with a unique beauty, and he could also put his own ideas together with a singular facility, although not always with unsparing self-criticism. They derived from too many unacknowledged or unspoken premises. This is why some of his theoretical constructs, delightful and "elegant" though the metaphors were, sometimes left some of his more pedestrian and literal-minded friends and colleagues (myself included) puzzled and even baffled.

This catholic tolerance was of special use to him in his role as friend, consultant, and advisor during the survey of psychoanalytic institutes and education, which he and Helen Ross conducted jointly, brilliantly, and with such generosity. Temperamentally it was impossible for them ever to play the role of investigators from a central "Inspector General's Department." To the institutes they were best friends. Therefore they could be frank critics, but never hard or intolerant, always more like the ideal analyst to the patient. Where things had gone wrong, their concern was not to "crack down" but to understand how and why, as a basis for a gradual, therapeutic rectification of error. Because both were gifted with such emotional tolerance for differences, and because they refused to play the role of agents whose duty it was to report back to headquarters, everyone trusted them and confided in them. This special human quality was what made the survey itself supremely creative, therapeutic, and healing, as Bert was himself.

Together with all of his wonderful qualities, Bert sometimes showed a sad and vulnerable side. One of these grew out of his tendency never to appreciate adequately his own special quality. This self-depreciating attitude also showed itself at times in speech, gesture, and body posture; in those quick, half-apologetic, Charlie Chaplinesque gestures with which we were so familiar and for which we loved him, whether he was on the lecture platform or in a discussion with some friend or colleague. I saw it mystify Adolf Meyer, who over my angry protests always underestimated Bert. Meyer took these self-depreciating gestures at face value; not realizing that they were part of the same Bert who could never treat pretentiousness with reverence.

IV

Death came suddenly, mercifully, and exactly as Bert himself would have wished it. In his last years because of glaucoma and other visual difficulties, night driving had not been easy for him, especially in winter. Also a puzzling shadow had been found in the X rays of his chest. For a long time his doctors had feared that it might be malignant; but the final decision was that it was only a scar left by his illness during the flu epidemic of 1918. Nevertheless, in his last years it had deleterious effects on his breathing and heart action. The morning of his death his plan was to drive to a nearby inn where he would leave his car and where the local taxi was to pick him up and drive him to the airport for a trip to Florida first to visit his daughter and her family and then to join some friends for a restful time on an island in the Gulf, thus escaping the rugged weather of the winter months. At about 9:00 A.M. he had chatted with a neighbor on the phone, and commented that it was too early to start for the inn, and that he would first have another cup of coffee. The hours passed and he did not reach the inn to meet the taxi. Finally, in mid-afternoon the caretaker came by to close up the house and found Bert sitting at his desk, a half-emptied cup of coffee by his arm. At first the caretaker thought that Bert was dozing (as I had often seen him doze at his desk during my last visits). But on entering and coming closer he found that Bert's book had slipped from his hand and that in reality the end had come to him swiftly and painlessly as he sat at his desk in that most characteristic posture.

In 1928, I was living in a tiny English hotel while studying in London. There was a stocky little Cockney waitress, with whom Bert used to banter gaily when he visited us there. The day came for him to leave for the States; and she stood watching him going down the stairs and out the door. As the door closed behind him, she shook her head sadly and in her inimitable Cockney said, " 'E was hever so haffable."

Marian Cabot Putnam

ELEANOR PAVENSTEDT, M.D.

MARIAN CABOT PUTNAM DIED ON THANKSGIVING NIGHT IN 1971 OF A heart attack. She was 79 years old. Fortunately she lived to see the publication of *James Jackson Putnam and Psychoanalysis*. During her last years, preparatory work on this book, the selection of letters, and the collaboration with Nathan J. Hale, Jr., its editor, had preoccupied her most of the time. At the party celebrating the publication of this book, she spoke with devotion of her father, whom she deeply revered. She was strongly identified with him and shared his clinical and scientific interests.

Following in his footsteps, she went to medical school. When Harvard Medical School refused to change its policy of not admitting women—despite the protest voiced by James Putnam— she followed other young women from New England to Johns Hopkins.

Just a year before Molly's graduation from medical school in 1921, Edwards Park was invited to Yale to head up the newly established department of pediatrics. Molly joined him in Europe that summer to visit pediatric services. Ned Park subsequently asked Molly to be one of his first interns. The head resident of this group, Martha Eliot, still remembers Molly's sensitive approach to children who invariably responded. It was the human side of pediatrics that interested Molly and in particular the relationship between the child and his parents.

Lecturer in Psychiatry, Tufts University, Columbia Point Health Center, Department of Preventive Medicine, Dorchester, Mass. Professor of Psychiatry, Boston University School of Medicine.

Marian Putnam remained at Yale from 1921 to 1938. Never entirely satisfied with pediatrics alone, she spent several years away: one at Johns Hopkins to train in psychiatry under Adolf Meyer; another at Boston Children's Hospital where she wrote a treatise with Bronson Crothers on "Obstetrical Injuries of the Spinal Cord." In 1933 her interest in psychoanalysis took her to Vienna for psychoanalytic training. She returned to Yale as Assistant Professor of Psychiatry and Mental Hygiene.

A paper written with Ruth Washburn in 1932 entitled "Child Care in the First Two Years of Life" reveals her later spheres of interest. Having studied a small group of children intensively in a well-baby clinic, Molly focused on "behavior expressive of emotional states." Finding the mothers little interested in this aspect of their children's development and failing to follow suggestions, she advocated that mothers be given more education in this important area of child care. She found the mothers equally unprepared for individual differences in the development of their children and learned that their ensuing anxiety could itself create problems in the children. She was eager to study "atypical behavior" in the early months and sought to learn whether this might be predictive of later behavior deviations.

In 1938 Molly returned to her native Boston to concentrate on clinical problems in children during the first 4 years. Her ability to present child development in a warm and lively manner led to her becoming Lecturer on this subject at Harvard and Boston University Medical Schools, at the Massachusetts Institute of Technology, and the Simmons School of Social Work.

While she was on the staff of the Judge Baker Guidance Center, her earlier interest in preventive work grew. She was very optimistic about the modifiability of young mothers, particularly with their first child, and was confident that personality and behavior patterns could be altered during the first 5 years. Out of this conviction grew her determination to found a center where young children could be with their parents in a homelike atmosphere, there to be observed, studied, interviewed, and treated by a multidisciplinary team.

Marian Putnam succeeded in stimulating the interest and support of foundations and friends in her pioneering venture of establishing the first nursery school-child guidance center in this country. In 1942 she acquired a large, old, rambling house in a poor neighborhood and set about canvassing the families of the community with regard to their priorities for their young children. Even then the need for day care and residential care during crises was voiced. During the early years of the center, 60 percent of the referrals came from the catchment area.

The Children's Center was founded in 1943. The original plan was to give nursery care to children of broken homes, to children of unmarried mothers who had unstable relationships to their children and to society, and to children from otherwise strained and unstable families. The nursery setting was to be used for observation as well, so that consultations on young children could be more meaningful than in a psychiatrist's office.

The Center undertook training of students in various fields of child care who were given the opportunity of observing and studying "emotional growth of young children and the beginnings of conflicts which lead to neurosis and delinquency." Training in the treatment of young children and their parents was offered to all allied professionals.

In 1944 when Beata Rank became co-director, the emphasis shifted to young children who were already emotionally disturbed. The nursery school work was closely integrated with the therapeutic process with the child and the casework with the mother. Some mothers remained at the Center for many weeks.

From its inception, the Center had planned to maintain careful case records, which were to be used in research. The main topics investigated were children of psychotic parents, children with atypical development, hyperactive and destructive children, children without fathers. These researches resulted in a number of publications.

In 1946 the Center was incorporated as an independent institution under the name James Jackson Putnam Children's Center. Its existence and prestige had a wide impact. Many clinics for young children were subsequently established around therapeutic nursery schools, and many child guidance clinics throughout this country added a nursery group to their establishment.

In 1949 a Well-Baby Clinic was added to explore the importance of the mother-child unit, and Marian Putnam became its director and served in that function until her retirement in 1955. By this time half the staff of the Center was devoted to the treatment of children with atypical development.

Marian Putnam was on the Editorial Board of this Annual from its inception in 1945. She was on the Board of Trustees of Radcliffe College from 1950 to 1955 and was honored with its Founders Award in 1967.

Those of us who were privileged to share in the early work of the Children's Center were inspired by her devotion to extending our knowledge of early child development, to teaching, to adapting this knowledge to child care education, therapeutic intervention, and to social programs.

Marian Putnam's high-mindedness, self-effacement, utter honesty, and steadfast reliability made her a model for those who knew and worked with her. She was a worthy successor of her father, a pioneer of psychoanalysis in the United States.

ASPECTS OF NORMAL AND PATHOLOGICAL DEVELOPMENT

The Preoedipal Infant-Father Relationship

DOROTHY BURLINGHAM

SOME OF THE MATERIAL USED IN THIS PAPER HAS BEEN EXTRACTED from the literature, i.e., from publications where relations between fathers and their infants are described. Other material comes from personal observations of fathers' attitudes and their behavior toward their young sons and daughters. More important still, it comes from young men who were in analytic treatment or in training at the time their infants were born; I am much indebted to them for their communications. Beyond this I owe the greatest debt to the Baby Department of the Hampstead Child-Therapy Clinic. The staff of the Infant Welfare Clinic, Dr. Josefine Stross, pediatrician, and her assistants Irene Freud and Elizabeth Model have provided a wealth of careful reports in which interaction between the parents and their infants are noted and described in a most useful manner. That in these examples the boys far outnumber the girls is purely accidental.

This paper was presented at a general meeting at the Hampstead Child-Therapy Clinic, London, on January 24, 1973.

The author is on the staff of the Hampstead Child-Therapy Clinic, an organization which at present is maintained by the Field Foundation, Inc., New York; the Foundation for Research in Psychoanalysis, Beverly Hills, Calif.; the Anna Freud Foundation, New York; the Freud Centenary Fund, London; the Grant Foundation, Inc., New York; the National Institute for Mental Health, Bethesda; The New-Land Foundation, New York; the Andrew Mellon Foundation; and a number of private supporters.

Part I

MOTHERS AS CARETAKERS

Mothers as the bearers and caretakers of their infants are considered to be the most important persons in their infants' lives. Motherhood has been depicted in literature and in art as a relationship of beauty, self-sacrifice, and tenderness. Psychoanalytic studies abound on the one hand in descriptions of how mothers love, nurse, and handle their infants, and how infants respond to these ministrations by forming the close mother-infant bond. On the other hand, they portray the serious consequences that ensue when mothers reject or neglect their infants. But, on the whole, whatever is written by most analysts on the early years of children's lives, the important persons described are the mothers—the fathers remain in the background, unimportant, and, apart from the early, primary identification, scarcely mentioned until they come into their own when the children reach the phallic-oedipal phase of development.

I cannot help feeling that this comparative neglect of the preoedipal father not only does an injustice to his role but actually distorts in some manner the fate of the infant-mother relationship. We have to understand on the one hand the existing unity between infant and mother, and on the other hand trace the infant's gradual emergence from this symbiotic state. I have no doubt that the child's relationship to a second person, the father, is instrumental in helping to bring about the progress toward individuation.

Nevertheless, in psychoanalytic writings, the preoedipal father is accorded a minor role. This may be due to numerous observations of cases where an infant at the beginning of life meant little to the father. In many marriages, what is most important to the father at the time of pregnancy and birth is his relationship to his wife, while his attitude toward the offspring of the marriage takes second place. In such cases the father's relationship to the infant proceeds via his relationship to the wife and in response to her needs and moods. Such father-infant relationships can also be pleasurable for both sides, even though they are not built directly on the cues given by the child, but rather are based on the father's wish to keep in tune with his wife's involvement with the baby.

Nevertheless, long before the child has reached the oedipal stage, much has gone on between fathers and their infants. It is the purpose of this study to follow the development of this relationship.

LEGENDS AND FAIRY TALES

In many legends and fairy tales the father is represented as king, as giant, as a ferocious animal, that is, as a masterful being who can destroy, kill, and punish, has power over life and death, and is finally conquered by the hero, the child. The force behind these fantasies is probably oedipal. The child, however, is also pictured as admiring the powerful male, as wishing to copy and emulate him, i.e., the phase in a child's life which precedes the oedipal one.

Equally numerous are the tales of the unwanted infant who represents a threat to the father and is put out to die by him. The best known examples of these themes are the legends of Moses and of Romulus and Remus.

EARLY CULTURES AND PRIMITIVE SOCIETIES

In searching the literature on customs and habits of early cultures and primitive societies only very little is found concerning the role of the father during the infant's early years. Margaret Mead (1957) writes:

> In very primitive societies it is not unusual to find fathers taking a good deal of care of small infants. So among some Australian aborigines, the father, after his morning hunt has been successful, will carry the young infant while the mother gathers vegetable foods. However, no complex society, so far as I have been able to ascertain, no complicated society with a written tradition has ever expected the man of stature and education to care for a baby. Mothers, nurses, female relatives, children, even eunuchs, but not fathers, had the physical care of young infants. So it has been possible to say that there seemed to be no instinctive basis for fatherhood comparable to the instinctive bases of maternal behaviour [p. 374].

In contrast to this, Margaret Mead also describes the male as having an instinctive urge to rescue a small creature in distress, just as in legends and folklore:

> Ethology provides us with many instances of the way in which the male, who pays no attention to his own offspring as such, may respond to the cry of distress of any infant of the same species [p. 375].

Where infants are abandoned to death as a threat to the race, for example, among the Eskimos and Spartans, it is the father who carries out the deed of exposure. Such customs can be found in the case of abnormal infants, the blind, malformed, even twins.

We leave it to the anthropologists, historians, and sociologists to connect the changes in human customs and ways of life with the changes that have occurred in family life and the interactions between family members. We have occasion in our own times to observe far-reaching alterations in the roles of father and mother. I refer here to what is happening in many young couples, especially in the professional classes in the United States, who espouse the Women's Liberation Movement, which so often means liberation from the chores of household and child care. I also refer to the changes brought about by what is called "planned parenthood," and the pill.

THE ROLE OF THE FATHER IN FREUD'S WRITINGS

In Freud's writings the father appears in a variety of roles, though here too stress is laid on the later years of childhood, especially the phallic-oedipal stage, rather than on early infancy. I quote in what follows what I have found under the most appropriate headings: the father as an early object of love, admiration, and identification; as giving bodily care; as a powerful or even omnipotent godlike being; as a comforting protector; as a threatening castrator and inhibiting authority opposed to the child's autoerotic activities and object-directed oedipal wishes; finally, as the authoritarian figure that has to be overcome before adulthood and independence can be reached.

The Father As an Object of Love, Admiration, and Identification

> As regards the prehistory of the Oedipus complex . . . we know that period includes an identification of an affectionate sort with the boy's father [1925, p. 250].

A little boy will exhibit a special interest in his father; he would like to grow like him and be like him, and take his place everywhere. We may say simply that he takes his father as his ideal. . . . It fits very well with the Oedipus complex, for which it helps to prepare the way [1921, p. 105].

[T]here is always an identification with the father in early childhood. This is afterwards repudiated [1939, p. 125].

This leads us back to the origin of the ego ideal; for behind it there lies hidden an individual's first and most important identification, his identification with the father in his own personal prehistory. [Corrected to: his identification] 'with the parents'; for before a child has arrived at definite knowledge of the difference between the sexes, the lack of a penis, it does not distinguish in value between its father and its mother. . . .

At a very early age the little boy develops an object-cathexis for his mother, which originally related to the mother's breast and is the prototype of an object-choice on the anaclitic model; the boy deals with the father by identifying himself with him [1923, p. 31].

The Father As Giving Bodily Care

But this father, whom he [Little Hans] could not help hating as a rival, was the same father whom he had always loved and was bound to go on loving, who had been his model and his first playmate, and had looked after him from his earliest infancy [1905, p. 134].

It is clear that being made to widdle—having his knickers unbuttoned and his penis taken out—is a pleasurable process for Hans. On walks it is mostly his father who assists Hans in this way; and this gives the child an opportunity for the fixation of homosexual inclinations upon him [*ibid.*, p. 20].

The Father As a Powerful or Omnipotent Godlike Being

The common man cannot imagine this Providence otherwise than in the figure of an enormously exalted father. Only such a being can understand the needs of the children of men [1927, p. 74].

[A] man makes the forces of nature not simply into persons . . . but he gives them the character of a father. He turns them into gods . . . not of an infinite prototype but a phylogenetic one [*ibid.*, p. 17].

It had laid open to view the father who had all along been hidden behind every divine figure as its nucleus. Fundamentally this was a return to the historical beginnings of the idea of God. Now that God was a single person, man's relation to him could recover the intimacy and intensity of the child's relation to his father [*ibid.*, p. 19].

The Father As a Great Man

Although in Freud's writing there is little specifically related to fatherhood in the infancy of the child, there are many passages referring to childhood which could be taken to include infancy.

The decisiveness of thought, the strength of will, the energy of action are part of the picture of a father. . . . One must admire him, one may trust him, but one cannot avoid being afraid of him too . . . who but the father can have been the 'great man' in childhood? [1939, p. 109f.]

The Father As a Protector

For once before one has found oneself in a similar state of helplessness: as a small child, in relation to one's parents. One had reason to fear them, and especially one's father; and yet one was sure of his protection against the dangers one knew [1927, p. 17].

As we already know, the terrifying impression of helplessness in childhood arouses the need for protection—for the protection through love—which was provided by the father [*ibid.*, p. 30].

The doctrine is, then, that the universe was created by a being resembling a man, but magnified in every respect, in power, wisdom, and the strength of his passions—an idealized super-man. . . . Our further path is made easy to recognize, for this god-creator is undisguisedly called 'father'. Psycho-analysis infers that he really is the father, with all the magnificence in which he once appeared to the small child. . . . For the same person to whom the child owed his existence, the father . . . also protected and watched over him in his feeble and helpless state . . . under his father's protection he felt safe. . . . He therefore harks back to the mnemic image of the father whom in his childhood he so greatly overvalued [1933, p. 162f.].

The Father As a Punishing Figure, a Threatening Castrator, and Inhibiting Authority

In infantile experiences . . . the father appears as an interferer with the satisfaction which the child is trying to obtain; this is usually of an auto-erotic character [1911, p. 55].

Lying in bed with his father or mother was a source of erotic feelings in Hans just as it is in every other child [1909, p. 17].

His father had told him the lie about the stork and so made it impossible for him to ask for enlightenment upon these things [*ibid.*, p. 134].

But if we look for the roots of such hostility to a father in childhood, we shall recall that fear of a father is set up because, in the very earliest years, he opposes a boy's sexual activities [1916–1917, p. 189f.].

The essential part of this course of events is repeated in the abbreviated development of the human individual. Here, too, it is the authority of the child's parents—essentially, that of his autocratic father, threatening him with his power to punish— which calls on him for a renunciation of instinct and which decides for him what is to be allowed and what forbidden [1939, p. 119].

We have heard already that his [the Wolf-Man's] father had been his admired model. . . . This object of identification of his active current became the sexual object of a passive current in his present anal sadistic phase. . . . By bringing his naughtiness forward he was trying to force punishments, . . . and in that way to obtain from him the masochistic sexual satisfaction that he desired. His screaming fits were simply attempts at seduction [1918, p. 27f.].

It must be that a sense of guilt was attached to the satisfaction in having gone such a long way: there was something about it that was wrong, that from earliest times had been forbidden. It was something to do with a child's criticism of his father, with the undervaluation which took the place of the overvaluation of earlier childhood [1936, p. 247].

While the relationship of son to father is well documented in its reality and fantasy aspects in Freud's writings, there is less to be found concerning the corresponding one of father to child—the father's fantasies in the period between impregnation and birth, and during the first weeks of the infant's life; the father's hopes and expectations concerning the child's growth and development; his jealousies of the mother's preoccupation with the infant; the arousal of his own feminine attitudes; the impact on all these attitudes of his own latent memories of his own father relationships.

By now much has been contributed in these respects from the more recent analyses of adults, and further useful illustrations can be supplied by direct observation. What I quote of the latter is mainly based on experience gathered in the Infant Welfare Clinic of the Hampstead Child-Therapy Clinic (Baby Clinic).

Part II
Relationship of Father to Infant

THE FATHER'S FANTASIES BETWEEN IMPREGNATION AND BIRTH

According to my own experience in direct observation and analytic treatments of a number of fathers, their fantasies concerning the expected child were built around the wish that the boy should be a strong powerful male like the ideal of himself; if a girl, that she would respond to his own loving feelings.

Concerning a firstborn child, fantasies appear to be of two types: that the child should be physically perfect and excel as an athlete, or have superior intellectual gifts, i.e., in both cases, should become famous; that the child should be a loving companion sharing adventures and interests.

Long before overcrowding of the universities rendered this necessary, fathers would apply for their sons' admission to their colleges as soon as they were born.

1. A father of a boy repeatedly imagined taking his son skiing and the pleasure he would have in sharing this sport, which he enjoyed so much himself.[1]

---

[1] In the illustrative examples the source of the material is identified in

2. A former crew captain imagined his son of a few weeks, born with one leg shorter than the other, partaking in a boat race. When he expressed this fantasy, he hesitated and then questioned, "Would this be possible when he is deformed?" His overwhelming wish for his son to be an athlete like himself could be seen, and was soon followed by the narcissistic hurt.

Fantasies regarding daughters frequently concern the many suitors that she will have, the latter obviously representing the father himself.

Other examples show the father's imagined enjoyment of teaching the child, introducing him to the beauty of nature, the fascination of science, objects of art, taking him along on trips around the world.

3. A father fantasied taking his child to the farm which had been so pleasurable for him as a little boy, and showing him all the places where he had hidden treasured possessions. He actually did this when the boy was older.

4. A biologist planned to take his infant where he had collected specimens.

FATHERS DURING MOTHERS' PREGNANCY
AND FIRST WEEKS AFTER BIRTH

Most fathers take little interest in their children until some weeks after birth. The infant remains a part of the mother for a considerable period of time, before he becomes an individual in his own right. However, there are some fathers who experience the infants as their own very much earlier.

One father reported to me that he felt the infant was *his* as soon as the mother knew she had conceived; another, as soon as he was aware that the infant was moving in the mother's body; still another developed this feeling, two weeks after birth, as soon as he could feel the mother was safe.

JEALOUSY OF THE MOTHER'S PREOCCUPATION WITH THE INFANT

During the first months of an infant's life, fathers very often feel unwanted or outcast, because of the mother's preoccupation with

---

parentheses. When such identification is lacking, the material derives either from direct observation or personal communication.

her infant. Feelings of this kind are in direct contrast to the common adoration of the "Madonna with the child," an adoration which may well serve to deny the opposite emotions of jealousy. These jealousies may find a variety of expressions.

5 (Baby Clinic). Tom's mother reports that her husband resents her attention to the new baby and makes angry demands on her.

6. A father timed his wife while she nursed her infant, allowing the infant so many minutes at each breast, and interrupting with the words: "That's enough."

7 (analysis). This father made little mention of his wife's pregnancy and childbirth in his associations, but at home his irritability with his wife was extreme and he turned to incessant piano playing. His wife understood this as an expression of his jealousy and his analysis revealed it as a form of withdrawal to a sublimated form of masturbation.

THE FATHER "MOTHERING" THE CHILD

During the last and the beginning of this century, it was considered unsuitable for a father to be openly involved with the infant's care, as if taking the maternal role in this respect was undignified for a man and betrayed a lack of masculinity. It was considered natural for the man to be repulsed, especially by the infant's eliminations or his vomit, and to hand him over to the mother for cleaning up, diaper changing, etc. Some of these former attitudes are still reflected in the attendancies at the Baby Clinic, where mothers are more conspicuous than fathers. To quote a few figures:

Out of the 42 families attending the Baby Clinic at present,
21 fathers never attended,
14 attended occasionally,
5 frequently,
2 regularly.

The fathers who attend frequently, or regularly accompany their wives, are found to do so for a variety of reasons; they may have an unusually intense involvement with the infant and therefore have a special urge to do so; or they may feel, with or without justification, that the mother is inadequate in some way and cannot be trusted on her own; or they may substitute for the mother to prevent her from missing work; or they may be motivated by their own feminine tendencies and envy of the wife's mothering role.

The fathers who appear in the Baby Clinic only occasionally usually do so because of an emergency in the home, such as illness or hospitalization of the mother, lack of any domestic help.

Nevertheless, on the whole attitudes have changed dramatically in the present generation of young parents who experience it as wholly natural for both partners to take turns in looking after the infant's need, and not to distinguish between a maternal and paternal role in this respect.

8 (Baby Clinic). Stephen's father had shared in the baby's care to a larger extent than is usual. One reason for this was that the mother had a damaged elbow from an accident in the child's early months.

9. A father of twins, a teacher, was the greatest support to his wife who had no one else to help her. When the mother returned from the hospital with just one twin, he helped in caring for this child in every way he could. Later when the other twin came home and he was not teaching, he cared for one twin while the mother cared for the other.

10 (Baby Clinic). Doris's father (the husband of a partially sighted wife) reported at the Baby Clinic that he himself was one of 13 children, his mother having done everything. However, with his infant he supported his wife and helped care for the baby. Nevertheless, when the girl was $5\frac{1}{2}$ months old, he reported that he ceased to feed the baby, this being his wife's job now. This father showed his willingness to care for the baby so long as it was a necessity, but desisted when the need was no longer present.

11. Both father and mother were studying for their degrees and it was financially important for them to finish as soon as possible. The parents arranged to take turns in studying and caring for the baby.

12 (Baby Clinic). John's mother was a musician before marriage. She took up work again to enable the father to finish his studies while at the same time minding the baby.

13 (Baby Clinic). The mother of Jack had worked before the baby was born, and had enjoyed the contact with other workers. Now she resented that she was so much alone, cooped up with the baby. She found part-time work and arranged for a baby-minder. Although this proved a failure, she continued to look for work and a place where she could leave her child. Thus emergency situations arose when the father had to care for the child. Finally, he took on nightwork to be free to care for the child during the

day. This did not prevent the child from deteriorating markedly, after having made good progress under the mother's care.

14 (analysis). A young architect, married to a woman who had worked before her marriage, would find his wife unhappy, irritable, and depressed in the evenings, reproaching him for his involvement with his work, for being always away from home, for having no time for her. Unable to soothe her, he found comfort in mothering his child.

15 (Baby Clinic). Both parents of George were lecturers, and it was possible for the father to care for his son in his free time. The mother minded giving up her work and weaned the baby at 5 months. In the first year the father took over a great deal of care of the baby, fed him and even prepared his bottles. It was the father who went to George at night as he could settle him better and the infant turned to him for comfort. At 14 months the report from the Clinic was that the infant was developing remarkably well.

The Father's Own Maternal Attitudes

In some instances the choice of partner in marriage was found to be based on the father's maternal attitudes and their corresponding absence in the mother; this gave the husband the opportunity to take over a role which coincided with his own wishes. From the beginning it resulted in interferences with the mother's management, criticism of the way she handled the child, and competition with her in the care of the infant. Such fathers may love the actual handling of the child's body as shown in the following examples.

16 (analysis). Simm's father told how he loved the feel of the baby in his arms and how he loved to kiss him.

17 (analysis). Tom's father could not stand the crying of his child and enjoyed his ability to soothe him. Like other fathers of this type, he was apt to respond to the child's crying in the night before the mother did.

18. Jeremy's father told how he loved to stroke the baby.

19 (analysis). The analysis revealed the father's wish to play the woman's part and take over all the mothering activities, such as bathing, feeding, potting, getting the children to sleep, even doing the washing.

20 (analysis). The father frequently investigated the child's testicles, allegedly to see whether they had descended or not. In this case, as in similar ones, the father's use of the child to satisfy his own needs is obvious.

THE IMPACT OF THE FATHER'S RELATIONSHIP TO HIS OWN FATHER

What cannot be left out is the impact of the father's relationship to his own father and the determining influence of this on his relationship to his child even as an infant. We have found that whatever handling the father experienced from his own father, whether it has been loving, unfeeling, secure, lenient, understanding, or inconsistent, this affects his own attitude and behavior toward the child. Such similarities of behavior are often noticed and remarked upon by members of the family, uncles and aunts. Exclamations such as the following are frequent: "Why must you be so strict with John? You do just as your father did with you." "Can you not stop spoiling Mary?! You were spoiled in just the same way by your father."

Fathers occasionally tell that they are themselves aware of imitating their fathers. At other times they consciously attempt to behave differently but may act just as their fathers did, although this is against their better judgment. The unconscious determinants of such behavior show up in analysis.

21. A father reported how his wife objected to the passionate way he kissed his little child—he reported that his father had kissed him in that way.

22. A mother told of how her husband had suddenly shaken the baby because she cried so unceasingly—she added, "not like him at all." Some time later he remembered how his father used to get cross with him and suddenly shake him.

Part III
Relationship of Infant to Father: Interactions

After dealing with the father's adjustment to the expectation and birth of the baby, I turn now to the actual interactions between father and infant.

EYE CONTACT

One of the earliest contacts between father and child is through looking at each other.

23. At 5 months, Jane was reported by her father to be looking at him while nursing, then turning back to mother's breast. When she saw her father and was hungry, she turned away from him, but at other times greeted him with smiles and laughter.

24. Julie's mother reported that when Julie was at the breast she would look up at her father and then return to nursing.

25 (Baby Clinic). At a few months, Morris seemed to have a special relationship with father through their looking at each other.

26 (therapist's observation). Father and Morris (7½ months) seemed to communicate with each other by looking at each other from a distance, laughing and just looking.

SMILING RESPONSE

It is not only the mother's relationship to the child which is strengthened and confirmed by the infant's smiling response. Fathers, in a similar way, are encouraged in their actions by the child's answering smile or other, similar reactions.

27. A mother of twins reported that at the age of 6 weeks, while she was feeding one twin, the father was giving the bottle to the other, and it was he who received the twin's first smile.

28 (Baby Clinic). At 6½ months, father nuzzled Carol and made farting sounds with his lips. She responded with big smiles and began to move her legs and arms.

29. The father of baby Tom (See #5), who was reported to be jealous of his wife's attention to the baby son, started to pick him up as soon as the infant began to smile at him. It seemed that this smiling contact was irresistible—and a bond between them was created.

30 (analysis). A father was afraid of handling the infant in case he might hurt him, but lost this fear when his son began to smile at him.

This budding relationship grows further according to the amount of time and attention the father devotes to the child.

31 (Baby Clinic). As soon as father comes into the room, Jane (4 months) laughs at him.

32 (Baby Clinic). Mother reports that John (4 months) babbles like mad to his father.

33 (Index). Mother reported that father had said that Clare was out to charm him as early as 5 months, and by the time she was 6½ months old, father was devoted to her.

Like mothers, who generally have the inclination to soothe, cuddle, and show affection in gentle ways, fathers also commonly handle their infants gently in the beginning, often due to fear of hurting the baby.

34 (Baby Clinic). Father's envy of Morris does not seem to interfere with his pleasure in him, for it is he who discovers many different ways in which the baby enjoys physical stimulation.

FIRST FEELING OF CONTACT

35. One father felt this in the first weeks when the baby snuggled in his arms.

36. From the 12th week, this father felt the baby relaxing in his arms. He used to sing and hum to the baby while holding her in his arms.

37. This father used to walk about with the infant in his arms, who responded to smiles.

38. This father handled the baby tenderly, enjoying his ability to soothe the baby when his wife was unable to do so. He enjoyed soothing the crying child and liked to stroke him.

STIMULATION AND ENJOYMENT

As the fathers' confidence grows, they become increasingly active in producing pleasurable responses from their children. They bounce, tickle, and tease them at an early age, and the answering chuckle or excited laughter invites the repetition of this type of amusement.

Since at this early age there is little difference in the muscular development of boys and girls, fathers react to this and make little differentiation in the way they play with either. We might say that the infant, whether male or female, is treated by the father as if it were a symbiotic addition to his own masculinity.[2]

39 (Baby Clinic). Father was gentle with Anne (3½ months), rocked and bounced her.

40. Mother reported that from the time Arthur was 6 weeks old, father stroked Arthur's head and tickled his chin, which invariably evoked a smile and later laughter.

41. Father would take his twin sons in turn doing acrobatic leaps with

---

[2] Of course, this lack of differentiation between boys and girls does not extend to other areas of the fathers' interaction with them. So far as the fathers themselves are concerned, they usually react to their male children as replicas of themselves, whereas they relate to their daughters in more complex ways, influenced by their attitude to femininity in their early object relationships and the feminine part of their own natures. It remains an open question how far there are innate qualities in the little girls' attitudes to which the fathers respond.

them in his arms to a Gilbert and Sullivan tune, the twins laughing uproariously.

42 (Baby Clinic). When Donald was 9½ months old, the father asked his wife to get a ball; holding his son by his arms, he swung him so that his legs hit the ball. Donald greatly enjoyed being swung around and hitting the ball with his legs.

43 (Baby Clinic). When Morris was 10 weeks, his father stroked the soles of Morris's feet while holding the foot in his hand, which Morris seemed to like and which seemed to pacify him.

44. Father enjoyed dangling his 8-month-old daughter above him in the air as he lay on the floor. She greatly enjoyed this.

45. At 11 months, the daughter enjoyed father teasing, tickling her, and playing with words.

Much more than mothers do, fathers tend to stimulate and excite their children. They not only lift them, but swing and toss them in the air, catching them again or even pretending to let them fall, which provokes frightened, but at the same time pleasurable, excited laughter. As the child grows older, the father can allow himself more freedom in his handling and become rougher in answer to the child's evident pleasure. Observers usually react with an exclamation of fear that the child will be hurt.

46 (Baby Clinic). Caroline (6 months 3 weeks) was irritated and then cried, but when the father picked her up, held her, and lifted her up in the air, she calmed down and became preoccupied with him.

47 (Baby Clinic). While Derek (9½ months) was being changed, the father held him on his lap, then lifted him up in the air.

48 (analysis). A woman patient, who observed her brother tossing his little daughter high in the air, could not understand how this could be allowed and wished to interfere.

49 (analysis). As a latency child John reported a recurring nightmare of a tall, bearded man with a "terrible face" who terrified him by lifting him up high, then dropping him. He had a sleep disturbance from 2 years.

50 (treatment). Basil, a borderline child in treatment, often talked of the lovely games mother's friend played with his younger brother, like tossing him in the air, which he longed to have done to him. It seemed as if Basil could not conceive of gaining pleasure and well-being in any but the most primitive experiences of body contact, and feeling states aroused by being adored and admired. Whenever experiences he must have enjoyed, like being tossed up in the air by his father, were reconstructed, Basil's face lit

up with pleasure and he often remarked: "I like going back to these old days."

That games of this kind cause specific sensations in the child is not an unknown factor as the following quotations from Freud's writings show:

[T]he existence, then, of these pleasurable sensations, caused by forms of mechanical agitation of the body, is confirmed by the fact that children are so fond of games of passive movement, such as swinging and being thrown up into the air, and insist on such games being incessantly repeated (1905, p. 201].

[They relate, that is, to games involving movement, which are extraordinarily attractive to children. . . . There cannot be a single uncle who has not . . . [played] by holding him up high and then suddenly pretending to drop him [1900, p. 271].

Once when Pharaoh had taken him [Moses] in his arms and playfully lifted him high in the air, the little three-year-old boy snatched the crown from the king's head and put it on his own [1939, p. 32].

And from a different source:

Shu . . . with his twin sister . . . was created by Ra. . . . He threw them violently apart and elevated Nut high into the air, where he maintained her with his upraised arms.[3]

It remains an open question whether for the infant these pleasurable activities increase sensations already stimulated by the mother or whether they awaken new and different ones, specific to the father relationship; for the fathers these overtures are expressions of active impulses of their own, and we may assume that the child's whole body symbolizes for the father part of his own body, i.e., the penis, its erection.

As the child matures and acquires motility of his own, he himself may become the initiator of games, thereby *reversing the role of father and child.*

---

[3] *New Larousse Encyclopedia of Mythology* (London: Hamlyn, 1968, p. 13).

It appears that in watching the two main figures in a ballet, the moment of greatest pleasure is when the man at the height of the dance lifts the woman high in the air and holds her there for a moment. This may be in adulthood a replica of the early father-child experience.

In games such as these, the child now actively takes over the father's former method of attracting attention, i.e., by teasing and provoking. The former play, far from being given up, has now become a true interaction, i.e., *reciprocal.*

51. Richard, a toddler, sits on his father's lap and tries to open his father's mouth; when the father allows him to do so, he jerks away as if frightened and attempts to get off the father's lap.

52. Jane (2½ years) is behind her father's chair, father reading his newspaper. She peeks around looking at him. When he notices her and makes to pick her up, she scuttles away screaming—clearly inviting him to chase her.

53. John (2½ years) notices father is holding his teddy, snatches it from him, and runs away with it, expecting his father to catch him.

54 (Baby Clinic). Morris reaches up to father's empty mug, and he and father have a game. Father pretends to give the empty mug to Morris while holding on to it. They alternately blow into it, making a variety of noises, which Morris seems to enjoy. There is also a good deal of looking at each other from a distance, or standing close together. Father sometimes holds him in a mothering way.

55. This game started when the baby girl was 6 months. Father made a tent out of the bedclothes, which later developed into playing "house" together, the little girl putting blankets over chairs.

PREFERENCE FOR THE FATHER

Although we normally expect the infant's early tie to the mother to be closer than that to the father, this is not always the case. Preference for the father may begin for many reasons, usually at a time when father *substitutes* for mother during her absence, her hospitalization, or any other limitation of her care, either temporary or permanent. The child then turns to the father, expecting from him what the mother is unable to provide.

56 (Baby Clinic). This mother was an immature person, but with her second child, Mark, she was more secure and the father was less involved in the care of the second child. At 1¼ years, Mark was very attached to his father and would always leave his mother to go to him. At 1½ years, he preferred his father when he was upset, called for him, and stopped crying as soon as he was lifted up by him. At 1¾ years, in the course of a medical examination, he called through his tears, "Daddy come here!"

57 (analysis). At 17 months, this little boy continued to turn to father for comfort. He had had a strong reaction following a measles vaccination and only wanted his father when he felt miserable.

58 (Baby Clinic). Simon's mother said that at 2 years, he was very attached to his father: "He has fun with my husband; he calls through the letter box to my husband when he is not at home."

59 (Baby Clinic). Peter's mother reported that when Peter was completely weaned (11½ months), he refused the bottle from her, but took it from father.

60 (Baby Clinic). Doris's mother is partially sighted; at the Baby Clinic, it was the father who could quiet the baby (at 11 months) and who carried her more securely (at 22 months).

61 (Baby Clinic). Jack was a baby who had been deserted by his mother. When he was being vaccinated at 2 years, his father could comfort him and yet be firm enough to avoid a battle and mounting panic.

62 (Baby Clinic). Simon's mother had a damaged elbow which during his early months made it difficult for her to handle him. When Simon was a little over 3 months old, she reported, "I think Simon likes it with my husband; he has more fun with him." At 11 months, when Simon was held by his mother, he struggled to get away from her to father.

63 (Baby Clinic). When Robert was 7½ months old, his mother had to nurse an ill relative. During the month she was away Robert enjoyed being cared for by his father. After she returned home, Robert refused to go to her for some time. She was pleased when he finally turned to her spontaneously and stopped crying for his father.

64 (Baby Clinic). At 11 months, Morris protested when his father left him. He crawled after him, kept looking at the closed door, and cried.

65 (Baby Clinic). Brian (15¼ months) was very fond of his father. He watched with fascination while the father was shaving himself; and he liked to talk to his father while he was having his bath.

66 (Baby Clinic). Jake was unwanted by both parents. The parents had passionate quarrels in which they used the infant as a bone of contention. The mother told us about one such scene when Jake was 18 months old. The father snatched the baby away from her, and she tried to pull Jake back while Jake was clinging to his father and screaming that he wanted to be with his father.

We have found that, as the child gets older, he shows more and more pleasure at the thought of the father, in expectation of his arrival and in his presence. He turns away from accustomed daily routines to new and exciting experiences that father gives him.

That such preferences need not always be occasioned by a failure of the mother is shown in the following observation as reported by the father of a toddler whose tie to the mother is an extremely happy and good one. I quote in what follows the father's report from 8 months onward:

1. In situations which might be termed stressful or anxiety-evoking, Erik definitely turns to me and not to his mother for comfort when he has a choice. Such situations include people who are relative strangers to him visiting our home; his catching his finger in some painful way; his falling and hurting himself, etc.

2. When my wife and I are together at home, he will cry much more vigorously at my leaving than at her leaving.

3. Recently, in the past months or so, he has required that he be held on the lap before falling asleep. Clearly he prefers me to his mother.

4. When people who are strangers to him visit our home, after an interval period of distress, Erik does try to play up to them and make friends. Here too he prefers my lap to his mother's as a "base of operations" to which to take flight until he feels fully comfortable.

Thus, a child may turn to his father, rather than to his mother, for comfort even in situations which might be termed stressful and anxiety-provoking.

GREETING FATHER AFTER ABSENCE

67. Before Dorothy was 1 year old she showed great joy whenever her father entered the room. She would ecstatically shout, "Daddy, daddy," and stretch out her arms to be picked up.

68 (Baby Clinic). By 5 o'clock Susan (2 years) is usually tired and cross, but as soon as her father comes home she is happy again.

69. Arthur (23 months) is always expectant when he sees a black car, hoping Daddy is in it.

70. Mother reports that both twins, from an early age on, were always delighted to see their father.

71 (Baby Clinic). Father arrived unexpectedly. Susan (11½ months) was delighted to see him, smiled, held up her hands to him, and when he took her, did not want to go back to mother.

72. The father yodeled as he came to the house. Jane (1 year) was

having her bath as usual. Hearing her father, Jane got very excited, bouncing on the tub as toddlers do on their chairs while waiting for food.

73 (Baby Clinic). Martin's father came home after a three-weeks' concert tour and woke Martin up. Martin (16 months) was happy to see him and stayed awake for hours.

DEMANDING FATHER'S CARE FOR SPECIFIC REASONS

It seems that infants turn to their fathers when their mothers are overanxious or depressed. The infant reacts to the atmosphere of strain created by the mother's excessive anxiety, which the infant experiences as unpleasant and as unresponsive to his needs. The depressed mother is involved with herself, not with the child, leaving the infant feeling empty and dissatisfied. In these circumstances, if the father is available, the infant turns to him for comfort, security, and pleasure. This has many times been observed and especially noted in the Baby Clinic.

74 (Baby Clinic). At 13 months, John turned to his father for comfort, probably because the mother tended to be overanxious.

75 (Baby Clinic). At 16 months, David settled better at night if his father went to him when he woke up. His mother is an anxious mother.

76 (Baby Clinic). The father is very important to Tom, whose mother has a severe depression.

77 (Baby Clinic). Barry turns more to father when mother is disturbed and father calm.

78. Teddy's father was most concerned about mother's needs and her moods. He would try and amuse the child to spare mother, or to let her get on with household chores.

DEMANDING FATHER'S CARE FOR SPECIFIC SERVICES, OR AT SPECIFIC TIMES

79 (Baby Clinic). John's mother does not cuddle him, but the father does, and John turns to father for this sort of affection.

80 (Baby Clinic). At 2 years 1 month, it is father who puts Susan to bed. Mother finds it difficult to accept that Susan prefers father at bedtime.

81 (Baby Clinic). At 2¼ years, Tom wants his father in the mornings.

Some fathers will take over the infant's care at night to spare the mother, and some will hear the child crying before the mother does.

Some infants will prefer the father's care at this time, and will be more easily comforted by him. This may or may not be due to the mother's resentment of having her sleep disturbed.

82 (Baby Clinic). Mother reports that father is always the first to hear David (7 months) and usually the first to go to him.

83 (Baby Clinic). Donald (16 months) settles better when father goes to him in the night.

84 (Baby Clinic). Sarah (18½ months) sleeps well once she knows that father is in the house.

85 (Baby Clinic). Martin (2¾ years) tends to have bad dreams if he is upset, and at these times settles more readily if he is handled by his father.

86 (Baby Clinic). Susan's mother started to put her to bed later, as she felt the child never really settled until father came in.

87 (Baby Clinic). David, at 16 months, woke two or three times in the night and settled better if father went to him. Quite often it was enough if father picked him up, walked downstairs with him, told him everything was in its place, and put him back in his cot.

At 17 months, David still woke up at night, but father could settle him very quickly.

NEGATIVE REACTION TO FATHER

Infants do not always respond with pleasure to the father's overtures. At the age of 8 months when stranger anxiety sets in, it is often the father who is the first recipient of this reaction. Children may panic when the formerly much-loved father enters the room. The fathers are deeply hurt by this, even if they are knowledgeable enough to realize that the reaction is a differentiation of one person from another, the mother, and that it is a forward step in development.

Other reasons for the child's turning away from the father are the father's changing moods, anger shown in behavior and manner of speaking, going too far in rough games, disharmony and noisy quarrels between the parents.

88 (Baby Clinic). Barry at 2¼ years no longer liked the rough games with his father.

89. As an infant, he loved the bear hugs his father gave him, but as a toddler they became too much for him and he appeared afraid. It is

interesting that this same child, as an adolescent, greets his father with these bear hugs which are now too fierce for the father to enjoy.

CONCLUSIONS

I feel that it is these mutual relations between infant and father, as well as the impact of this interaction, which had to be added to what we already know about the infant's emotional life: on the one hand, to the infant-mother relationship and its implications; on the other hand, to our knowledge of early primary identification with a powerful father figure and the child's much later oedipal rivalry with the father.

According to the clinical experiences described above and the examples given, the infant's emotional responses to the father differ from those to the mother in the degree to which their personalities, their roles in caretaking, and their types of handling differ. Maternal care is more gentle, soothing, and comforting, while paternal involvement is more active, exciting, stimulating, and occasionally also arouses discomfort and anxiety. With regard to maternal care, the infant is above all a passive recipient, while paternal care is more likely to produce active reactions in the child.

I agree with the objection that this generalization may be misleading insofar as it is based on the idea of predominantly feminine mothers and predominantly masculine fathers, i.e., a constellation which is not matched by what we meet in many ordinary families. Moreover, the distinctions between motherly and fatherly care are further lessened by present-day attitudes and realities. Our picture changes where the infant's care is indiscriminately divided between the parents, both fulfilling the same needs and tasks, according to time, work, or other preoccupations. The result in the child's mind might well be the "combined parent" image which at one time used to figure prominently in analytic literature. Or, the father, according to his personality, may be the gentle, comforting agent, the mother according to hers the livelier, rougher, and exciting one. Such a reversal of roles between the parents will naturally lead to reversed responses in the child. In all those instances where the special care of the children weighs heavily on the wife and interferes with her more lighthearted responses, the husband, less burdened, may be more ready to enter with a purely pleasurable father-infant relationship.

In any case, I cannot help feeling that in spite of and beyond the complexities of parental characters, and also in spite of the alleged modern equality of the sexes, many of the either female or male characteristics of the parents will continue to exist and, in response to them, the infant's differentiated emotional reactions and differentiated experiences of pleasure. If it were not so, the decrease in variety of experience might well prove to be a loss to the child and show up later in the development of a flatter, more uniform, and less rich affective life.

BIBLIOGRAPHY

FREUD, S. (1900), The Interpretation of Dreams. *Standard Edition*, 4 & 5. London: Hogarth Press, 1953.

——— (1905), Three Essays on the Theory of Sexuality. *Standard Edition*, 7:125–243. London: Hogarth Press, 1953.

——— (1909), Analysis of a Phobia in a Five-Year-Old Boy. *Standard Edition*, 10:3–149. London: Hogarth Press, 1955.

——— (1911), Psycho-Analytic Notes on an Autobiographical Account of a Case of Paranoia. *Standard Edition*, 12:3–82. London: Hogarth Press, 1958.

——— (1916–1917), Introductory Lectures on Psycho-Analysis. *Standard Edition*, 15 & 16. London: Hogarth Press, 1963.

——— (1918), From the History of an Infantile Neurosis. *Standard Edition*, 17:3–123. London: Hogarth Press, 1955.

——— (1921), Group Psychology and the Analysis of the Ego. *Standard Edition*, 18:67–143. London: Hogarth Press, 1955.

——— (1923), The Ego and the Id. *Standard Edition*, 19:3–66. London: Hogarth Press, 1961.

——— (1925), Some Psychical Consequences of the Anatomical Distinction between the Sexes. *Standard Edition*, 19:243–258. London: Hogarth Press, 1961.

——— (1927), The Future of an Illusion. *Standard Edition*, 21:3–56. London: Hogarth Press, 1961.

——— (1933), New Introductory Lectures on Psycho-Analysis. *Standard Edition*, 21:3–182. London: Hogarth Press, 1964.

——— (1936), A Disturbance of Memory on the Acropolis. *Standard Edition*, 22:239–248. London: Hogarth Press, 1964.

——— (1939), Moses and Monotheism. *Standard Edition*, 23:3–137. London: Hogarth Press, 1964.

LEONARD, M. R. (1966), Fathers and Daughters. *Int. J. Psycho-Anal.*, 47:325–334.

MEAD, M. (1957), Changing Patterns of Parent-Child Relations in an Urban Culture. *Int. J. Psycho-Anal.*, 38:369–378.

STOLZ, L. M. et al. (1954), *Father Relations of War-Born Children.* Stanford: Stanford University Press.

WEISSMAN, P. (1963), The Effects of Preoedipal Paternal Attitudes on Development and Character. *Int. J. Psycho-Anal.*, 44:121–131.

The Primal Scene

A Review and a Reconsideration

AARON H. ESMAN, M.D.

AMONG THE CLINICAL CONSTRUCTS OF PSYCHOANALYSIS FEW HAVE BEEN more widely entertained than that of the "primal scene." The view that the child's observation of parental sexual intercourse will have a critical, and usually damaging, effect on his subsequent development has been extensively enunciated in the literature. It has had a significant effect on child-rearing procedures and domestic arrangements, at least among middle-class Western families, and child guidance practice has been materially influenced by it. In recent years a number of writers have proposed far-reaching evolutionary and cultural derivatives of this individual experience; on the other hand, Freud suggested a phylogenetic base for its emergence in the individual's life.

It will be the purpose of this essay to review the background of this concept of primal scene trauma, to trace its evolution in the literature of psychoanalysis, and to reassess its status within the framework of current thinking in psychoanalysis and behavioral science in general. I shall begin by reviewing Freud's thoughts on the matter and then survey the contributions of other analysts. I shall also review some of the relevant anthropological and cultural data, and refer briefly to some recent pertinent contributions to the theory of trauma.

Dr. Esman is Chief Psychiatrist, Jewish Board of Guardians, and a member of the Faculty of the New York Psychoanalytic Institute.

REVIEW OF THE PSYCHOANALYTIC LITERATURE

FREUD'S IDEAS ON THE PRIMAL SCENE

From the very beginning of his psychoanalytic work Freud was impressed by the pathogenetic import of what he called "primal scenes." In his letters to Fliess of 1896–1897, he referred repeatedly to the influence of such repressed mental content on the development of hysterical symptoms. The arousal of a "sexual scene" would lead to a surplus of sexual excitation, which would result in a conversion symptom as a pathway of discharge (1950, p. 230). The repressed "primal scenes" tend to generate impulses which threaten to break into consciousness and must be warded off by the conversion process (p. 247f.).

The first clinical report of the pathogenic effects of the observation of the primal scene appeared in the case of Katherina in *Studies on Hysteria* (1893–1895). The young peasant girl dated the onset of her hysterical attacks to observation of sexual intercourse between her uncle and his paramour. The overwhelming stimulation experienced on that single occasion was the source of the sexual excitement contained, and yet disguised, in her symptoms.

It was in *The Interpretation of Dreams*, however, that Freud (1900) made the most explicit statement of his early views on the significance of the primal scene. In the course of analysis of a dream in which a primal scene observation at age 9 was reconstructed, he stated, "It is . . . a matter of daily experience that sexual intercourse between adults strikes any children who may observe it as something uncanny and that it arouses anxiety in them. . . . [W]e are dealing with a sexual excitation with which their understanding is unable to cope . . . and which is therefore transformed into anxiety" (p. 585). Needless to say, Freud conceived of the traumatic effect of primal scene observation here in the terms of his then current anxiety theory, i.e., that undischarged sexual excitement is transformed into anxiety.

In *The Psychopathology of Everyday Life* (1901) Freud described a young woman who "suddenly flung open the door of the consulting room" while the previous patient was still there. This reproduced in the analytic situation "the curiosity that in the past had caused her to make her way into her parents' bedroom" (p. 214). Nothing is said here of the pathogenic effects of any observations thus made.

In the Dora case, however, Freud (1905a) once again offered a reconstruction of a specific connection between the patient's adult symptomatology and a childhood primal scene experience. "Dora's symptomatic acts and certain other signs gave me good reason for supposing that the child, whose bedroom had been next door to her parents', had overheard her father in his wife's room at night and had heard him . . . breathing hard while they had intercourse. Children, in such circumstances, divine something sexual in the uncanny sounds that reach their ears . . . in many cases, as in Dora's, I have been able to trace back the symptom of dyspnoea or nervous asthma to the same exciting cause—to the patient's having overheard sexual intercourse taking place between adults" (p. 79f.).

Although Freud had by now repeatedly delineated such connections, it was not until the publication of *Three Essays on the Theory of Sexuality* (1905b) that he linked another crucial element to his view of the special significance of the primal scene. "If children at this early age witness sexual intercourse between adults . . . they *inevitably* regard the sexual act as a sort of ill-treatment or act of subjugation: they view it, that is, in a sadistic sense" (p. 196; my italics). In "The Sexual Theories of Children" (1908) he reiterated this idea and suggested that the sadistic view of coitus may be derived from or supported by certain actual phenomena such as: (1) real "sex battles" in the foreplay; (2) the mother's real resistance in many marriages; (3) the actual presence of constant quarreling and fights between the parents in the daytime; and (4) seeing blood on the sheets or the mother's underclothes.

This formulation—that the child's impression of parental intercourse derived from observation of the primal scene is inevitably sadistic—dominated not only Freud's later thinking on the subject, but that of most of his associates and followers in the years to come. Although Freud indicated some of the actual events that might lead the child to such an interpretation, the general tendency was to assume its "inevitability," and to this theme I shall return.

Other elements in the total experience were, however, incorporated into Freud's reflections. Thus, in "A Case of Paranoia" (1915) he noted that the patient's fantasy of being observed in the course of her sexual excitement derived from an unconscious identification with her mother in the primal scene, and a projection of her own scopophilic impulses. Both of these themes—the identification with one of the observed parents and the special role of looking in the primal scene experience—recur in later writing.

As is well known, the fullest elaboration of Freud's thoughts on the primal scene appeared in the case of the Wolf-Man (1918). Not only the Wolf-Man's spectacular childhood anxiety dream, but the whole form and content of his infantile neurosis were shown to have been derived from the traumatic impact of a single primal scene observation at age 1½. The boy's interpretation of this scene as a sadistic assault by the father on the mother determined his wolf phobia and his unconscious homosexual orientation.

Aware of the theoretical difficulties posed by this formulation, Freud considered at great length alternative explanations, concluding finally that "this question [whether the primal scene is a fantasy or a real experience] is not in fact a matter of very great importance. These scenes of observing parental intercourse . . . are unquestionably an inherited endowment, a phylogenetic heritage, but they may just as easily be acquired by personal experience" (p. 97). His conclusions from this case are summarized in a passage in the *Introductory Lectures* (1917) where he stated of primal scene images, ". . . or if, as happens most frequently, it turns out to have been intercourse from behind, *more ferarum,* there can be no remaining doubt that the phantasy is based on an observation of intercourse between animals . . . and that its motive was the child's unsatisfied scopophilia during puberty. . . . It seems to me quite possible that all the things that are told us to-day in analysis as phantasy . . . the inflaming of sexual excitement by observing parental intercourse . . . were once real occurrences in the primaeval times of the human family" (p. 369ff.).

Here, of course, we are dealing not only with Freud's concern about the inherent implausibility of the child's traumatic response to a primal scene experience so early in life, but also with his disillusionment with the accounts of infantile seduction that figured so largely in his early work. The idea of such primal traumas as phylogenetically determined fantasies offered a solution to his dilemma and it represented a position from which Freud never deviated in his future work. Thus, in 1925, he said, "analysis shows us in a shadowy way how the fact of a child at a very early age listening to his parents copulating may set up his first sexual excitation, and how that event may, owing to its after-effects, act as a starting-point for the child's whole sexual development. . . . It is impossible, however, to suppose that these observations of coitus are of universal occurrence, so that at this point we are faced with the problem of 'primal fantasies' " (p. 250f.).

In the last work published in his lifetime, Freud (1939) returned to the influence of the sadistically perceived primal scene. He cited the case of a little boy who "had repeated, and indeed regular, opportunities of observing sexual acts between his parents." Prematurely aroused by such observations to aggressive masculinity and to phallic masturbation, he was led to attempt sexualized attacks on his mother in identification with his father as he perceived him in the primal scene. After puberty he was impotent, with his sexual activity limited to "psychical masturbation" accompanied by sadomasochistic fantasies. His adult character was "egoistic, despotic, and brutal"—all determined by the above-mentioned identification with the primal scene image of the father (p. 78ff.).

Freud's statements about the primal scene can be summarized as follows:

1. Observation of parental intercourse, even on a single occasion, can be traumatic and will at least evoke intense sexual excitement which will be transformed into anxiety.
2. The child's conception of the act is inevitably a sadistic one which will decisively affect his sexual fantasies and probably his adult sexuality.
3. The child is likely to identify with one or both of the participants in the primal scene. This will lead to the development of special features of his character.
4. If the primal scene is not actually perceived by the child, he will develop fantasies about it anyway; these will be determined by hereditary phylogenetic influences and will operate intrapsychically just as would actual perceptions.

OTHER PSYCHOANALYTIC CONTRIBUTIONS

References to primal scene observation and its consequences are legion.[1] I shall cite here only a sampling to indicate general trends.

Abraham (1913) described the case of a 9-year-old girl whose neurosis set in following an attack of pavor nocturnus during which she told her mother, "A man wanted to murder you in bed, but I saved you." Abraham traced this to her having recently seen the primal scene and interpreting it sadistically. He mentioned, but did not assign significance to the fact, that the parents had recently been quarreling in bed and that the child had slept in the parents' bedroom all her life without visible effect. Similarly, he cited (1917) a case of ejaculatio praecox which, he believed, was also due to a primal scene observation sadistically interpreted. The patient did not want to do to women what he thought his father had done to his mother and so avoided penetration. Finally, in 1924, he described the case of a woman with kleptomania and pseudologia fantastica whose pathology he traced to a primal scene observation at age 6, which, he said, "increased her scopophilic tendencies greatly, until they were overtaken by an intense repression" (p. 483). Further, she lost emotional contact with her father, but retained a compulsive interest in his penis; her kleptomania represented an unconscious wish to bite it off. No other determinants of this severe and complex pathology were offered by Abraham and no explanation of the oral fixation evident here was proposed.

Nunberg (1920), in his analysis of a catatonic patient, interpreted a dream referring to a "shark" that was a "spy." The patient's associations included a statement of fear that "someone could see me and become aware of me." This, Nunberg concluded, justified an assumption that the patient had eavesdropped on parental intercourse and that he had projected his own role of observer to the outside world. Nunberg did not state whether he offered this interpretation to the patient, or whether his assumption was ever verified.

In a classic paper on child analysis, Jenny Waelder Hall (1930)

[1] Dr. Henry Harper Hart has provided me with a bibliography containing over 300 references; this is admittedly incomplete.

told of little Anton, who "starts up in terror at night at the time when he knows that his father is taking his mother into bed . . . his starting up in bed is above all an attempt to prevent his parents from having intercourse" (p. 224). Waelder Hall mentioned the fact that the parents fought all the time, that the father was a brutal alcoholic, and that he had often overtly threatened little Anton with castration.

Schmideberg (1931) reported three cases of sexual pathology in which there was a pathogenic primal scene of destructive quality. In all cases the parents were described as "abnormal" people who were violent and fought all the time. Similarly, Buxbaum (1935) ascribed the perverse behavior of little Poldi in large measure to his frequent observations of the primal scene, "which was frequently accompanied by quarreling and fighting" (p. 168), a condition which, as she points out, characterized all the family interactions, not only those between the brutal father and the frigid mother but also those between both father and mother and the boy. And Eisler (1937), who ascribed the multiple phobias of his patient to repeated auditory primal scene experiences between the ages of 10 and 16, noted without comment that what his patient heard were mostly her parents' quarrels in the bedroom.

M. Klein (1932) referred repeatedly to primal scene experiences and fantasies in the genesis of infantile neurosis. Not only did she subscribe to Freud's idea of innate, phylogenetically determined primal scene fantasies, but she assigned them to the first half of the first year of life, where they make up a portion of the mental contents of the depressive position. In addition, she did describe cases of pathogenic primal scene observations, such as that of the boy whose "rage . . . at witnessing his parents' coitus was already expressed in his first hour by his wanting the two horses who were going to sleep to be 'dead and buried' " (p. 45). Klein offered no other possible determinants or interpretations of this wish.

Graber (1935) reported a case of a woman who as a child was "spoiled" by her parents in many ways, including being allowed into their bed at night. She thus was repeatedly exposed to the primal scene which, Graber believed, generated the wish for the father to "play" with her as he did with the mother. This led to the development of a character based on wishes (1) to separate the parents and (2) to get from the father what the mother had gotten; i.e., to a tyrranical, sadistic, domineering character. Graber does not discuss the influence of other aspects of the "spoiling" his patient received in generating this narcissistic character, nor does he reflect on the obvious ego disturbance of his patient.

Fenichel (1945), after epitomizing Freud's theoretical views as outlined above, cited a number of cases in which the primal scene is stated to be of traumatic import. One, originally reported in 1929 by Y. Kulovesi, is that of a tiqueur whose symptom was determined by a single primal scene observation. "In the excitement attending this experience, the frightened little boy suppressed certain motor impulses, particularly impulses to scream and weep. These motions . . . occurred subsequently . . . in the form of a tic. He remained fixated on the primal scene, and regressed to it whenever he suffered a disappointment in later life" (p. 321). Another case cited by Fenichel was that of a man who warded off the original reaction to the infantile primal scenes, hostility toward both parents, "by means of an increasing indifference toward the world. The identification with the mother and the passive homosexual inclinations found a distorted expression in this indifference" (p. 423). This patient became a hebephrenic schizophrenic; no other determinants of his psychosis were suggested by Fenichel. In addition, he ascribed some types of voyeurism to a fixation to primal scenes. Such patients develop a hunger for "screen experiences" and attempt to master the original trauma by repeating the frightening scenes in slightly altered form (p. 347f.).

In his exploration of mania and allied states, Lewin returned repeatedly to primal scene traumas. In 1932 he reported a case of hypomania ushered in by the patient's eavesdropping on the analyst and imagining his having intercourse with a female patient. The hypomania was, he believed, the acting out of a coitus from the standpoint of both sexes (i.e., a double identification) culminating in the fantasy of taking both roles in the sexual act at practically the same time. This patient had slept in the parents' bedroom until age 6 when she was displaced by a younger sibling. It appeared to Lewin that she was attempting to reinstitute this infantile position in her symptom. In his book on elation (1950) he deepened his interpretation of this relationship, suggesting that, universally, the young child will interpret the primal scene in oral terms either as a reciprocal cannibalism or a reciprocal suckling. The primal scene is often the event that is reproduced in adult depression and elation. It disturbs the child's sleep, leading to a wish on his part to return to sleep, to stay asleep, or to deepen sleep; in any case, the oral triad (the wish to sleep, to eat, to be eaten) is activated. Insomnias, too, can often be traced back to primal scene memories, the insomnia or wakefulness of the child in the primal scene being equated with the sleeplessness of the unfed baby.

In the course of his exposition Lewin subjected the Wolf-Man's dream to reappraisal in terms of his concepts. Thus, for him, the dream reveals the wish to stay asleep in the closed window that *opens* in the dream. Lewin related this closed window to his concept of the dream screen/breast, which is evoked in the dream to defend against the interruption of sleep by the primal scene.

In a number of papers Anna Freud has dealt in passing with aspects of the primal scene and its consequences. She relates one type of feeding disturbance to typical fantasies of the phallic phase: "children escape [oedipal] anxiety by regressing . . . to the earlier pregenital levels. . . . This leads to the conception of parental intercourse by mouth, a phantasy which is frequently reinforced by actual observation of fellatio acts" (1946, p. 131). In addition, she attributes certain types of social maladjustment and delinquency to the acting out of a variety of fantasies, e.g., "when an *observation of intercourse,* or fantasies of intercourse between the parents, have had a traumatic effect on their sexual development. Influenced by his own crude pregenital urges, the young child conceives that intercourse is a violently aggressive, sadistic act which is continued until one of the partners, or both, are severely damaged. The fantasies expressing these ideas are then displaced on the environment and acted out. Such children impress the community as belligerent, truculent, quarrelsome, always up in arms against something or somebody" (1949, p. 201).

However, she also has raised a challenging problem in her discussion of children reared in her war nurseries who, in their play, acted out coital fantasies which "every analyst would have assessed . . . as the result of imitation of coitus observations in the parental bedroom." These children had been in the nursery since the age of

10 days, and had never seen their parents alone together or known
of the existence of a private bedroom. "With stimulation from
outside thus excluded, play of this nature appears to be the
expression of innate, preformed, instinctual attitudes, a suggestion
which—if found to be true—would throw doubt on some of our
analytic reconstructions of early witnessing of the primal scene"
(1951, p. 28f.). Nunberg (1932), too, considered the question of
patients who "could never have observed parental intercourse" and
who still report it as a memory. He attributed these to "primal
fantasies" whose sources are unknown but which may derive from
infantile sexual investigations where curiosity finds no satisfaction
in reality (p. 74f.). Clearly, he was uncomfortable with Freud's
concept of phylogenetically determined fantasies.

Clinical and theoretical reflections on the primal scene have
continued to emerge in the past 30 years; indeed, recently there has
been an upsurge of interest in the subject. Of particular note are the
observations of the child analysts, whose vantage point would seem
to place them at reasonable proximity to the postulated traumatic
event. Mahler (1942) attributes the syndrome of pseudostupidity *in
part* to a defensive response to primal scene observation ("I didn't
see it, I don't know anything about it, but I can still be around to
watch"), but she adduces a number of other determinants as well,
including the child's compliance to the mother's wish for him to be
stupid. Geleerd (1943) traces several aspects of the compulsive
masturbation in her patient to repeated primal scene observations,
but she describes innumerable additional determinants, including
repeated observations of quarrels between the parents, repeated
genital manipulation by the mother, and repeated beatings by the
mother as punishment for masturbation.

Erikson (1937) describes an 8-year-old patient who actually
recalled having seen a man perform intercourse with a woman who
sat on him, and who observed that the penis looked shorter
afterward. The boy's first impression was that the woman had
defecated on the man's umbilicus and had done some harm to his
genitals. At second thought he concluded that the man had
eliminated part of his penis in the woman's rectum. His castration
anxiety could be traced to this experience. However, this was a boy

who had previously had symptoms of soiling and masturbation
followed by defecation, and who had been circumcized at age 5
or 6.

Wulff (1951) reports an interesting case of a "preoedipal" child
who, entering the parents' bedroom while they were having
intercourse, began to make strange sounds. The parents were struck
by her "tense" expression, which they interpreted as "fascinated
fright." The child immediately developed a phobia of a previously
loved dog and shortly afterward began to show fearful reactions to
the father. "The little girl experienced strong fear of the father at
the sight of the primal scene and then displaced the anxiety onto
the dog" (p. 170f.). He does not describe the parents' reaction to the
child's invasion of their bedroom, but he ascribes the child's phobic
reaction not to traumatic overstimulation but to the (presumably)
sadistic interpretation of the act.

In her report of the analysis of Frankie, Bornstein (1949)
interpreted his screaming attacks and his violently aggressive play
as reactions to "audible primal scene experiences" and to the
fantasies about intercourse derived therefrom. "His games presented scenes of attack duplicating those which he *undoubtedly*
assumed were taking place in the parents' bedroom" (p. 192; my
italics). As is so common in child analysis, no direct confirmation of
these interpretations is reported.

Fraiberg's (1952) report of an acute neurosis in a 2½-year-old girl
leans heavily on the fact that the symptoms began after the child
had seen her grandparents in the sexual act. The child appeared to
interpret the scene as a sadistic attack by the grandfather and a
castration of the grandmother. Fraiberg mentions, but does not
seem to consider of consequence, the fact that the grandfather
responded to the child's intrusion by *spanking* her. She does observe
that there had been a premorbid history of sadistic fantasy,
associated with hatred of her younger sibling and with the discovery
of her mother's bloody sanitary napkins.

Furman (1956), too, describes a case of severe pathology in a
3¼-year-old which she attributes to multiple primal scene exposures, especially incidents of fellatio. I have the impression that
Furman appears to have considered these to be of greater traumatic

significance than the repeated overt seduction by the child's uncle who, in a quasi-rape, forced the child to accept his penis in her mouth.

Other authors (Esman, 1962; Coren and Saldinger, 1967) have ascribed major predisposing and precipitating significance to primal scene experiences in the genesis of visual hallucinoses in young children. In both essays it is, however, suggested that violent aggressive stimuli are of equal or greater importance in this regard; Coren and Saldinger emphasize the crucial significance of the resonance of the precipitating event with the child's current developmental conflicts. Similarly, Nagera (1966) states that some sleep disturbances may occur during the latency period when "the child has a sadistic conception of the sexual relationship between the parents that has been reinforced by early primal scene observations *and* by an unsatisfactory hostile relationship between the parents" (p. 435; my italics).

In both clinical and theoretical writings, the analysts of adults, too, continue to use the primal scene as an explanatory factor. Rose (1960), for example, contends that the criminal behavior of a murderer-rapist he studied was a reenactment of sadistic primal scene observations from his childhood. His patient had, however, been thoroughly brutalized by a sadistic father, was possibly epileptic, and had serious ego defects; further, the primal scenes were never recalled by the patient, but were postulated by the analyst. Friedman (1954) and Bird (1954) are among those who report cases in which primal scene observations were implicated and reconstructed in the course of analytic work, but were never actually remembered by the patient.

Jacobson (1943) presents one of the rare instances in which an actual memory of a primal scene experience appears to have emerged. In her patient there was a vague recall of seeing "something terrible" happening in the parental bedroom, with the father naked and angry with the little girl. Jacobson emphasizes that the primal scene itself was one of many determinants of her patient's depression and that the father's anger and seductiveness were crucial elements, particularly since there was constant quarreling between the parents. Reich (1954) also reported such a case, where her young male patient observed the parents' intercourse during a beach vacation in his 5th year. His unconscious concept of the sexual act involved the man cutting the woman's genitals. It is noteworthy, however, that this patient's father was a gynecological surgeon and it would appear that this lent a significant element of reality to the young man's fantasies.

Calef (1954) discusses the appearance of color in dreams as reflecting "unsuccessful attempts . . . to deal with the impulses aroused by being witness to the primal scene" (p. 458). In emphasizing the role of *violent* primal scene experiences in the childhood of his patient who reported "red" in a dream, he passes lightly over the fact that the patient's mother was psychotic and that her father was overtly seductive.

As would be expected, primal scene experiences have been particularly implicated in the genesis of sadomasochistic disorders. Schuster (1966) is categorical in his assertion that the primal scene has a predominant influence on the formation of identifications during the phallic period. "Whether seen, heard, or fantasied, it is the model for the sadomasochistic polarities of the phallic period" (p. 366). Niederland (1958) finds that beating fantasies have a latent primal scene core; he interpreted his patient's memory of being beaten by the father in the parental bedroom while the mother was outside pleading for him as a disguised primal scene fantasy. Niederland argues, however, that noises themselves may be threatening and overwhelming to the young child and may later be linked to the primal scene events (e.g., the booming voice of the father, the soft moaning sounds of the mother). "While primal fantasies about coital violence are bound to develop in the child's mind . . . no recourse to the idea of preformed or inherited fantasies may be necessary" (p. 496). Actual observation of the primal scene may be traumatic if it stirs up earlier auditory anxieties. Needless to add, questions of special sensitivity become relevant here. Thus Knapp (1953) cites a case of a man especially sensitive to sounds, who could recall eavesdropping on noises from the bathroom but became anxious at the thought that he also "must have" listened to sounds of intercourse. Whether his sensitivity to noise was the cause or the consequence of his special auditory interest would be a matter for speculation.

In the case of a sadomasochistic fetishist, Greenacre (1955b) also implicates early primal scene observations, but it is to be noted that these were actually overtly sadomasochistic in character, and that the patient had also witnessed and overheard abortions performed in her home in childhood. Greenacre has, in fact, returned repeatedly to the influence of primal scene experiences on the developmental process. Thus in her discussion of penis awe (1953) she includes such observations among the conditions under which the little girl may develop this attitude. Indeed, the phallus as such may not be observed, but the child may be caught up as a passive, frightened participant in a scene of excitement fraught with fears of punishment. If the girl observes the tumescent phallus during the primal scene, she may develop a terror of the organ because of its size and a fear of being torn apart by it, especially if she has previously experienced enemas or severe constipation. Primal scene observations can interfere with the development of the sense of identity, as in Greenacre's (1958) case of a woman who had until age 2½ been kept in the parental bedroom in "gleeful primal scene participation." The resultant sexual excitement led to frantic masturbation, which induced the parents to subject the child to multiple medical examinations and manipulations of the genitals. This was followed by a tonsillectomy which coincided with the child's sudden ejection from the parental bedroom. The girl developed a state of chronic bewilderment and made frantic efforts to reach the parents and to see their genitals again.

In another paper (1960), Greenacre suggests that "infants who slept habitually in bed with their parents were stimulated by primal scene activity and took on through vision, hearing, and kinesthetic sensory responses the excitement of the motility, incorporating it into general body excitability. . . . Certainly young infants react markedly and in highly individual ways to both motion and sound" (p. 216). These formulations correspond to the speculations of Fries and Woolf (1953) on the differences in response to primal scene experiences of infants of different activity types. They suggest that the congenitally quiet infant may not respond as much, and therefore may not need to employ such intense defenses, as the more active infant, who may tend to withdraw or use denial. Similarly, the more active infant might seek to discharge the tensions stimulated by primal scene observations through motor activity, provoking reprimand, while the quieter infant might not.

Greenacre (1963, 1966) contends that the long-range effects of repeated exposure to the primal scene can be seen in the analytic situation by way of the transference. Patients who show attacks of acting out in the transference have a background of oral and speech problems, derived from abnormal closeness to one or both parents, and from constant inclusion in both primal scenes and *chronic marital quarreling*. This combination, she suggests, interferes with the infant's sense of the safety, reliability, and even reality of the parents. Patients who overidealize the analyst also have a history of constant, repetitive exposure to the primal scene from the first few weeks of life until puberty or beyond. This leads to a serious disturbance of later sexual interests and of passive and aggressive attitudes. Selective denial and amnesias are common among patients who have shared the parental bedroom into latency. Greenacre is almost unique here in considering the reasons why parents might keep the child in the bedroom for so long a time—that they may narcissistically enjoy having him at hand as a plaything; that a sexually inhibited mother might keep him there as a barrier to sex; that a neurotically anxious parent might need to reassure himself (or herself) of the child's safety.

Although Zetzel agrees that early and repeated exposure to the primal scene may affect learning and responsiveness by heightening intellectual defenses and diminishing aesthetic receptivity, she notes that neither of the thus-exposed patients she describes was severely neurotic or characterologically impaired (see Niederland, 1965). Rosen (1953, 1955) also considers the damaging effects of early primal scene observations or fantasies on the learning process, but concludes that his patient's special mathematical talents and flashes of "illumination" were fostered by, and represented reaction formations against, the impact of such experiences.

By and large, however, the emphasis in the literature is on the pathogenicity of primal scene experiences. Kanzer (1952) implicates them in the etiology of paranoia; Perestrello (1954) in the genesis of headaches; Fink (1968) in the production of multiple Isakower phenomena. It is Stern (1953a, 1953b) who has most systematically developed the theory of the traumatic aspect of the primal scene. Drawing on Selye's stress concepts, Stern (1953a) posits the primal scene as the "primary traumatic situation in sleep or half-sleep due to sexual overexcitation" (p. 204). It "is a *primary pavor nocturnus* and represents the *basic infantile trauma*. . . . [The] *pavor nocturnus* attacks (nightmares) have to be understood as *repetition of the basic infantile trauma,* due to a failure of its reparative mastery" (p. 206). Stern, like Freud and others, acknowledges that "whether the primal scene is an actual occurrence or belated elaboration of sexual experiences and fantasies or dreams or a conglomeration of all these, can probably never be fully cleared up" (p. 205).

Most recently Edelheit has, in a series of communications (1967, 1969, 1971), considered the role of what he calls "the primal scene schema" in normal and pathological development. In essence, Edelheit assimilates to his schema all the by-now-familiar elements —the sadomasochistic concept of the act, the exhibitionistic and voyeuristic components, the regressive (oral and anal) elements fused with the phallic percepts—deriving many of the concomitant polarities from the double and shifting identification with the partners. He suggests, in addition, that the primal scene schema determines the imagery of certain socially pervasive fantasies and that, among these, crucifixion fantasies are the most important, having an almost universal distribution in our culture. The primal scene schema, he believes, enters into both normal and pathological development.

It would appear, then, that the psychoanalysts who followed Freud have by and large accepted and maintained his views about the primal scene—that it constitutes a traumatic event or sequence in the child's development; that it is extensively implicated in the genesis and structure of psychopathology; that it is virtually always interpreted as a sadomasochistic event; and that it appears in fantasy whether actually experienced or not.

The primal scene has been indicted as the primary pathogenic agent in virtually every form of psychopathology. Mania, depression, paranoia, hebephrenia, phobia, hysteria, compulsive neurosis, character disorder, learning disturbance, asthma, headache, delinquency—all have been explained as reactions to single or multiple exposures to the primal scene. One is moved to wonder whether we are here confronted by one of those situations in which a theory, by explaining everything, succeeds in explaining nothing. Certainly, we would seem to be dealing with reductionism of a high order, in which the genetic fallacy appears to reign supreme.

The Primal Scene in Culture and History

That primal scene imagery extends beyond the consulting room needs no further demonstration than the opening scene of Fellini's recent film, *The Clowns*. A little boy (Fellini himself as a child) is awakened by rhythmic grunting noises outside his room. He goes to the window (cf. the Wolf-Man's dream) and sees in the field outside a circus tent in the process of erection. As he watches, the huge tent slowly rises in the air, to the accompaniment of continued grunts (presumably those of the stevedores). The whole scene is bathed in a soft yet sharply defining light, like that which so often characterizes screen memories.

A number of writers have considered some of the ramifications of the primal scene outside the realm of psychopathology and individual development. Pederson-Krag (1949) has interpreted the detective story as a concealed primal scene, in which the reader, identifying with the detective, discovers and "sees" the criminal event. Bonaparte (1935), too, sees the murder in Poe's "Murders in the Rue Morgue" as a repetition of a primal scene, and concludes that Poe had observed his parents in coitus. Greenacre (1955a) traces the development of a screen memory with primal scene themes through the work of Lewis Carroll and suggests that the scary ogres that people children's fantasies and children's literature are representations of the primal scene with the sexual images of the parents fused into frightening or awe-inspiring figures. Edelheit (1971) explores the contribution of his "primal scene schema" to myths and rituals such as the riddle of the Sphinx and to artistic productions such as drawings by Picasso and Oldenburg and recent films and works of imaginative literature.

Edelheit draws extensively on the work of Roheim who, more than any other investigator, was occupied with the impact of the primal scene on culture. Thus Róheim (1934) states: "The repression and sublimation of the primal scene is at the bottom of totemistic ritual and religion. Children do not originate from parental intercourse but from the 'tjurunga,' from the reincarnated ancestor" (p. 403). Similarly, "I have always found that the primal scene plays a very important role in the dreams of most patients. After all, the dream means *seeing something,* and on the oedipal level the most important thing to see is the primal scene" (1952, p. 39). And just as with patients, so with the Australian aborigines and other primitive cultures he studied, primal scene imagery is rife in dreams, rituals, and fantasies.

A reading of Róheim's material makes it difficult to avoid an impression of tendentiousness and arbitrariness in his work. Thus, in citing the Yuma Indian saying that "If somebody is skilful and clever, he probably kept his eyes open when his parents had intercourse," Róheim (1934, p. 393) concludes that their ideal is founded on the repression of emotions accompanying the primal scene. But here he assumes *a priori* that these emotions are negative, ignoring the clear implication that cognitive development and adaptive skills are aided by primal scene observation. Similarly, in the above-mentioned observations on the Australian view of the origin of children, Róheim assumes it is the primal scene that is repressed. But he describes at some length the seductive behavior of the aboriginal mother toward her son, and it thus seems at least as likely that what is repressed is not the primal scene as such but the oedipal fantasies engendered by the mother's seductiveness.

Indeed, although Róheim emphasizes the traumatic nature of primal scene observation, he observes elsewhere (1958) of his Australian subjects that, despite the fact that children see their parents having intercourse all the time, "In summary, we may say that, on the whole, [the pattern of their sexuality] is quite favorable. The sexual life and potency of the Australian male is far more 'normal' than the sexuality of the European male . . . there are no cases of frigidity or psychosexual impotence. . . . Sadistic and masochistic tendencies are not absent . . . [but] do not exist as independent perversions" (p. 244).

Mead (1928) arrives at similar conclusions in her appraisal of sexuality in Samoan culture. Sex was easy, casual, and without shame, unmarred by extensive adolescent turmoil. Little homosexuality could be observed. Overt sexual behavior, then, seemed undisturbed by the inevitability and frequency of childhood primal scene observation in a culture in which privacy was unknown, clothing little used, and bodily functions completely open. Nydegger and Nydegger (1963) report similar observations among the Ilocos of the Philippine Islands. On the other hand, Mead (1930) points out, the Manus of New Guinea take great care not to let their children observe adult intercourse. "In their one room houses this is difficult to accomplish, but the children soon learn the desirability of dissembling their knowledge. This clandestine knowledge is as shamed and marred by a sense of sin as is their parents' indulgence" (p. 164). The Manus are a puritanical, warlike tribe, noted in earlier times for the total submission of the young to the elders.

Among the Gusii of West Africa, parental intercourse occurs only when the children are supposed to be asleep (LeVine and LeVine, 1963). Evidently they are awake often enough to perceive the manifest reluctance and resistance of the woman, who regularly claims to be hurt, and the aggressive attitude of the man who "imposes" sex upon her. (Indeed, during the wedding night he actively seeks to inflict pain.) Identification with the parental sexual roles clearly occurs, but whether this is the product of the primal scene observations or whether it is systematically inculcated by tribal educational procedures might be open to question.

Boyer (1964), too, described the impact of primal scene observation on psychological development, in this case among the Apaches. Apache children are witness to repetitive exhibitions of sexual and aggressive actions on the part of adults; incorporating the excitements of both sexes, they are unable to repress and modify their archaic instinctual urges and to develop a clear sexual identity. Boyer carefully points out, however, that these experiences occur in a context of drunkenness, violence, and social disorganization, as well as a developmental experience marked by a sharp break between early oral indulgence and later maternal neglect.

Although Devereux (1951) is careful to deny any effort to minimize the intrinsically traumatic nature of primal scene observation, he notes that the Mohave children he studied "do not seem to be *severely* traumatized by the frequent witnessing of the primal scene. The most obvious factors which tend to *attenuate* these expected traumatic effects are the early sexual enlightenment of children, the commonplace nature and frequent recurrence of their primal scene experiences and the knowledge that they will not be punished for their scoptophilic activities. . . . An even more important attenuating factor may be the . . . relative freedom from guilt of the adults whose sexual act the child is witnessing" (p. 97f.).

Anthropological data are derived primarily from observations of overt behavior and interpretation of conscious communications and therefore are uncertain bases for the confirmation or refutation of psychoanalytic hypotheses about unconscious mental processes. Bradley (1967), undaunted by such cautions, offers sweeping conclusions on the effects of primal scene observations on human evolution. Suggesting that such experiences are universal, and accepting the classic view that they are inevitably interpreted sadomasochistically, he concludes that "such observation has been significantly responsible for the brutality that has been a character- istic of barbaric peoples" (p. 36). Though he quotes Rickman's description of a Russian child being slapped in the face for peeping at parental intercourse, he does not appear to entertain the possibility that the influence he delineates may be reversed—that parental brutality may determine the child's perception of the sexual act as a sadistic performance.

This question arises with particular force in the case of a striking instance of the effect of the primal scene on history—the origins of the Shaker movement. Of Mother Ann Lee, the founder, it is said in one of the classic Shaker texts (Bishop, 1816), "In her early youth she had a great abhorrence of the fleshly cohabitation of the sexes, and so great was her sense of its impurity, that she often admonished her mother against it, which, coming to her father's ears, he threatened, and actually attempted to whip her . . . upon which she threw herself into her mother's arms and clung around her to escape his strokes" (p. 44). Growing up in the industrial slums of 18th-century Manchester, Ann Lee undoubtedly had ample occasion to observe or intuit parental coitus, marked by the violence and brutality that her father evidently displayed. Add to that the fact that her own four children died in infancy—i.e., as a punishment for her sexual indulgence—and one can readily understand the urgency with which Ann Lee insisted on her doctrine of celibacy in the formulation of Shaker ideology.

Some Observations on Trauma

It would be inappropriate to undertake a comprehensive review of the concept of trauma in this essay. A number of recent contributions are, however, germane to my particular topic. In his survey of the field, Furst (1967) defines psychic trauma as an overloading of the ego by stimulation which puts the ego out of action so that the organism is suddenly forced back to the use of pre-ego mechanisms for dealing with the internal and external environment. He points out that "it has not been conclusively demonstrated that any known psychic change or condition is *unique and specific to trauma* . . . the role played by trauma in pathogenesis depends on a host of separate but related variables" (p. 42f.; my italics).

Kris (1956), who distinguished between "shock" and "strain" traumas, emphasized Anna Freud's observation that "what the analytic patient reports as an event which has taken place once ["shock" trauma] appears in the life of the growing child as a more or less typical experience, which may have been repeated many times ["strain" trauma] . . . analysts tend to be misled by the telescopic character of memory. . . . The problem is further complicated by the fact that the further course of life seems to determine which experience may gain significance as a traumatic one" (p. 73). Earlier, Hartmann, Kris, and Loewenstein (1946) had pointed out that "a stimulus that was of little relevance in one phase of . . . development may be of decisive relevance in another" (p. 18). And Anna Freud (1967) notes that in the usual clinical situation, "the traumatic event becomes pathogenic mainly through the triggering off of an ordinary neurotic conflict or neurosis that has lain dormant" (p. 245).

Sandler (1967) attempts to codify such formulations in his concept of "retrospective trauma," by which he means "that the perception of some particular situation evokes the *memory* of an earlier experience, which under the present conditions becomes traumatic. A typical example of this is the traumatic reactivation of a primal-scene memory during the phallic-Oedipal phase. The perception of the primal scene need not in itself have been traumatic, and it may have remained as a memory until a new link between it and the later sexual fantasies of the child occurs. . . . Here the memory functions as a present perception. *The operation of retrospective trauma must present a further hazard to the accurate reconstruction of the child's infantile experiences by the analyst"* (p. 164; my italics).

Greenacre (1967), developing the influence of ego psychology on concepts of trauma, proposes that "the undermining of the firmness of mental development in the earliest months after birth is probably the most important factor in increasing the reaction to trauma in the remaining pre-Oedipal years" (p. 152). It is such considerations as these that undoubtedly contributed to George Klein's question whether primal scenes are equally traumatic in every case and whether the original ego endowment does not play a role in determining their traumatic significance (see Niederland, 1965).

DISCUSSION

As the above synopsis makes clear, the idea that the child's observation of adult—especially parental—sexual intercourse will have profound, immediate, and long-range effects on his development has been a staple of clinical theory ever since Freud first enunciated it. The consequences of primal scene experience would appear to be protean; it has been said to affect not only individual character development and psychopathology but also the cultural development of the human race itself.

The primal scene, in this view, assumes a place alongside the oedipus complex as one of the universal nuclear factors in human psychological development. Unlike the oedipus complex, however, its—usually baleful—influences can be exerted after even a single incident and its intrapsychic elaboration follows a circumscribed and predetermined course. Indeed, it appears that even where actual primal scene experiences have not occurred, the child's fantasies about it will lead to the same results. Thus, not only the event but the fantasy may be traumatic, or at least pathogenic, regardless of the extent to which it is supported or reinforced by reality.

There is good reason to believe that primal scene fantasies are, indeed, universal in human experience. In fact, the vast majority of humans, reared in the one-room huts of the "primitive," the one-room shacks of the peasant, or the one-bedroom flats of the urban poor, have been regularly and repeatedly exposed to the sexual lives of their parents. That small minority of the world's children whose families' favored circumstances include the notion of privacy may or may not occasionally undergo such encounters; but even where they do not, they are likely, in attempting to grasp the complexities and imponderabilities of the oedipal situation, to apply their cognitive and imaginative capacities to the construction of fantasies about what goes on in their parents' bedrooms.

It is not surprising, then, that primal scene material appears in the content of virtually every analysis. Commonly, it presents itself in the guise of "curiosity" on the part of the patient, or of fantasies of being spied upon or overheard by the analyst (or his agents) in the waiting room or bathroom. One of my adult patients expressed what appeared to be her primal scene interests in both these ways; she was constantly curious about what went on between me and other patients—who she always imagined were female—and always, like Cherubino, she "tried not to listen" when sounds were audible in the waiting room. At the same time she sedulously avoided using my bathroom because she imagined that I would somehow observe what she did there—even though a long hallway separated that room from my consulting room.

This woman readily, even eagerly, accepted interpretations related to the primal scene. She could easily imagine herself, an only child, intensely concerned with her parents' intimate relationship, feeling excluded, wanting to be present as they performed their conjugal mysteries, and, perhaps even spying on them at times. Never was she able to remember such incidents consciously, however, despite her conviction. As is so often the case, one could not determine where fantasy stopped and reality began. There are few matters credited with such analytic weight about which this is true. Freud himself found it possible, in time, to distinguish fantasies of seduction from genuine incidents. With the primal scene, however, he as well as many of his followers have had to accept the Scotch verdict—*"non liquet."*

Granted, then, the universality of primal scene experiences and fantasies, what can we conclude about their influence on normal and abnormal development? The customary view is that they are (1) traumatic; (2) laden with sadistic and masochistic content; and (3) responsible for confusion in sexual identity because of the double and shifting identifications they generate.

Observation of the primal scene is said to be traumatic because it floods the childish ego with overwhelming and unmanageable sexual excitation. This excitation which cannot be discharged is transformed, Freud said, into anxiety, and the various defense mechanisms deployed to deal with the anxiety lead to one or another variant of symptom formation. This formulation is, of course, derived from Freud's first anxiety theory, in which undischarged libido or sexual excitation was thought to be the source of anxiety. Despite Freud's abandonment of this theory and its replacement by that of signal anxiety is the context of ego psychology, many analysts appear to have held to the earlier theory with respect to the primal scene.

It may be said that those who maintain the view of the primal scene as traumatic have recast their thesis in ego-psychological terms—i.e., that the overwhelming sexual excitation it engenders is experienced as a danger situation which in turn mobilizes signal anxiety, etc. Strikingly, however, the experience is said to be equally traumatic regardless of the age or ego resources of the subject; at least until quite recently, little or no consideration was given to the child's capacity to deal with the situation through cognitive or other adaptive means. Loewald (1971) as well as Rapaport (1953) have pointed out the crucial role of active mastery versus passive suffering in determining the outcome of infantile experience.

I have reported (1971) how a comparable stimulus (repeated observation of the father's phallus) was dealt with differently by a pair of fraternal twin girls. One of them, favored with normal or advanced ego development, appeared to have adapted to and integrated the experience through verbal communication and attempts at cognitive mastery, while her sister, less well developed, was unable to ask the necessary questions but instead identified with the father and his phallus and showed signs of an early and pathological transsexual identity formation.

In this regard, one cannot avoid astonishment at the fact that no suggestion appears in the literature that the child may ever interpret what he observes or imagines as an act of love. He is said inevitably to understand the parental goings on as a sadistic assault on the mother or castration of the father. The principal reasons for this misinterpretation (where it is one) are said to be the violent physical activity which is redolent of aggression, and the child's own phase-specific or regressive anal-sadistic fantasies that color what he observes. It seems to me, however, that an equally cogent and persuasive case can be made for the impact on the child of day-to-day (or night-to-night) fighting between the parents, or their violence and hostility toward the child himself. If the child perceives the parents as violent and combative during the day, it is not unlikely that he will so picture them in the secret interactions of the bedroom; if the father is sadistic or abusive toward the child, the latter will have good reason to expect that he will behave similarly toward the mother. In case after case of "primal scene traumatization," references are made to the father's brutality or the parents' frequent quarrels.

Elsewhere I have described (Esman, 1968) two cases in which the child's sadistic concept of the primal scene was clearly a reaction to the audible fighting and bickering in which the parents engaged in their bedrooms. Even in Fraiberg's case, it may be argued that what traumatized Sally was not merely her observation of the grandparental intercourse but the slap which her grandfather administered and the guilt and fear which the grandparents imposed upon the whole experience. Where, among slum children, repeated primal scene experiences do seem to be associated with impaired development, there seems good reason to suppose that the blame can be laid to general, not merely sexual, overstimulation and, indeed, that the aggressive and violent elements that generally accompany the primal scene form an integral part of the total life experience of the slum child.

Actually, the anthropological evidence would seem to suggest that in cultures where sex is less laden with conflicts than it is in ours, and where the child is repeatedly exposed to the primal scene, he quickly grasps its significance as a pleasurable act and seeks to carry it out himself. In so doing the boy or the girl clearly imitates one or the other of the parental pair, but that this constitutes a true identification would be difficult to prove without psychoanalytic investigation. No reports of which I am aware suggest that, in their own reenactment, the children behave sadomasochistically, with the possible exception of LeVine's description of the Gusii where, it will be recalled, the adult sex act itself is culturally enacted as a sadomasochistic performance. Further, such reports generally emphasize the absence of (overt) evidence of perversion or confused sexual identification.

This is not to suggest, of course, that the child's notions about the sexual act are determined entirely by external influences. The child brings to his efforts to grasp the mystery the cognitive equipment available to him and the fantasies characteristic of his developmental phase. As Nunberg (1932) put it, "Every stage of development has its own means of expression, its own language" (p. 76). Thus, as noted, Lewin (1950) emphasizes the oral-incorporative and oral-sadistic elements in such interpretations and fantasy formations, while Freud and most of his followers have stressed anal-sadistic and phallic aspects. Erikson's anally fixated patient interpreted the primal scene as both a fecal attack by the woman and an anal penetration by the man, while an 8-year-old phobic girl whose treatment I supervised played out a clear primal scene fantasy in terms of mother and father battling over the possession of a large pencil, which the "baby" finally recovered from the mother and returned to the father. This child was certain that "200 years ago both men and women had penises, but nature took them away from women because they didn't use them."

Such constructions are applied not only to the data of actual observations, but also to the hints and suggestions that come from childhood gossip and, as suggested above, to the child's own efforts to solve the mysteries of procreation, childbirth, and male-female relations. In the course of his development, therefore, every child will form some notion, expressed in conscious as well as unconscious fantasy, of the primal scene, irrespective of any exposure to the actual event. It is because of just such observations that it appears to be unnecessary to postulate, as Freud did, phylogenetically determined innate primal scene fantasies, or even actual primal scene observations among the bulk of middle-class Western individuals.

Differences in cultural setting seem to have a great deal to do with conflicting views about the effects of the primal scene. So much is this so that, as noted above, Greenacre states that repeated primal scene exposure throughout childhood is likely to be traumatic, while Devereux, writing of the Mohave, believes that repeated and regular exposure to the primal scene tends to mitigate its traumatic character.

Among those who have postulated a special role for the primal scene in psychic development, Edelheit's arguments are perhaps the most ingenious and convincing. In developing his concept of the "primal scene schema," however, he is careful to note that universally it derives from fantasy as well as from actual observation, and that psychic events external to it will determine its evolution in normal or pathological directions. He does not suggest that it is in itself traumatic or pathogenic.

Why is it, then, that observation of the primal scene is so often cited as a specific determinant of psychic illness? It is hard to avoid the impression that Freud's authority is a major factor in determining this. The general view as repeatedly cited in the literature over the past 70 years echoes Freud's formulation in every detail and without question. Certainly, the primal scene concept has offered a ready and persuasive explanation for phenomena that would otherwise be perplexing. In another context, Weinshel (1970) suggested, "At times . . . one has the impression that those factors which the patient emphasizes are really 'red herrings' that are invoked to provide causality and a sense of mastery" (p. 315). Every analysis will, if carried far enough, yield primal scene material, because every child speculates on the primal questions. It is usually the analyst who, based on his own preconceptions, assigns special weight to certain material, and the analyst, too, may have a need for "causality and a sense of mastery." In a personal communication, Beres has suggested that what to the analyst appears traumatic may not have been so to the patient. He has further raised the question (1969) "whether we do not as a result of our cultural background regard certain experiences as traumatic to the child which, in other cultures, do not lead to symptom-formation or other pathology" (p. 135). I suspect that this may be particularly true with reference to the primal scene.

Conclusions

The following propositions seem to be warranted at this time:

1. Primal scene content, derived either from observation or fantasy, seems to be a universal element in the mental life of postoedipal humans.

2. Evidence that observation of parental intercourse is *per se* traumatic to the child is not convincing; certainly, no specific pathological formation can be ascribed to it.

3. The "sadistic conception" of the primal scene, supposed to be inevitable, appears to be largely, if not entirely, determined by other elements in the parents' behavior—in particular, by the amount of overt violent aggression they exhibit. It is this aggression, not the sexual act itself, that "is responsible for the brutality that has been characteristic of barbaric peoples" (Bradley).

4. The child's response to such observations will be determined in large measure by the cultural setting and emotional set that surrounds him. In many non-Western cultures the experience seems to be handled adaptively and without evident conflict or pathological consequences.

5. The child's ego resources, particularly his cognitive functions, special sensitivities, and capacities for active mastery, play a major role in determining the fate of whatever fantasies and affects are aroused by primal scene experiences.

Perhaps Greenacre (1966) summed it up most succinctly when, in speaking of the "shock" reaction of the child to sporadic, chance participation in the primal scene, she said, "the impact . . . depends very much on the age of the child, the actual nature of the primal scene exposure itself, the circumstances surrounding it, and the reactions of the parents to the child's intrusion" (p. 754).[2]

---

[2] Only after the completion of my work on this project did I learn that a section of the Kris Study Group of the New York Psychoanalytic Institute, under the chairmanship of Dr. Martin Wangh, had carried out a similar survey some time earlier. That my version of the story has achieved publication earlier than theirs is an accident of history. A summary of their study is expected to appear in the Kris Study Group Monograph Series.

BIBLIOGRAPHY

ABRAHAM, K. (1913), Mental After-Effects Produced in a Nine-Year-Old Child by the Observation of Sexual Intercourse between Its Parents. *Selected Papers*. London: Hogarth Press, 1927, pp. 164–168.

―――― (1917), Ejaculatio Praecox. *Ibid.*, pp. 280–298.

―――― (1924), A Short Study of the Development of the Libido, Viewed in the Light of Mental Disorders. *Ibid.*, pp. 418–499.

BERES, D. (1969), Review of *Psychic Trauma*, ed. S. Furst. *Psychoanal. Quart.*, 38:132–135.

BIRD, B. (1954), Pathological Sleep. *Int. J. Psycho-Anal.*, 35:20–29.

BISHOP, R. (1816), Testimonies of the Life, Character, Revelation & the Doctrines of the Blessed Mother Ann Lee and the Elders with Her. Quoted in: H. Desroche, *The American Shakers*. Amherst: University of Massachusetts Press, 1971.

BONAPARTE, M. (1935), The Murders in the Rue Morgue. *Psychoanal. Quart.*, 4:259–293.

BORNSTEIN, B. (1949), The Analysis of a Phobic Child. *This Annual*, 3/4:181–226.

BOYER, L. B. (1964), Psychological Problems of a Group of Apaches. *The Psychoanalytic Study of Society*, 3:203–277. New York: International Universities Press.

BRADLEY, N. (1967), Primal Scene Experience in Human Evolution and Its Fantasy Derivatives in Art, Proto-Science and Philosophy. *The Psychoanalytic Study of Society*, 4:34–79. New York: International Universities Press.

BREUER, J. & FREUD, S. (1893–1895) Studies on Hysteria. *Standard Edition*, 2. London: Hogarth Press, 1955.

BUXBAUM, E. (1935), Exhibitionistic Onanism in a Ten-Year-Old Boy. *Psychoanal. Quart.*, 4:161–189.

CALEF, V. (1954), Color in Dreams. *J. Amer. Psychoanal. Assn.*, 2:453–461.

COREN, H. Z. & SALDINGER, J. S. (1967), Visual Hallucinoses in Children. *This Annual*, 22:331–356.

DEVEREUX, G. (1951), Primal Scene and Juvenile Heterosexuality in Mohave Society. In: *Psychoanalysis and Culture*, ed. G. B. Wilbur & W. Muensterberger. New York: International Universities Press, pp. 90–107.

EDELHEIT, H. (1967), Discussion of A. J. Lubin: The Influence of the Russian Orthodox Church on Freud's Wolf-Man. *Psychoanal. Forum*, 2:165–166.

―――― (1969), The Primal Scene Schema. Presentation to Kris Study Group. New York Psychoanalytic Institute.

―――― (1971), Mythopoiesis and the Primal Scene. *The Psychoanalytic Study of Society*, 5:212–233. New York: International Universities Press.

EISLER, E. R. (1937), Regression in a Case of Multiple Phobia. *Psychoanal. Quart.*, 6:86–95.

ERIKSON, E. H. (1937), Configurations in Play. *Psychoanal. Quart.*, 6:139–214.

ESMAN, A. H. (1962), Visual Hallucinoses in a Young Child. *This Annual*, 17:334–343.

—— (1968), Marital Psychopathology. In: *The Marriage Relationship*, ed. S. Rosenbaum & I. Alger. New York: Basic Books, pp. 133–134.

—— (1971), Transsexual Identification in a Three-Year-Old Twin. *Psychosoc. Proc.*, 1:77–79.

FENICHEL, O. (1945), *The Psychoanalytic Theory of Neurosis*. New York: Norton.

FINK, G. (1968), Analysis of the Isakower Phenomenon. Abstr. in: *Psychoanal. Quart.*, 37:326.

FRAIBERG, S. (1952), A Critical Neurosis in a Two-and-a-Half-Year-Old Girl. *This Annual*, 7:173–215.

FREUD, A. (1946), The Psychoanalytic Study of Infantile Feeding Disturbances. *This Annual*, 2:119–132.

—— (1949), Certain Types and Stages of Social Maladjustment. In: *Searchlights on Delinquency*, ed. K. R. Eissler. New York: International Universities Press, pp. 193–204.

—— (1951), Observations on Child Development. *This Annual*, 6:18–30.

—— (1967), Comments on Trauma. In: *Psychic Trauma*, ed. S. S. Furst. New York: Basic Books, pp. 235–245.

FREUD, S. (1900), The Interpretation of Dreams. *Standard Edition*, 4 & 5. London: Hogarth Press, 1953.

—— (1901), The Psychopathology of Everyday Life. *Standard Edition*, 6. London: Hogarth Press, 1960.

—— (1905a), Fragment of an Analysis of a Case of Hysteria. *Standard Edition*, 7:3–122. London: Hogarth Press, 1953.

—— (1905b), Three Essays on the Theory of Sexuality. *Standard Edition*, 7:125–143. London: Hogarth Press, 1953.

—— (1908), On the Sexual Theories of Children. *Standard Edition*, 9:205–226. London: Hogarth Press, 1959.

—— (1915), A Case of Paranoia Running Counter to the Psycho-Analytic Theory of the Disease. *Standard Edition*, 14:261–272. London: Hogarth Press, 1957.

—— (1917), Introductory Lectures on Psycho-Analysis. *Standard Edition*, 16:358–377. London: Hogarth Press, 1963.

—— (1918), From the History of an Infantile Neurosis. *Standard Edition*, 17:3–123. London: Hogarth Press, 1955.

—— (1925), Some Psychical Consequences of the Anatomical Distinctions between the Sexes. *Standard Edition*, 19:243–258. London: Hogarth Press, 1961.

—— (1939), Moses and Monotheism. *Standard Edition*, 23:3–137. London: Hogarth Press, 1964.

—— (1950), Extracts from the Fliess Papers. *Standard Edition*, 1:175–280. London: Hogarth Press, 1966.

FRIEDMAN, L. J. (1954), Regressive Reaction to the Interpretation of a Dream. *J. Amer. Psychoanal. Assn.*, 2:514–518.

FRIES, M. E. & WOOLF, P. J. (1953), Some Hypotheses on the Role of the Congenital Activity Type in Personality Development. *This Annual*, 8:48–62

FURMAN, E. (1956), An Ego Disturbance in a Young Child. *This Annual*, 11:312–335.

FURST, S. S. (1967), Psychic Trauma: A Survey. In: *Psychic Trauma*, ed. S. S. Furst. New York: Basic Books, pp. 3–50.

GELEERD, E. R. (1943), The Analysis of a Case of Compulsive Masturbation in a Child. *Psychoanal. Quart.*, 12:520–540.

GRABER, G. H. (1935), Primal Scene, Play and Destiny. *Psychoanal. Quart.*, 4:467–475.

GREENACRE, P. (1953), Penis Awe and Its Relation to Penis Envy. In: *Emotional Growth*, 1:31–49. New York: International Universities Press, 1971.

——— (1955a), "It's My Own Invention": A Special Screen Memory of Mr. Lewis Carroll. *Ibid.*, 2:438–478.

——— (1955b), Further Considerations Regarding Fetishism. *Ibid.*, 1:58–66.

——— (1958), Early Physical Determinants of the Development of the Sense of Identity. *Ibid.*, 1:113–127.

——— (1960), Considerations Regarding the Parent-Infant Relationship. *Ibid.*, 1:199–224.

——— (1963), Problems of Acting Out in the Transference Relationship. *Ibid.*, 2:695–712.

——— (1966), Problems of Overidealization of the Analyst and of Analysis. *Ibid.*, 2:743–761.

——— (1967), The Influence of Infantile Trauma on Genetic Patterns. *Ibid.*, 1:260–299.

HARTMANN, H., KRIS, E., & LOEWENSTEIN, R. M. (1946), Comments on the Formation of Psychic Structure. *This Annual*, 2:11–38.

JACOBSON, E. (1943), Depression. *Psychoanal. Quart.*, 12:541–560.

KANZER, M. (1952), Manic-Depressive Psychosis with Paranoid Trends. *Int. J. Psycho-Anal.*, 33:34–42.

KLEIN, M. (1932), *The Psychoanalysis of Children*. New York: Grove Press, 1960.

KNAPP, P. H. (1953), The Ear, Listening and Hearing. *J. Amer. Psychoanal. Assn.*, 1:672–689.

KRIS, E. (1956), The Recovery of Childhood Memories. *This Annual*, 11:54–88.

LEVINE, R. A. & LEVINE, B. B. (1963), Hyansongo: A Gusii Community. In: *Six Cultures*, ed. B. Whiting. New York: Wiley, pp. 15–202.

LEWIN, B. D. (1932), Analysis and Structure of a Transient Hypomania. *Psychoanal. Quart.*, 1:43–58.

——— (1950), *The Psychoanalysis of Elation*. New York: Norton.

LOEWALD, H. W. (1971), Some Considerations on Repetition and Repetition Compulsion. *Int. J. Psycho-Anal.*, 52:59–66.

MAHLER, M. S. (1942), Pseudo-Imbecility. *Psychoanal. Quart.*, 11:149–164.

MEAD, M. (1928), *Coming of Age in Samoa*. New York: Morrow.

——— (1930), *Growing Up in New Guinea*. New York: Morrow.

NAGERA, H. (1966), Sleep and Its Disturbances Approached Developmentally. *This Annual*, 21:393–447.

NIEDERLAND, W. G. (1958), Early Auditory Experiences, Beating Fantasies, and the Primal Scene. *This Annual*, 13:471–504.

—— (1965), Panel Report: Memory and Repression. *J. Amer. Psychoanal. Assn.*, 13:619–633.

NUNBERG, H. (1920), The Course of the Libidinal Conflict in a Case of Schizophrenia. In: *Practice and Theory of Psychoanalysis*, 1:24–59. New York: International Universities Press, 1965.

—— (1932), *Principles of Psychoanalysis*. New York: International Universities Press, 1955.

NYDEGGER, W. F. & NYDEGGER, C. (1963), Tarong: An Ilocos Barrio in the Philippines. In: *Six Cultures*, ed. B. Whiting. New York: Wiley, pp. 693–867.

PEDERSON-KRAG, G. (1949), Detective Stories and the Primal Scene. *Psychoanal. Quart.*, 18:207–214.

PERESTRELLO, D. (1954), Headache and Primal Scene. *Int. J. Psycho-Anal.*, 35:219–223.

RAPAPORT, D. (1953), Some Metapsychological Considerations Concerning Activity and Passivity. In: *Collected Papers*. New York: Basic Books, 1967, pp. 530–568.

REICH, A. (1954), Early Identifications as Archaic Elements in the Superego. *J. Amer. Psychoanal. Assn.*, 2:218–238.

RÓHEIM, G. (1932), Animism and Religion. *Psychoanal. Quart.*, 1:59–112.

—— (1934), The Evolution of Culture. *Int. J. Psycho-Anal.*, 15:387–418.

—— (1952), *The Gates of the Dream*. New York: International Universities Press.

—— (1958), The Western Tribes of Central Australia: Their Sexual Life. *Psychoanalysis and the Social Sciences*, 5:221–245. New York: International Universities Press.

ROSE, G. J. (1960), Screen Memories in Homicidal Acting Out. *Psychoanal. Quart.*, 29:328–343.

ROSEN, V. H. (1953), On Mathematical "Illumination" and the Mathematical Thought Process. *This Annual*, 8:127–154.

—— (1955), Strephosymbolia. *This Annual*, 10:83–99.

SANDLER, J. (1967), Trauma, Strain, and Development. In: *Psychic Trauma*, ed. S. S. Furst. New York: Basic Books, pp. 154–174.

SCHMIDEBERG, M. (1931), A Contribution to the Psychology of Persecutory Ideas and Delusions. *Int. J. Psycho-Anal.*, 12:331–367.

—— (1932), Some Unconscious Mechanisms in Pathological Sexuality and Their Relation to Normal Sexual Activity. *Int. J. Psycho-Anal.*, 14:225–260, 1933.

SCHUSTER, B. (1966), Notes on 'A Child is Being Beaten.' *Psychoanal. Quart.*, 35:357–367.

STERN, M. (1953a), Trauma and Symptom Formation. *Int. J. Psycho-Anal.*, 34:202–218.

—— (1953b), Trauma, Projective Technique, and Analytic Profile. *Psychoanal. Quart.*, 22:221–252.

WAELDER HALL, J. (1930), The Analysis of a Case of Night Terror. *This Annual*, 2:189–227, 1946.

WEINSHEL, E. M. (1970), Some Psychoanalytic Considerations on Moods. *Int. J. Psycho-Anal.*, 51:313–320.

WULFF, M. (1951), The Problem of Neurotic Manifestations in Children of Preoedipal Age. *This Annual*, 6:169–179.

"He Can But He Won't"

A Psychodynamic Study of So-Called "Gifted Underachievers"

C. JANET NEWMAN, M.D.,
CYNTHIA FOX DEMBER, PH.D.,
AND OTHILDA KRUG, M.D.

WHEN CLEVER, ARTICULATE AND BEGUILING CHILDREN WHO OBTAIN high scores on both IQ and achievement tests experience prolonged academic failure, adults are puzzled and concerned. They sense the existence of strong adverse influences which oppose the natural impulses of most children to learn, master, and achieve. When gifted children fail miserably, something must be seriously amiss. Shakespeare said that "Lilies that fester smell far worse than weeds."

Our interest in this problem was stimulated by experience with several highly intelligent children in intensive inpatient treatment at the Children's Psychiatric Center in Cincinnati. Although these children had IQs ranging from 130 to 160 and were generally able to read well and hence to acquire information, they had serious disabilities around academic performance and achievement. The fact that these children frequently showed unusual expressive ability and verbal fluency suggested that intensive diagnostic and

From the Children's Psychiatric Center of Cincinnati, a joint activity of the Jewish Hospital and the Department of Psychiatry, College of Medicine, University of Cincinnati, Cincinnati, Ohio.

therapeutic work with them might yield increased understanding about the development and use of intelligence. Furthermore, clinical experience with these children suggested that aspects of their intelligence itself seemed in some ways to contribute to their personality problems, which in turn influenced their intellectual functioning. We had the distinct impression that the same constellation of historical genetic factors contributed both to high scores on intelligence tests and to underachievement.

Since then, we have been confronted in clinical practice with ever-increasing numbers of children, especially boys, at different levels of intelligence, whose academic achievement is grossly below their so-called potential. In this context we undertook a pilot study of 15 underachieving gifted children. In this essay we shall review some of the background of our thinking, describe briefly the nature and procedures of this study (in the Appendix) and then report and discuss in detail those of our findings that are relevant for our understanding of some of the pathogenic influences on the development of intelligence and the ability to achieve.

The underachieving gifted child epitomizes the child of whom parents and teachers alike complain desperately: "He has so much potential, but he won't use it," or "He can, but he won't!" What is it exactly that the underachieving bright child "can" do and what is it that he "won't" do?

He can obtain high scores on IQ and achievement tests, which typically require immediate short answers, often to multiple choice questions, using simple pencil marks. He can and he does. The "won't" does not apply to these procedures at all, but rather involves an entirely different set of tasks with entirely different psychological requirements. These typically are assignments, projects, lengthy compositions, and, more generally, work or tasks requiring planning, effort, the integration of a large body of material, and sustained activity toward a goal. The child does not do these things. Sometimes a child pleads that he can't when he really means, consciously or unconsciously, that he won't. But rather than assume that he "can but won't" or "won't even though he says he can't," we must consider the possibility that he truly can't and that such a disability may lie at the core of his seemingly willful "won't."

Rather than looking upon him as a child who, possessing measurably high intelligence, can therefore use it appropriately (except for "laziness" or neurotic conflict), it might be well to consider alternative hypotheses:

1. The child can do some things well, and cannot do other things well. Leaving motivation aside temporarily, we suggest that perhaps some of his ego functions are well developed, and others are not. What he cannot do well threatens him greatly, but he maintains defensively an attitude of being in control of his disability, and thus does everything in his power to make it appear that he "won't" even at the cost of external punishment and criticism.

2. We have considered the "won't" as a mask for "can't." Another possibility is a vicious circular relationship in which the early and constant repetition of negativistic "won't" attitudes prevent the child from "practicing" certain functions and developing them to higher levels of competence. Ultimately this may lead to fixations in severe disability of the "can't" variety. In this sense, failures of motivation at early levels during critical phases of ego development lead to actual structural deficits in the ego later on. Over a span of years the developmental story would unfold like this:

> "I can, but I won't"
> "I won't, so I don't"
> "I don't, so I can't"
> "I can't, but I'll say I won't"

Although the theoretical implications will be discussed later, it is evident that such simple questions and phrases have led us to the heart of ego psychology ("can and can't") and motivation theory ("will and won't").

We now realize that intelligence is not purely defined by a set of ego functions anymore than achievement is determined solely by motivational factors. Nor can the relationship between intelligence and the motivation to achieve be expressed in simple arithmetic terms. The study of underachieving gifted children leads us to consider the ever-changing, subtle, complex, and mutually inhibitory or facilitating interactions that occur between intelligence and achievement within the psychodynamic matrix of the developing personality.

Underachieving gifted children have been extensively studied primarily from an educational point of view. The phrase itself is an educational descriptive one. The term "gifted" was used by Hollingsworth (1929) to describe children with IQs over 130, while Terman (1925) generally used the figure 140 as his cutoff point. "Underachievement" refers to a child achieving significantly below the level statistically predicted by his IQ. In spite of hundreds of studies these children continue to pose many thorny problems for research design, educational methodology, etiological understanding, and psychotherapy (Goldberg, 1965).

Recent works have challenged and refined the concepts of "overachievement" and "underachievement." Thorndike (1963) points out that "underachievement" and "overachievement" really refer to the limitations of our predictions: "In much of the work on prediction of academic achievement, educators (and psychologists) have suffered from a kind of single-minded obsession with intelligence or scholastic aptitude tests as predictors. . . . There has been a tendency to forget that the aptitude test is, after all, only one sample of behavior from which another, usually somewhat larger and somewhat different sample is being forecast" (p. 3). He suggests that "as we are able to extend our understanding of the relevant factors, . . . and so reduce overprediction," we will automatically reduce "underachievement" (p. 5).

The point of view of the present clinical and theoretical study of this area has been well summed up independently by Goldberg (1965). Replying to statistical and conceptual criticisms such as those suggested above, she states that "no matter how much of the discrepancy is due to errors of measurement and to statistical artifacts, a part of the dissonance between prediction and achievement probably lies within the social-psychological makeup of the individual" (p. 33).

Piaget's monumental work on the development of intelligence emphasized the vital importance of a stimulating environment in the adaptive development of ever more complex stages of intelligence (1936, 1937, 1945). His work has been lucidly interpreted by J. McV. Hunt (1961) and applied by others to studies of the roles of cultural deprivation and compensatory stimulation in affecting intellectual growth. Bayley and Schaefer (1964), in studying longitudinally the correlations of maternal and child behaviors with the development of mental abilities, made the intriguing discovery that boys' intelligence is strongly related to environmental factors, namely, the love-hostility dimension of maternal behavior, in contrast to the intelligence of girls. Another significant longitudinal study which points to the role of motivation in intellectual development is that of Kagan et al. (1958) who found that children with higher achievement motivation scores had IQ scores which had increased over a 4-year period, while those with lower achievement motivation scores had decreasing IQ scores. Other pertinent studies linking personality with cognitive styles include those of Gardner et al. (1960) and Witkin et al. (1962).

Conceptual formulations about achievement motivation as well as about the motivational aspects of intelligence are themselves contingent upon the authors' basic orientations in motivation theory. The wide range of theoretical positions concerning motivation seems to be evoked with special intensity around the very issues of achievement and mastery. These theoretical positions have special relevance to our study since we wish to keep in mind intrapsychic as well as environmental and educational factors affecting the development of intelligence and achievement. Briefly stated, in psychoanalytic theory, motivation arises from basic unconscious, tension-producing drives, and intrapsychic conflicts play a vital part in stimulating ego development and achievement. As Anna Freud (1936) succinctly stated, "instinctual danger makes human beings intelligent" (p. 163).

Hartmann (1939) introduced the concept of the adaptive, conflict-free autonomous functions of the ego, placing great emphasis on achievement as a vital part of the adaptive side of the ego. He spoke of intelligence and achievement on the one hand, and of defense mechanisms on the other, as mutually interacting; and, indeed, as often reflecting two aspects of one and the same ego process. Robert White (1960) has carried a view of motivation as independent of instinctual drives to its ultimate degree in his theory of effectance or competence motivation, and described developmental stages of competence along lines exactly parallel to psychosexual and psychosocial stages. Rapaport (1960), in responding to the challenge of White's theory, clearly reserves the psychoanalytic meaning of "motivation" for drive motivations, and subsumes all other factors influencing behavior (such as curiosity and exploratory activity) under the nonmotivational phrase "causes of behavior." Wolff (1960) attempts a synthesis between the two major motivation theories by postulating "long-range forces" which correspond to instinctual drives and "short-range forces" which correspond to ego functions relating directly to the external environment.

Psychoanalytic approaches to learning and performance problems (Pearson, 1954; Liss, 1955; Klein, 1949; A. Freud, 1965) have referred to repression, fantasied omnipotence of thought and speech, intellectualization, obsessional thinking, inhibition or restriction of ego functions out of shame and fear of narcissistic injury. These workers have also dealt with success neurosis involving fear and guilt over competition, conflict of parental ego ideals, or excesses and deficiencies of ego ideals, and more general problems of identification. The relevance of the superego is suggested by the labeling of such children as "academic delinquents" (Gowan, 1957). Halpern (1964) stressed parental narcissism and overcontrol as preventing the separation and individuation of the child, and making "achievement for his own sake" impossible.

Keiser (1965) and Khan (1965) discussed the way in which high intelligence can produce hypersensitivity to otherwise nontraumatic stimuli, as well as the role of intense symbiotic mother-child relationships in fostering certain unusual forms of high intelligence which remain unproductive. Keiser (1969) subsequently developed this dynamic relationship further.

Closely related to these emerging concepts, and of central importance to our study, are the heuristically fruitful concept of "focal symbiosis" proposed by Greenacre (1959) and A. Freud's (1965) description of ego disharmonies in terms of separate "developmental lines." It is to the psychodynamics of such uneven development of different functions as shown in so-called gifted underachievers that this study addresses itself. It is based on the comprehensive appraisal of 15 low-achieving (grades of C or below) high IQ (130 and above) boys who were referred because of our special interest in this area.[1] Details of the criteria for referral and the method of study are presented in the Appendix.

FINDINGS

After briefly describing some general characteristics of the sample, we shall focus on the outstanding verbal and performance patterns as manifested both in the current functioning of these boys and in the parents' histories of their child's early development.

GENERAL CHARACTERISTICS

All subjects were boys, since no girls were referred to the project although they had not been excluded in the criteria for referral.[2] The boys ranged in age from 7 to 13, most were between 9 and 11. Ten of the 15 boys had birthdays in the last four months of the year and started school at a somewhat younger age than the average child. Ten were oldest boys in their families, and of these 10, 7 were oldest children as well. The only 2 who were youngest sons belonged to the only two Jewish families in the sample.

In school, the boys read unusually well but performed poorly in arithmetic and in writing. Their teachers described them with terms such as: "He's lazy." "He goofs off." "He messes around." "He's obviously bright." At home, these boys read avidly, showed no initiative about homework, preferred to play with younger children, and enjoyed roaming alone in open country or woods.

Socially and culturally, many boys came from ambitious families who had made major moves geographically in search of economic betterment. Relative work instability or multiple occupations were frequent among the fathers of the boys, and the mothers often

---

[1] The authors wish to thank personnel of the Cincinnati Public Schools for their cooperation in locating and referring children for this study.

[2] The referral of only boys probably reflects in part the preponderance of boys over girls in the usual latency-age clinical population. In addition, it is consistent with the clinical impression that in boys academic problems are more likely to be manifested in latency, whereas girls are more apt to show similar problems at later developmental stages and in different dynamic constellations.

complained about what they considered to be their husbands' lack of success. The mothers often viewed marriage or the birth of their first child as an interruption of their own educations or careers.

CHILDREN'S VERBALIZATION

These boys all spoke easily, rapidly, fluently, and glibly. They enjoyed talking, had an impressive command of language for their age, and spoke with considerable social facility. Their speech was often picturesque; word plays and jokes were frequent; and on the spur of the moment they could become verbally engaging, entertaining, and disarming. At the same time they obviously derived much narcissistic and exhibitionistic pleasure from their own verbalizations. Their verbal fluency and high level of language utilization, however, did not reflect the kind of organization of knowledge and level of abstraction that are typical in children with such verbal skill.

These boys showed marked gaps in information when closely questioned, so that the knowledge they had paraded was actually patchy and inconsistent. In their areas of special interest, their vocabulary was highly technical, but their actual grasp of the concepts behind the words was judged to be no more than age-adequate by those who knew something about the specialized area. The boys' verbal cleverness petered out when any lengthy or sustained attention to the topic was attempted. They often blocked on the TAT and especially on the Rorschach, to which there were very few movement responses—those most clearly indicative of imagination and of the use of thought in place of immediate impulse expression. In a general way, the intellectual quality of their responses in less structured psychological tests did not conform to what is typically found in well-functioning youngsters with IQs as high as theirs.

Most of the boys had been described by their parents as having, outside the regular school curriculum, strong individual interests about which they knew a great deal. When, however, in the educational group experience, they were each given the opportunity to work on individually chosen projects of high personal interest, their results were uniformly poor.

To a more than ordinary degree these boys seemed to use speech for defensive rather than communicative or thought-clarifying purposes. Thus, these boys' glib speech often covered up their fundamental lack of knowledge in situations where they could not perform adequately. At times, they very skillfully diverted attention from their failures with facile apologies and amusing jokes.

Speech also was divorced from its appropriate function when used primarily for affective discharge in an intellectually challenging, academic situation. Here the boys, in a manner very immature for their ages, used speech that was egocentric and highly colored emotionally. Thus, during a flower-dissection project, the spontaneous comments, included: "The gooey stamen," "I smashed my ovules," "My pollen just fell off." It appears that academic material lent itself to readily verbalized, primitive associations.

Still another quality of their use of speech was their tendency to talk in an adult fashion and to intellectualize in response to questions about feelings and fantasies, often missing or avoiding the central issue. Thus, one 9-year-old, talking about sex differences, observed:

> They're an entirely different sex. I heard that girls react quicker than boys, they function quicker; . . . they don't have the muscular development. . . . I was studying doctoring books in school with a bunch of other kids who are interested in medical care, heart surgery, and stuff like that; I'm much more interested in bone structure.

Empty intellectualization emerged on psychological tests as well, where the boys gave lengthy, detailed, but essentially simple, irrelevant, and banal responses.

In summary, speech was used for narcissistic and exhibitionistic gratification, for impulsive affective discharge, and as a defense against anxiety and shame rather than as a means of age-appropriate thought clarification, communication, and emotional expression in dealing with the central issues of the moment.

CHILDREN'S NONVERBAL BEHAVIOR

Physical appearance and motor behavior contrasted sharply with verbalization. The boys appeared languid, lounging, and droopy;

they often slouched in their chairs, tiredly resting their heads in their hands, and working slowly and carelessly with one hand rather than two. Simultaneously, they displayed a great deal of small fidgeting movements such as finger-tapping, wriggling, or kicking their feet. They often used pens and pencils as objects to suck on or play with rather than as instruments of writing, and they had many hand-to-face mannerisms. In academic sessions characterized by unstructured class discussion they looked physically apathetic even as they spoke freely and fluently, but during formal paperwork they temporarily became still, tense, and in a sense immobilized. Thus, paradoxically, they often appeared both lethargic and restless.

Consistent with this picture is the fact that on psychological tests, these boys emphasized to a greater than usual degree images of leaning, lying, sitting and looking, looking and then doing nothing, and sleeping. Such imagery occurs typically in the records of people who are relatively inactive and have problems around inhibition or lack of energy.

At the level of actual motor performance, these boys displayed notably poor penmanship and generally sloppy-looking and unorganized paperwork. Their scores on the coding subtest of the WISC, the only subtest that requires use of a pencil, were the only scores that were almost uniformly low. It was noteworthy, however, that on their psychological tests they did not show even slight signs of any actual motor incoordination, and their total test performance was in no way suggestive of the presence of minimal brain damage.[3]

In the social diagnostic group, these boys gravitated toward immature activities. On the playground they showed little competitive interest, relied completely on adult leadership, and had uniformly poor athletic skills, as judged by an experienced recreational worker.

[3] Subjects' WISC scores tended to be somewhat lower than their Binet Scores (as might be expected statistically, because of regression to the mean and because of differences between the tests). While their Performance IQs were typically somewhat lower than their Verbal IQs they were nevertheless well above average, in the superior range.

PARENTAL ATTITUDES ABOUT SPEECH DEVELOPMENT

In their responses to questions about speech,[4] both parents concurred remarkably as they spoke of their son's precocity, emphasizing the clarity of speech and the excellent vocabulary. The mothers especially glowed with pride and saw these boys as wonderful conversational companions. Quite interestingly in both joint and individual interviews, the mothers were far more loquacious and verbally productive than the fathers. The mothers had a great need to talk and almost uniformly complained of a lack of verbal companionship and interaction with their husbands while emphasizing their verbal rapport with their sons. The extent to which these parents "adultomorphized" their infants was striking. They attributed to their boys not only a precocious vocabulary, but a greater degree of intentionality and adult motivation than such young children could possibly possess. In some cases the child reinforced this by pretending to know even more than he really did. The exploitation of the child for adult narcissistic or interpersonal needs was conspicuous. The following is a composite of parents' typical responses when asked how and when their sons began to talk:

> He talked like a little man. Speech has always been clear, there was no baby talk. . . . He liked to keep people entertained and laughing. . . . He could talk his way out of any responsibility and had a way of twisting words around to suit his own purpose. . . . He picked up grown-up words and we laughed. . . . He could recite 25 pages at age 2½ and make like he was reading. . . . He was witty and sharp. If he didn't know the answer, he made one up.

[4] These responses were regarded not primarily as objective data about early events in the family and developmental histories, but as projective material which might reflect basic characterological attitudes of each parent toward the many unfolding aspects of the child's development. Thus, a mother, while stating that her son spoke very early, might use glowing terms, revealing her strong subjective pleasure. Her emotional response was considered to be "psychologically true" even though the chronological statement might or might not be accurate. This is analogous to viewing a person's responses on projective tests as revealing his psychological reality, rather than his external reality. The "early parental memories" were especially revealing when mother's and father's views were incongruent.

Similar patterns were found in other underachievers who were not included in this study since they were slightly below the required IQ of 130. For example, one mother said: "He was a beautiful talker at age 2; he said things I couldn't. At 3 he corrected our English; it floored me. He could talk so intelligent, when he wasn't even toilet trained. I couldn't adjust that fast, first like talking to an adult, then to a baby."

An adolescent boy who was a very gifted underachiever, but overage for our clinical sample, explained in a therapy hour that as a child he had learned to use words which visibly impressed his parents, but that he had no idea what they meant. He recalled at age 4 asking them to their great astonishment, "What is relativity?" but he was not interested in listening to the answer. Instead, he was searching for his next impressive word.

As so clearly stated by these parents, their special emphasis was on their children's early speech as an end in itself, on its plainness, its adultlike qualities, its entertainment value, and its cleverness, even implying a cleverness in pretending to know. Some parents even admired their children's ability to use language to exploit and manipulate adults. By contrast, these parents expressed relatively little pride or delight, as most parents of bright children do, in the intrinsic qualities of the child's intelligence, in his ability to understand concepts and ideas, in his capacity to solve problems, and in the potential development of his intellect. In essence they said: "he talked clearly" rather than "he thought clearly." They seemed unaware of the existence of thoughts and feelings behind their child's words. It appears that these parents were easily satisfied with superficial appearances of intelligence, and with an image of the child as having already achieved the status of a small but highly verbal "adult" at age 2. They conversed with him on a level far beyond his years. They seemed unaware of the need for further growth and did not view their child as a developing toddler with bright future possibilities. Several of the boys responded to this parental view of them by pretending to know more than they really did.

PARENTAL ATTITUDES ABOUT EARLY MOTOR-MUSCULAR ACTIVITY
AND THE DEVELOPMENT OF SPHINCTER CONTROL

There was less uniformity in the responses relevant to these developmental areas than those about speech development. In marked contrast to the many positive expressions of pleasure and delight in the child's speech, we saw no enthusiasm about physical activities and only a few instances of pride around the child's acquisition of sphincter control. Parents valued passivity, recognizing no problem if their children were quiet but complaining of severe problems in active children. In either case they implied that they viewed activity and autonomy as problem areas.

Six mothers who described the boys as having been relatively quiet and passive saw them as "good babies, causing no trouble." One mother retrospectively expressed guilt, feeling she had neglected her son who had demanded little and had played contentedly in his playpen. She explained he had been "no bother," thus attributing negative qualities to activity.

In the 7 boys who were described as very active or even hyperactive, it was the nuisance value of the activity that was stressed. In one instance, the mother said that her son had always been harder to handle than his sister, who was quieter and less active. She attributed his greater activity to his masculinity. She described him as exceedingly active, walking at 9 months, and a curious child, "eager to get into everything and hard to keep up with."

In those cases where we noted the vivid description of energy and activity, it was difficult to estimate whether the boy was really so unusually active or whether the mother was basically intolerant of the child's activity, experiencing it as dangerous, demanding or fatiguing to her. In either case, however, the total parent-child interaction in this area appeared to be one of displeasure or ambivalence.

In summary, although the parents described their child's activity as ranging all the way from passive to hyperactive, they invariably expressed conflictual or negative attitudes toward activity. It is therefore not surprising that only 2 out of the 15 boys showed even average athletic ability. Many fathers expressed disappointment about this deficiency.

Questions about toilet training elicited a variety of responses. The 7 boys who were trained in the age range from 8–18 months caused "no difficulty" or "no major problem." (One of these boys who caused "no difficulty" was later described as having caused "a difficulty in the neighborhood when he stopped up a sewer.") When mothers did express pride, it was because of the child's early and total acquiescence. For example, they used phrases like "I got him conquered completely" and "he was quite proud of his accomplishment." Since this achievement was said to occur at 8 months, one must wonder whose pride it was!

The toilet training of 4 boys, which began at 1 year and was completed at 3 years, was admittedly a battleground. Two of the boys had defiantly and exhibitionistically urinated on the floor in front of mother, and one had dramatically defecated in front of her. One boy, trained very early, was remembered for having sat on top of an elaborate chocolate cake placed high on a cupboard beyond his reach. His mother remembered having cried about this, but could not be angry because "he simply wanted a place to sit down." Four of the 15 boys had episodes of acute or chronic soiling in later childhood.

From the descriptions, training was evidently a source of exasperation in many of the mothers, and a source of conflict in the boys. Feelings of pride related to conquest of the child. Parents' feelings of pleasure about either their sons' physical activities or autonomous sphincter control were conspicuously absent. There were echoes of these early tensions and disappointments in the later years of school, with the parents of all 15 of the boys frantically urging, to no avail, that their boys "sit down and do their homework."

DISCUSSION

Intensive study of 15 underachieving gifted children revealed that these boys are verbally fluent and skillful while physically clumsy and inept. Indeed, they are poor doers in general. This consistently uneven pattern of ego development was retrospectively described by parents as occurring already in the second year of life. Since the parents knew that the interviewers were investigating the origins of current underachievement in their gifted children, it is possible that retrospective distortions or rationalizations play a significant part in these developmental histories. Nevertheless, we feel the picture that emerged in this specific area, that is, the convergence of markedly positive attitudes toward verbal skills and the active discouragement or passive neglect of performance skills, was so consistent that it is a useful hypothetical pattern to test in further controlled and longitudinal studies.

As a powerful vehicle for achieving positive social reactions, the boys' speech greatly impressed parents, teachers, and other professional persons, at least initially. From the vantage point of intelligence tests, they ranked in the very superior range, especially in the verbal areas. The verbal fluency which they showed reflects a kind of intelligence which pays off well on the verbally loaded IQ tests. Examination in depth of the boys' intellectual functioning showed that they lacked the other intellectual abilities that are usually associated with good verbal skills and which taken together constitute high intelligence. Verbal fluency is indeed the only outstanding ego ability these boys demonstrate. Witkin et al. (1962) described a certain subgroup of less well-differentiated children whose personality characteristics appear remarkably similar to those of the boys in the present study. He described them as follows: "Despite the high level of verbal skills of these 2 boys, in their interviews they gave an unmistakable impression of a low level of cognitive clarity. Both had a wide fund of information on many subjects, but the information was poorly assimilated. They gave the impression of trying hard to impress adults and, as far as the personnel of the laboratory was concerned, they succeeded in this attempt" (p. 266).

Thus, so-called verbal intelligence in these children can be viewed as having developed considerably beyond all other functions. The discrepancy or disharmony between the levels of development of ego functions in these boys is striking. Speech became a prominent but relatively isolated function, significantly detached from action, rational thinking, and emotional expression. The precocious preeminence of speech emerges as a vital focal point of parent-child experience. Many genetic factors may lead to this specific pattern of ego development, but once established it gives rise to dynamically important ramifications.

Our further discussion will focus on (1) aspects of early ego development which facilitate ego disharmony; (2) dynamically important ramifications of such skewed experience in subsequent personality development; and (3) implications for psychoeducational programs.

ASPECTS OF EARLY EGO DEVELOPMENT
WHICH FACILITATE EGO DISHARMONY

The Separateness of Early Ego Functions

The ego is comprised of a large number of autonomous functions, the basic elements of which initially develop separately in a process of differentiation out of an early diffuse, unorganized state. Only later are they coordinated into an ascending hierarchy of higher functions. Important conceptual formulations of the separate early development of emergent ego functions have been described by Glover (1956), Vygotsky (1934), and A. Freud (1965). Piaget's formulations of the stages of intellectual growth parallel and may be fruitfully coordinated with the phases of ego development.

Glover contended that the earliest ego tendencies are derived from numerous scattered instincts which converge gradually, probably about the age of 2. "As development proceeds, the nuclei [of the primitive ego structure] merge more or less (it is always a case of more or less with ego-synthesis) and a coherent and complicated ego structure appears" (p. 318).

Piaget, in his studies of early sensorimotor intelligence, gives numerous examples of functions which develop separately at first, and later become reciprocally coordinated to form more complex behavioral units. For example, the infant is slowly developing skill in grasping objects and in looking at them, but he does not look at what he grasps, nor does he grasp what he sees. It is not until the age of 5 months that a mutual coordination takes place between seeing and prehension, and the child can now "see what he grasps and grasp what he sees."

A specific example of the separateness of early functions,

especially relevant to our study, has been described by Vygotsky (1934), who states: "In their ontogenetic development, thought and speech have different roots. In the speech development of the child, we can establish a preintellectual stage, and in his thought development, a prelinguistic stage. Up to a certain point in time, the two follow different lines, independently of each other. At a certain point these lines meet, whereupon thought becomes verbal and speech rational" (p. 44). When "at about the age of two the curves of development of thought and speech, till then separate, meet and join to initiate a new form of behavior . . . the child 'makes the greatest discovery of his life,' that 'each thing has its name' " (p. 43).

Finally, Anna Freud's (1965) concept of developmental lines emphasizes that the development of the child from infantile to adult patterns proceeds along numerous dimensions or lines of personality, comprised of both drive and ego contributions, and that discrepancies between different levels reached along different lines produce many normal and pathological variations. She states that under the influence of external and internal factors, these lines of development may proceed at a fairly equal rate, i.e., harmoniously, or with wide divergences of speed which lead to varying kinds of imbalances, variations, and incongruities of personality development. Among her examples, she gives one particularly relevant to our topic; namely, that of excessive speech and thought development with infantilism of needs, fantasies, and wishes. Nagera's (1966) concept of "developmental interference" also suggests that excessive stimulation of a function (as well as lack of stimulation) can interfere with normal development.

Thus, several authors have formulated the concept that ego functions develop separately at first, each at its own pace and influenced independently by internal and external factors. As the function matures, it may be coordinated with other concurrent functions to form a more complex unit. Each function has it own critical period as it emerges when it is most vulnerable to influence. Similarly, crucial reciprocal and synthetic coordinations of functions also have critical periods; for example, prehension and vision at 5 months; vocalization and thought at 2 years.

Three Possible Fates of Separate Ego Functions: Enhancement, Conflict, and Silent Compliance

In the emerging personality each separate ego function, before it becomes coordinated with others, may have a specific individual dynamic course which will influence its fate. These kinds of influence may be conceptualized as enhancement, conflict, and silent compliance.

Basic to all development, certain innate factors play an important role at least in limiting the upper range of maturation of a given function. Below this limit, however, environmental factors have crucial impact. The proportion of hereditary-environmental influences may vary from one function to another. Thus, walking has a maturational timetable less subject to environmental influence than speech. As A. Freud (1952) has observed, walking and motor development are more conflict-free than speech, which in turn is more conflict-free than sphincter control. Those functions which are more subject to environmental influence are more vulnerable to conflict situations. Families and cultures bring greater pressures to bear upon the innate maturational curves of some functions than of others.

The complex, ambivalent attitudes of parents toward their children find numerous outlets for expression in the emergence of separate ego functions. For example, motor development may be encouraged by the positive attitudes of a sports-minded father, while simultaneously intellectual tendencies may be inhibited as "sissyish." For a dependent, depressed mother, her son's speech may serve as a gratifying avenue for companionship, which she may foster excessively. A phallic, narcissistic mother will enhance those traits in her son, such as physical prowess or intellectual achievement, which best express her own unconscious masculine wishes. A mother's eagerness to serve protectively as her child's "accessory ego" may stunt her child's development of autonomy. In an academically striving family, a child's early speech may elicit the parents' unusually strong investment, which then further enhances verbalization. A child's sexual interests and curiosity may stimulate guilt in the parent and evoke a repressive response.

Parents cannot be characterized simply as "rejecting mothers" or "dominating fathers." A mother may express ambivalence by behaving rejectingly toward some functions in the child while accepting or even encouraging others, or she may express such ambivalent attitudes to the same function at different times (e.g., valuing the 2-year-old's compliance and berating the 10-year-old's lack of initiative). The wide array of functions of the child's growing ego serves as a keyboard for the playing out of a broad range of parental attitudes, unconscious wishes, hopes, and conflicts (Coleman et al., 1953).

Our study of 15 underachieving gifted boys revealed important discrepancies in parental attitudes toward the ego functions of speech, motormuscular skill, and autonomous sphincter control, all of which initially develop separately in the second and third years and ultimately become integrated.

In reference to early speech in these boys, it appeared that the uniformly positive parental responses of delight and pride enormously fostered verbal development. Thus, enhancement was the basic parental influence upon this particular ego function. In this study several dynamic-genetic factors seem to lead to this enhancement. Most of the boys were firstborn, which ordinal position has been correlated with early development of speech because of closer parent-child relationships (Koch, 1954). About half of the mothers had been significantly depressed in the boys' first year of life. Their depressions were not severe enough to cause them to turn totally away from their babies; rather, they sought excessive gratification from them. They complained about their husbands' aloofness and marked lack of verbal communication. It is likely that the mothers' dependency needs and depressive tendencies were assuaged to some degree with the onset of speech in their boys. Each mother reported great pleasure in conversing with her toddler son as though he were a little adult.

Another factor favoring enhancement of speech was the mother's own ambition for scholastic success. Many mothers reported that they had interrupted their educations to get married. It may well be that they had displaced their academic ambitions to their sons. Many of the mothers had intellectualized relationships with their own fathers and had thereby erotized intellectual functions generally, but they had, not surprisingly, often made nonintellectual or regressive "preoedipal" marital choices of relatively passive husbands. Most of the husbands had histories of school difficulties and relative occupational failures. In their sons, these mothers sought anew those elements that had been important in their earlier relationship with their fathers. Thus, they eagerly fostered verbalization as a sign of intellectual precocity and masculinity.

Parental narcissism is another speech-enhancing factor. The vocabulary used in mother-son conversations appears to have been slanted toward mature-sounding words clearly enunciated with little regard for meaning or content. A 9-month-old infant, according to his proud mother, was said to have used the word "flyswatter." A 4-year-old repeated the word "relativity." This type of superficial overstimulation of speech may produce an artificial "hothouse" or "early blooming" quality which does not stand the test of time. Such artificial, external enhancement results in a totally different quality from that which occurs when speech is the timely expression of images, feelings, and internal concepts. At times the emptiness and hollowness of such speech remind one of the parroted words which are sometimes used by the congenitally blind when they speak of colors.

The mother's enhancement of her child's speech might be considered a hypercathexis of a particular ego function. It might be compared to Mahler's (1952) description of the peculiar hypercathexis of one part of the body encountered in many symbiotic children, often corresponding to the type of parental overstimulation which occurred during prolonged symbiotic relationships. She stated that in these "symbiotic cases the adult partner very often seems to be able to accept the child only as long as it belongs as a quasi-vegetative being, an appendage, to her or his body" (p. 293). Greenacre (1959) dealt with a similar phenomenon in her concept of focal symbiosis, which she conceived as an intensely strong interdependence, usually between mother and child, which is limited to a special and circumscribed relationship rather than a nearly total, enveloping one. Although the concepts of hypercathexis and focal symbiosis have been generally applied to the parental hypercathexis of bodily parts of the child, we have found these concepts useful in conceptualizing the mother's strong need to enhance or exploit a particular ego function, mental capacity, or cognitive style in her child.

The ego functions of motor-muscular activity and sphincter control in our study sample were not subjected to the same process of unambivalent parental enhancement which we have described above for the function of speech. Nor did the mother and father have essentially similar or compatible responses to these areas as they did to the function of speech. The mother-son interactions around activity and performance fell into two major patterns, each of which served in its unique way to bring about a common outcome of apparent passivity in the child.

In the case of the active and independent boys, a developmental interaction of *neurotogenic conflict* arose, leading to later character patterns of passive aggression, covert resistance, apathy with underlying hostile fantasy, and a high incidence of chronic depressive symptoms and traits, all of which were evidenced in the current assessments of these boys.

In the case of the passive boys, a subtle but noteworthy mode of mother-child interaction involved hidden pleasure in and exploitation of the child's passivity, which fit so well with the neurotic needs of the mother.

Such an interaction does not have the intensity of enthusiasm and narcissistic pleasure and other positive affects openly expressed in the *enhancement* mode, which characterizes the development of speech in these families. Nor does it have the quality of the *open conflict* (so visible in early development) which, when internalized, may become part of the child's neurosis. The apparent lack of pathology, or façade of normality, obscures a subtle underlying pathogenic process specific to these ego functions. Here, an innate tendency or disposition of the child dovetails with a neurotic need of the parent, so that the "line of least resistance" results in a gradual, imperceptible, and conflict-free amplification of a basic trend (i.e., passivity) to a pathological degree. The parent makes no attempt to increase the child's active strivings by stimulation or education. This is the hidden symptom of which the mother does not complain. "He was a good baby, he caused no trouble." "He was quiet, he was no bother." Somewhat like the older child in the classroom who, though withdrawn, does not disturb the teacher into seeking help, this type of infant is unwittingly allowed from birth onward to become deficient in some function because of the parent's hidden compliance for his own gratification. Rationalizing "that was just the way he was," the parent is really feeling, "He was just the way I wanted him to be." Naturally, parents have a blind spot in perceiving this behavior as a symptom, since it is so family-syntonic. The concept of *compliance* is especially useful here. In psychoanalytic theory, somatic compliance means that the psychological state of an organ happens to parallel or comply with a neurotic pattern in the individual, and lends itself to a continuation of the neurosis. Hartmann (1939) coined the term "social compliance" in analogy.

The parent-child interaction described above can be conceived still further analogously as *familial compliance* to a deviant trait in the child. The pathology of such a trait, obscured within the family dynamics, emerges into visibility only when the child leaves home and enters school. How often parents say, "There was nothing wrong with him until he went to school!" Often the sudden appearance of difficulty is not related primarily to the new experience of going to school. Instead, the child's tendencies, with which the family complied, finally encounter a lack of such compliance in the wider social world.

Ego Functions, Considered Separately and Together, with Special Regard to Future Conflict Formation and Eventual Insufficiency in Synthetic Function

As described above, the concept of "focal symbiosis" was especially helpful in understanding the possible dynamics leading to *enhancement* of speech. In contrast to speech, the functions of motor activity and sphincter control were subjected to influences resulting in either *conflict* or *compliance.* In an important sense, it is an oversimplification to identify an ego function as either completely "conflicted" or "conflict-free." It has become clear that even if several functions develop individually in a "conflict-free" manner, the fact that some are subjected to enhancement while others are subjected to compliance lays the groundwork for both intrasystemic and intersystemic conflict in the future. Hartmann (1951) urged: "To the study of the ego's relations with the id or the superego, that is of the intersystemic conflicts and correlations, we shall have to add a more detailed study of the intrasystemic correlations." He believed that it was crucial to study various aspects of structure within the ego, such as "the relative preponderance of certain ego functions over others" (p. 145). Accordingly, the discrepancies in the developments of the speech and activity functions of the boys in this study can be viewed as producing an "intrasystemic conflict" within the ego. These conflicts within the ego can develop in several ways and take several forms.

Piaget has shown that sensorimotor activity is the firm foundation for genuine intellectual flowering later. Among these boys, however, "intelligent-sounding speech" developed early, but in relative isolation from physical activity, and thus speech developed on its own, unanchored by intelligent sensorimotor activity. The child, of course, does not initially perceive that his enhanced speech function is superior to others of his functions, or to the speech skills of other children. But sooner or later he must unconsciously become aware of his own development and of the special significance that his skills and deficiencies have for his parents. At this point, secondary conflicts (e.g., guilt over success, shame over inadequacy, resentment against parental vicarious gratification, rebellion against parental exploitation of his own function) appear to cluster around the very function which was *enhanced* in a conflict-free manner early in development. Thus, many factors contribute over a period of time to changing *enhancement* from an initially conflict-free mode to one which is ultimately intensely conflict-producing.

Likewise, parental compliance with an ultimately maladaptive trait in the child appears to be a situation totally free of conflict. Everything proceeds amiably. It is only later when the maladaptive nature of the trait becomes socially visible, usually outside the family, that an insidious neurotic conflict may belatedly focus around this area. The particular ego function whose development has been inhibited in this subtle manner probably has a high degree of resistance to later remedial efforts. The dynamics involved are similar to those described by Johnson (1949) as leading to "superego lacunae," but in this case we are speaking of a kind of "ego lacunae," unwittingly fostered (rather than "unconsciously condoned") by the parents.

It is possible, ironically, that openly visible conflict between parent and child around an ego function is the least pathogenic interaction of the three described above. *Enhancement* and *compliance* are influences which promote delayed, but severe, neurotic conflicts.

When these delayed conflicts finally become visible in the oedipal or latency periods, we are often misled into attributing the sources of the conflict to problems originating in these stages of development. But as noted, the conflict originates much earlier in the preoedipal period, out of distortions stamped initially on the ego alone.

It is important to consider not only the conflict potentials of individual ego functions but also those of the several functions together, as a disharmonious cluster which facilitates intrasystemic conflict within the ego. Of special importance is the potential impoverishment of a function which grows out of phase with other contemporaneous but deficiently developing functions and cannot gain strength and richness from them. Normally, functions of speech, thought, and action develop crucial, mutually enriching coordinations across harmoniously developing phases. But when marked enhancement takes place, the function develops in isolation, to its eventual detriment.

Among the principal tasks of the healthy ego are its executive and mediating functions among the id, superego, and external reality. Since it mediates between potentially conflictual demands of the psychic structure and external reality, and is itself party to neurotic conflict, it must be strong, integrated, resilient, and harmonious. In its executive function, it must ideally "speak as one mind." When moderate conflict or disharmony is present, the healthy ego has a synthetic function which can creatively construct, or impose, a high degree of unity in overall functioning. If these master functions of the ego are served by a number of supporting functions such as speech and motor activity, which are highly discordant, a high level of synthetic or integrative activity must take place within the ego before it is applied outside the ego, or between the ego and other psychic agencies. The ego which is occupied with unusually difficult synthetic or integrative functions within itself will have little to lend to the task of conflict resolution between itself and other agencies.

In the boys described, the discrepancy between verbal and performance functions was so great that we hypothesized a relative insufficiency of the synthetic function, which, even if strong, appeared unequal to the integrative task. The development of the synthetic function was thus impaired by its repeated lack of success in integrating the enhanced function of speech with the inhibited function of activity. We might also suppose that the familial conflicts in our cases were sufficient to diminish the child's synthetic function by libidinal deficiency. The boys were frequently depressed and highly unorganized in many ways.

A disharmonious ego is especially vulnerable to the influences of narcissism, which selectively rewards and reinforces a child's pleasure-producing abilities, and shuns shame-producing deficiencies, thus powerfully aggravating the vicious cycle of spiraling disharmony. "The rich get richer and the poor get poorer." In the long run, this disharmony was at the expense of the total healthy narcissism.

In summary, neurotic conflict within and between the parents may be acted out in various ways upon the fabric of the child's immature ego. Libidinization and enhancement of one function, and open conflict or subtle compliance with regard to other functions, lead to pathological developments of the individual functions involved and to faulty coordinations among them. The development of actual conflict may be subtle and delayed. Disharmony and discrepancy among component ego functions lead to mutual incoordination and impoverishment of these functions, relative insufficiency of the synthetic function, and intrasystemic conflict. Narcissism accentuates the process, setting in motion an intrinsic motivational system which enhances a skill area and aggravates deficiencies still further.

The pattern or syndrome of ego disharmony transcends the traditional diagnostic classifications. In the present series of cases the pattern was part of overall clinical pictures which included borderline states, narcissistic personality disorders, and passive-aggressive personalities. Oedipal conflicts were flamboyant but not primary (see below), and sexual confusion was common. While these diagnostic groups require different kinds of therapeutic approaches, in each case the disharmony itself must be recognized and special attention paid to its often central role in the ongoing (though sometimes delayed) pathological progression of the personality. While the ultimate bedrock of ego disharmony is very difficult to modify, awareness of its complex ramifications in character structure is important in planning therapy and special education.

THE RAMIFICATIONS OF EARLY EGO IMBALANCE
IN SUBSEQUENT DEVELOPMENT

We have described how a particular group of related ego functions, which normally develop separately, concurrently, and interrelatedly in the second year of life, have been subjected to different fates, depending in part on varying types of parental influences, three of which we have described as *enhancing, familial compliant,* and *conflictual.*

From an early period, the skew in the ego appears well established. Some parents may in fact relate to the child's budding ego more pathologically than to his id, perhaps imposing their own distortions on some aspects of the new and still malleable ego, rather than on the child's instinctual drives. The interactions of this rigidly skewed segment of the child's ego with other aspects of his growing personality may produce serious pathology. The particular variety of ego disharmony described above appeared to have a number of different but interrelated ramifications, which can be considered according to developmental sequences.

The Narcissism-Depression Axis

The narcissistic attractiveness of a precocious talent with all its glamour and glitter compels attention and detracts from less remarkable skills and capacities. Thus, a single ego function, if precociously developed (even if only in the eyes of the parents), may be subject to a form of the psychology of the exception (Freud, 1916), in which, because of the exceptional nature of the gift, everything else is tolerated or even condoned. The narcissism in these cases appears peculiarly lopsided, even while retaining its infinite quality. On the one hand, as the child becomes aware of his superior capacities of verbalization and the value and power of these capacities, he cultivates them still further. Parental narcissism, his own narcissism, and his own verbalization enhance one another actively in a spiral of motivating rewards. On the other hand, sometimes behind the scenes, sometimes openly, the child's defects in performance feed a cycle of shame, low self-esteem, and injured narcissism, which depresses performance still further. The child's ego disharmony parallels a dynamic system of affects involving both heightened narcissism and readiness for narcissistic injury; these may balance each other or alternate cyclically, each serving periodically as a defense against the other. The resulting depression is a focal form of that described by Bibring (1953) as "narcissistic injury." The depression may express itself through a region of the ego which is poorly developed. The so-called giftedness reflects narcissistic aspects and the so-called underachievement reflects depressive trends, both of which are evident in the current functioning of these children. Recurring sequences of enthusiasm and apathy are constantly noted and are often entirely attributed to current, secondary effects of underachievement. But this cycle operates at a deep level of the personality.

The Sense of Omnipotence

The heightened sense of omnipotence in these children is closely related to the problems of narcissism described above. In immature stages of development, words are typically endowed with magical and omnipotent powers. This is even more the case in those children whose words have had such powerful effects upon parents. Using only words, the child finds he can evoke enormous gratifications from his parents. Often parents will say, "Of course he is not a genius, but. . . ." The repeated experience of feelings of omnipotence associated with the act of talking also contributes to the child's exaggerated expectation in school that talking alone will see him through. "He feels he can talk his way out of and into anything." Often, of course, parents have anticipated great academic success solely from the child's early verbal skills, only to discover belatedly when he went to school that other very different skills are also required. By the time the parents are disillusioned with the power of words, the defect in the ego is well established.

When the child's verbal activities are accompanied by dangerous omnipotent fantasies, he also has at hand a ready mechanism to disarm himself, to forestall retaliation, and later to placate or bribe his superego. Verbal omnipotence or omniscience seems safer because of the relative inability to perform. Much as the dreamer can dream powerful images and scenes because pathways to motility are blocked in sleep, the ideational life of the verbalizer may actively be facilitated by his very ineptness of performance. This use of verbalization is akin, in some ways, to the defensive use of thinking processes in obsessional patients. Clinically, our subjects sometimes had obsessional symptoms as part of their total personality functioning. However, they were clearly not obsessional personalities.

Acting Out Through Words

A lag in motor skills may itself influence the use of words. Where channels for motor discharge of impulses have been inhibited or underdeveloped, there may be a strong substitutive use of the verbal channel for impulse expression. Greenacre (1952) termed this phenomenon "acting out through words," and described how speech becomes degraded and exploited for purposes other than communication. She stated that the emphasis on the cuteness of speech and its use for exhibitionistic purposes may occur in children with precociously clear verbalization, sometimes based on their amusing imitations of elders. The overloading or contamination of one ego channel may be seen as the developmental failure of another. The burden placed on language by its use in "acting out" may weaken its effectiveness as an agent for other functions such as impulse delay and emotional control.

The Reality Principle and the Capacity to Delay

The capacity to delay, so vital to the development of the reality principle, is seriously handicapped in the child whose particular skill of verbalization so frequently produces "instant gratification" in everyone. Speech requires little physical effort. As one mother explained, her clever son made her think of the following Biblical quotation: "Consider the lilies how they grow, they toil not, they spin not; and yet I say unto you, that Solomon in all his glory was not arrayed like one of these." The child's instantaneous success "unmotivates" him or renders unnecessary the use of other, slower, more effortful means of securing parental praise. The need to develop the capacities to delay, to play, and to work, has been short-circuited in the overly praised verbal child. (This is not unlike a similar problem which arises in beautiful children.) One boy, intensely aware of his high intelligence, stated that "Just knowing my potential has the soothing anesthetic effect of straight A's." His very gift of words has chained him to their evanescent use. Intelligence and verbalization may become such an "end pleasure" in themselves that they are no longer used as a means to an end.

Furthermore, in a family atmosphere where only final success is praised, the early and intermediate steps of patient and painstaking endeavor, clumsy trials, and initial failure will tend to be avoided. Weaker, slower-developing areas will give way to the more rapidly rewarded areas of strength, unless the handicap is so glaring as to evoke special solicitude and remediation.

Ambivalence

Ambivalence originating at any level, in relation to any pair of drives, finds a natural outlet in this particular type of ego imbalance. Love of a parent may be readily expressed with verbal offerings of charm and affection, while the simultaneous hostility finds unspoken but behavioral (nonverbal) expression in failure and inadequate performance. Likewise, activity is expressed in vivacious verbal fluency, while passivity is expressed in behavior. The child who must deal with double-bind messages from one or both parents can resolve his dilemma by responding to one of the messages verbally, and to the other, behaviorally. This kind of unconscious compromise may preserve the personality from a deeper rupture.

Fantasies Projected upon the Ego

Fantasies and unconscious imagery originating at all stages of development may be experienced symbolically in various ego functions. A child who is aware at some level that he speaks fluently and well, while he is clumsy and ineffectual in his actions, can easily associate oral feelings of plenty with his words, and feelings of emptiness with his deficits.

At an anal level, the child can "let go" verbally (logorrhea) while withholding the activities so eagerly desired by the adults around him. Many clinical studies of children have related poor perform-ances to stubborn withholding or retentive modes, or to passive aggression and passive resistance. In addition, nonperformance deriving from some other level may be misinterpreted as "anal"; thus the child who "can't" is often perceived as the child who "won't."

Phallic fantasies can readily seize upon "outstanding" abilities as "phallic" and on deficits as feminine or castrated. In these boys, early verbalization had often been enhanced and exploited because the strong phallic strivings in the mothers were both expressed and defended against in intellectual derivatives, long before it could acquire this significance in the mind of the child. However, as the child entered this phase, he might make the symbolic equation on his own, or unconsciously respond to the mother's equation, and develop secondary conflicts at this level.

The Role of Ego Imbalance in the Genesis of Defense Mechanisms

The imbalanced ego profile can be an important structural precursor in the subsequent genesis of various defense mechanisms. Verbal skills and defective performance lend themselves well to the mechanisms of isolation, to defense by denial, reaction formation, and "acting out." As mentioned above, speech itself can be a subtle form of acting out. Certainly, these children used speech in primitive and impulsive ways. At the same time, their verbal skill greatly facilitated at later stages of development the use of intellectualization and rationalization. This study revealed that the early impulsive use of speech was only partly superseded by defensive intellectualization and lacked adequate development of the intervening stage of the communicative and thought-clarifying functions of language. These children differed, as a group, from obsessive-compulsive children whose mentation or inner speech is so important in their defense structure. It was the mixture of the impulsive and the intellectual which appeared overly impulsive in academic settings and intellectualized in emotionally charged settings. In fact, their speech is used increasingly for defensive purposes and becomes ever less adaptive once the child moves outside of his family.

The Parents' Leveling Tendency

The child's development is impeded not only by the ego disharmony but also by the parents' tendency to maintain the *status quo* of the "little genius." When the parents view early verbalization as mature and adultlike, they may easily generalize to see their child as almost a little man, therefore a finished product. This perception, although it increases current expectations, reduces expectations for further growth, de-emphasizes the need for intervening stages of development, and hinders continued emotional development of the child. A compellingly evocative image of the child's future is absent. How can he *become* what he already is? In fact, having started with adultomorphic perception of the child in his earliest years, parents often resist inevitable change and growth as regressive as he turns more to his peers as identification models for standards of behavior. Furthermore, by using their sons as quasi-adult confidants, they may stimulate and intensify their sons' anxieties. Later, precocious knowledge may intensify anxieties and guilt reactions in the oedipal phase. Or, a precociously intellectual vocabulary may prevent the child from experiencing the full emotional impact of a phase. Premature verbalization serves as a kind of "defense before the fact"; experience and activities normally *precede* the naming or verbalization process.

Precocious intelligence may also lead to tendencies in the child to force hasty premature closure in his thinking, as he anxiously avoids trial and error while he strains to maintain the appearance of superior competence. He uses his intelligence for quick solutions, he seeks problems which have flash-answers, not daring to show uncertainty, anxiety, ignorance, and searching behavior, which are a necessary part of larger tasks. This is akin to Christine Olden's (1946) concept of "headline intelligence."

Influence on Separation-Individuation Phase

Ironically, the very same boys described as adultlike in their early speech are in later years perceived by everyone as immature and infantile. Of course, the parents' neurotic need to see maturity in the infant is related to their own anxieties about maturity in the larger growing boy and to their subsequent depreciation of adult masculinity. As long as a little boy can serve as a phallic extension of mother, by visibly enhancing her through his verbal precocity, he arouses unambivalently positive feeling. But to the extent that he seeks to become an autonomous male on his own, mother's underlying castration anxieties and envy are newly evoked and intensified. There appears to be a crucial "tipping point" in early boyhood toward the conclusion of the separation-individuation phase when the masculinity which had been pridefully proclaimed and assiduously promoted in babyhood now becomes threatening to mother. For such a mother, separation-individuation in her son means his emergence not only as an independent person but as a male, separate from herself. The disruption of the tie reactivates castration anxieties within the mother, and then retaliatory castration wishes and secondary guilt which may lead to depression. The special separation conflict in both mother and son is often resolved by a compromise in which the son becomes verbally close to his mother while behaving freely by "messing around" and "roaming about" for himself. This behavioral independence and manifestation of masculinity are so precious that the boy later has special difficulty in submitting to further educative influences, especially those of women teachers.

The Oedipal Period and Castration Anxiety

The total constellation of factors that led to early ego imbalance thus far described may be an especially fertile substrate for conflicts in the oedipal period, and may render the child vulnerable to a particular pattern of faulty resolution of this crisis. These oedipal conflicts may then appear so blatant as to obscure the underlying ego disharmony and confuse the clinical diagnosis. The boy described as a "little man" early in his childhood can be thought of as having received an unearned "oedipal victory," long before the development of his own oedipal strivings. This early apparent triumph through verbalization makes the oedipal strivings more guilt-producing and the inevitable defeat more humiliating. The same boy who posed a castration threat to his mother as he attained some forms of independence from her now enters the oedipal phase to face not only his inevitable inadequacy but the hidden wrath of a depreciated, passive father whom he "deposed" long ago, and with whom it is dangerous to identify lest he suffer the same depreciated fate. The mother who accepted her son as a phallic extension will continue to accept obsequious and clinging aspects of his present attempts to live out his oedipal relationship to her, so that even as she often freely pets and seduces him as her "baby," she at the same time will vigorously deny or repress any sexual implications. He is blocked not only by his fantasies of father's rage against him for oedipal feelings but also by the poor masculine identification figure afforded by his father.

In this type of impasse, the boy again exploits the ego disharmony to the fullest. The child may use verbalization to further his emotional tie to a verbal mother, and he may use his relative physical inadequacies as a provocative defiance of his father.

The verbal tie to mother serves as a defense against oedipal impulses, yet at the same time affords some vicarious gratification through the intimate, subtle, verbal rapport. Family therapy sessions may highlight the mothers' and sons' mutual understanding of fine verbal nuances while the father remains remote and insensible on the periphery. Mother and son are often aware that they share the same "cognitive styles." One mother whose own hobby was writing highly imaginative poetry responded very warmly to what she viewed as poetic imagery in her son—in reality this was primary process type of primitive thinking common in children—and she considered it more clever and "creative" than his more advanced, realistic, and rational expressions. She enhanced primary process expressions at the expense of secondary process verbalization. Another mother unconsciously cultivated all mathematical expressions ever uttered by her son, hoping he would become a scientist.

Additional layers of defense become necessary when the boy, beginning at last to sense erotic implications underlying his intellectual closeness to mother, develops guilt about this now erotized verbal intimacy. Thus, an additional obstacle to successful conflict-free intellectual achievement arises. It is probably at this point that the boy's speech becomes pedantic and excessively intellectual. Many of these boys had intense, special, intellectual interests, often similar to their mothers', which they expressed primarily at home in a secretive manner. However, similar projects developed in the diagnostic school setting were sloppy and of poor quality. It was not clear whether this was because the actual interest was a superficial, facile one, admirable only in the biased family, or because the interest was too highly erotized and guilt-laden to display publicly.

While verbalization was an important tie with mother, the physical inadequacy of these boys was especially significant in relation to their fathers. Most of the fathers were extremely perturbed by their sons' lack of athletic skills, sensing the latent hostility which this basic ego deficit had acquired in the oedipal phase. The boys expressed hostility passively by not achieving, thus causing shame and helpless rage in their fathers. The fathers often responded as though they were incapable of producing a vigorous masculine son. The boys avoided competition in father's areas of strength, either intellectual or physical. When the parents each had different intellectual interests, the boys commonly followed mother's line of interest rather than father's. However, mother's interest was typically a masculine one. Thus, one boy's interest in military history and the Civil War paralleled his mother's adolescent hobby.

Superego and Ego Ideal

The basic disharmony between the ego's verbal and performance functions is related to the development of the observing and participating functions of the ego. All of the boys clearly showed immaturity and inadequacy in the participating functions of the ego. Several, but not all, had relatively strong powers of self-observation. They could describe fluently, in some detail, superficial aspects of their own behavior, feelings, and intentions. This was especially true of the group of boys who had internalized the conflict with respect to activity. In such cases the observing ego not only was well developed but served to "report" to a harsh superego (itself a substructure of the relatively overdeveloped ego) about the boys' inadequacies.

A destructive, reciprocal, and spiraling influence operating between verbal intelligence and physical ineptitude occurs when the intelligent child observes that his own performance does not and cannot measure up to his intellectual vision. His observing ego casts scorn and criticism upon the other participating and performing functions. His ego ideals along intellectual lines run far ahead of his executive abilities, and so the shame over clumsiness is doubly strong. It is well known that the superego is unusually endowed with aggression and severity in cases where aggression outward is not tolerated. The internal battleground between superego and ego is then all the more intense.

In all boys, feelings of guilt and shame seemed to be especially closely related. When a boy feels he cannot do something, he feels shame, but as soon as he uses his inability to express hostility, guilt becomes more prominent. In these boys the oscillations between guilt and shame, which were used as defenses against each other, seemed unusually rapid. In either case the boy readily castigated himself in a rich vocabulary of self-criticism, more often for errors of omission than commission. The transgressions are against the "thou shalt's" rather than the "thou shalt not's." Underachievers carry out their rebellion against family and society by neglecting academic tasks rather than by active social transgressions. The boys were ready with self-accusations of neglect, such as "I was messing around" and "I was goofing off."

In addition to the "errors of omission," there was another frequent category of "error." In the sphere of physical action, the boys were particularly inept and clumsy. However, clumsiness may serve as a disguise for crude but intentional acts of hostility. A boy who bangs into a desk or a person or disrupts another's work may immediately excuse himself on grounds of accidental clumsiness. The ambiguous unconscious ties between intentionality and ineptitude pose difficult problems for adults who feel they must arbitrate fairly, or be forever "understanding." Parents and teachers often make mistakes in the direction of underestimating the degree of malicious intent in apparently clumsy behavior.

After either acts of omission or so-called clumsy accidents, the boy typically makes no attempt to initiate restitutive behavior. As usual, the sphere of action of the participating ego is avoided and again the child resorts to his verbal stronghold. In a way that parallels his tendency to act out through words, he enacts or "acts out" his restitutive feelings through words. After the first phase of verbal self-castigation, the second restitutive phase (which would normally be undertaken in *acts* of correction or restitution) occurs verbally in a profusion of fluent alibis, glib resolutions, and pious promises.

Meanwhile, the dissociated undeveloped portion of the participating ego, the "doing" part of the personality, undertakes no alterations, fails to live up to the latest resolutions, and continues to underachieve. The verbal side of the personality has had further reinforcement through self-accusation and expressions of atonement. Ironically, an interesting variation of the mechanism of "doing and undoing" operates in this two-phase sequence, with the "doing" consisting of actually nondoing, and the "undoing" consisting of talking!

The concept of bribery of the superego is applicable here. The boys' promises and spoken good intentions serve to placate not only his parents and teachers but also his own superego. Superego lacunae result from the child's ability to fool himself with words. Convincing verbalization is the principal talent; and even when everyone, including the child himself, becomes aware of the emptiness of repeatedly broken promises, there is always the tantalizing hope that the words might be true "just this once."

Latency and Entrance into School

On entering school, these boys are confronted with unusually complex problems in adaptation. Although chronologically of latency age, none of the boys was psychologically in latency. It was striking that two thirds of the boys in this study had birthdays in the months between September and December. Verbally adept but behaviorally immature, these particular boys had the added burden of being among the youngest in their classes. Some of the parents had questioned whether it was better to have the child enter school early or to "hold him back until next year." This very general problem of timing of school entry affects our selected group in several specific ways.

Many of the boys were given intelligence tests to determine the readiness for school entry. In fact, this examination was for many families the earliest formal, objective indicator of the boys' high IQ, which evoked all kinds of parental attitudes, e.g., anxiety, ambition, competitiveness, confirmation of early hunches or hopes. Interestingly, the responses of mothers and fathers were often quite different.

The high IQ often led to decisions for early school entry, even though a few parents expressed some trepidation. Many studies have shown that for many bright children early school admission is the wise decision (Reynolds, 1962). But these boys are in part the casualties of this decision, which overlooked their severe immaturities. Overly trusting of the predictive value of the IQ, parents and teachers alike felt that the apparent "potential" guaranteed success in school if the otherwise immature child entered early. In addition, the IQ automatically increased the adults' expectations of the children. (Even when parents were not told the exact test score, they were usually informed of his relatively high standing which had opened the door to early admission.)

Regardless of the birth dates of their sons, the mothers of the group were ambivalently ambitious for their sons and were caught in an unconscious conflict about the wisdom of "holding back" or "going forward." This conflict brought about increasing tension in the parents and often between the parents, at the very moment when the child faced the new experience of school entry, with all its challenges to achieve mastery of separation anxieties and competition with peers, to learn to read, and to tolerate success and failure. The boys probably sensed their parents' underlying uneasiness at this crucial time when they needed even greater assurance and confidence that leaving home and entering school would be a step they could master. The emotional support that a confident parent can offer a child in making the important transition to school was often absorbed in anxious inner debates over his readiness to succeed in school.

Throughout the first year of school, which is an academically "critical period," the boys' progress, report cards, and teachers' reports were anxiously scrutinized by parents. While signs of success were eagerly sought, difficulties were magnified. All academic and social performance became charged with anxieties which generated further difficulties in the child. One couple, who anticipated being told that their precocious son would skip a grade, was shocked and dismayed to learn that his behavior had been so immature that the teacher was at her wits' end. Neither she nor the parents could understand why such a bright boy could not "work up to capacity."

Adding to the anxieties around school achievement are the different, sometimes conflictual attitudes of the parents toward the uses of intelligence. The mothers frequently felt that the ideal use of intelligence was in scholarly achievement, while the fathers often

felt that practical success in the business world was a far better use
of intelligence. In such cases the child was torn between the values
of his parents and found himself unable to please both of them.

In summary, the child who showed such ego imbalance at the age
of 2, later at age 9 or 10 can read at a sixth-grade level, do
arithmetic like a third-grader, and behave like a nursery schooler.
His sense of self-esteem is vulnerable, he fluctuates between
expansiveness and depression, and is a source of puzzlement and
perplexity to his parents and teachers.

IMPLICATIONS FOR PSYCHOEDUCATIONAL PROGRAMS

Experience with these children, both in inpatient residential
settings with special education, and in outpatient psychotherapy or
analysis combined with collaborative efforts with teachers in public
schools, have demonstrated that underachieving gifted children
present difficult therapeutic problems. Treatment plans must be
tailored according to the needs of the individual child.

In considering questions of placement, the parents and school
worry excessively "did we decide correctly"—as if there were a
simple right or wrong answer. In fact, extremely verbal children
with behavioral immaturities are often misfits in the usual school
system and challenge the concept of "appropriate grade levels."
The idea that all children can be divided by age and intelligence
into grade levels and subgroups assumes that all the "mental ages"
of all the many ego and drive functions within the child are more or
less identical. In school, certain academic tasks are expected in
settings where certain levels of behavioral competence are also
expected. Principals, teachers, and parents often face the dilemma
of pushing the child ahead or holding him back. The child is pulled
hither and yon by this recurrent conflict in the adults' attitudes
toward him. His self-concept seesaws constantly; middle grounds
are hard to find, and yet he needs them desperately.

Current concepts of "ungraded education" frequently offer the
best solution for such children. A program must take into account
the profound discrepancies within the child and help to develop all
functions, the "bright functions," the "deficit functions," and the
often obscure "average functions."

Although these children obviously need special educational programs, it is crucial not to overlook the underlying dynamic conflicts, anxieties, and deficits. Often teachers may be helped to gain understanding of these aspects of the child's personality through consultation and collaboration with child psychiatrists and psychologists. In addition, individual psychotherapy or analysis is frequently indicated for the child as well as help at some level for the parents.

Psychotherapeutic and educational work with these children is complicated by specific problems which grow out of their particular personality configurations. These problems are related to the frequent underestimation of the depth of the child's pathology and to the unrealistic and illogical attitudes these children elicit from therapists and educators alike.

Teachers and therapists share certain "countertransference pitfalls" in their professional relationships with underachieving gifted students. Both professions place high value on verbal skills in attaining social and vocational goals. They enjoy the fluency, expressiveness, and "intelligence," which they feel bode well for either learning or psychotherapy. Thus, to some extent they readily duplicate the preexisting parental attitudes toward speech. The boys' capacity to charm and entertain adults, and to tantalize them with glimmers of verbal "giftedness," be it for "knowledge" in class or "rich fantasies" in the office, evoke enthusiasm and delight early in the adult-child relationship. However, disappointment, frustration, and counterhostility soon follow as a frequent countertransference sequence.

In the classroom there is the tendency to "fall for" and exploit the verbal reading skills of these children. Teachers often expect great achievements from a child who reads at a very advanced level. In fact, however, skill in reading is not always associated with comparable achievement in spelling, arithmetic, or other subjects (Haggard, 1957). Teachers may enthusiastically enrich and stimulate the "gifted child" with more of what he already does in some ways too well for his own good. Fox example, they give him even more advanced, technical books to read while they may unwittingly, in subtle ways, condone his lack of performance because "he is gifted" or "is bored." Another approach, sometimes adopted in

punitive desperation, is a grimly, purely remedial effort; the bright
area is neglected as spurious, the child is not praised, he is made to
read and write at a lower level, and his deficits are intensively
"remedied" by special educational techniques in the attempt to
equalize and harmonize his abilities. But now the child himself is
crestfallen. No longer perceived as gifted, he experiences a narcissistic injury which brings about inner rage, depression, and apathy;
and he invests little in the dreary remedial exercises. In turn, the
teacher feels angry, incompetent, guilty, and finally resorts to
dramatic, emotional, or even bizarre attempts "to reach" these
bright children. The child in turn senses, as he had with his mother,
that his teacher is seeking in part a personal professional triumph
where all previous teachers have failed. Autobiographies of teachers
describe the special pedagogical delights of having identified and
fostered talent in a child. Sometimes teachers are seeking, among a
class of 30 children, one hidden talent for just this purpose. The
temptation to exploit another's intelligence, reaction formations
against envy or awe about intelligence itself, or unconscious
competition with the child, may all play an important part in the
teacher-child relationship. When the underachieving child continues to fail, the teacher's initial enthusiasm and delight are
followed by excessive disappointment, hostility, and guilt. The child
often suffers from educational efforts which have been influenced by
these irrational attitudes. Both teacher and student subsequently
experience apathy and a sense of helplessness and resignation
following further failure. The relationships between parents and
school under these conditions often deteriorate, and blame is easily
projected back and forth.

Therapists have likewise experienced countertransference attitudes of excessive enthusiasm followed by frustration. They enjoy
listening to the keenly verbal child, and rarely feel the need to
utilize play techniques in treatment because the child is sufficiently
fluent in producing the vivid fantasy material which they feel is the
well-trodden path to insight and therapeutic success. The therapist
may sometimes wonder about the fluidity or primitive quality of the
fantasy material, but the patient can also elaborate theoretical or
encyclopedic discussions, thus showing evidence of structure and
ability to abstract. It takes a while for the therapist to notice that

the child rarely thinks in practical realistic steps toward a concrete goal. Verbalization for these boys is linked with neither underlying and unnamed affects nor with underdeveloped actions. Thus, the task of translating verbalized intellectualized insight into character and behavioral change is even more formidable than usual. As the therapist becomes aware of the relative emptiness of the child's speech, he is challenged to find nonverbal avenues to therapy and to build connections between feelings, words, and deeds. It might be important for the analyst to view certain forms of "acting out" in a positive, favorable light. The use of concrete work and play materials in the office may be crucial with such children.

Another common problem in both classroom and psychotherapy is the gross underestimation of the depth of pathology. In the classroom, the "underachieving gifted" child's difficulties are usually viewed as problems for educational management and responsibility. Aware of complex "motivational" or "personality factors" in achievement, educators have assumed, often effectively, the task of "motivating for learning." However, for these underachieving students direct extrinsic motivation rarely helps and often hinders. They suffer from real incapacities or retardations which exist side by side with ability or talent in other areas. It is helpful to think of these students as simultaneously "partially gifted" and "partially retarded." It is clear that a level of capacity in one area does not necessarily guarantee capacity in another, even though such correlations typically exist in well-integrated personalities. It is precisely in poorly organized children that such prediction works least well.

With insight the teacher may find it easier to relinquish the isolated IQ as a yardstick for academic expectancy or "potential." He could help the student best by relating to him as a complex child with long-standing problems. Traditional teaching has not and will not solve the problem by itself. The child often needs a combination of specialized education and psychiatric or analytic treatment to make substantial academic progress.

The psychiatrist also tends to underestimate the depth of the pathology. Too often the central conflict of underachievement is seen to lie at the oedipal level, with problems around such issues as curiosity, competition, and success. However, in these cases, vivid oedipal pathology often obscures the more fundamental pregenital problems.

Psychotherapy in which only the obvious oedipal fantasies, conflicts, and regressions are interpreted is too superficial. Even when the problem is seen to lie at a preoedipal level, it may be erroneously viewed as predominantly conflictual. Conflict-free developmental factors often play a preponderant role. The remediation of such deviations in individual ego functions, and ultimately in the synthetic function, often requires a combined psychotherapeutic and educational approach. Remedial and educational efforts around skills neglected at a very primitive level of ego development, especially in the face of other precocious functions, typically evoke in the child intense feelings of narcissistic injury, shame, and anxiety. It is at this point of emotional turmoil aroused by attempts at renewed educational development of very early functions that the therapist and educator must collaborate most carefully and closely.

Therapy with the parents involves working through the pathogenic aspects of such seemingly innocuous, nonneurotic attitudes as enhancement and compliance toward specific ego functions of the child. The intrapsychic neurotic origins of these parental attitudes are difficult to reach and change, for they are solidly ego-syntonic. Parents often have a natural defense in their focus on the child's illness or disability, and when this disability combines low achievement and high IQ, it is especially easy to project blame upon the school system. Guilt is a frequent parental response when the child does not utilize talent. The guilt is misplaced, for neither the talent nor the underachievement is quite genuine. Each is a component of the child's personality and each requires and reinforces the other. The parental guilt may actually revolve around some half-hidden realization of the unusual intensity of early and continuing narcissistic exploitation of selected elements of the child's own personality.

These findings of familial pathology when transposed onto the larger social scene have implications that relate to the values, emphases, and goals that currently permeate thinking about early childhood education. There is growing self-consciousness, narcissistic investment, and national competitiveness around the rearing and education of children, and intensified zealousness of purpose around the early cultivation of specific kinds of abilities. The current emphasis on cognition is obvious in both professional and popular literature. The findings of this study indicate that selective emphasis in early personality development will inevitably have unanticipated, far-reaching consequences.

As new, more "efficient" ways are found to mold, enhance, induce, condition, exploit, inspire, stimulate, discipline, and acculturate children, or even simply to permit them to grow, it is important to recognize that there is a price to be paid for each apparent gain and to consider what this price might be. Perhaps it is even fortunate that each generation does not have the full power to shape the next one according to its own images of the future.

APPENDIX

CRITERIA FOR REFERRAL

Children were referred to this project for intensive study by public elementary schools in Cincinnati as well as through the usual range of referral sources. This study was restricted to 15 latency-age children. The arbitrary definition of giftedness was a Stanford Binet IQ of at least 130, the cutoff point suggested by Hollingsworth (1929) in her classical definition of giftedness. Underachievement is an educational term which means significantly poor school performance either as reflected in achievement test scores or, more commonly, in school marks. For the purpose of this study, grades of C or below in the major classroom subjects were chosen as the criterion of underachievement. It was our assumption that, although an intelligence test is clearly imperfect as a predictor of school grades, the discrepancy between an IQ of 130 and grades of C and below is large enough to unequivocally reflect "underachievement" in any of the usual senses of the term.

METHOD OF STUDY

The comprehensive diagnostic assessment included a detailed history of the child's illness, his developmental history, an explorative interview of the child, and interviews with both parents in which both family relationships and the background histories of the parents were obtained. Children were given a battery of psychological tests. The specific procedures were as follows:

1. *An identical structured interview questionnaire was given to both mothers and fathers, separately.* Previous clinical experience highlighted the fact that fathers often tended to be overlooked as informants of the child's early developmental history. Having both parental points of view on the child's early history facilitated the delineation of congruent and conflicting parental attitudes to all kinds of needs, activities, and traits in their children, including those relevant to intellectual development. Questions were especially designed to elicit parental responses concerning early hopes and fantasies about their child, attitudes and expectancies about speech and motor development, and attitudes toward achievement and the utilization of intelligence. The parents' own intellectual and achievement histories were given emphasis. The questionnaire was so extensive that it often required 4 to 5 separate hours of interview time. By the end many parents expressed spontaneous fresh insights into areas and relationships they had never even previously considered.

2. *Interviews with children.* In addition to the usual attention to the child's appearance and behavior, content of thought, etc., these interviews tapped the child's understanding of his problems and of himself, his own perception of his intelligence and performance, and his ideas about his own difficulties in these areas. Feelings and attitudes were elicited about family members and homelife, and especially awareness of and attitudes toward father's work. The child was asked about his teachers, school peers, friendships, various subject areas, school activities, recess, homework, grades, sports, hobbies, and special interests. Direct questions and play techniques were used to elicit information about particular anxieties, worries, misconceptions, favorite reading material, fantasies, and ambitions.

3. *The psychological test battery* included the Wechsler Intelligence Scale for Children, Rorschach, and TAT. These tests provided data on multiple aspects of intellectual functioning including attention, concentration, judgement, visual-motor coordination, verbal fluency, ability for conceptual thinking, for sustained effort, for analysis and synthesis. They also provided information on style of affective expression and control, articulation of emotion, capacity for impulse delay, nature of interpersonal relationships, and content of fantasy life. Typically, a fairly comprehensive picture of the child's current functioning was obtained.

4. *School reports and cumulative records* were collected for each child in interviews with teachers and principals. Since these children came from many different schools, it was difficult to compare the records systematically. Details of the child's style of performance in schoolwork and in play needed for the pilot study were of necessity unavailable from teachers of

large classes. To meet the need for more systematic observation of academic behavior, we adapted a group method used in this and other centers to enrich initial diagnostic evaluations (Maas and Schreiber, 1969).

5. *An educational and social diagnostic group*[5] was developed and composed of 7 of the underachieving gifted children who met as a group (on 4 consecutive Saturdays for 3-hour sessions). The staff included teachers, recreational workers, and group workers. A wide variety of academic and social activities was provided. These varied in degree of structure and included cooperative group efforts, competitive situations, and individual projects. Both participant and nonparticipant observations were made.

BIBLIOGRAPHY

BAYLEY, N. & SCHAEFER, E. S. (1964), Correlations of Maternal and Child Behavior with the Development of Mental Abilities: Data from Berkeley Growth study. *Monogr. Soc. Res. Child Develpm.*, Serial #97, Vol. 29, #6.

BIBRING, E. (1953), The Mechanism of Depression. In: *Affective Disorders*, ed. P. Greenacre. New York: International Universities Press, pp. 13–48.

COLEMAN, R. W., KRIS, E., & PROVENCE, S. (1953), The Study of Variations of Early Parental Attitudes. *This Annual*, 8:20–47.

FREUD, A. (1936), *The Ego and the Mechanisms of Defense.* New York: International Universities Press, 1966.

—— (1952), The Mutual Influences in the Development of Ego and Id. *This Annual*, 7:42–50.

—— (1965), *Normality and Pathology in Childhood.* New York: International Universities Press.

FREUD, S. (1916), Some Character-Types Met with in Psycho-Analytic Work. *Standard Edition*, 14:309–333. London: Hogarth Press, 1957.

GARDNER, R. W., JACKSON, P. N., & MESSICK, S. J. (1960), *Personality Organization in Cognitive Controls and Intellectual Abilities* [*Psychological Issues*, Monogr. 8]. New York: International Universities Press.

GLOVER, E. (1956), *On the Early Development of Mind.* New York: International Universities Press.

[5] Grateful acknowledgment is made to C. Caroline Maas, R.N., M.S.W., Director of Milieu Therapy and Group Services, and Edward Requardt, M.A., Director of Special Education, for their planning of, participation in, and critical evaluation of the Educational-Social Diagnostic Group. This portion of the study was supported, in part, by a Research Fund in memory of Dean Rohovit, M.D., former child psychiatry Fellow, Department of Psychiatry, University of Cincinnati.

GOLDBERG, M. L. (1965), *Research on the Talented.* New York: Bureau of Public Teachers College, Columbia University.

COWAN, J. C. (1957), Dynamics of the Underachievement of Gifted Students. *Except. Child.,* 24:98–101.

GREENACRE, P. (1952), General Problems of Acting Out. In: *Trauma, Growth, and Personality.* New York: International Universities Press, 1969, pp. 224–236.

——— (1959), On Focal Symbiosis. In: *Dynamic Psychopathology in Childhood,* ed. L. Jessner & E. Pavenstedt, New York: Grune & Stratton, pp. 243–256.

HAGGARD, E. A. (1957), Socialization, Personality and Achievement in Gifted Children. *School Rev.,* 43:318–414.

HALPERN, H. (1964), Psychodynamic and Cultural Determinants of Work Inhibition in Children and Adolescents. *Psychoanal. Rev.,* 51:173–189.

——— & HALPERN, T. (1966), Four Perspectives on Anti-Achievement. *Psychoanal. Rev.,* 53:407–417.

HARTMANN, H. (1939), *Ego Psychology and the Problem of Adaptation.* New York: International Universities Press, 1958.

——— (1951), Technical Implications of Ego Psychology. In: *Essays on Ego Psychology.* New York: International Universities Press, 1964, pp. 142–154.

HOLLINGSWORTH, L. S. (1929), *Gifted Children: Their Nature and Nurture.* New York: Macmillan.

HUNT, J. McV. (1961), *Intelligence and Experience.* New York: Ronald Press.

JOHNSON, A. M. (1949), Sanctions for Superego Lacunae of Adolescents. In: *Searchlights on Delinquency,* ed. K. R. Eissler, New York: International Universities Press, pp. 225–245.

KAGAN, J., SONTAG, L. W., BAKER, C. T., & NELSON, V. L. (1958), Personality and IQ Change. *J. Abnorm. Soc. Psychol.,* 56:261–266.

KATAN, A. (1961), Some Thoughts About the Role of Verbalization in Early Childhood. *This Annual,* 16:184–188.

KEISER, S. (1965), Role of Trauma in Gifted Patients with High IQ's. Presented at Annual Meeting of the American Psychoanalytic Association, New York.

——— (1969), Superior Intelligence: Its Contribution to Neurosogenesis. *J. Amer. Psychoanal. Assn.,* 17:452–473.

KHAN, M. M. (1965), In Panel: The Concept of Trauma. Annual Meeting of the American Psychoanalytic Association, New York.

KLEIN, E. (1949), Psychoanalytic Aspects of School Problems. *This Annual,* 3/4:369–390.

KOCH, H. L. (1954), The Relation of "Primary Mental Abilities" in Five- and Six-Year-Olds to Sex of Child and Characteristics of His Siblings. *Child Develpm.,* 25:209–223.

LISS, E. (1955), Motivations in Learning. *This Annual,* 10:100–116.

MAAS, C. & SCHREIBER, G. (1969), Use of the Group Work Method as a Dimension in the Assessment of Children Referred for Diagnostic Evaluation in a Psychiatric Treatment Center. Presented at Annual Meeting of the American Association of Psychiatric Services for Children, Boston.

MAHLER, M. S. (1952), On Child Psychosis and Schizophrenia. *This Annual*, 7:286–305.

MILLER, M. M., ed. (1961), *Guidance for the Underachiever with Superior Ability*. Bulletin #25, U.S. Department of H.E.W.

NAGERA, H. (1966), *Early Childhood Disturbances, the Infantile Neurosis, and the Adulthood Disturbances*. New York: International Universities Press.

OLDEN, C. (1946), Headline Intelligence. *This Annual*, 2:263–269.

PEARSON, G. H. J. (1954), *Psychoanalysis and the Education of the Child*. New York: Norton.

PIAGET, J. (1936), *The Origins of Intelligence in Children*. New York: International Universities Press, 1952.

—— (1937), *The Construction of Reality in the Child*. New York: Basic Books, 1954.

—— (1945), *Play, Dreams, and Imitation in Childhood*. New York: Norton, 1951.

RAPAPORT, D. (1960), On the Psychoanalytic Theory of Motivation. In: *Nebraska Symposium on Motivation*, ed. M. R. Jones, Lincoln: University of Nebraska Press, pp. 173–247.

REYNOLDS, M. C., ed. (1926), *Early School Admission for Mentally Advanced Children: A Review of Research and Practice*. CEC Special Publication, The Council for Exceptional Children, NEA.

SHAW, M. C. & McCUEN, J. T. (1960), The Onset of Academic Underachievement in Bright Children. *J. Educ. Psychol.*, 51:103–108.

TERMAN, L. (1925), *Genetic Studies of Genius*. Stanford: Stanford University Press.

THORNDIKE, R. L. (1963), *The Concepts of Over and Underachievement*. New York: Bureau of Publications, Teachers' College, Columbia University.

VYGOTSKY, L. (1934), *Thought and Language*. Cambridge: M.I.T. Press, 1962.

WHITE, R. W. (1960), Competence and the Psychosexual Stages of Development. In: *Nebraska Symposium on Motivation*, ed. M. R. Jones. Lincoln: University of Nebraska Press, pp. 97–140.

WITKIN, H. A., DYK, R. B., FATERSON, H. F., GOODENOUGH, D. R., & KARP, S. A. (1962), *Psychological Differentiation*. New York: Wiley.

WOLFF, P. H. (1960), *The Developmental Psychologies of Jean Piaget and Psychoanalysis* [*Psychological Issues*, Monogr. 5]. New York: International Universities Press.

Some Thoughts on Childhood Psychosis, Self and Object

HERMAN ROIPHE, M.D.

ALICE, A PSYCHOTIC GIRL, WAS $3\frac{1}{2}$ YEARS OF AGE WHEN SHE WAS started in an intensive treatment program, as part of a research investigation of the separation-individuation phase in normal and psychotic children (Mahler, 1952; Mahler and Gosliner, 1955; Mahler and Furer, 1960; Pine and Furer, 1963). In spite of impressive therapeutic movement, the treatment after two years of intensive work, was ultimately unsuccessful in that she could not be integrated back into the family and was, on the parents' own decision, institutionalized. However, her treatment afforded the opportunity to make a number of observations about the centrality of bowel and bladder functioning and the developing self and object relationship which may be of general interest in understanding some features of psychotic functioning and may, perhaps, even throw light on some aspects of early normal development.

Alice was a well-developed child and physically attractive, except for the vacant, unfocused gaze and immobile features which gave her appearance a curiously unappealing quality. While she was

The data on which this paper are based were collected at The Masters Children's Center. The interpretation of these data is entirely my own and in no way reflects the views of Margaret S. Mahler, M.D., Director of Research of The Masters Children's Center.

Assistant Clinical Professor of Psychiatry, Albert Einstein College of Medicine.

largely oblivious of her human environment, unless it impinged too closely or vigorously upon her, she carried with her everywhere a burdensome collection of plastic baby bottles, a shredded blanket and toy duck, objects from which she could not bear to be parted. Her activity alternated between aimless wandering around the playroom and a concentrated and almost endlessly repetitive filling and emptying of her baby bottles with dried peas, beads, and dirt painstakingly collected from crevices in the concrete-floored playground.

It is noteworthy that even this psychotic child, whose object life was very highly compromised, clung so tenaciously to this collection of inanimate objects. The repetitive filling and emptying of the baby bottle do seem to suggest some primordial definition of those central polarities of inside-outside, self-nonself and, by virtue of this, do point to a relationship to that intermediate area of experience which Winnicott (1953, 1965) so felicitously described in his paper on transitional objects and phenomena. In firm concrete form, these psychotic transitional objects reflect some central inner core of self and object, fragile and staunchly guarded, which through its very crystallization tends to constrict further development (Modell, 1968; Fintzy, 1971).

The transitional object in normal development makes its appearance during a period of rapid growth and expansion which necessarily involves increasing separation from the mother, a step that cannot be accomplished without some measure of strain. The transitional object serves as a support to the infant and promotes the expansion and deepening of the child's autonomy and object relatedness. In psychotic development, the transitional object has a much more focal and rigid defensive function and the child's involvement with it, frequently to the exclusion of any relationship with the actual object, serves to impair object relatedness.

Alice was the firstborn child, whose development, in retrospect, was already aberrant in the second half of the first year. Although her physical growth was entirely normal, her social responses were atypical. She was from a very early time on a sober-faced child who rarely smiled. When she awoke either in the middle of the night or in the early morning, she never cried or called to her mother, but would sit quietly in her crib until someone came for her. Even when she had an ear infection which on physical examination revealed an angry, red, bulging eardrum, the child did not cry. By the end of the first year the pediatrician, who had seen Alice since birth, made the diagnosis of childhood autism. She did develop speech in the beginning of the second year, but did not appear to use it in a communicative fashion. Her parents divorced when she was 2 years old. Thereupon her use of speech, such as it was, quickly diminished, so that when she appeared for treatment a year and a half later, she was mute except for unintelligible vocalizations and shrieks. She was at 3½ incontinent and wore diapers during both day and night. She never appeared to manifest any awareness of bladder or bowel functions even after her mother had made an effort to train her around 2. In this regard, she behaved much more like an infant in the first year rather than a 3-year-old child whose incontinence stemmed from anal phase conflicts. Such children, while not performing on the toilet, show a fluctuating degree of awareness of bowel and bladder functions and at least give some evidence of bowel and bladder patterning of their activity.

As indicated above, Alice's parents were divorced when she was 2 years old after a marriage of some 4 years' duration. Her father, a boyish-looking, rather ineffectual young man in his late 20s, probably a borderline character, was cut off from a very considerable inheritance when he took a Jewish wife. After the divorce, he maintained an irregular contact with Alice in which he always seemed affectionate and gentle if somewhat vague. Alice's mother, in her mid-20s, was a woman of considerable intellectual and musical achievements. She remarried shortly after her divorce and, by the time Alice was 5, had two other children, who seemed as best we could tell to be bright, attractive, and normal youngsters. She managed with these two infants, the difficult older psychotic child, without much domestic help, quite admirably. In her handling of Alice, she frequently seemed to be quite detached and often asserted wryly that our efforts would come to naught since she believed that Alice was an organically compromised child. As evidence she offered the observation that at 11 months Alice would hold a few blocks against a vertical surface, let go, and after the blocks, as they inevitably must, fell to the floor, repeat this over and over; according to her mother, Alice did not even know what was up from what was down. Such remonstrances seemed, in my judgment, less an evidence of her rejection of the child than a reflection of the profound narcissistic insult and sense of guilt which compelled this woman to prove that the child was organically damaged rather than compromised as a result of inadequate mothering. Adherents of the "schizophrenogenic" mother will have to make the most of these bare bones, in this instance at least.

The initial phase of the treatment was taken up with a painstaking and tactful effort to establish a relationship with this child. After several months of extremely patient work with her warm, sensitive, and devoted therapist, Alice began to show some cracks in her autistic shell. She began to use the therapist to fetch objects which were out of reach, to join in mutual rhythmic play, and occasionally burrowed herself in the therapist's embrace in a relaxed, dreamy, infantile attitude. While she periodically retreated into her autistic shell, particularly when she was frustrated or angered, she was just as often driven outward again by her object hunger.

A particularly remarkable observation was made on a number of occasions, during this phase of the treatment when Alice could no longer retreat into her autism. Several times Alice manifested a mounting rage when she was frustrated by her therapist. The rage state would abort and the child would collapse in a heap on the floor, all her large muscles extraordinarily limp, her breathing labored with prominent asthmatic wheezing. This observation seems particularly significant for our understanding of psychosomatic reactions. In this child whose object relations were now sufficiently solid so that she could no longer retreat into her autism, the mounting tension from frustration found discharge in rages which became body-bound in the large muscle atony and the life-threatening involvement of the respiratory mechanism. I would imagine that the abrupt somatization of the mounting rage state serves to protect that inner core of the self and object world. This may be a crucial mechanism in such a child whose libidinal attachment to the object is still quite fragile and whose ego lacks the strength and integrity to interpose less compromising psychological defense mechanisms. I would imagine that in instances of true psychosomatic disease such a reaction tendency must be very much enhanced by some organic compliance (Reiser, 1966).

In this general climate of self and object involvement, Alice was one day observed frantically running about the playroom with a searching, darting gaze as if she were looking for something. She suddenly stopped, her gaze seemed to focus inward, she momentarily strained at a bowel movement, and then resumed running about as before. Previously, as indicated above, Alice had not shown even the slightest awareness of bowel or bladder functions, nor had she shown any observable behavioral reflections of these functions. When it was pointed out to her that she was looking for something outside herself when, in fact, what she was responding to was the inner stimulus of bowel urgency, Alice flew into a panic tantrum of awesome dimension. From that time on, it was possible in an emotionally meaningful climate to delineate for Alice such primal ego discriminations as inside-outside, self-nonself, animate-inanimate. In the process, the behavioral concomitants of and her attitudes toward the bowel function became sharply focused in a well-defined sequence of cause and effect, such as had never before been observed in her autistically organized state. For a time this sequence of bowel urgency-interpretation-panic tantrum occurred much more frequently so that the several hours which Alice spent daily at the treatment center were entirely consumed in the most intense conflict over holding on and letting go.

In the clinical sketch of Alice's developmental progress in her therapy up to this point, her relationship to her own stool paralleled and was directly bound up with the level of her object relations. The first behavioral reflections of a bowel movement, the frantic searching outside, and the momentary, rigid straining were manifested only after months of therapeutic work, which resulted in a relatively solidly established need-satisfying relationship with her therapist. We had the interesting confirmation of this stool-object equation from the mother's own report. Beginning at this period, whenever Alice's mother had to leave her alone in the bath momentarily either to answer a telephone or to check something on the stove, Alice had a bowel movement in the bath, something that had not happened previously. Early during this period, she would completely ignore the stool on her mother's return; but later, when her relationship with her mother was warmer, she would pick the stool up with a beaming smile and in the friendliest fashion offer it to her mother.

The passing of the bowel movement was clearly the equivalent of the mother's leaving and would, I should think, reflect the depletion of the self which the separation involved. The early, total ignoring of the stool on the mother's return bespeaks Alice's obliterating anger at being left in much the same way as the hospitalized child's nonrecognition of the mother does. The later, friendly proffering of the stool to the returning mother bespeaks the growing warmth of her object relations as well as a greater tolerance for separation.

There are interesting, although inexact parallels in the normal infant's developing relation to his bowel movement. Early in the first year, the infant tends to have his stool during feedings or shortly thereafter, and usually there is no attention to or behavioral reflection of the bowel movement. Toward the end of the first year and certainly early in the second, there very commonly is a tendency for a certain general body rigidity, some straining, not infrequently a brief stilling of other body activity, and withdrawal of attention from the outside. It is a commonplace with our normal 14- to 15-month-old children to note a sudden fascination with the toilet and particularly the flush, with the highly exciting and absorbing observation of the controlled disappearance of the stool, toilet paper, or a toy.

This shift in the child's relation to his own bowel movement seems to follow the normal and at this age typical emergence of a separation conflict with all this implies about the consolidation of the internal self and object representations. Until 8 or 9 months, the child's self differentiation is extremely rudimentary and the relation to the object is essentially a symbiotic one. With the onset of the differentiation subphase, there is a rapid quickening in the whole process of self, particularly the body-self, schematization and the separation of the infant from his mother (Mahler, 1963, 1968). It is at this stage with the new level of self and object differentiation that the bowel movement is singularly situated and suited to express the double-faced, developing inner concept; something which is part of the self can be felt inside, has a movement and yet is not alive, has a climactic expulsive pattern, a texture, a smell, etc., and very importantly a relationship to the nourishing object, and yet when expelled is neither self nor object. Its movement, texture, and consistency are subject to the vicissitudes of health and sickness, loving and hating feelings toward the object; and the ultimate control of the whole toilet process waits on some partial resolution of the separation conflicts, the independence conflicts, and the conflicts over self dissolution and object loss. The whole process of attention to the bowel movement and the new relation to it follows from and is a reflection of the newly developing self and object relationship and is in this sense quite independent of any demand from the parents, either explicit or implicit, for control of these functions. In fact, the reasonably well-attuned parent will wait for the emergence of this naturally occurring shift in the child's own relationship to his stool, taking the cue from the child, to support and encourage this new and developing control with all that this implies in the process of consolidation of the developing self and object relations.

The early evidence of bowel patterning in Alice, the stilling of body activity, the shift of attention from outside to inside, and the straining have already been described. As work with the bowel conflict proceeded, the patterning effects of the bowel movements on a variety of ego functions became richer and more comprehensive. She began under the influence of bowel urgency to gather toys from all over the playroom into a pile and later would build towers ten blocks and higher. The first time she successfully built a tower of blocks, she shrieked, in exultation, "I can do it." This was the first time she had ever spoken a complete sentence and the first time she had ever referred to herself as "I." The tower building became for quite some time an absolute indication of bowel urgency. Her body posture at these times regularly showed a good deal of rigidity and her body movements were very stiff. Clearly, the block building, the toy gathering, the postural rigidity and stiffness of movement all reflected the inner muscular tension and perhaps even the column of stool.

The association of certain patterns of body rhythm, movement, muscle tone, as well as particular configurations of play with underlying anal function is supported by Werner and Kaplan's

(1963) work on symbolism. These authors compare the dynamic-vectorial nature of patterns of early psychic functioning with the qualities of direction, force, balance, rhythm, and enclosingness which are easily distinguishable in the early patterns of sensorimotor development. Galenson and Roiphe (1971) further stated, "We follow the process of displacement from the original zonal site to another body area. The next step is externalization to outside objects which are then utilized as concrete semisymbolic representatives of the bodily experience. It is through this link with the original zonal area that we hope to document, from data of direct infant observation, the assumption that play, as all other infant behavior, is patterned by the instructual drives" (p. 199). (See also Galenson, 1971.)

It may be worthwhile to stop at this point and to consider the block building described above in some more detail. It will be remembered that when Alice's mother tried to assert that Alice was organically damaged, she gave as evidence the child's efforts to build a tower of blocks only from a vertical surface. On more detailed questioning the following story emerged. When Alice was 11 months old, she attempted to build a conventional tower of three blocks from the floor up. When this tower collapsed as she placed the third block, the child broke into an inconsolable sobbing that lasted for over half an hour. She was not seen to attempt again to build a tower from a horizontal surface until she did so in the course of the therapeutic work. However, it was shortly after this incident that she was observed by her mother to hold a few blocks against a vertical surface, let go, and when they, of course, fell to the ground, repeat this patiently and persistently, over and over again.

It seems to me that this does not reflect any confusion in spatial orientation. It was precisely because it was recognized as an impossibility that it could be repeated, in spite of failure, without the profoundly shattering effect produced by the original effort to build the tower from the horizontal surface. I would be inclined to think that the intense anxiety provoked by the failure of the original effort to build the tower from the horizontal surface may have followed from the likelihood that this external event had the inner resonance of the threat of total object loss and self dissolution. It may well be a characteristic of the fragile psychotic ego that the skin between the outer world and the inner world may be too thin in just this sense, that is, the external occurrence may have the literal resonance of an inner event.

For many months the conflict around the stool-object raged. Alice could not ignore it and she could not resolve it. Whenever her attention was verbally drawn to the bowel urgency, she burst out into prolonged and painful shrieks and danced back and forth over the threshold of the playroom. The playroom led onto a hallway and a short distance down the hall was the bathroom where her diapers were emptied when she did finally have a bowel movement. During this period, it was repeatedly noted that when the first signs of the urgency were observed, only a direct verbal reference to the bowel urgency or movement would evoke the panic tantrum. However, somewhat later when presumably the urgency became increasingly more intense and peremptory, not only the direct reference to it evoked the tantrum behavior but an increasing catalogue of words related to the word for the bowel movement either by clang association or by contiguity, that is, in primary process fashion, served to produce the same result, whereas earlier they did not.

It is indeed striking how so many of the situations, in which we have reason to believe Alice was confronted with the potential shattering of her inner object world and with a concomitant depletion of the inner sense of self, led directly to a primitivization of the thought process as exemplified by the shift from secondary process to primary process thought patterns, to an undermining of her reality sense and, very particularly, the sharp delineation of the primal modalities of inside and outside. The defensive and restitutive aspects of this inside-outside confusion, for example, are quite clear. When Alice was frantically looking around for something outside while, in fact, she was responding to the inner bowel urgency, the inside-outside confusion served to deny the imminence of the catastrophic loss of the stool-object. The looking outside tends to emphasize the restitutive aspect of the behavior with its shift to a visual incorporation, a taking into the body rather than the giving up of the stool-object.

Painstaking interpretive work dealt with a variety of reincorporative and destructive preoccupations. During this phase of treatment, there emerged a rampant coprophagic behavior. It was only with considerable difficulty that Alice was kept out of the garbage, from eating dirt, leaves, lint, etc. In her therapy, she could not bear to have her soiled diaper changed and shrieked in the most unbridled protest when her stool was emptied into the toilet to be flushed. She frantically stuffed her mouth with toilet paper and would, if permitted, have eaten the stool. Her therapist fed her instead with chocolate and raisins which Alice consumed in prodigious quantities, usually taking in so much that it was difficult for her even to chew what she had in her mouth. The ingestion of the chocolate and raisins seemed to make the flushing of the stool tolerable, although this was still a highly anxious situation.

The emptying of the diaper and the flushing of the stool were accompanied by an interpretation to the effect that she was frightened because this had for her the meaning of object loss and a depletion of the self. The ingestion of chocolate and the raisins, the toilet paper, garbage, etc., made her feel full again. This interpretation was offered the child, in a rather unvaried fashion, every day for over a week since this seemed so clearly to be the meaning of her behavior. However, the panic and protest continued unabated and her ingestion of chocolate and raisins continued. Finally, the therapist, in discouragement and despair at the failure of the interpretation to affect the behavior, one day changed the soiled diaper, fed her the chocolate and raisins, and flushed the stool, but did not accompany this with the usual interpretation. Alice looked at the therapist quizzically and expectantly. When the therapist realized the import of this, she gave the expected interpretation and Alice beamed broadly. From this time on the coprophagic behavior diminished and largely disappeared, and the anxiety over the flushing of the stool abated considerably.

During this phase of the treatment, I had the distinct impression that the interpretation, in addition to the usual requirement that it correctly and accurately express the unconscious meaning of the patient's behavior, also had certain formal requirements. That is to say, the frequent and relatively unvaried interpretive response to specific elements of Alice's behavior set up an island of causal anticipation and regular expectation in this little psychotic girl's otherwise chaotic world. It did so in much the same fashion as the regular feeding of the hungry, crying infant serves not only to still the hunger pangs but also to organize the infant's world and ultimately become an indication of the object world and reality.

With the partial working through of these conflicts, the ego's margin of control was enhanced, as manifested in the gradually improving sphincter control. Alice seemed to resolve the bowel conflict by withholding her bowel movement until nighttime, when she was asleep in her bed, wearing diapers. Much of the interpretive ground was touchingly confirmed when during this period Alice had her first bowel movement on the toilet. With this loss, she developed, for the first time, a profound sadness, which could be empathically recognized as such, and which lasted for several days.

As the conflict over bowel urgency receded, behavior and conflict very similar in many details, at least at the onset, were manifested around urinary urgency. Much the same interpretive ground was covered as was the case with the bowel conflict. Naturally, the primal polarities of self-nonself, inside-outside were traversed in a much more telescoped fashion, but the problems of the threat of object loss and of the dissolution of the sense of self, particularly the body-self, were only painfully slowly and partially worked through.

The patterning effect of the urinary urgency was just as remarkable and characteristic as had previously been that of the bowel urgency. There was of course the typical dance of the full bladder, observable even in normal children, jiggling back and forth and jumping up and down. In addition, Alice tended to dart around the playroom with a lightning rapidity and suddenness that was breathtaking. She also tended, with the same incredible rapidity, to scatter all the toys over the entire playroom in a brief few seconds. The room looked as if a cyclone had hit. What striking contrast to the stiffness and rigidity, the gathering, collecting, piling and towering characteristic of the bowel urgency.

During this phase of treatment, her attention seemed almost constantly to be riveted to her bladder and she would wet herself two, three, or four times in a morning. In this respect she looked very much like a normal youngster in the midst of her bladder training in that the urgency seemed so marked and so frequent. It was only in its extremity and the profound anxiety that she experienced that one could see the difference. When Alice was anxiously beset with a full bladder, she would drink water so that her cheeks literally bulged with the retained water. When she could no longer contain the urinary urgency and wet herself, she would swallow the mouthful of water, occasionally also dribbling some of it from her mouth. What a neat solution, indeed, for this child who could not bear to lose and give up part of her body content. While she ultimately could not control the discharge of the bladder to the outside, the other cavity, the mouth, bulging with water could be controlled and could be made to empty into the inside of the body.

In this general setting, with the gradual withholding and control of the urinary function through the acceptance of the use of the toilet, a new development emerged. As Alice became increasingly able to withhold the immediate discharge of bladder urgency, she began for the first time to manifest unmistakable and unambiguous indications of a marked genital arousal. For the first time she was observed to masturbate openly, and she began to examine with extraordinary curiosity and concentration the genital area of the playroom dolls as well as her own genitalia. There also were signs of a developing penis-envy syndrome. She could be seen to interrupt her masturbation and dart into the adjoining playroom of a little boy, where she would steal a model airplane, a car or a toy soldier of his, and return to her room in an excited and euphoric mood (Roiphe, 1968).

From this point on, Alice who had still to deal with important residues of unresolved pregenital conflicts over object loss and self-dissolution had, in addition, with the sharp genital arousal, to cope with a castration reaction of formidable proportions, a loss of another but related kind. In line with the developing penis envy described above, Alice demonstrated a decided displeasure with and avoidance of any broken toys or crayons. This new vector of loss very much complicated the still ongoing urinary conflict, and for that matter the bowel as well, by investing these functions with a new castration significance. It is my impression that in many cases of rather intractable enuresis, where the child has never adequately developed bladder control, we are confronted with just this double-faced conflict. As a result of some configuration of early experience in the first year and a half of life, such as bodily illness, surgical intervention, birth defect, which contributes to an unstable and fluctuating outline of the body-self; or parental loss, maternal depression, or other grossly inadequate mothering which results in an unstable object representation, a sharp castration reaction develops in the wake of the normal genital arousal of the second year. Such a concatenation of experiences tends, among other consequences, to make a solid and reliable control of the urinary function unusually difficult to establish (Roiphe, 1968; Roiphe and Galenson, 1972, 1973; Galenson and Roiphe, 1971).

During this whole phase of treatment which dealt with Alice's anal conflicts, there was a marked expansion in this heretofore mute child's understanding and use of speech. While her exclamation, "I can do it," on her first successful building of a tower of blocks, was somewhat unusual in the complexity of structure, there was a considerable growth in the use of single words and two- or three-word phrases. Moreover, she used these appropriately for the purpose of communication. However, a most remarkable and persistent device which Alice adopted most commonly to communicate complex thoughts and, particularly, emotional states was to hum songs, the text of which conveyed her meaning. It is probably significant that her mother was a musically gifted person who sang a wide variety of children's songs to Alice. In this connection, Greenacre (1969) stated:

> I am also impressed with the early age at which babies react with ease and seeming relaxation to unsharp sounds such as crooning, or to the rhythm of simple tunes. By six months of age or even earlier the baby may initiate a swaying or rocking motion as he sits on the floor, if a rhythmic tune is played on the victrola. . . . Winnicott has remarked that sometimes a tune serves as a transitional phenomenon. It is probably the dependability of the rhythm, the familiarity of the sound, and the conditions associated with comfort from the mother which are the basis of selection of such a transitional phenomenon as a tune [p. 152].

It is indeed interesting that Alice's most complex and differentiated communications took place through this channel, which by virtue of its transitional nature implicitly contains an indication of the comforting, nurturing object. How much is this an aspect of normal speech acquisition?

Unfortunately, with Alice, it was not possible to do anything but to begin interpretively to attack the new but progressive dimension of sexual conflict. For shortly after this, her parents made the decision to discontinue Alice's treatment and institutionalize her. We were left with the heartbreaking task of presiding over this new situation, but unfortunately with a child who could no longer retreat into an autistic world and with a child who was fully capable of experiencing the depths and pain of sadness. She would dolefully wander about the playroom humming songs which dealt with the anguish and despair of parting.

BIBLIOGRAPHY

FINTZY, R. T. (1971), Vicissitudes of the Transitional Object in a Borderline Child. *Int. J. Psycho-Anal.*, 52:107–114.

GALENSON, E. (1971), A Consideration of the Nature of Thought in Childhood Play. In: *Separation-Individuation*, ed. J. B. McDevitt & C. F. Settlage. New York: International Universities Press, pp. 41–59.

———— & ROIPHE, H. (1971), The Impact of Early Sexual Discovery on Mood, Defensive Organization, and Symbolization. *This Annual*, 26:195–216.

GREENACRE, P. (1969), The Fetish and the Transitional Object. *This Annual*, 24:144–164.

MAHLER, M. S. (1952), On Childhood Psychosis and Schizophrenia. *This Annual*, 7:286–305.

———— (1963), Thoughts about Development and Individuation. *This Annual*, 18:307–324.

———— (1968), *On Human Symbiosis and the Vicissitudes of Individuation*, Vol. 1: *Infantile Psychosis*. New York: International Universities Press.

———— & FURER, M. (1960), Observations on Research Regarding the 'Symbiotic Syndrome' of Infantile Psychosis. *Psychoanal. Quart.*, 29:317–327.

———— & GOSLINER, B. J. (1955), On Symbiotic Child Psychosis. *This Annual*, 10:195–212.

MODELL, A. H. (1968), *Object Love and Reality*. New York: International Universities Press.

PINE, F. & FURER, M. (1963), Studies of the Separation-Individuation Phase. *This Annual*, 18:325–342.

REISER, M. F. (1966), Toward an Integrated Psychoanalytic-Physiological Theory of Psychosomatic Disorders. In: *Psychoanalysis—A General Psychology*, ed. R. M. Loewenstein, L. M. Newman, M. Schur, A. J. Solnit. New York: International Universities Press, pp. 570–582.

ROIPHE, H. (1968), On an Early Genital Phase. *This Annual*, 23:348–365.

———— & GALENSON, E. (1972), Early Genital Activity and the Castration Complex. *Psychoanal. Quart.*, 41:334–347.

———— & ———— (1973), Object Loss and Early Sexual Development. *Psychoanal. Quart.*, 42:73–90.

WERNER, H. & KAPLAN, B. (1963), *Symbol Formation*. New York: Wiley.

WINNICOTT, D. W. (1953), Transitional Objects and Transitional Phenomena. *Int. J. Psycho-Anal.*, 34:89–97.

———— (1965), *The Maturational Process and the Facilitating Environment*. New York: International Universities Press.

The Infantile Fetish

HERMAN ROIPHE, M.D.
AND ELEANOR GALENSON, M.D.

FETISHISM, ONE OF THE MOST BIZARRE AND FLORID PERVERSIONS OF the human sexual instinct, has attracted the attention of many psychoanalytic and psychiatric investigators. The fetish is an inanimate object which is adopted as a necessary prop to insure adequate sexual performance in adult life. Tracing the development of adult fetishists in analysis, several authors have found that the fetish first emerges in the phallic phase and during latency (Gillespie, 1952; Bak, 1953, 1968; Greenacre, 1970).

Any discussion of the genetic and dynamic roots of fetishism must start with Freud's original contributions to this topic, which occupied him over a period of 35 years. In 1905 Freud described fetishism as an "unsuitable substitute for the sexual object." He stated: "What is substituted for the [normal] sexual object is some part of the body . . . which is in general very inappropriate for sexual purposes, or an inanimate object which bears some assignable relation to the person whom it replaces" (p. 153). He wrote that a certain degree of fetishism is normal and ubiquitous, as in the overvaluation of the love object which inevitably extends to everything associated with the beloved. The condition becomes pathological only in those cases in which the fetish replaces the normal object. He also alluded to intermediary states in which the sexual partner must have certain distinct qualities, e.g., a particular hair coloring.

Assistant Professor and Associate Professor of Psychiatry, Albert Einstein College of Medicine.

In footnotes added to later editions of the *Three Essays,* Freud further extended our understanding of fetishism. In 1910 he pointed to the importance of the coprophilic pleasure in smelling as one determinant in the choice of the fetish. In this footnote, Freud also alluded to the role of the castration complex in fetishism: "Another factor that helps towards explaining the fetishistic preference for the foot is to be found among the sexual theories of children: the foot represents a woman's penis, the absence of which is deeply felt" (p. 155). Freud emphasized the central and organizing role of the castration complex in the precipitation of fetishism in his definitive paper on "Fetishism" (1927), in which he offered several additional considerations. He asserted that the fetish becomes the vehicle for both denying and affirming the fact of castration and in this manner brings about a split in the ego, a point which he further elaborated in 1938. In addition he wrote: "Affection and hostility in the treatment of the fetish—which run parallel with the disavowal and the acknowledgment of castration—are mixed in unequal proportions in different cases, so that one or the other is more clearly recognizable" (p. 157).

A number of other authors, while recognizing the organizing role of the castration complex in the structure of fetishism, have tended to emphasize the preoedipal threads in the fabric of the fetish. Abraham (1910) stressed the importance of sadomasochistic elements. His patient had a tendency to retain his excreta and had a lifelong fantasy in which he was forced to refrain from relieving either bowel or bladder. Bak (1953) demonstrated that his patient's relation to his fetish contained currents which condensed the tactile sensation of his mother's skin, her body smell, the smell of feces, and an illusory phallus.

In a series of papers on fetishism, Greenacre (1953, 1955, 1960) emphasized a specific combination of genetic influences. She pointed to disturbances in the first 18 months of life which produce an instability in the formation of the body image, lead to uncertainty of outline and fluctuations in the subjective sense of size, and by bringing about complementary disturbances in the phallic phase result in an exaggeration of the castration complex. The genital area of the body image is less certain in the early years of life than most other parts of the body. In normal development the genital schematization becomes consolidated during the phallic phase, due to an increase in the spontaneous endogenous sensations arising at that time. Under the conditions of disturbed pregenitality which she described, the overly strong castration anxiety of the phallic phase is combined with the body-disintegration anxiety from the earlier phases and depletes rather than reinforces the genital schematization.

This brief review of the literature on adult fetishism serves to underline the main thematic outlines in the precipitation of the fetish during the phallic phase or during latency. An unusually sharp castration complex is generally agreed to be the central, organizing nucleus in the structure of fetishism; this development occurs on the basis of severe disturbances in the preoedipal libidinal and aggressive drive economy, object relations, and body-self schematization.

Greenacre (1960, 1969, 1970) has in addition pointed to fetishistic phenomena such as some partially automatized autoerotic habits, the amulet or magic objects, the symbolic object in religious rites, the token in romantic love, and some special properties of children's play. In these fetishistic phenomena the "fetish" is not related specifically to genital sexual performance. This conceptual extension, while it does not blur our understanding of fetishism as a perversion of the sexual instinct, offers the possibility of understanding a wide range of individual and cultural practices, as well as fetishisticlike phenomena in children which may or may not be the forerunners of adult fetishism.

Wulff (1946) presented observational vignettes of phenomena which he termed infantile fetishism. Two of the five cases which he reported were seen by himself and three were observed by colleagues: Friedjung (1927–28), Idelsohn (personal communication), and Sterba (1935). The first case described by Wulff was that of a boy a little over 4 years old. When this youngster had a pain, or was in a bad humor, or could not tolerate his mother's leaving, he only had to be given his "magic blanket"; he would then wrap his head in it and fall asleep peacefully and happily. Ever since he had been weaned from the breast, this warm, soft coverlet was prized by him more than anything in the world. Wulff's second case was that of a boy who was not quite 2 when he was separated from his mother and admitted to an orphanage. He became inseparably attached to his chamber pot and readily complied with the most difficult and disagreeable demands of upbringing so long as he was allowed to keep his pot, the most precious object in his world.

Sterba reported on a little girl who clung tenaciously and lovingly to a drooling bib which she had worn when she suckled at the breast. Since she was weaned at 6½ months she would press this drooling cloth against her cheek and suck her thumb, contentedly falling asleep. It was her comforter and her protector when she was hurt, when something was taken from her, or when she was in a strange environment.

Idelsohn reported on a little boy, age 15 months, who showed a special interest in a particular feeding bib. Whenever he went to bed, he took this bib, smelled it, and sucked it; under no circumstances would he be parted from it. When he was 2½ years old this bib disappeared, and for some time thereafter he was in low spirits and had great difficulty in falling asleep. He refused to accept a substitute and promptly became a regular bed wetter. At the age of 4, he became attached to his mother's handkerchiefs, whereupon he stopped wetting the bed. While he did not insist on a specific handkerchief, it had to have some residual odor of his mother's eau-de-cologne. He often stuffed it in his pajamas, holding it pressed against his penis, saying that in this way it could not get lost.

Finally, Friedjung reported the case of a little boy who during the first year of his life was accustomed to fall asleep with his mother's worn nightgown pressed between his hands, thumb in his mouth. At some point in the second year he began to prefer a brassiere or stocking which his mother had used.

Wulff calls each of these special infantile objects a fetish, clearly implying that they are for the infant a necessary aspect of the object which stands for the mother and her nurturing function. It would seem to us that such a terminology involves a considerable conceptual unclarity and ambiguity in that it fails to demonstrate any genetic and dynamic continuity with the fetish of the phallic phase and of the adult perversion, at the core of which virtually all investigators agree that the castration complex is the organizing nucleus.

In the cases of the drooling cloth, the feeding bib, and the magic blanket, it would seem that Winnicott's (1953, 1965) concept of transitional objects, with its emphasis on the normal, healthy, and ubiquitous nature of this infantile construct, is a much more appropriate one and avoids the ambiguity of Wulff's explanations. In the case of the 2-year-old boy and his chamber pot, we lack sufficient developmental data to make a reasonable decision about the meaning of this behavior. In Idelsohn's case, on the other hand, the boy's use of the handkerchief is a clear instance of fetish formation in a 4- to 5-year-old, but this does not help us to answer the question whether there is an infantile fetish which makes its appearance earlier than the phallic phase.

We have of course no information that would help us decide whether such fetish formation appearing at the ages of 4 and 5 indicates some widespread pathology or foreshadows later perverse development. It may be that such fetishes in the phallic phase appear much more commonly than we have heretofore suspected. Such quantitative factors as the intensity of the castration anxiety and the degree of disturbance in the preoedipal years may ultimately be crucial for the differentiation of those cases in which the fetish goes on to become an obligate prop for sexual functioning in adulthood and those in which this childhood manifestation finds a more normal resolution.

Of all the cases, Friedjung's is perhaps the most evocative as far as its bearing on the subject of the infantile fetish is concerned. This little boy's transitional object of the first year, his mother's nightgown, shifted in the second year to a brassiere or stockings which had been worn by her. When Friedjung communicated his unusual observations to Freud, he received the following reply: "It has been shown beyond doubt . . . that the fetish is a penis substitute, a substitute for the missing penis of the mother, and hence a means of defense against castration anxiety—and nothing else. There remains to test this in the case of this child. If proof is to be forthcoming the boy must have had ample opportunity to convince himself of his naked mother's lack of a penis" (quoted by Wulff, p. 462). Freud's expectations were completely fulfilled. The parents, whose bedroom the boy shared, undressed in his presence, in order, as the mother put it, to accustom him to their naked bodies and to enable him to recognize the difference between the sexes. Freud, then, would seem to have accepted this use of stocking and brassiere in a 16-month-old boy as definite evidence of a fetishistic defense against castration anxiety.

Wulff raised an understandable objection to Freud's formulation in this case, an objection which cannot be wished away. He states that such a possibility "is in complete contradiction to our very certain and well-established knowledge concerning the development of the child and its various phases." He quotes Freud (1923): "It seems to me, however, that the significance of the castration complex can only be rightly appreciated when its origin in the phase of *primacy of the phallus* is also taken into account."

Greenacre (1970) was well aware of this conceptual dilemma and offered the following special solution:

> It is my impression that early fetish formation does not develop unless the accompanying disturbances have been so undermining as to produce a severe preoedipal castration problem, whether through illness, operative procedure, or severe parental mishandling. It is significant that at the early age of one to two years there is a general body responsiveness to discomfort or physical insult, and discharge of tension may occur through whatever channels are available at this special time. If the disturbance is so severe, however, that ordinary discharge mechanisms are inadequate, premature genital stimulation may be induced. This is most likely to occur during the second year. This tends then to promote sadomasochistic elements in the incipient erotic response. Some fluidity between pregenital and genital responses remains, and gives rise to a tendency to persistent polymorphous perverse reactions as well as increasing later castration problems [p. 336].

In brief, then, she states that under the special conditions of a highly disturbed preoedipal development there may be during the second year a premature genitalization and a severe preoedipal castration problem with the emergence of an infantile fetish. This represents a revision of her earlier thesis that experiences in the first 18 months of life which result in an instability in the formation of the body image lead to an overly strong castration anxiety in the phallic phase and a need for bolstering the genital outline of the body through the fetish (1953, 1955, 1960).

The construct of the infantile fetish as a true genetic forerunner of that in the adult perversion would then require that we can demonstrate the existence of a fetish that has the same general dynamic outline as the adult fetish and that appears with some regularity earlier than the phallic phase. It would then be necessary to show that the infant's profound attachment to the fetish object follows the development of a preoedipal castration problem and that the fetish becomes identified with the child's own phallic body image and with the missing phallus of the mother. Anna Freud (1965) in her discussion of the fetish of childhood and its relation to the adult perversion correctly cautions us:

> Seen from the side of the analyses of relevant adult cases, there is no doubt of the early origin of their fetish and of its persistent nature. . . . Seen from the side of clinical experience with children, on the other hand, it is equally obvious that the number of childhood fetishes is far greater than that of the true fetishists of later years [p. 211].

Unfortunately, the literature is replete with many confusing references to an infantile fetish when the clinical observations or the theoretical arguments clearly suggest that what is being considered is a transitional object, with its emphasis on the ubiquitous and healthy aspect of the phenomenon. We would agree with Winnicott (1953) in his discussion of Wulff's paper when he states:

> There is a difference between my point of view and that of Wulff which is reflected in my use of this special term [transitional object] and his use of the term 'fetish object'. A study of Wulff's paper seems to show that in using the word fetish he has taken back to infancy something that belongs in ordinary theory to the sexual perversions. . . . I would prefer to retain the word fetish to describe the object that is employed on account of a *delusion* of a maternal phallus [p. 96].

In this paper we offer an alternate explanation to Greenacre's for the appearance of a true infantile fetish in the preoedipal stage. On the basis of experiences gained in the treatment of psychotic children and observations of normal development in the second year of life, Roiphe (1968) has proposed a more general solution. He suggested that children between the ages of 16 and 24 months, normally and regularly, experience a sexual arousal as evidenced by a significantly increased frequency and intensity of the manipulation of their own genitals, including frank masturbatory activity, as well as a significantly increased curiosity about the genitals of other children and adults. This early sexual interest seems to be involved with the consolidation of the object representation and the body-self schematization, particularly a primary genital outline of the body. As far as can be determined, this early sexual interest is free of any oedipal resonance (Roiphe and Galenson, 1973).

Roiphe also found that certain children during this period may develop moderate to severe castration reactions, which phenomenologically cannot be distinguished from those familiar reactions arising during the phallic phase. Such children will show a symptom complex which includes increased negativism and heightened dependence on the mother, sleep disturbances, bowel and bladder disturbances (e.g., loss of previously attained bowel and bladder control or severe constipation), nightmares, fleeting phobias of being bitten by horses, birds, dogs, etc.; the verbally expressed fear, in boys, that the penis will fall off; and in girls, the heartbreaking query why they do not have one; and interminable play sequences which clearly derive from the underlying castration complex (Roiphe and Galenson, 1972).

At this juncture of development, the castration anxiety converges with and is indissoluble from the anxieties of object loss and self annihilation; we do not find one without some resonance on the other plane. In the phallic phase, with the further solidification and constancy of the self and object representations, the castration fear, powerful and organizing as it may be, no longer carries the immediate, more global meaning of threatened object loss and self annihilation as is the case in the early stage of sexual development. Ordinarily, a child will pass through this early period of sexual interest and activity with only low-keyed behavioral reflections of the underlying, important currents of this phase. However, symptomatic castration reactions, at times of extreme violence, will develop when there is a confluence of the following three conditions: (1) Indications of the normal sexual arousal have already appeared, usually between 16 and 24 months. (2) The child, in the context of this sexual arousal, has had the opportunity to observe the anatomical difference between the sexes. (3) The child has earlier had such experiences as birth defects, severe illness, surgical intervention, loss of a parent, or in general, not "good enough" mothering, which have resulted in an instability in the self and object representations.

In order to test and investigate these hypotheses, we have established a research nursery at the Albert Einstein College of Medicine and have by now systematically studied the longitudinal development of 35 children throughout the second year of life. In the course of this work, we have come on a set of observations on the development of the infantile fetish during the second year which seems to us to fulfill all the requirements of a true fetish formation.

OBSERVATIONS

Suzy was a dainty, small-boned, little girl of 13 months when she entered the nursery (Roiphe and Galenson, 1972). This very pretty child had already worked as a model for several months and not only was capable of making the rounds of the children's modeling agencies with her mother in a quiet, poised manner but was able to sit through photographing sessions of one to two hours patiently doing as she was expected. Her early development was of good quality. She had already been walking for 3 months prior to her entering the nursery and was competent, sure-footed, and agile.

To observe the emergence of sexual behavior and curiosity in Suzy required very little imagination or sophistication. During her 13th and 14th months it was possible to establish a clear baseline during which her interest in her own genitals was either absent or very casual. When she was almost 15 months, she rather abruptly began to show an implacable curiosity about the genital anatomy of other children. As soon as any child was taken to the changing table Suzy was there, scrutinizing the whole process with great fascination. With an unwavering gaze, fixed on the genital of the child, she would demonstrate by consistent gestural indications a clear apprehension of the anatomical difference between the sexes. During this period and until she was 19 months, she progressively engaged in more intense sexual activity, as our own observations in the nursery and the mother's report of Suzy's behavior at home indicate. She engaged quite regularly whenever she was undressed in more or less prolonged masturbation. Beginning at 17 months and reaching a peak at 19, there was clear evidence of a developing castration reaction which profoundly affected a broad spectrum of other areas of her personality development. The disruptive influence on the developing object relations was decisive and far-reaching. The overwhelming anger and disappointment with the mother were reflected in the development of an almost paralyzing dependence on her. The child almost literally clung to the mother and demonstrated a sullen distrust of other adults and children which did not auger well for the age-appropriate individuation thrust.

Concurrent with the undermining of the child's developing object relations was the indication of an interference with and a weakening of several aspects of the maturing ego functions. Most dramatic was the pervasive inhibition of Suzy's curiosity in general, and sexual curiosity in particular; this was paralleled by a marked inhibition and deterioration of symbolization and play. An outstanding effect of this early castration reaction was a decisive loss in self-esteem and the emergence of a depressive mood (Mahler, 1963, 1966).

For the purpose of our discussion of the infantile fetish, the story begins at Christmastime when Suzy, aged 16½ months, was given, among other gifts, a battery-operated, walking-talking doll almost as large as she was. Suzy was at first somewhat taken aback by this rather formidable toy, but when a flap in the doll's back became unhinged and the batteries fell out, the child broke out into intense, frightened crying. The doll was quickly repaired, but Suzy would have nothing to do with it anymore and it was put away in a closet in her room. Some 6 weeks later the family moved to a new, larger apartment. While Suzy did not overtly show any particular anxiety in connection with this move, she asked to have this doll in her crib and fell asleep clinging to the doll and a soft woolen coverlet to which she had previously had no special attachment. The new attachment to the doll and coverlet continued, unabated, for the remaining 5 months that we observed Suzy. She would fall asleep pressing the coverlet with one hand against her cheek and sucking her thumb, and holding her other arm around her doll. Whenever any other children visited, she very generously permitted them to use any one of her toys—with the exception of this now very precious doll. She could not tolerate having any child touch this doll.

Ruth, one of our nursery children, was discovered to have a congenital dislocation of her hips at 2 months (see Galenson and Roiphe, 1971). A corrective pillow was placed beneath her diaper and thenceforth was removed only during bathing and diapering. This pillow remained as a quasi-body part until its use was discontinued when she was 12 months old. No further corrective device was required until 15 months when a Dennis-Brown bar and shoes were prescribed for nighttime use only. Although the pillow did not limit movement of the whole body, it certainly interfered with leg mobility and probably with lower trunk movement as well. Large muscle development fell within the late normal range; she stood with support at 7 months, crawled at 8, walked with support at 12, and achieved unaided locomotion at 16. However, all of these were characterized by the rather grotesque position of widely separated thighs and lower legs, clearly visible and distressing to her mother. In her crawling, Ruth made remarkable accommodation to the wide lower segment of her body. Her awareness of spatial relations and fine motor coordination showed precocious development.

A very early and pronounced wariness with strangers accompanied by intense visual inspection of every unfamiliar person had not yet abated when Ruth entered the research nursery at 12 months. It took several weeks before the two staff members assigned to her were able to break into her orbit. Her favorite activities with them consisted of looking at picture books and pointing to pictures on the wall toward which she was then carried. Beginning at 14 months Ruth began to show much more open aggression such as temper tantrums and negativism toward her mother, biting her own arms and pushing and scratching the face of her observers. With this development, she seemed to become much freer with adults and children, was heard to laugh out loud for the first time, and lose the anxious look which had previously been characteristic of her.

At 17½ months, interest in her own genitals made its appearance. Her mother reported that Ruth now actively touched her genitals with her fingers. When other children in the nursery were diapered, Ruth immediately ran over and asked to be lifted up in order to get a closer look. She tried to lift the skirts of several female staff members in order to peer under them. In her very active doll play, she pointed to the crotch of dolls, insisting that her mother remove their clothes and especially their panties. She would then look at the crotch area intently. After some 5 weeks of intense sexual activity and curiosity, she seemed to develop a rather intense inhibition of any direct sexual interest. Her curiosity was displaced from the genital area, first to the umbilicus, and then to inanimate objects such as knobs and other protuberances. She developed a distinct dislike for broken crayons and toys.

A slow deterioration in her mood set in; she became irritable and increasingly less able to tolerate even slight frustrations. Her aggression was not directed against her mother as it had been earlier, but instead she teased and provoked other adults and again began to bite her own fingers in a renewed emergence of self-directed aggression. The earlier fear of strangers and the clinging to her mother returned in ever-mounting intensity.

At this point, a new obligatory object made its appearance in the form of a doll which Ruth called "boy." She insisted that this doll, which resembled her other girl dolls in every way, be seated next to her at all meals, and that "he" receive a mouthful of food each time she fed herself. Her favorite inanimate companions became a number of dolls which she carried along without using them in play.

Billy was a sturdy boy of 11 months when he entered the nursery (Roiphe and Galenson, 1973). He crawled everywhere, babbling as he went, apparently unconcerned by the strange environment and the many unfamiliar adults and children. When he was 9 months old, his father left for army service and did not return until after Billy's second birthday; the youngster apparently showed no direct reaction to his father's leaving. His development during the first year was generally of good quality, except for an emergent and quite persistent sleep disturbance. He virtually never slept through the night, waking usually at least once and quite frequently three and four times throughout the first two years of his life that we were able to follow.

When Billy was 13 months old there were distinct signs of a developing and expanding separation reaction, which exploded in intensity and extent when he was 16 months old, following an actual separation from his mother of two weeks' duration. One of the homely consequences of his early intolerance for separation was that his mother, who had no regular domestic help, was no longer able to use the toilet behind a closed door. Billy then had the repeated and daily experience of seeing his mother exposed on the toilet.

At 14 months, his mother began to report and we began to observe in the nursery that Billy with increasing frequency and intensity manipulated his penis whenever he was exposed. Of particular interest during this interval of early sexual activity was Billy's tendency to clutch his penis through the diaper whenever he was frustrated and seriously angered.

When Billy was 15 months, he developed an interesting bedtime ritual which persisted throughout the ensuing months that we observed him. Holding his bottle pressed against his penis, he would lie down in prone position and fall asleep. The ritualized holding of the bottle suggested a transitional phenomenon, with the bottle standing for the object. The associated clutching of the penis, however, suggests a concomitant castration reaction. It will be remembered that on numerous occasions he had had the opportunity to see his mother exposed.

From the age of 16½ months on, Billy developed, in addition to the sexual behavior described earlier, a clear-cut genital masturbation practice. He would lie prone on a ball or some other toy, hands tucked underneath in the genital area, and rock back and forth in a concentrated and withdrawn manner. It is certainly of more than passing interest that the whole form of this preferred masturbatory posture was similar to that of the bedtime ritual.

We are grateful to Dr. Daniel Feinberg for permitting us to read and discuss with him an unpublished manuscript, "An Analysis of Intractable Nightmares in a Two-Year-Old Boy." The case material affords us a very vivid and interesting example of an infantile fetish in the process of formation. At 26 months, this boy developed a profound sleep disturbance as a consequence of repetitive nightmares, so that he averaged only two to three hours of sleep at night. During the long periods of wakefulness, he was overactive but not in a prolonged panic. His parents had divorced when he was a little over 12 months of age, and for roughly 4 months after the separation he suffered a mild sleep disturbance. His nighttime awakenings were frequent but not persistent or prolonged and unaccompanied by nightmares as best one could determine. At that time his mother's reassurance would enable him to return easily to sleep.

At the onset of the severe sleep disturbance which led him to treatment he threw all the stuffed animals with which he had previously been accustomed to fall asleep out of his crib, calling them "No good." In their place, he insisted on taking to bed with him each night his toy trucks and cars.

We could clearly establish that this little boy had for several months shown a real interest in his penis and had developed open genital masturbation. It was also established that he had recently had the opportunity to see his mother and a little girl cousin exposed. The precise details and timing could not be ascertained, except that this had all taken place before the boy fell ill. The interesting therapeutic work with this boy disclosed the nuclear role of the castration complex in the entire symptomatic picture; it also provided clear evidence that the infantile fetishes, the toy trucks and cars, stood for the penis, the absent father, and the missing penis of the mother.

DISCUSSION

In each of the cases presented above, we have been able to muster reasonably convincing evidence of a primary sexual arousal. That is to say, with the increase in spontaneous, endogenous genital sensation, the child's attention is increasingly drawn to the genitals, which as a consequence gradually attain a greater and more distinct narcissistic importance in the general body schema than does, for example, the toe or the elbow. Roiphe (1968) suggested that with the delay in the immediate discharge of bowel and bladder tension that takes place in the early part of the second year, independent of any parental efforts to establish toilet control, there regularly and normally occurs a spread in excitation to and arousal of the genital organs. Greenacre (1968) presented a strikingly parallel formulation when she wrote, "I have thought that toward the end of the second year there was regularly some enhancement of genital sensitivity (phallic or clitoral) that occurred simultaneously with the increasing maturation of the body sphincters" (p. 304).

In a later paper, however, Greenacre (1970) offers what seems to be a contradictory formulation when she states that under the special conditions of a highly disturbed preoedipal development, there may be a premature genitalization and a severe preoedipal castration complex.

> The transitional object is a support in the period at the inception of autonomous ego development and object relatedness, and furthers the union of the (nonhostile) aggression of growth with loving tenderness. . . . It would appear, however, that when the infant has suffered unusually severe deprivation or mistreatment, i.e., when the mother has not been good enough to neutralize this, the hostile elements in the aggression appear in mounting tension from frustration, and the energy cannot be sufficiently used in the forward movement of growth. It then finds discharge in rages, or it may become bodybound, gradually causing premature sadomaso-chistic erotization associated sometimes with precocious genitaliza-tion under strain [p. 336].

While we have certainly seen evidences of such development, e.g., Billy's clutching his penis through his diapers whenever he was frustrated or seriously angered, we would tend to view this behavior as a special and particular variant of the normal sexual arousal which regularly occurs during this period of life.

In any case, the child's reaction to the anatomical difference between the sexes is by no means just a consequence of the fact that this is where the difference is. We believe that castration reactions frequently appear at this period in life precisely because the genitals normally attain a particular and heightened narcissistic valence as a consequence of the regular genital arousal. We do not think that a castration reaction appearing at this time of life is of necessity a major pathological complex which bespeaks an ominous disruption in development. We believe that the intensity of the castration reaction and its consequent effect on subsequent development vary as a function of the severity of the insults which the child has experienced in the object and body spheres, whether through maternal mishandling or birth defect, illness or operative procedures.

In the three research children described above, there was less than good-enough mothering during the first year, which resulted in an uncertain sense of self and object. Suzy's mother was an immature and highly narcissistic woman who was inordinately proud of her little daughter's appearance and accomplishments and reacted grievously to each bruise, cut, or scar. From the age of 11 months on, Suzy regularly showered with her parents and we have consistent reports that Suzy started to hold food in her mouth in spite of her mother's mounting frustration and irritation. So long as her pretty little daughter was passive and compliant and showed off well, the mother was more or less able to read Suzy's cues and provide adequately for her needs. However, when Suzy developed a will of her own and moreover seemed to react massively to the narcissistic insult implicit in her observation of the anatomical difference between the sexes, there developed a growing gulf between this mother and daughter.

We assumed that Ruth had arrived at only a marginal stability in her object representation, compromised during her early months by the early and abrupt weaning, the less than optimum mother-child relationship, and the limitation of aggressive motor discharge due to the corrective device she wore.

In Billy, the absence of the father from the age of 9 months through the second year must be implicated in the unduly sharp object-loss anxiety which this boy demonstrated. His mother, whose husband was away for an entire year, suffered greatly from loneliness and consequently became involved in a more inseparable closeness with her little boy than might otherwise have been the case; that is, she may have resisted the child's maturing tendency to grow away from her. The major developmental thrust at the end of the first year is the separation from the infantile symbiotic relationship to the mother, in the process of which the child leans increasingly heavily on the father. With the absence of his father and his support in this whole process, Billy was much more than ordinarily threatened by his maturing independent strivings.

Normally, the sexual arousal which is characteristic of the second year concerns itself with the expansion and consolidation of the self and object schematization. In these three children with their uncertain sense of self and object, the discovery of the anatomical difference between the sexes and the emergence of severe castration reactions served to disrupt and seriously interfere with the whole individuation thrust as well as with some of the major aspects of ego development such as play, symbolization, defense, and frustration tolerance.

In the two little girls the awareness of the genital difference produced the additional burden of disappointment and anger, which very much intensified the ambivalence that is characteristic of this stage of development. In all three, the intensification of the ambivalence resulted in a weakening of the developing object representation and the intervention of the pathological defense mechanism of the splitting of the maternal image with the projection of the bad object (Mahler, 1966). This was reflected in each child by the explosive expansion of the fear of object loss and a recrudescence of the fear of strangers. All the children developed a heightened dependence on their mothers, almost literally clinging to them and demonstrating a sullen mistrust of other adults and children, which did not auger well for the age-appropriate individuation thrust.

Simultaneously, a split in the self representation seemed to have occurred, with the obligatory infantile fetish serving to bolster the genital outline of the body. In the two girls, the walking-talking doll and the doll "boy" served to deny the absence of their own penis. In the little boy, the bedtime ritual with the bottle served not only to deny the absent penis of the mother, but also to bolster the genital outline of his own body in the face of the confusion which must arise from the two competing genital schemata, the tactile, visual, and sensorimotor schema of his own body and that which arises through a primary identification with the visual percept of his mother's genitals.

The intense hostile aggression in these children arises as a result of the early disturbance in the mother-child relationship as well as the castration reaction. The intense ambivalence in these children not only has the above-described effect of weakening the developing self and object schemata, but also seems to call forth a turning of aggression against the self, a mechanism which was particularly notable in Ruth, but also quite prominent in Suzy. Finally, the heightened ambivalence would seem to foster an early sadomasochistic erotization as was indicated, e.g., by Billy's tendency to masturbate when frustrated or angered and the distinct development of teasing in Suzy and Ruth.

Concurrent with the undermining of the children's developing object relations is the indication of an interference with and weakening of several aspects of the maturing ego functions. Most dramatic in each of these children was the pervasive inhibition of curiosity in general and sexual curiosity in particular. Parallel with this was the marked inhibition and deterioration of symbolization and play. In Billy, where the castration reaction seemed to have developed quite early, there was a very decided retardation in the development of symbolic fantasy play. Both Suzy and Ruth, who early showed a flourishing of such play particularly in relationship to the beginning stage of sexual discovery, soon demonstrated a dramatic deterioration and impoverishment in their symbolic play.

SUMMARY

In each of the children we have described, the appearance of the infantile fetish in the second year of life was preceded by definite indications of a sexual arousal, the observation of the anatomical difference between the sexes, and a distinct and prominent castration reaction. We have, therefore, been able to demonstrate that there is a true infantile fetish, which has a clear dynamic continuity with the fetish arising later in life. The fetish serves to define and supplement the body schema, particularly the genital outline of the body. This reparative construct is precipitated and split off as a result of the undermining of the sense of body integrity which follows from the observation of the anatomical difference between the sexes at a time in life when the genitals have already assumed a distinct narcissistic importance in the general body schema.

It may even be that the infantile fetish and fetishistic phenomena are much more common than we have tended to think. Perhaps in all but the most severe castration reactions of early life, the young child's reliance on the fetish as a supplement to the body schema is ultimately diffused through its extension into play, fantasy, character formations, and other less tangible and concrete defensive forms. It may be that the fetish goes on to become an obligate prop to later sexual functioning only in those children who experience some further major castration insults during the oedipal phase.

BIBLIOGRAPHY

ABRAHAM, K. (1910), Remarks on the Psycho-Analysis of a Case of Foot and Corset Fetishism. *Selected Papers on Psycho-Analysis.* London: Hogarth Press, 1948, pp. 125–136.

BAK, R. C. (1953), Fetishism. *J. Amer. Psychoanal. Assn.,* 1:285–298.

—— (1968), The Phallic Woman: The Ubiquitous Fantasy in Perversions. *This Annual,* 23:15–36.

FREUD, A. (1965), *Normality and Pathology in Childhood.* New York: International Universities Press.

FREUD, S. (1905), Three Essays on the Theory of Sexuality. *Standard Edition,* 7:125–243. London: Hogarth Press, 1953.

—— (1923), The Infantile Genital Organization. *Standard Edition,* 19:141–145. London: Hogarth Press, 1961.

—— (1927), Fetishism. *Standard Edition,* 21:149–157. London: Hogarth Press, 1961.

—— (1938), Splitting of the Ego in the Process Defence. *Standard Edition,* 23:271–278. London: Hogarth Press, 1964.

FRIEDJUNG, J. K. (1927–28), Wäsche-Fetischismus bei cinem Einjährigen. *Z. psychoanal. Päd.,* 2:25–26, 235–236.

GALENSON, E. & ROIPHE, H. (1971), The Impact of Early Sexual Discovery on Mood, Defensive Organization, and Symbolization. *This Annual,* 26:195–216.

GILLESPIE, W. H. (1952), Notes on the Analysis of Sexual Perversions. *Int. J. Psycho-Anal.,* 33:397–402.

—— (1956), The General Theory of Sexual Perversion. *Int. J. Psycho-Anal.,* 37:396–403.

GREENACRE, P. (1953), Certain Relationships Between Fetishism and the Faulty Development of the Body Image. *This Annual,* 8:79–98.

—— (1955), Further Considerations Regarding Fetishism. *This Annual,* 10:187–194.

—— (1960), Further Notes on Fetishism. *This Annual,* 15:191–207.

—— (1968), Perversions. In: *Emotional Growth,* 1:300–314. New York: International Universities Press, 1971.

—— (1969), The Fetish and the Transitional Object. *This Annual,* 24:144–164.

—— (1970), The Transitional Object and the Fetish. In: *Emotional Growth,* 1:335–352. New York: International Universities Press, 1971.

MAHLER, M. S. (1963), Thoughts About Development and Individuation. *This Annual*, 18:307–324.

—— (1966), Notes on the Development of Basic Moods. In: *Psychoanalysis—A General Psychology*, ed. R. M. Loewenstein, L. M. Newman, M. Schur, & A. J. Solnit. New York: International Universities Press, pp. 152–168.

ROIPHE, H. (1968), On an Early Genital Phase. *This Annual*, 23:348–365.

—— & GALENSON, E. (1972), Early Genital Activity and the Castration Complex. *Psychoanal. Quart.*, 41:334–347.

—— & —— (1973), Object Loss and Early Sexual Development. *Psychoanal. Quart.*, 42:73–90.

STERBA, E. (1935), An Important Factor in Eating Disturbances of Childhood.

WINNICOTT, D. W. (1953), Transitional Objects and Transitional Phenomena. *Int. J. Psycho-Anal.*, 34:89–97.

Wulff, M. (1946), Fetishism and Object Choice in Early Childhood. *Psychoanal. Quart.*, 15:450–471.

CLINICAL
CONTRIBUTIONS

The Son of a Refugee

SYLVIA BRODY, PH.D.

THIS CASE PRESENTATION IS INTENDED TO SHOW SOME CONNECTIONS between a specific historical event, a father's escape from Nazi Germany, and one aspect of his son's neurotic conflict during adolescence.

The analysis began when the boy was 9, because of his extreme irritability, negativism, restlessness, and psychogenic stomach pains.[1] At school he was a loner, evasive, unhappy, and depressed. Despite his superior intellectual abilities and high aspirations, his academic achievements were erratic. As treatment proceeded, phobic and counterphobic behavior appeared. After about five years all of the symptoms except some irritability and a free-floating anxiety had subsided, and gradually both were found to be related to the boy's unconscious fantasies about the father's escape. Insight into those fantasies, which did not emerge clearly until the last year of treatment, finally dispelled his irritability and diminished his anxiety, checked certain faults in his superego which had been attracting him to delinquent acts, and contributed to a resolution of his oedipal conflict.

Clinical data regarding the patient's body image, sibling status, psychosexual development, and transference manifestations are

Adjunct Professor of Psychology, Graduate School of the City University of New York. An earlier version of this paper was presented to the Long Island Psychoanalytic Society on November 8, 1971, and in the Workshop, "Children of Survivors," at the Annual Meeting of the American Psychoanalytic Association in New York, December 19, 1971.

[1] The stomach pains were found to occur mainly before leaving for school in the mornings, and to be related to events of the day that aroused anxiety. They gradually disappeared without specific analysis.

omitted from this account. The material of the first years of analysis
is summarized, however, insofar as it bears upon the patient's fears
of detection, his unconscious ideas about the father's status as a
refugee, and the subject of escape. Emphasis is to be placed mainly
upon the patient's manifold resistances in order to show the extent
to which repressed ideas about his father as both a representative
and an opponent of Hitler were embedded in his character
structure. It was late in the analysis that the theme of *getting away
with something* became prominent, and led to the uncovering of the
repressed material. As will be shown, the uncovering was the end
result of repeated efforts to understand the intensity of the patient's
conflictful interest in getting away, getting to safe places, and
traveling itself.

The patient's mother was an American physician, engaged in
public health work. She was an energetic woman with humor,
sensitivity, and competence. She resumed professional work when
the patient was in elementary school, but remained closely attentive
to the needs of her children. His father was a radiologist who was
born and educated in Germany and was seriously dedicated to his
work. Although the father was kindly and gentle, he was not at ease
with details that arise in the care of young children and left them
completely to his wife. He suffered from a chronic depression, which
began after the holocaust. The depressive periods lasted for several
months at a time. Remissions were brief, usually no more than 6
weeks in the patient's childhood, but longer in his mid-adolescence;
yet even in those periods the father rarely was free to communicate
with his children in a light-hearted or informal way. Psychiatric
treatment, including medication, had provided little relief.

Shortly after the father had completed his medical studies he had
had to leave Germany suddenly. Some critical remarks he had
made about the Nazi regime were reported to the authorities, who
were searching for him. In the beginning of the analysis the patient
had referred with mild pride to his father's dramatic escape by a
back door of the building where he had been working. The story fell
among his many reports of "Believe It Or Not" anecdotes that
intrigued him. Now and then he mentioned that his father spoke
warmly about his boyhood in Germany, but that, in contrast, he

disliked being asked about the Nazi period and became gloomy if it was mentioned.

The intensity of the patient's anxiety was difficult to understand because both parents were consistently and affectionately concerned with their children's growth and development, and the family life appeared to support sound object relationships and good possibilities for sublimation. The only known experiences that might have provoked excessive anxiety were two hospitalizations of the mother when the patient was age 2 and age 7.

In the preschool years the boy, Leon, was petulant and demanding. By mid-latency he was discontent, said he hated school, was nothing but a bum, and wished he were dead. At home he became vexed when his mother went out, but mostly if she did so while his father was at home. He demanded her help or her attentiveness from waking until bedtime, and accused her very frequently of not providing for his needs. However, it was only to her that he confided his ambitions to be a great inventor or to make great discoveries. Except during school hours, he hovered about one or another family member with a grumbling attitude, but shied away from direct verbal, visual, or physical contact with any of them. His uneasiness at being separated from his mother was aggravated by the criticism he earned from his brothers (two older and one younger than he) for being as cantankerous as he was. He regularly gave them cause to call him a jerk, a nut, a pest, a dope; and by age 9 he had a solid reputation as a grouch. He avoided his father most of all.

The mother was aware of two possible reasons for Leon's neurosis, and they are noted here to provide a more adequate background for its development. The main reason was his father's depression, which made the father irritable, silent, and withdrawn, although it never interfered with his work. In periods of depression he sat alone and read, and communicated adequately, though minimally, only with his wife. He avoided contacts with his two younger sons. The two older sons he often nagged and upbraided, and whenever he did so in Leon's hearing, Leon disappeared from sight. The second reason was that Leon had from birth strongly resembled one of her brothers, who had become a successful industrialist but whose unkindness to her had angered her throughout her girlhood. From material in her own psychotherapeutic treatment she surmised that because of that physical resemblance she might have been overly tense with Leon and engendered his feelings of being neglected by her. Although Leon's fears of his father and his uncle were confirmed in the analysis, they were not enough to explain the formation of his symptoms.

In our first meeting he was friendly but also jumpy, tense, and guarded. He disparaged the accounts of his behavior as told by his parents and teachers, but as he was troubled by the stomachaches and felt "nervous" at times, he responded to the offer of analysis with a begrudging acceptance. It was important, as will become clear in connection with his preoccupation with traveling, that the family lived in another state. This meant that unless he could be brought by automobile he had to take two buses and two trains to get to his sessions, so that the trip usually took about 2 hours each way. He was driven to them for most of the first few years—a drive of about 40 minutes—and after that only occasionally. In spite of these inconveniences he came with almost perfect regularity to his 3 hours each week.[2] The analysis lasted more than 8 years, and no

---

[2] The fear of traveling emerged early in the analysis, when he was being driven by car to his sessions, and when we did not foresee that he later on would have to make the trip alone. It first transpired distinctly as a fear on a day when the regular elevator of my building was in repair, so that Leon had to use a service elevator and a slightly different route to the waiting room. He became frightened that somehow he would get lost on the way to me. This fear was traced to an experience in the former home of his maternal grandmother. As a younger child, Leon had been extremely resentful and fearful of the grandmother's scolding him for being so restless and jumpy, and jealous of the attentions she received from Leon's mother. (Feelings about his grandmother and his father were almost identical.) The grandmother had had a private elevator in her house, and on one occasion Leon, just after feeling rebuffed by her, had been terrified of being stuck in the elevator, left in the house with her, and separated from his mother. The fear of riding in the elevator in my building was one of his first clear negative transference reactions. In the same early phase of the analysis Leon often reported dreams and daydreams of "fun rides," perilous skating and skiing trips, traveling *to* places, and sometimes mischievous pranks on roads that would scare drivers into thinking Leon had been knocked down and needed to be picked up and carried to safety. (See footnote 4.) Thus phobic and counterphobic ideas mingled and alternated; but there was no material to indicate that Leon's fear of traveling either originated in or was increased by the trip to the office. The practical

doubt was protracted by the excessive intervals between hours. Not until the final year did we come to understand the relationship between Leon's extreme self-consciousness, his concern with traveling, and the father's escape.

From the beginning of treatment he blamed his bad moods on his father: the father was inaccessible, faultfinding and bad-humored; moreover, he acted as if Leon didn't exist. All that made Leon nervous. He wished his father just weren't around at all, and shrank from the idea of my seeing his father often. And he wished to say no more about it. In fact, he frequently said, he tried never to think about his father. Until the last 2 years of the analysis, the same kinds of statements were reiterated peevishly, without elaboration. Other references to the father were exceedingly scarce; those initiated by the analyst were discounted. The father's depressions were never reported directly by the patient, not even their onset or their waning. For him, it was as if no remissions ever occurred, until the last phase of treatment. Although the chronic depression gradually came to play a large part in the analysis, it never became a central theme in his daily life; because he skillfully avoided his father's presence, and because he was able to devote his attention to many other persons and their activities—his brothers and their friends, and his mother and her friends and colleagues. The household was a busy one, providing Leon with many distractions, though of course none satisfied him.

Leon tried in other ways to deny or to rationalize his anxieties, but he failed. He could not suppress the worries that arose on his way to and from hours, of carsickness, traffic, tunnels, and tailgating. He chafed at any delay in getting home from anywhere. He feared open places and crowds or being "stuck" in rooms, buildings, or elevators. He pondered about the emotions Houdini must have felt, knowing he had to get out of a box or suffocate. He was perpetually afraid of being left alone somewhere and conspicuous, e.g., if he was the last to remain seated at a dining table. An open car window in hot weather agitated him because he feared being suffocated by hot air or gasoline fumes. An open window in

---

difficulties did yield masochistic satisfactions, and did nourish his already existing ambivalence about traveling.

my office made him nervous because of noises from outdoors. Open curtains made him worry that people across the street might become curious about him. He blamed his parents for making him angry because they did not get him home from places quickly enough, took him to places he would rather avoid, and talked to him when he wanted to be alone; and he blamed his brothers for bothering him with needless questions, e.g., where he had bought a ball. And he worried daily and hourly about every impending event, whether it involved fun or duty. He resisted any admission that the source of these ever-present anxieties was internal.

The pressure to decry the importance of his anxiety was increased by an acute self-consciousness, attributed by Leon to his conviction that he was a freak—skinny, freckled, and flat-footed. Being noticed, looked at or heard, at home, in school, or on the street made him nervous. In the analytic office he felt caged and exposed. For many months the most pervasive and intense fear during sessions was that his mother would forget to call for him or would leave the city thinking he had somehow gone home alone. He tried to manage his anxiety by repeatedly looking out of the window to watch for her car, filling the session with complaints about the difficulties of the trip, and brooding about the possible alternative routes she might take.

It was typical that no sooner did he utter a complaint or speak of something which made him feel tense than he launched into some form of verbal undoing—he negated, denied, or retracted what he had just said, or altered the complaint to apply to something different. Interpretive comments, however tactful, produced an impatient, "Oh, *that's* not it!" and a sullen refusal to speak further; then a compulsive interrupting of any effort on my part to say anything; or a period of mumbling. Sometimes he tried to control his rising tension by rapid shaking of his hands, or crumpling papers, or squeezing pencils, or incessant scribbling, or drawing complex mazes. For the better part of a year he ensconced himself behind a table during entire sessions, avoiding physical proximity or eye contact with me, hammering away with a pencil on paper and making fierce, indiscriminate markings—a kind of busy work intended to mask feelings of unworthiness, and a powerful resistance against introspection and communication.

Even more than he showed anxiety, Leon made fun of himself as if trying to persuade me not to take him too seriously. For example, with an overly jolly manner he would set up small block structures in such a way that they had to crash, and when they did he would cry out with a broad grin, "Timber!" Or, with an intense facial expression, and a grand display of athletic power and skill, exaggerating the technique of a basketball star, he would take precise aim in order to toss crumpled balls of paper into the wastebasket. Some such clowning became part of most hours. He was making fun of popular heroes, and wishing me to recognize that he was too sophisticated for such idolatry. But soon he was telling me his fantasies of being watched by me while he performed on TV, and of the prowess I should see and admire as he performed with extraordinary skill in sports, oratory, or magic tricks. If I was going to look at him, he was going to make sure I should be amused or impressed.[3] Occasionally, in reflective moods, he told of writing letters to a class president, a school librarian, or a town official, regarding some educational or civic improvement. Problems of government, and especially of social justice, attracted his attention. When I showed my interest in his ideas, he usually belittled them, as he had belittled his earlier aspirations toward invention and discovery.

By the third year he realized that his feeling of freakishness had to do with a defective body image and with an unpleasant "half-mind, half-body" sensation that came with erections. He knew, too, that his worries about not getting home had to do with the old fear of separation from his mother, and that his incessant demands for her presence and care covered a wish to have her at home to protect him from being alone with his father.[4]

---

[3] While traveling to his hours by automobile his defense against being observed in traffic took the form of rating songs heard on the radio, or counting passing cars and trucks. He liked to imagine that the cars put themselves in his view because they wanted to be seen and counted. Probably the passive locomotion, as well as the rating and counting, helped to ease his conflict about being seen.

[4] Material regarding his unconscious oral-passive wishes to achieve intimacy and safety with his mother at the end of long and treacherous journeys were prominent in dreams and hypnagogic phenomena. They have been described elsewhere (Brody, 1964a, pp. 124–129).

He then began a conscious struggle against his ambivalence toward his father, maintaining that his father probably was a superior physician, but at home he was awful, always scolding, always too tired, always demanding quiet; he cared only about reading the newspaper and didn't speak to anybody civilly.

Leon often had eavesdropped on his parents' conversations with each other, somewhat mischievously, somewhat defiantly, and in such a way as to make his father notice him, become annoyed, and send Leon away; Leon would then leave the room with a slight show of triumph. He now began to watch my techniques, with due complaints, and tried to provoke me to speak my thoughts while keeping his own secret. He posed inconsequential questions, fretted when I did not answer them, angrily told me to "Forget it!" and then loudly justified his decision to say nothing more until I spoke first. He admitted that he wished to make me lose my temper while he was to remain unmoved—neutral, he said, like Switzerland with its natural and safe boundaries. His efforts to remain distant and composed were in vain because he could not well tolerate his or my silence, just as he could not tolerate either closeness to or distance from his father. His agitation increased and his provocations became more plentiful. He fidgeted, kept adjusting his clothing, hemmed and hawed, repeatedly changed his seat, temporized, or scowlingly demanded that I tell him what to talk about. Or he informed me that he had a thought—should he say it? It didn't matter—I wouldn't understand it anyway.[5] Then he would resort to scribbling silently or to crumpling paper and kicking it around, sometimes sulkily, sometimes laughingly. Frequent reminders that he could succeed in blocking all further insight by such acting out usually enabled him to resume reasonable communication with me in the given hour.

At age 12 or 13 he began coming to his hours alone. He was very proud of getting to know his way about New York City. Still he dwelt upon his fears of riding in vehicles where he might be trapped or caught in traffic, or in tunnels where escaping gas might cause an

---

[5] Several years later he verbalized his reluctance to speak: "By being silent I prolong my life expectancy. I'm providing for the future." The need to withhold could then be related to fear of apprehension by the (Nazi) police.

explosion or where, in case of an accident, he might have to get out by having to walk on the narrow side ledges. He recalled his fascination, when younger, upon reading about a man who walked across Niagara Falls on a tightrope, and as a result became a "mental case" for the rest of his life. He marveled at the idea that some men must once have crossed from Alaska to Asia; or at the safe completion of other long and dangerous journeys across continents.[6]

A coronary attack suffered by his father when Leon was nearing 13 hardly disturbed him overtly. It led, however, to many elaborations of fantasies reported earlier in the analysis about his father's "X-ray vision," which might be lethal to both the father and his patients. As long as Leon could remember, he had felt awe at his father's capacity to see into others' bodies, and amazed when he learned that his father had seen him inside his mother before he came into the world. One of his fantasies about getting out of a tunnel was that the guard in the glassed-in alcove would put up a sign as Leon came along, saying, WATCH OUT FOR IDIOT! The guard represented his father observing him just before his passage through the birth canal. Leon once had read that all of the people on the earth could be packed into a box one-half cubic mile in size. If that was true, then his father, by means of his deadly machine, had the power to enjoy the "supreme ecstasy" of spying on the entire world population at one time and killing them all as well, with impunity. That joy was comparable, he said, to one he had imagined now and then, of pleasantly falling through endless space. The two fantasies contained identifications with the visually penetrating, sadistic father who could go unpunished, and with the exposed victims. Both identifications were linked to fantasies of watching his parents in the dark of early morning. Thus, although the father's illness did not arouse overt anxiety, it did evoke awareness of a wish for his father's love and respect. In the train of that wish he developed positive transference reactions: a cranky

---

[6] The claustrophobic and agoraphobic ideas also were related to fantasies about conditions prior to his birth; and to a confusion he had experienced as a young child, when major building renovations in his house were made, and spaces were oddly changed for him.

curiosity about my personal life and my capacity to detect his thoughts. In that mood he showed markedly improved behavior at home and in school. At first he identified me, admiringly, with a detective in a TV serial who was strongly on the side of justice. For a school assignment he wrote a serious account of the Dreyfus case, and acknowledged to me his old interest in social justice. The position of Dreyfus was of less importance to Leon than the fact that Dreyfus lost interest in his own defense while Zola persevered in it. Dreyfus represented his father, a Jew falsely accused for political reasons; more importantly, he represented the Leon who was well enough to end analysis, while I was the unrelenting Zola. No sooner was this understood than the patient's negative attitudes toward analysis reappeared. His irritability rose, he renewed his complaints about the traveling and his ridicule of the analyst. He had to spar with me, to provoke my impatience, and then to scold me, with a great sense of injury for having taken note of his negativism.

His provocations deserve more description because there was scarcely an hour for at least 7 years when they did not occur in some form or degree. A few instances may suffice: he would begin a session by boldly stating that he had nothing to say; would repeat that several times, looking at me furtively for a reaction; would ask me to tell him what to say; would then report that he had a dream last night—did I want him to tell it? Well, he wouldn't. He just didn't want to. Suddenly, with huge annoyance, he would bang his fist and throw a pillow across the room because I hadn't told him whether to tell the dream—he might as well leave. Whereupon he would jump up, kick a wastebasket, clench his fists and glare at me, then sigh and smile, then quickly frown again. After a few minutes he might hum or might allude to a few events at home or in school, superficially, adding that he didn't really care about them—he actually would rather look at my books than talk. So he would browse through a few, come back to his seat, and announce that he was now waiting for me to speak. Finally he would shout at me in a fury that I hadn't been listening to him at all, would stamp his foot, stride to the door, again shout, "Are you going to listen to me or not?!" Any number of times he threatened to leave, marched to the door, opened it, closed it, and returned to his seat, often with a grin; and many times I lost patience and told him that he might indeed defeat the analysis by his conscious unwillingness to make any effort to control this sadomasochistic behavior. He seemed to want again and again and again to justify a right to leave and a right to return; to provoke, to deny guilt and yet to demand absolution. These frequent tantrumlike episodes never reached a peak. It was often impossible to tell whether he was truly angry or upset or only pretending to be overexcited, because a grin or a sigh or a look of perplexity so often followed quickly upon his outbursts. He himself could not say whether the anger was real, but he did recognize that his disorganized activity served to distract him and me from awareness of his inner states and from a sense of personal contact with me.

Another form of acting in the hour developed. When he sat in an apparently relaxed manner and was about to speak, or during pauses, he grimaced, distorting all of his features as if he were deeply involved in thoughts he could not articulate, or mimicking that kind of thoughtfulness. He would knit or arch his brows, suck in his cheeks, poke his tongue into his cheeks, move his lips up, down, sideways or forward, clench his teeth, move his lower jaw in various directions. The grimaces would alternate or coincide, and repeat themselves; and often would abruptly be erased by a natural frown or a grin. The facial contortions had a compulsive quality, although after instant flare-ups, when I called them to his attention, he could often control them. They were like variations, in miniature, of the ways he had of flinging his limbs or his body around, and they had the same purpose of avoiding eye contact or diverting attention from self-observation or observation by me. They had appeared gradually, and were caricatures of the earlier comic facial shows of surprise or dismay when his block structures fell or his paper grenades did not make the basket. He offered the explanation that the grimaces, like his unfocused large body movements, helped him not to explode. He sometimes wished that his body were made of rubber, so he could bounce easily, or else were like a block of wood that could not move at all. The sexual significance of the physical activities was clear, but they expressed something more particular: he was afraid that his body was trapping his emotions, and he had to release them, to get away from them, by constant motion of one kind or another, or he would suffocate. The grimaces also had the virtue of providing a disguise through alterations of his facial appearance.[7]

The fear of emotional suffocation was analogous to the fears of suffocation in traffic or tunnels. Now, in a counterphobic way, he practiced riding long distances on his bicycle, often uphill. If he reached the summit, he was beset by a fear of heat prostration, maybe a heart attack. Or he might feel observed by some hostile watcher; or he would imagine that the sun was trying to get at him,[8] and so would find himself in a panic. His excited involvement with bicycle riding, like his physical movements, had a sexual and aggressive base. It also fed his obsessional thoughts about where and how extensive traveling could be undertaken safely and on short notice.

When Leon was 16 college entrance and termination of analysis rearoused his separation anxiety. If I greeted him a minute late, if I did not consent at once to explain a cartoon he had puzzled over in the waiting room, if I did not decide whether he should get a new bicycle for his summer trip—any of these was seized upon to make him shout at me, throw something or pretend to, expostulate, and threaten leaving for good. It became almost unbearable to be with me or without me, to listen to me or be listened to, or look at me or be looked at. Maybe, he said, he would have to kill me and get away because he would know too much about me (he referred to a bit of extra-analytic information learned from a friend by chance). As a matter of fact, though he realized he had never spoken about it, the idea of getting away, of *getting away with something*, had always intrigued him. This realization advanced his analysis significantly.

He began to report, with cautiousness and mild boasting, about classmates who got away with very minor car accidents, staying out late, or participating in drug parties. He himself had been getting

---

[7] At about age 11 or 12, Leon regularly wore cowboy boots. They had the quality of a disguise, or a costume, being quite out of keeping with his usual, casual and appropriate dress or his interests. Their meaning was not analyzable at that time. He became hugely annoyed at any comment from me about them, and declared that he just liked them. (At that time "crazy" adolescent attire was not yet in vogue; nor was Leon prone to faddishness at any time.) Later it seemed possible that they, too, provided a disguise for his "ugly" (flat) feet.

[8] As with Schreber (Freud, 1911), the sun represented the father.

away with drinking hard liquor when at home alone. Soon he informed me, with a challenging air, that he was ignoring school assignments and staying out of school now and then, and when I alluded to his wish to *get away* from the analytic work by his acting out, he became unexpectedly depressed, admitting that he would be getting away with nothing. He still felt like a freak, he still got edgy in the presence of his father; and he felt that his negativism and sarcasm—which he had always gotten away with—had aggravated the trouble of his next older brother and the depression of his father. He really did wish he were a nicer person, less grouchy, less aggressive, and less apt to worry about every little thing. His father was getting gray. Leon was glad, sometimes, that his father got angry with him, it was only right. *He should not get away with it.* When I interpreted that he feared his father might have another heart attack and die without their making peace, Leon hid tears. He began to perceive that his ambivalence toward his father unconsciously had motivated him to identify himself with the father as the imagined aggressor. He had had to irritate me, to scold me, and then to withdraw from me; and he also had projected to me his own feeling that, especially in comparison to his father, he was a stupid freak.

Anxiety about college superseded his capacity for introspection. While he argued that there was no point in going to college because he had no goals, in the transference he expressed a wish to be guided toward maturity by his father. No sooner was confirmation of positive feelings for the father recognized than there came fresh outbursts of rage at me. He denied any positive feeling for me, denied that leaving the analysis had any meaning whatsoever for him, and became hypercritical about everything I said or failed to say. He overreacted wildly to the slightest hint of frustration that he endured in my office or even in my building, convinced that I cared nothing about him or his agitation. Eventually he made a turnabout: he really was a "clod," a defective creature not worth caring about. It was only right that he should get away from both of his parents as well as from me. In such episodes of grumbling, petulance, anger, and self-accusation, again and again he obfuscated much that had been worked through about his oedipal conflicts and his castration anxiety. As already described, at every point in the analysis when insight was gained fresh anxiety was stirred up and he oscillated between accusing others and himself. The first step was to mock the analytic procedure, subvert it, confuse it, and threaten to leave it, until, in the second step, anxiety forced him to set aside the negativism and turn his aggression mainly against himself, and have a siege of worrying. Thus, as tension about his impending summer trip arose, he sought relief again. He spoke exclusively about various aspects of the trip that made him anxious, i.e., his clothing, his physical endurance, his companion, and the adequacy of every part of his bicycle. He did, however, ride across Canada and back with a friend, kept a careful log of every place he went, and swelled with pride at his success and his independence during the journey.

He began the last year of analysis with a frank statement that his fear of his father was now his main problem. Almost immediately he assured me that was not correct. The only worry was whether he would pass his driver's test; but no, he was confident of passing it, and there was nothing further to understand. He looked forward to driving the car alone, going places, and feeling free. Once again there was a wave of clowning or of scoffing at me, at analysis, and at all the "gimmicks" analysts used. For example, one day as I entered the waiting room to greet him, he pretended surprise at the sight of me, abruptly strode past me with arms swinging as if at the end of a long race, and with a mock carelessness glanced at things on my desk; next he sat on my desk chair, put on a scowlingly serious expression, and placed his feet on the desk top; then turned to me with a broad smile. A warning that the hour would end immediately unless he made a sincere effort to halt his pseudocomic defiance sobered him. But a few days later he responded to my greeting by sticking his tongue out at me. He found it ridiculous of me to mention that. School and grades were also ridiculous. In fact, he rarely did homework anymore, and often stayed out of classes or out of school. When finally he listened to my reminder that this near-delinquent behavior was out of character for him, he became depressed again, even abject. He conceded that he really did want to understand what made him so flippant while inwardly he was so fearful that no one would ever care for him, not even the girls who clearly were attracted to him. Many times he had spoken of his conviction that I could not possibly have any positive feeling for him, but never before had he been able to say that he cared about it. The feeling made him jittery, but he decided to take himself seriously, and to do so by using the couch regularly—a decision soon followed by invectives against me for saying so many preposterous things: he might just put some signs around saying, "Dr. Brody is a buffoon!" Maybe, with my other patients, he would start a revolution against me. He was disgusted with me, he said, for being serious, dashed to the door, then reconsidered and returned to the couch. Such swings in the working alliance made for repeated delaying tactics, almost to the last months of treatment.

Being on the couch revived memories of nervousness when feeling he might be watched by his father, disapprovingly. He would rather watch me. He thought of how often he had wondered about the possible course of his own and his father's life if not for Hitler. Imagining the danger his father must have been in when sought by the Gestapo, Leon perceived that in his watching of his father he had identified himself with the Nazi police. A few days later, at home alone, he secretly examined his father's life insurance policies. The wish and fear regarding the father's arrest and death, and the enactment of both in the hostile transference resistance, were patent. By means of his disruptive behavior in the analysis he had been successfully blocking the "final solution," as he said, i.e., termination, which required that he tolerate the conflictful affects stemming from his aggressive and libidinal fantasies about his father.

Analysis of the aggressive fantasies produced the information that his compulsive drinking of liquor, reported a year ago, had occurred only at home; and that the liquor had been taken only from the liquor cabinet in his mother's office. His drinking unconsciously had been intended to get from her a strength that she had (from the father); that would enable him to save himself from condemnation and castration by the father. The libidinal fantasies were less threatening; they were experienced as reassurances of his love for his father. They helped him know that he was still trying to ward off tender affect: that is, nobody, especially his father, should know that he *cared*. He rather would show that he could get away without needing conventional approval of any kind. In this reflective and partly defensive mood, he one day ended an hour with a cheerful report that Haynsworth's nomination to the Supreme Court had been rejected by the Senate. My response, "So not everybody gets away with things," bewildered him. He could not leave before I explained my implication: that the news about Haynsworth came to Leon as a reassurance that he, too, might be found out, stopped from getting away with something—actions, feelings, or ideas—and relieved of secret guilt.

In his next hour Leon was denigrating the use of the couch. It was frightening; it was stupid; it was corny; and anyway, he was sure I didn't really believe in "that stuff." The worst was that by lying on the couch he would be in my control, or he might lose his control, destroy my things and run away. A few days later he told, with elation, about experiencing a tremendous excitement, the night before, when he helped his brother catch a plane. The 10-minute account of speeding in the car and frantic racing through the airport, straining to hold on to heavy luggage, was a dramatic example of Leon's exhilaration at the idea of catching transportation and escaping, just in the nick of time. So he went on struggling with the thought that getting away with something came from an intense need to get away as fast as possible from awareness of affects that the analyst might interpret, because the analyst was perceived as an all-seeing and vengeful father.

I have cited these repetitive periods of acting out, defensiveness, and resistance to show the stickiness of the patient's position. Almost every time any interpretation was offered, the split in his ego had to be renewed and he had to be preoccupied with ridding himself of everwhelming guilt for something he could not name.

In this advanced phase of the analysis his thoughts turned to the safety he still sought with his mother, and which he might have got if he had looked more like his father. According to his childhood memories, his father had always "gotten away with it," that is, with cranky behavior when mother was out of the house. But mother never blamed father for those bad moods. She even asked the children to be more tolerant of him. A sudden realization that she thus might have increased his fear of his father was soon followed by a report that recently his father had talked with him about radiology, and it had dawned upon Leon that to follow his father's example, and to emerge as the most scholarly of his father's sons, would make him very proud and happy. He began to feel freedom to initiate conversations with his father; sometimes he even acknowledged to me, with pride and pleasure, that his father really did have a sense of humor. Right after this access of positive feeling for his father, Leon added new details to the story of his father's escape, as he knew it.

The father had been one of the last Jewish students to receive a medical diploma in Germany, in 1933 or 1934. He may have been involved in anti-Nazi activities. At least he made critical remarks about the regime to a fellow student, who betrayed him to the Gestapo. Shortly afterward, he heard that the SS men were searching for him. When suddenly he was warned that they were at the front door of the hospital in which he was working, he escaped out of a window on the ground floor,[9] traveled immediately to his hometown many miles distant, and left for America the next day, leaving his parents behind. He was befriended by people in Philadelphia who were vaguely known to relatives of his family. He could speak no English at all, and had to learn it in order to pass his state board examinations and become able to practice. He served in the American army in World War II. When I remarked to Leon that his father thus had come to fight against his own homeland, Leon became very angry. He defended his father as not being a German anymore, but an American—well, maybe a misfit. It troubled him to see that unconsciously he also had entertained an idea that his father really had been a bad German who had to escape due punishment. He then related that in World War I his paternal grandfather served in the German army, was captured by the French, and perhaps because he spoke French well, managed to be freed after just one day. This meant to Leon that both his father

---

[9] Leon was sure of the window escape, although at a younger age he had said it was from the back door. The detail about the window clarified one of Leon's preoccupations. In dreams, fantasies, and reports of actual events he had told of being watched or feeling watched, through windows; had described windows from which one could jump safely; and had mentioned mischievously that when playing ball he had broken yet another window of his house, and as each broken window had to be boarded up for a time, nobody inside could see what was going on outside.

and grandfather had succeeded in getting away from enemy authorities, but it also left him with confusion as to what was a good German or a bad German.

Following these disclosures Leon experienced an emotion entirely new to him, a sudden desire not to be a loner, a wish to do favors for people, and to be needed by somebody. He imagined successfully defending himself in physical fights in his mother's behalf or mine. But even as he noted new phallic attributes, he felt fear that his sexual abilities or excitements might be perceived by his father. And when he compared his new feelings with the real capacities of his father, he felt discouraged. Surely he would not have courage like his father, who at Leon's age rode down the Danube in a kayak (traveling). Surely nobody would have dared to oppose his father as a young man. I interjected that the Nazis did, and Leon became deeply upset. He did not want to hear or speak about that. It made him imagine horrible things, such as his father going on a train to a concentration camp. When I suggested that Leon sometimes must have wondered about his father's state of mind during the sudden voyage to America, he affirmed that his father had been very upset; he knew it from a photograph taken on the day of sailing, in which his father had looked very worried indeed.

The more tolerance Leon felt for his father, the more he expressed oedipal fantasies and became "nervous." Should he jump up from the couch when he got so jittery? Break a window? Get the key to the liquor cabinet? He felt, above all, a need to do something desperate, and was sure that the feeling had to do with getting away with something, and then probably being caught, because otherwise, "You always live with it." Turning to me, half-laughing, he asked, "Will you gimme shelter?" That question led him to understand that his chronic worries about the practical aspects of the trips from his home to mine had covered a worry that he might not find safety with me or with his mother. At the same time, the worries gave him an opportunity to experience a stress while traveling that was vaguely comparable to that which his father had endured. It was not unimportant that the family in Philadelphia which had befriended the father upon his arrival in America was the same one that also introduced him to Leon's mother.

Ambivalence and masochism still permeated the awareness of

identification with the father. For one day Leon impulsively accused a classmate of being a Nazi, and then felt frightened of repercussions. He was perplexed by his provocation—who was the Nazi, really, the classmate or Leon himself? On the instant he felt a great urge to get away, to stay out of school, to hide at home, or to take a bicycle trip somewhere. So he wondered whether his father, too, unconsciously might be identified with the Nazis—as a little boy Leon had felt confused as to which side his German father had fought on in World War II—and if so, he might see into Leon's aggressive thoughts, and get after him. Perhaps Leon's brothers, like Hell's Angels, would be his father's buddies, like Nazi aides. And then Leon, having to run away from his father's vengeance, would lose his mother as well—what a waste that would be!

On another day in school he aggressively defended an anti-Zionist position, like that of his father. In his hour he argued that as his father was natively a German, he could be regarded not only as anti-Zionist but as anti-Jew, and therefore as a Nazi. Leon wrote a social studies report showing that he himself was neither a typical Jew nor a Nazi, and could be a free person. It was all very unsettling to him. His father was Hitler (we remembered Leon's fantasies of all the people in a box whom his father could kill easily: Leon's way of alluding to what went on in the extermination camps), and Leon was the Jew; or Leon was Hitler, aiming to get rid of his Jewish father. He alternated roles in his hours, at times being the growling, fussy tyrant, and at times feeling that he was the terrified victim. He recalled that in the period of his childhood when he probably already knew about his father's refugee status, he was often mischievous during automobile rides. His father would threaten to stop the car and go on without him. Later his mother and brothers used the same threat. Maybe, thought Leon, those collective experiences of fear of being left behind contained another source of his lifelong interest in maps, roads, and solitary travels across continents. If one could walk around the whole world, the world would seem smaller, distance would not matter, one could conquer the world and always be safe. However, if one were lost in a crowd, one might lose family and home; there was something good in that, though—at least one could get lots of traveling experience.

Leon became tense as he planned another summer bicycle trip, this time in Europe. He plied me with repetitive and unanswerable questions about the trustworthiness of his bike, the value of buying a new one or new parts, where, when, and for what price. He brooded about possible accidents that might leave him trapped in some hospital far from home. He would rather be sent home to the hospital where his father was a member of the staff. The big question was whether he would be able to cope with all of the difficulties that might arise, as if doing so would confirm that he really could get away without castration. The fear of an accident during the trip was libidinized, just as the tension he had suffered about countless daily crises, and which usually had little or no basis in reality, had been libidinized. The daily crises which daily were solved facilitated a perpetual reaffirmation of mastery over anxiety, giving him temporary assurance each time that he had gotten away with something and had controlled his fate. The defensiveness, antics, and aggressive clowning throughout treatment signified the presence of overwhelming conflict regarding escape. The ultimate escape was to evade the dissolution of the oedipal conflicts, positive and negative, in the transference.

He was sad as he contemplated that he was going on a holiday to a place from which his father had had to flee alone and in fear. To tell the truth, he said, his father was not so bad. He had not even seen the dent on the car fender that Leon's friend had made; and when Leon had hesitatingly shown it to him, his father merely said that it wasn't even noticeable. Leon supposed that he must have overreacted to the actual dangers emanating from his father—actually, his father might even fear Leon! because Leon had behaved so badly to him. In the final weeks he expressed guilt about not staying at home to help his father mow the lawn and attend to household repairs. Several amiable talks with his father, during the same period, made Leon consider going to medical school.[10]

A year after the analysis ended, Leon questioned his father and verified that the father did escape from the Nazi police by jumping out of a window and over a nearby wall, then traveling at once to

---

[10] As this report goes to press, the patient has in fact applied to medical school.

his own parents' home several hours away, where he could expect to be safe temporarily because of the grandfather's status as the much-loved and respected town physician. He then completed a year's internship at a hospital in a neighboring city, during which time he had to report periodically to officials in his hometown. As they were cordially familiar with his family, they never took the investigations of his conduct seriously. Seeing the dangers ahead, the father left Germany as soon as he finished his internship. Several years later he persuaded his parents to follow him to America, just in time, for many relatives and friends never escaped. So we learned that only in Leon's fantasy had the father fled from Germany in panic, and that Leon had projected his oedipal fear of capture and retaliation. He also found out that his paternal grandfather had been a prisoner of the French in 1918 for 6 months. It was in 1939, when he was trying to leave Germany, that the Nazis held him for only a day before releasing him. Leon had fused the two events in his memory, according to his fantasies of narrow escape from castration.

The wish to get away with something is seen among delinquents, and among narcissistic or infantile personalities who take pride, often mischievously, in their ability to elude authority. The quality of the wish in Leon was different. It had neither the isolation of affect and the rebelliousness typical of the delinquent, nor the light-heartedness and the excitement of the child or adolescent. Leon was in fact a responsible person, more than usually concerned with social justice, and he adapted increasingly well to the demands of home and school except in the period of acting against school routines. His need to get away with something had an intensity that drove him to a brinkmanship he could not explain. He discovered it in himself as a feeling, as something earnest in itself, only after he had become able to work with interpretations of his fear of tender affect. What he might get away with was unimportant: only the continuous feeling that he must get away. In the transference the inchoate desire was transformed into a specific wish to get away with analysis of his castration anxiety. It was expressed in his pervasive attitude: "Am I guilty or not? I must be! What of? You're wrong! But maybe you're right! I'd better get away—fast!"

DISCUSSION

Analytic material (not presented here) pointed to the likelihood that early in the phallic phase, before age 3, the patient's libidinal impulses toward the father probably were repressed and his aggressive impulses were mainly acted out or turned against himself. Identification with the depressive elements in his father's personality was present, but not yet dominant. During latency, eruptions of sadomasochistic behavior increased. A faulty perception of his father's experiences added to his earlier awe of his father's uncanny power to see and know that which was invisible to others, and apparently evoked the unconscious idea that if he were quick and clever enough to elude detection, he could show a special capacity to challenge dangers with impunity. In spite of his father's cleverness in seeing into others' insides, he himself had not been able to escape detection, had faced arrest, and was depressed. The patient, by displaying cheerfulness, nonchalance, and freedom from care, would appear not to feel guilty or to suffer for his crimes. So he would show greater stamina than his father had. Repeatedly he had to experience a triumph in getting away with something, either castration by those he provoked or the pain of his own anxiety states. Nevertheless he could not bribe his own superego. He felt unworthy and made others confirm his poor estimate of himself.

Probably the deepest contribution to his neurosis was the father's depression. It made identification with the father unsafe and aggravated his fear of separation from the mother. Fear of the father's oedipal retaliation was reciprocally reinforced by the patient's unconscious recogniton of the murderous impulses that lay beneath the father's depression, and by his fantasies about the father's real "power to kill" with his X-ray machines.

To the extent that experiences at the hands of the Nazis were a factor in the father's depression—and that possibility is suggested by numerous references of the patient to the father's avoidance of the topic and becoming morose when it was mentioned [11]—the experi-

---

[11] The paternal grandparents were depressed after their forced emigration to America, and the father's depression became severe after the holocaust ended and after he served in the European theater in World War II.

ences could be said to have affected the quality of the superego development of the son. If so, then even a relatively benign insult by the Nazis, such as the forced escape, can be said to have disturbing effects upon the children of the victim. Only gathering of material from many cases can tell us whether there are universal dynamics inhering in such a context. Some years ago I described (Brody, 1964b) an analogous situation, in which a boy's father had been a political prisoner for a year in the patient's infancy. The imprisonment had followed the death of the father's elder brother. The boy's unconscious idea that his father in fact was guilty of having murdered the uncle and deserved to be in prison was an important factor in his turn toward delinquent behavior and in his interest in ancient wars and mystery stories. As with Leon, the aggression against the father took the form of an unconscious suspicion that the police were justified in their effort to apprehend the father; in this way it contributed to a superego defect in the sons.

A hypothesis can be formulated that in cases where the father has been sought by police, i.e., has been regarded as a criminal regardless of actual guilt, that external reality is sufficient to facilitate the son's projection of his oedipal wishes to the father and to perceive the father as the oedipal criminal. This reversal of the normal situation is of course only an overlay upon the inevitable oedipal structure. The real historical event shapes the defenses, contributes to character formation, and permits the patient to play a double role, that of the detective and the suspect.

BIBLIOGRAPHY

BRODY, S. (1964a), *Passivity*. New York: International Universities Press.
——— (1964b), Aims and Methods in Child Psychotherapy. *J. Amer. Acad. Child Psychiat.*, 3:385–412.
Freud, S. (1911), Psycho-Analytic Notes on an Autobiographical Account of a Case of Paranoia. *Standard Edition*, 12:3–82. London: Hogarth Press, 1958.

A Contribution to Assessing the Role of Infantile Separation-Individuation in Adolescent Development

ERNA FURMAN

THERE ARE MANY ASPECTS OF ADOLESCENT BEHAVIOR AND MENTAL functioning which remind us of the toddler and which form parallels between these two different periods of psychic growth, e.g., the intensity of the drives, the presence of pregenital drive components, the use of primitive defenses, the changes in the nature of the self and object representations and the cathectic shifts which accompany them, the new identifications and new investments of the body image and of ego activities. Such similarities between toddler and adolescent are striking enough to make it important to explore and understand the relationship between the two developmental phases. Our interest is further heightened when, as analysts and parents, we are impressed by the extent of the adolescent's inner turmoil and his struggles for mastery and integration. The

A shorter version of this paper was presented at the panel on "The Experience of Separation-Individuation in Infancy and Its Reverberations Through the Course of Life: Adolescence and Maturity," sponsored jointly by the Association for Child Psychoanalysis and the American Psychoanalytic Association in Dallas, Texas, 1972.

From the Cleveland Center for Research in Child Development and the Department of Psychiatry, Case Western Reserve University School of Medicine.

adolescent often uses terms like "identity," "individual," "independent" to characterize his subjective strivings, just as the toddler insists on "me do it." At the same time, the evident similarities should not blind us to the important differences between the toddler who is in the process of earliest personality development and the adolescent who is becoming a mature adult.

During the last decade our understanding of early personality development has been considerably enhanced by Mahler's detailed and perceptive observations of young toddlers and by her theoretical formulations, particularly the concept of separation-individuation. Mahler's work has justifiably made a great impact on psychoanalytic thinking. Many analysts feel that it has not only shed light on the toddler period of child development but has opened a new view of personality growth and can be applied to other developmental phases. Some of the similarities between the toddler and the adolescent suggest that Mahler's approach could be utilized in an understanding of adolescence. In order to assess whether, and to what extent, this is suitable, it is necessary to consider Mahler's concept in detail. Mahler (1963) defined the separation-individuation phase as the infant's "hatching from the symbiotic membrane to become an individuated toddler" (p. 322).

The mental life of infants and toddlers is, as a rule, not directly accessible to the scrutiny of the analytic process. Anna Freud's and Ernst Kris's work showed us that data gained from direct observation by analysts can and should play an important part in our understanding of mental processes and contribute to our theoretical formulations. We consider ourselves clinically fortunate and scientifically sound when we are able to relate and compare observational data with those gained from the analyses of patients. Collecting and correlating observations and analytic material can be accomplished only·through continued laborious work, which we carry out in the anticipation that each step will bring us closer to our aim of understanding a mental phenomenon or process metapsychologically, i.e., its genetic, dynamic, economic, and structural aspects.

The concept of separation-individuation has, to my knowledge, not yet been fully related to all aspects of the toddler's personality and assessed comprehensively in metapsychological terms. Mahler herself was keenly aware of this from the start. She expressed regret that her observations had not made it possible to relate her concept sufficiently to the instinctual side of the toddler's personality, i.e., the predominant anal phase (p. 319). Geleerd (1969) attempted to correlate separation-individuation with reconstructive material from child analyses and to understand it in the wider context of total personality development. Insofar as Geleerd was able to confirm Mahler's findings, she stressed the important influence of the anal-sadistic impulses and their handling on the process of separation-individuation. Jacobson (1954) had earlier clarified some aspects of toddler development, particularly the differentiation, cathexis, and stabilization of the self and object representations. This process coincides with separation-individuation and explains some of its economic and structural aspects. In a more recent contribution Mahler (1971) fills some important gaps. She relates the process of separation-individuation to several aspects of the toddler's ego functioning, applies it to borderline phenomena in adults, and discusses the limitations of confirming preverbal psychic events from reconstructive verbal analytic material.

Although we are still working toward a fuller understanding of separation-individuation in infancy, analysts have become increasingly interested in the effects of this phase on later personality development and have also tried to apply the concept to other developmental phases, particularly to adolescence. Mahler herself did not relate separation-individuation to adolescence and apparently did not think that later phases repeated the specific changes in the development of mental representations and in the investment of ego functions and activities which she had described for the young toddler. Her only reference to adolescence in 1963 is in terms of a parallel period of developmental potentialities: "The rich abundance of developmental energy at the period of individuation accounts for the demonstrated regeneration of developmental potentialities to an extent never seen in any other period of life, except perhaps in adolescence" (1963, p. 322). More recently she discusses the influence of the rapprochement subphase on the personality. She states that the clinical outcome will be determined by later developments and experiences, including the "developmental crises of adolescence" (1971, p. 413).

In our study of adolescent processes we are not as handicapped as we are with the toddler. There is ample opportunity for analytic observation, for direct analysis during adolescence, and for reconstructive data from the analyses of adults. Nevertheless, it has not been easy to utilize adolescent clinical material toward a fuller understanding of infantile separation-individuation or to evaluate the adolescent phenomena in relation to it.

One such attempt has been made by Blos (1967), who applied the concept of separation-individuation to adolescent development as he understands it. In two different definitions he addressed himself to some aspects of the process: "Adolescent individuation is the reflection of those structural changes that accompany the emotional disengagement from internalized infantile objects" (p. 164), and "the individuation process [is] the ego aspect of the regressive task in adolescence" (p. 185). Blos did not attempt to extend the metapsychological understanding of infantile separation-individuation through adolescent analytic material, nor did he, on metapsychological grounds, justify his use of the term individuation in connection with adolescent psychic functioning.

Recently a panel discussion on "The Experience of Separation-Individuation in Infancy and Its Reverberations Through the Course of Life: Adolescence and Maturity" was sponsored jointly by the Association for Child Psychoanalysis and the American Psychoanalytic Association (1972). In this framework Spiegel addressed himself, among other aspects, to the effect of early phallic and later genital drives on the process of individuation. He pointed out that when the boy integrates his penis and its sensations into his body image and self representation, he has taken an important step in individuation. By contrast, when he fails to make his penis a permanent part of himself, his individuation is interfered with. Schafer (1973) contributed to our understanding of individuation by relating the terms self and identity to the self representation. In this context he pointed out that we cannot use the term individuation both for the differentiation of self and object representations and for the giving up of relations to infantile objects such as obtains in adolescence.

My own contribution does not aim at a comprehensive exploration of the concept of separation-individuation, either in its infantile form or in its effects on the adolescent. I merely try to illustrate clinically how, when, and why phenomena from the infantile separation-individuation phase manifest themselves in the psychic life of early adolescence in some cases. In the following two vignettes I highlight the impact of the genital drives and associated incestuous fantasies on the emergence of some of the genetic antecedents, on the interplay between progressive and regressive forces, on the changing pattern of identifications with the parents, and the effect of these factors on the therapeutic alliance.

CASE PRESENTATIONS

CASE I

Peter was 12½ years old when his parents sought help for him. During the preceding months Peter's difficulties had drastically increased. With his mother he was most defiant and tyrannical, with his younger brother, who had a minor congenital deformity, he was outright sadistic—so much so that his father occasionally stepped in and forcefully subdued Peter. Among his peers Peter joined those who engaged in excited-aggressive games. On his own he avidly gathered information about spies and criminals, reading long into the night. His tender and thoughtful side showed only in his care and concern for his dog. Of late Peter had also been preoccupied with his gun, toying with it in forbidden ways, threatening to kill and wondering to his parents whether they would care if he killed himself. His schoolwork had fallen to a minimum, way below his high capacities.

Handsome, athletic, and quite poised, Peter himself minimized his parents' complaints, but he wanted help with "things that troubled" him and admitted having wondered sometimes about being crazy. Most of all, however, he wanted to be independent of his "infantilizing" parents. Although he at once proved himself capable of analytic work with insight and humor, in most sessions he expected me to take the lead and ask questions which he could then evade or contradict. The initial work focused on Peter's tendency to externalize both ego and superego functions. I attempted to make him aware of the extent to which he was defeating his own purpose and making himself needlessly dependent on

adults by his contrary behavior. In time Peter became quite
talkative in his sessions. He regaled me with accounts of his own
and others' misdeeds and cruelties. He would appear detached or
even side with the callous villains, but watched me closely for signs
of upset and pity for which he derided me: "Only women get so
emotional." We began to see Peter's provocations as intended to
shock women, i.e., to excite them by his symbolic phallic-sadistic
attacks. At the same time, however, this behavior served to ward off
his passive homosexual excitement as he externalized his femininity
to the "weak ones" whom he then aggressively rejected. He
carefully hid his fondness for animals, an identification with his
mother, and stressed his heartless "cool," a caricature of some of his
father's attributes. Even simple words expressing feelings, for
example, sad or beautiful, were abhorrent to him as mushy and
womanish. Along with the words, Peter rejected the feelings. This
became a prominent obstacle to his analytic progress. The analysis
seduced him into having feelings. He was rather close to recognizing that feelings represented femininity to him, but he was far from
acknowledging that feelings also constituted an essential aspect of a
masculine genital love relationship. The regressive phallic-sadistic
position seemed safer.

Yet Peter's partial insights helped him to become more mature
and self-controlled in his daily life and he could allow himself
periods of positive cooperative work in his analysis. There were
many signs of manly charm in his approach to me. It was striking
how much he tended to belittle his new achievements and retreated
from praise and recognition for success. In the analysis, too, his
active sensitive work was usually followed by increased reversal to
toddlerlike provocative withholding and argumentativeness. Any
reference to this fear of success only tightened his regressive
defenses.

Increasingly Peter blamed me for trying to put ideas in his head.
One day he had a fantasy that surprised him: he saw me, in his
mind, as a nurse in white uniform, holding up something like a big
injection instrument. When I moved my office shortly afterward, he
behaved like a curious toddler in an unfamiliar house, explored
everything by touching, ran into every nook and cranny, and could
not communicate with me verbally. I suggested that his nurse vision

and his reaction to the new office were feeling memories of an old experience which the thinking part of him had forgotten. I suggested that we understand them so that he could become master of himself. Peter could not at all address himself to analyzing this material. He either strenuously rejected any interpretive approach like a toddler defending himself against an encroachment of his bodily integrity or, at other times, acted like a package to be handled with no will or verve of his own.

I learned subsequently from the parents that Peter, at 18 months of age, had been taken over for 2 months by a kindly nurse in another city while the parents vacationed. On their return he had begun to walk and talk, new achievements for him. In his early third year, his slightly deformed brother was born whose care preoccupied his mother. Then, just prior to starting public school, there was another long separation to which he reacted with a setback in ego activities, particularly an increased dependency on the mother and a difficulty in learning.

Peter's current analytic behavior suggested a connection with his toddler experience—the analyst and analysis representing the strange nurse to whom his parents had sent him, whom he perhaps had wanted to resist but had needed enough to have to succumb to her care. Peter could not work on reconstructing and integrating any part of this past. His successes diminished. His functioning deteriorated. He became passively resistant rather than aggressively provocative. At the same time, however, his references to explosions, to clandestine night activities, and to renewed gun play suggested that Peter had recently begun to have emissions. Although there still were occasional times when the active, mature, and thoughtful side of him showed in his analysis, more and more he slept in his sessions. He thought of this as shutting me out, but a strong wish for passive surrender obviously played a part. Signs of primary identification and fears of merging manifested themselves in feeling trapped and in allusions to suicide by jumping out the window. On the one hand he felt hopeless about his inability to carry through with any task at home or at school; on the other hand he insisted that he would be alright if nobody made unreasonable demands on him and allowed him to "handle things on my own."

Peter summoned just enough self-observation and activity to

decide that he did have many problems but that he just could not work on them in an analysis at this time. He thought that he might get help when he was older, but now, at 14, he had to go it alone.

CASE 2

Sally was 12 years old at the start of her analysis,[1] paralleling Peter both in age and in parental description. She was defiant, rude, and tyrannical with her mother, sadistic with her younger sister and brother, so that her father stepped in occasionally to punish her. Her peer relationships were characterized by highly excited inter-plays, often accompanied by minor delinquencies. In contrast to Peter, Sally extended this attitude even to pets. At school she achieved well below her capacity. She also had difficulty going to sleep. At times she talked of irrational guilt feelings and feared being attacked by imaginary creatures. Her parents were especially worried about her approaching adolescence which, they felt, had recently made her much worse.

A scrawny, unkempt, tense girl in tight boyish clothes, Sally herself stated that her main trouble was with her conscience. She felt intensely guilty about several accidents to others in which she was at most minimally at fault. By contrast, she either denied or loudly justified her outrageous provocations and attacks at home as well as her uncontrolled activities with peers. She insisted that her family was hateful and deserved to be mistreated, and that her misdemeanors were "okay because the other girls do it too." The analytic work focused on acquainting Sally with her mechanisms of isolating and externalizing her guilt. Her bad behavior always brought the punishment she unconsciously sought. Considerable general improvement followed this work and Sally began to reveal a true cause of her great guilt—her masturbation problem. She could not stop doing bad and dirty things although she was ruining herself.

Shortly, Sally entered the dreaded and wished-for junior high school, started social dancing, purchased her first bra (though she

---

[1] I supervised this case. The therapist was Mrs. Marilyn R. Machlup, who kindly agreed to my using the material.

did not really need one), and within a month reported the onset of menses. Her feelings in the analysis, however, centered on missing her mother at lunchtimes and longing for the simpler pleasures of childhood, such as doll play. In contrast to her family, the therapist sympathized with Sally's "little girl feelings" and Sally began to make the analysis her "safe" place. For months she discussed no daily events or conflicts but re-created an ideal, exclusive, early mother-child relationship, in which no anger or excitement interfered. This protected her from distraction while she did her homework and entertained the therapist with pretend tea parties and songs. On the positive side this regressive period helped Sally to remember a forgotten happy early time with her mother. She utilized it later in greatly improving her relationship with her mother and adapting herself to the new school setting. On the negative side was Sally's defensive use of this phase vis-à-vis her parents. She infuriated them by flaunting her carefree happy times with the therapist while refusing to work on her troubles and continuing much of her bad behavior at home. The parents were about to terminate her treatment. In this way Sally was again externalizing her conflicts and seeking punishment.

After much resistance her aggression to the therapist invaded her ideal analytic relationship. Among other signs she refused to attend Saturday sessions. It emerged that during the preceding weeks Sally had begun to draw closer to her father. He brought her to her analysis on Saturdays while mother slept late and Sally afterward accompanied him to his office. Sally's oedipal aggression to mother and therapist caused her unconscious guilt and fear of rejection. She was now rejecting the therapist before she herself would be deservedly dismissed for her disloyalty.

Unfortunately, Sally's real rejection came from her father. On the day of her dance party he, for the first time in his life, complimented Sally on her looks. Later that day, however, without provocation, he attacked Sally brutally and injured her in a temper outburst. Although denied by Sally, such incidents had occurred before, but in connection with severe provocation from Sally. This time, too, Sally hardly referred to the incident in her analysis, but the repercussions were profound. For the first time she began to bring into the treatment the sadistic, excited, harsh, and callous behavior which had been so prominent at home earlier and which she rigidly defended with projections and denials. Gradually Sally could gain insight into her now intensified identification with her father as a defense against feeling unloved by him. Her teasing of him was calculated to evoke a regressive sexual gratification from him. It also served to bring about his attack deliberately to avoid being surprised.

With increasing understanding, Sally's behavior improved greatly. She became soft, sad, and dejected. The better Sally acted, the worse her father became. He derided her crudely, predicted that she would become a prostitute and a drug addict, blamed her for depriving the family of happiness, insisted that the analysis was making her worse, and time and again actually attacked her or threatened to do so. His mental balance was very shaky, the danger to Sally was considerable as well as to the father, who threatened suicide. We learned that Sally had, from babyhood on, been the father's scapegoat and target of his disturbance. The family's denial of this had been helped during recent years by Sally's own difficult behavior which appeared to justify his retaliation. She, for her part, had assumed the guilt—in part displaced from her unconscious oedipal wishes, in part as a means of affording her imaginary control over the father and her fear of him.

As her defenses crumbled, Sally had to face the reality of the truly terrifying father, the recognition that his disturbance precluded a normal parent-child relationship with her, and the fact that her improvement contributed to his upset. Could she maintain her new reality testing alone and in opposition to her family? Would the father not terminate her analysis as a threat to himself, even if she wished to continue? "If only I could pay for the analysis myself and come on my own," sighed Sally, but this was impossible. Fortunately Sally's mother was finally able to lessen her own denial, came to Sally's aid by physically protecting her, and supported Sally's treatment.

Sally's conflict over continuing treatment, however, also had other roots. Her masturbation problem still plagued her. In connection with that she had confessed earlier that her great wish to baby-sit was marred by her fear of an exciting fantasy. She wanted to handle toddlers' genitals during cleansing. She had occasionally acted this out and experienced genital excitement with an urge to urinate. Sally was unable to analyze this material and refused to expose her thoughts about it to the analyst. She was adamant that she could "handle that myself."

The moment Sally had her mother's support for continuing treatment, Sally began to miss sessions and, apparently on the basis of the family situation, was about to stop altogether. Sally could be shown that she had transferred her feelings from the father to the therapist. She feared that if she exposed herself as a girl to the analyst, she would be attacked and rejected. She warded this off by leaving first. With this insight, Sally decided wholeheartedly to carry on.

The analysis revealed that, in her baby-sitting problem, Sally took the role of her father who had bathed her throughout her earlier years. By identifying with him she warded off the intense passive excitement he had actively stimulated in her and derided her for. The analysis was unconsciously experienced as a repetition of the bathroom. Her wish to handle the problem herself meant not only a resistance and flight but also a healthy striving for mastery. When she realized this, she became able to use her active participation in the analysis as a means toward independence. Her new identification with her father became more adaptive in that she integrated his best quality, i.e., his ability to work hard.

Discussion

Peter's and Sally's analyses include aspects of "adolescent individuation" according to Blos's definitions (1967). They also reveal genetic nuclei from the infantile separation-individuation phase as defined by Mahler (1963). The analytic material in both cases suggests that the role of these phenomena in the patients' psychic lives was shaped by the resolution of the oedipus complex and by current forces within the personality.

Freud (1905) stated that the adolescent's task is to achieve genital primacy and to divert these impulses to love objects outside the family. The above case examples, like other analyses of adolescents, confirm the central role of the genital instinctual impulses and the associated incestuous fantasies. The adolescent, in contrast to the toddler, has already experienced the oedipus complex, has structured his personality around it, and, as it were, knows what he is up against in coping with adolescent genitality. The preoedipal regressive phenomena in his life need to be considered not only in terms of developmental recrudescence but also in terms of defense against genital incestuous strivings. The significance of preoedipal genetic events, including the separation-individuation phase, depends greatly on how the adolescent deals with his current genital impulses and on how he earlier resolved his oedipal conflicts. Both Peter and Sally encountered great difficulty in coping with genital impulses. Repeatedly their preoedipal behavior and analytic material served to conceal and ward off their fear of genital developments.

When the adolescent genital impulses first emerge, they are associated primarily with oedipal fantasies and linked to the object representations of the parents. The adolescent task of diverting the genital impulses to love objects outside the family consists both of shifts in cathexis and of new identifications. According to Freud (1923), "the character of the ego is a precipitate of abandoned object cathexes" (p. 29). Whenever the child gains in independence, in the toddler phase, with the resolution of the oedipus complex, and during adolescence, he does so in part through identification. Mahler's observations on separation-individuation and Jacobson's discussion of cathectic processes in the toddler phase trace the investment of the self and object representations with narcissistic and object libido. They also describe the attendant primary and primitive secondary identifications. The adolescent task of cathecting new love objects is concerned with changes in the distribution of object libido and in the cathexis of object representations. Anny Katan (1937) described this process as "object removal." It involves the narcissistic investment of the self representation insofar as the object-libidinal cathectic changes are accompanied by new identifications with the parents.

These partial and selective identifications with the parents are developmentally much more advanced than the identifications of the young toddler. Their aim is to assist the decathexis of the incestuous aspect of the parental object representations and to enable the adolescent to become a sexual adult like his parent.

Peter's and Sally's analyses showed how their incestuous attachments affected the nature and content of their identifications with the parents. They were unable to head toward identifying with them as sexual adults and had to resort to pathological and primitive forms of identification instead. These regressive solutions were determined not only by their experiences as toddlers but also by their resolution of the oedipal phase and by their current problems with genitality and its associated fantasies.

These differences between the separation-individuation phase of infancy and the developmental task of adolescence are so great that I feel we are not justified in applying the term individuation or second individuation to adolescence.

For the purpose of detailed scientific study it is both legitimate and useful to single out specific aspects of personality functioning, such as individuation, and to trace their effect on later development. In our attempts to work with patients, however, and to gain understanding of the complexities of their psychic lives, we need to relate such specific aspects to the total functioning of the personality and to view the processes metapsychologically. Should we mistake the part for the whole or the effect for the cause, we would be in danger of diminishing rather than utilizing the value that can accrue from studies of specific aspects of personality functioning.

Summary

Mahler's concept of separation-individuation has not yet been sufficiently compared with reconstructive analytic material. It has also not been comprehensively discussed from a metapsychological point of view and related to the drive development of the toddler. In spite of this, the concept of separation-individuation has greatly furthered our understanding of early personality development and has been related to mental processes in later developmental phases.

Some authors view adolescent developments as a second individuation (Blos, 1967), i.e., a form of developmental repetition. Some suggest that the term individuation cannot be applied to adolescence (Schafer, 1973) since the giving up of love objects differs from the initial emergence of self and object representations. Clinically there are many similarities and parallels between the toddler and the adolescent which challenge the analyst to explore more deeply the nature of the relationship.

Two case vignettes serve to illustrate some aspects of adolescent psychic struggles. In the course of the analyses infantile behavioral manifestations and mental contents could be observed and related to their genetic antecedents. The current role of these phenomena appeared to be primarily defensive rather than developmental in the context of the adolescent's task of achieving genital primacy and object removal.

Clinical analytic study of the regressive developmental phenomena, within the total context of the adolescent's personality, will help us to understand better their relation to the separation-individuation phase of infancy. The differences between the toddler's and the adolescent's developmental tasks are so great, however, that the term individuation cannot be applied readily to adolescence.

BIBLIOGRAPHY

Blos, P. (1967), The Second Individuation Process of Adolescence. *This Annual*, 22:162–186.

Freud, S. (1905), Three Essays on the Theory of Sexuality. *Standard Edition*, 7:125–248. London: Hogarth Press, 1953.

——— (1923), The Ego and the Id. *Standard Edition*, 19:3–68. London: Hogarth Press, 1961.

Geleerd, E. R. (1969), Introduction to Panel on Child Psychoanalysis; The Separation-Individuation Phase: Direct Observations and Reconstructions in Analysis. *Int. J. Psycho-Anal.*, 50:91–94.

Jacobson, E. (1954), The Self and the Object World: Vicissitudes of Their Infantile Cathexes and Their Influence on Ideational and Affective Development. *This Annual*, 9:75–127.

Katan, A. (1937), The Role of Displacement in Agoraphobia. *Int. J. Psycho-Anal.*, 32:41–50, 1951.

Mahler, M. S. (1963), Thoughts about Development and Individuation. *This Annual*, 18:307–324.

——— (1971), A Study of the Separation-Individuation Process: And Its Possible Application to Borderline Phenomena in the Psychoanalytic Situation. *This Annual*, 26:403–425.

Schafer, R. (1973), Concepts of Self and Identity and the Experience of Separation-Individuation in Adolescence. *Psychoanal. Quart.*, 42:42–59.

SPIEGEL, L. A. (1972), The Experience of Separation-Individuation and Its Reverberations Through the Course of Life: With Special Reference to Adolescence and Adulthood. Presented at the Meetings of the Association for Child Psychoanalysis and the American Psychoanalytic Association, Dallas, Texas.

Children Who Were Raped

ANNY KATAN, M.D.

THE CHILD ANALYST RARELY HAS THE OPPORTUNITY TO ANALYZE
small children who at a very early age experienced a rape of oral,
anal, or genital kind committed by an adult. Only very few such
cases have been reported in the literature.

Erna Furman (1956) published the case of Carol, a case very
notable because the oral sexual trauma inflicted upon the child by
an adult occurred when the little girl was only 18 months old.
Robert Furman analyzed another child at our nursery school, a boy
who was seduced by a young uncle at the age of 4. After their
analyses, both children developed satisfactorily.

These cases have been followed up to the present time. Carol,
who is now 24 years old, became pregnant by the first boy with
whom she was involved. There was no doubt that this had to do
with the early trauma. On the advice of a psychiatrist, an abortion
was performed. Since then she has functioned well both in her work
and her relationships. She is now getting married.

The case of the boy was never published. He is entering law
school and doing well academically. He has sought help in
psychotherapy because of a sadomasochistic relationship with a girl,
doubtless a repetition of an old relationship he had with his mother.

It seems that the early analytic intervention in these cases has
mitigated the impact of the unsettling trauma.

Such cases have stimulated in me a particular interest: what
happens to children who have suffered the same kind of trauma

Professor Emeritus of Child Analysis, Case Western Reserve University School
of Medicine.

when this trauma remains unknown and therefore ununderstood and untreated?

In order to study the consequences and the vicissitudes of pathological development following such traumas, the analyst has to turn almost exclusively to adult patients. A thorough analysis then leads to the discovery of such traumas and permits the exploration of the truly disrupting effect upon personality development.

Phyllis Greenacre (1950, 1952, 1971) follows an interest similar to mine. The cases she explores concern individuals who have experienced stimulations of various sorts over the years, often from infancy on. Greenacre is primarily interested in the pathological results of these chronic stimulations. My interest is in a different type of case. Although in some of my cases, as in Greenacre's, more or less chronic stimulation was present, my patients were raped, an experience which proved to be completely overwhelming and shattering.

Oxman (1971) recently reported several patients who were subjected to very severe incestuous traumas, starting in infancy and continuing over many years. His cases, however, differ from mine in certain respects. One patient had a psychotic mother who abused the child from infancy on, and then other relatives followed suit. A second patient was diagnosed as a borderline case, paranoid, and continually projecting her own thoughts onto other people. The third patient had a mother who gradually withdrew from life and committed suicide when the patient was 16; this patient had a depression herself, with a history of taking alcohol and drugs. None of my patients had a psychotic parent or was a borderline case herself.

I shall present reports on two of my patients who are representative of six such cases that I have analyzed over the years.

Case Reports

CASE I

Mrs. A., a woman in her 30s, came to consult me in great despair. She suffered from constant agitation, anxieties, and depression.

Several attempts at analysis with male analysts had failed miserably. Her blatant aggression and gross provocation had abruptly
ended these attempts. Behind her aggression, extreme anxiety was
easily recognizable and was not denied by the patient. She could
not stand being alone with a man, especially if he was sitting
behind her. She could not endure her situation any longer and
begged for help. She felt sure that, with a woman analyst, her
anxiety would be bearable and therefore analyzable.

This story convinced me that this patient at an early age had
been seduced by a man who approached her from the rear, and
that the only possibility of treatment would be with a woman.

My patient was a middle child, with a sister 1½ years older, and
another sister 6 years younger. Both parents worked all day in a
small business. Mrs. A.'s mother returned in the late afternoon,
worn out and irritable, to do household chores which she despised.
Her patience with her children was very limited. Yelling and
spanking were her only means of upbringing. The oldest child was
active, loud, boyish, and provocative; she was held up by the
parents as an example to my patient, who was frightened, subdued,
and quiet.

The parents' marriage was a very poor one, owing mainly to the
extreme pathology of the father. He would seduce his children into
exciting games; the climax of these games occurred when he would
bite the child on the cheek or the upper arm. My patient
remembered that he broke the skin with these bites. He would start
out by caressing the little girl with his hands in her underpants.
While doing this, he would have the child seated on his lap, her legs
spread, her genitals touching his. His excitement would mount until
he would bite. He used to say, "Next to pleasure is pain. You will
remember me more if you have pain." The biting was preceded by
growls and grimaces. His ugly, excited mouth open, teeth bared, he
would come at her like an animal. "After he hurt me," Mrs. A. said,
"he would explain how much he loved me—would give me
chocolate bars. He once told us that mother did not let him bite *her*,
so he did it to us!"

What did it do to the child when the father openly admitted that
he abused her because the mother rejected him? With respect to the
mother, the child felt guilty. As far as her direct feelings toward the

father were concerned, she felt humiliated; she was not chosen for her own value, but only as a replacement good enough to fulfill the father's need for dirty pleasures. Hurting, father claimed, was part of a man's sex pleasure. He would also step on a child's toe on purpose, to make her give him an object which she did not want to relinquish. After such games with father that ended in biting, the girl would run to her mother. Mother would shout at him, but to no avail, and then would have the little girl sit down with her. But mother was helpless and perhaps therefore harsh to the child, expecting her to keep away from father, to be more reasonable than father was. No wonder my patient did not want to date or to marry anyone who excited her.

Of course, the child could not follow her mother's admonitions. Often in her analysis she would ask in anguish: "Why did father do it to me—excite me that much? I was afraid of my mother, feeling guilty, sure she was watching. When she was sick I felt I had killed her! Father never pointed out to me that he was unattainable. He encouraged me to think that he might be attainable. For years I couldn't think of anything else but my fears of father! Father was big, powerful, desirable, and unpredictable. He was also attainable —stood there, just waiting. Sex excitement meant hurting or being hurt!" The father also gave the child the impression that in his eyes the mother was completely inferior.

Often the child did not want to play the game; then she would be ridiculed by the father or he would threaten to go away and never come back. When she tried to keep away from him, he appeared to dislike her and would say she was like her mother—cold and aloof.

Once, when the patient was a teen-ager, her father crawled into bed with her and her older sister. His arms were around her from behind. The mother rushed in, screaming hysterically, "What is the matter with you!" He just muttered that he was sorry he had married this woman who was so opposed to fun.

When I questioned my patient about *her* feelings during this incident, she replied: "When father got into bed with me, I was all stiff, very uneasy about it. I felt his body against mine. He had no erection, he felt soft and warm. I felt there were no limits." She then remembered having often been in father's bed as a child; he would become quite rough, put his arms around her, snuggle up close, and put one leg around her. It was impossible to get away, but very exciting. His excitement would mount and would end in biting.

After some of these memories about the father emerged in the analysis, I thought that the pathology of this father well explained the pathology of my patient. But I learned differently. An incident, never fully forgotten, came to light, and more and more details emerged and were remembered as the analysis progressed.

While attending kindergarten at the age of 5, my patient once found herself alone in the school basement. A black man came from outside to the door and motioned to her to open it for him, which she did. He was smiling, told her to turn around, and then put his hands inside her pants. It was both frightening and exciting. He tried to introduce his finger into her anus; she turned around toward him, expecting, as she said, something pleasant to happen. But instead something very frightening happened: he introduced his erect penis into her mouth. She felt choked and tried to bite. The man had his hands around her throat and choked her to make her stop biting. He then withdrew his penis, and she remembered that its size had changed—it had become small. Mrs. A. was later convinced that the man would have killed her if at that moment the schoolbell had not rung and footsteps could be heard nearing the basement. The man fled. A teacher appeared, and the child in tears told her about a bad man who had done things to her. The teacher responded: "We will never tell anybody about this. Pull up your pants and no one will ever know." The parents, however, were informed of this incident by the school. The mother screamed hysterically: "She is damaged for life, ruined forever! Nobody will ever want her!" Mrs. A. went on to say: "After that, father walked me to school. But it was no reassurance. I was terribly frightened and I completely confused father with this man."

Some of the details of these incidents with the stranger and with her father were remembered through the analysis of an episode of acting out that had taken place a number of years before the patient's analysis started. She was then living in Europe, where she received some psychotherapy. While sitting alone in a café, she began to flirt with a young man at the next table. She walked away with him, and the two went into a building and necked. People could see them, however, so she went up in the elevator with this strange man and in the elevator they had anal intercourse. She described this as painful at first, but very exciting. The next day she picked this man up at work, and they went to a hotel, where they had intercourse. At the height of his excitement, the young man slapped her viciously several times. She was terribly frightened and stunned. Again sex had ended in being hurt.

As a 5-year-old, after the incident in the school basement, the patient felt ruined, no good, a "nothing." No man would ever want her! Until that time she had been a good eater. Afterward she became a very poor eater. She would gag, vomit, and could not swallow. Finally, she could eat only a very few special foods.

Besides the fantasies of nothingness and worthlessness, other types of fantasies emerged.[1] She had acquired a penis! When the erect penis of the black man was introduced into her mouth, it had been large; when it came out, it was small. The penis was inside her. She would carry a penis inside her all her life! It was her secret. She would not have to worry anymore about men doing hurtful things to her. Only women got hurt! She would be more accepted by father if she had a penis. He had always wanted a boy and did not even look at her when she was born because she was a girl. Now he would no longer ridicule her. Yet all her life she feared that a man would punish her for what she did to him.

When she was 6, a sister was born. The parents wanted a replacement for her! She was a worthless "nobody." "I tried desperately to be one or the other, a boy or a girl," Mrs. A. said, "but I never made it. After the incident I lost my identity. I was no longer a nice little girl in a middle-class family. I didn't belong in that society! I became an unnoticed nobody."

The fantasies of having acquired a penis at the age of 5 caused the child to turn to her mother in her sexual excitement. The mother, too, was often seductive: she would call the child into the bathroom when she was bathing or dressing. The patient's sister was born at a time when the patient wanted her mother sexually. During that period she often dreamed that her father would die.

---

[1] In the cases of Mrs. A. and Mrs. B., pregnancy fantasies were not prominent, although I found them in some of my other cases. Prostitution fantasies were very prominent, as Mrs. A.'s acting out certainly showed.

She had strong wishes to caress her mother's body, but tried to ward them off with disgust.

The overwhelming excitement aroused by the patient's father and by her seducer influenced every phase of her development and permeated every phase of her life.

Some of her disturbances while at work went far back to her relationship with her mother at the time of toilet training. Anything that appeared to Mrs. A. like a demand—and nearly everything did—was impossible to follow up and was put off; she could not get to it at all, or else it was left to be done at the very last moment. Work that was started would never get finished. She wanted to improve or to redo it. She felt there had been a threat during toilet training to produce—or else! Enemas were taken and applied frequently by the entire family. To produce only under threat was displaced to many situations. (After this piece of analysis Mrs. A. was able to finish work.) If some work seemed satisfying and pleasurable, she would become so agitated, excited, and anxious that she could not continue it. She could not deal with men in authority. Either she saw them as sadistic, attacking father figures who only wanted to take advantage of her—she would feel overpowered and hurt—or else she would expect to find a praising, interested, encouraging father such as she had always longed for, one who would take care of *her* interests. To be active herself in such situations meant being *like* father, and she could not function because her excitement and agitation were too overwhelming. She would also try to play an old game of childhood: "How excited, angry, out-of-control can I get him before he hurts me!" Either she was a victim or else she identified with the agitated attacker.

When agitated, she would get biting impulses. Then she would frantically eat chocolates (the father offered the child chocolate bars after he bit her) and fill herself up by ferociously chewing. After the incident in the school basement she masturbated with the fantasy of having taken the penis away from this man. Prior to that incident she had had the same fantasy about her father: she was taking away his source of power. "If I achieve a goal, I destroy a man," Mrs. A. said. That of course was displaced and made all achievements very much forbidden. She had to boycott being effective. Any success was dangerous and forbidden.

The patient's desire, after the incident, to repeat it, to relive the excitement, made her feel guilty, bewildered, worthless, and bad. She was terrified lest her father discover that she found the black man in the school basement exciting. Excitement should occur only with father!

To produce in her work meant showing a part of herself, revealing a secret that must never be revealed. The incident, the secret, must remain concealed. To uncover it would cause the greatest agitation. "People should say I'm all right, anyway! Someone should have said that to me after the incident—that I was acceptable, that I could be liked. To show myself and win approval is to this day most important." The patient felt the worst possible guilt because she wanted the incident to happen again. Everyone said it was so terrible, and yet she wanted to repeat it! This was the terrible secret she had to hide from everyone.

When the end of analysis was set a year ahead, the patient remembered that after the incident in the school basement she had expected her father to be pleased with her. After all, she had only done what he taught her. But instead her father avoided her. She could recognize now that he had to reject her because he had become so agitated. Father didn't want to touch her! When she came to him, he pushed her away. This was a terrible blow from which she could not recover. One day she tried again and crawled up on his lap. He could not control himself. She remembered that his penis was out and that she touched it, whereupon his penis or his finger touched her genitals. This was beyond what the father thought permissible to do with a daughter, and he threw the child away from him onto the floor. He yelled at her as if she had taken advantage of *him*. She had driven him to a point that even he considered too far. What a miserable girl she was! She kept quiet about it and never told her mother. She felt her mother would have thrown her father out, and the disruption of the family would have been her fault. Of course, she felt guilty and was afraid of her mother's rejection of her. She needed her mother desperately for protection against her out-of-controlness. She felt that her father was afraid of her, and she developed and felt hatred toward him and shame about the whole affair. Later she longed for an ideal father—kind, affectionate, trustworthy, one who would take care of her. "There is something hopelessly disrupted in my personality," my patient would say over and over again, "and there is nothing that can heal it!"

CASE 2

Another patient, Mrs. B., consulted me a long time ago at the age of 26. She had been in a completely unsuccessful analysis for many years, which ended with the sudden death of her analyst. The patient was helplessly crying, she was badly groomed, her hair hanging down untidily around her face, which was covered with acne. She wore thick eyeglasses, was 25 pounds overweight, and a chain smoker. Her complaints at the time were depression and a paralyzing anxiety about men. She could flirt with a man, but felt she became too inviting too quickly; then, as soon as the man responded, she would freeze, as she described it, be choked with fear, and incapable of responding.

Although Mrs. B.'s family was socially prominent and rich, she considered herself very much deprived. Her father, whom she had greatly admired as a child, was gifted, widely known, gave his time to his business and the community, and had no time left for his family. He was often very depressed and at times suffered from a phobia of being too poor to pay. Apparently money was his main interest.

The mother, disappointed in her marriage, had turned to social activities. Bridge was so important to her that she had little time for her children. She openly favored the patient's older brother, who in the mother's eyes could do no wrong, would often tell lies about the patient, and was always believed. A succession of nursemaids took complete care of the little girl and also shared a room with her. The mother was a compulsive person, and her interest in the child concentrated on toilet training and the importance of regular bowel movements. A sadomasochistic relationship developed between mother and child. Everything became a fight, and the little girl felt mistreated, victimized, and neglected.

The nursemaids were kind, but, being unsupervised, did not pay sufficient attention to the child to protect her against overwhelming sexual assaults. When she was 3, the nursemaid's boyfriend coaxed her into the closet off the bedroom and committed fellatio, ejaculating into her mouth. This incident was repressed, completely unconscious, and emerged in the analysis only after an episode of acting out. She then slowly recovered all the details of the scene. The man stimulated her genitals while his penis was in her mouth, her excitement was overwhelming, and she felt like choking. He also impressed upon her that she must never tell anybody. She remembered standing behind her mother sometime after the incident and asking herself over and over again, "Shall I tell her? No, I can't!" Severe eating difficulties developed, and overwhelming biting impulses. She remembered viciously biting her brother at that time. The family had an open bathroom policy, and the father's walking around naked unbearably increased the patient's excitement and aggressive impulses. Her father and the man in the closet became completely merged in the child's mind and were one and the same.

After this incident intensive masturbation started. Mrs. B. remembered how very pleasurable it was and how she could not keep from doing it. Her fantasies were many: she had rubbed away her penis; now she was "hopelessly a nothing forever." She had exciting fantasies of her father "doing it" with mother, and also "doing it" with her. But most exciting and frequent were fantasies in which she identified with her father and imagined herself engaging in sexual acts with her mother. Mother frequently excited the child by inviting her into the bathroom while taking a bath. These were the only times the patient remembered getting her mother's attention.

At the age of 7 she witnessed sexual intercourse between another nursemaid and her boyfriend. It took place in the child's bedroom, which the maid shared, in the adjoining bed. The little girl was awake and observed all the details. More than ever she was convinced that girls and women were victims of male attackers. Only the possession of a penis would make life safe! Her masturbation increased in intensity, and so did her guilt. A Catholic nursemaid told her she would go crazy and end up in an institution, whereupon the child's anxiety and guilt became unbearable.

She could not stop herself from masturbating. Her fantasy at the time was of ripping or biting off father's penis and, with this possession, doing to mother what she now knew father did. She felt completely and helplessly out of control.

At the age of 8 she visited a girlfriend overnight. While there, she masturbated, lost control, and wet the bed. The wetting represented to her the man's ejaculation at the height of excitement. She thought the man had urinated in her mouth when she was 3. She saw this losing of control (urination) as a realization of the nursemaid's threat that she would go crazy and lose her mind. To ward this off, she succeeded with the greatest effort in stopping her masturbation and never touched herself again. Later, as an adult, she returned to an attenuated form of masturbation, in which she did not touch herself but pressed her thighs together; this gave her a slight pleasure, but never approached in intensity the orgastic pleasure she had experienced in childhood (compare Greenacre, 1971, p. 56).

In addition to this form of masturbation by pressing her thighs together, she began to have thoughts in which she tortured herself. These represented masturbatory equivalents, which were as painful as the forerunner had been pleasurable. She would compulsively tell herself over and over again how worthless she was, what a complete failure she was, how nobody could like her, and on and on relentlessly. She could not stop herself, she wished somebody else would stop her, and feared she would go crazy. From the physical act of masturbation, which she was powerless to stop and which afforded her so much pleasure, she went to an emotional torture which she could not stop. This torture had obviously the goal of warding off masturbation. However, the self-torture acquired the features of the warded-off masturbation. The defense, being saturated with the warded-off, became a form of mental masturbation, without having an orgastic outlet. She became and acted like a victim in every phase of her life—with her parents, her friends, and later with her husband and children—until this self-torture could be understood and interpreted. When Mrs. B. finally improved and was less often a victim, she became capable of ending an unhappy marriage, in which she had been completely frigid, and of dealing with her children more firmly and reasonably. In the analysis my role was often that of the devilish seducer who would make her lose control again, and she had to fight against me and the analysis constantly.

Although Mrs. B. improved in many ways as a result of the analysis, she remained frigid vaginally. Her superego was one of the severest and cruelest I have ever encountered in a patient. Her main difficulty, of which she repeatedly complained in a hopeless way, was a feeling of being fragmented. "My love life can't be cured because I am fragmented! You can improve me here or there, but never as a whole, because I cannot be and never have been whole."

OTHER CASES

A detailed report of the analyses of the other four women who were raped in early childhood would not add substantially new material. I therefore merely state that of these four patients, two also were orally raped, one at the age of 3, the other at approximately the age of 4. The two other patients were masturbated by adult men who had their erect penis exposed. Some penetration occurred by finger. These adults were not incestuous objects. The little girls were 3 and 5 years old at the time of the assault.

DISCUSSION

When Freud found out that his patients' reports about their fathers' sexual seductions of them were fantasies, it led to his discovery of the oedipal conflict. Analyses at that time did not reach the depth they did later. I have often wondered whether these patients of Freud's had not been right about one thing. The sexual seduction or rape that victimized them in early childhood may well have been a reality but was attributed by them to the wrong person, to their fathers. Not only Mrs. A., whose father behaved so incestuously and abnormally, but five of my six patients attributed in their fantasies the sexual deeds to their fathers. It is amazing how many pathological tendencies and symptoms were shared by these patients who had experienced more or less the same traumas. All of them showed a marked tendency to repeat the traumatic incidents in various ways throughout life until their analysis.

Oxman (1971) stresses this: "Characteristic of practically all

these patients is the need to repeat over and over again the
traumatic act. This is described most vividly by Shengold (1963),
who considers such people as being fixated at and regressed to a
cannibalistic level of libido development, with concomitant malde-
velopment and regression of the ego. He says that overstimulation
continues as a central problem in their lives and is therefore also
seen in the transference as they operate continually under the sway
of the repetition compulsion." Some of my patients showed a
repetition compulsion even more dangerous than that described by
Oxman. They had the tendency to expose their own children to the
same experience, mostly by not protecting them when they should
have been protected. Their own overwhelming excitement severely
hampered their capability for mothering.

The tremendous excitement of these six women focused on the
fantasied acquisition of the penis and identification with men. Only
in this identification and excitement could they escape the
unbelievably low self-esteem they all had in common. Without the
penis, they felt themselves to be "nothing," and this made vaginal
gratification impossible. They could never feel themselves to be
women. In their low self-esteem, they felt that they were neither
men nor women, they were nothing. When they identified with the
man, they felt themselves to be, and sometimes *were*, aggressive
attackers. If this identification was interfered with, they became
victims vascillating between these two extreme feelings throughout
life.

Discussing regression and fixation, Greenacre (1971) says:

> When genital excitation is pathologically aroused by body-image
> or body-ego problems . . . , or by direct overstimulation (as, for
> example, by mothers who habitually manipulate the foreskin
> excessively in the process of cleaning, or nurses who stimulate the
> child's genital to quiet him)—then the development of early
> masturbation is a forced affair under strain and may interfere with
> or delay the full and adequate development of the libidinal phase
> which would naturally tend to mature at this time [p. 172].

In all my cases the early masturbation was a forced affair, as
described by Greenacre. A 3-year-old is on the way to the phallic
developmental stage. In my cases the trauma did not delay the

onset of this phase, but fixated these patients in an overwhelming phallic excitement. If, for whatever reason, they could not keep up their phallic fantasies, the disastrous drop in self-esteem just described would occur, with some suicidal impulses. Such tendencies were helped along by the harsh, even cruel superego of all my patients. Mrs. B. had the cruelest superego I have ever encountered. The tremendous excitement that was aroused in these patients made all their conflicts extraordinarily intense; hence the abnormal amount and quality of guilt they were forced to cope with.

All of the results and vicissitudes of childhood rape that I have mentioned so far were of minor importance compared with a disturbance of development that I shall now discuss. I am referring here to the development of aggression. In my opinion, the factor that causes the most severe pathology is a disturbance in the fusion of the drives. With regard to this factor Freud (1937) wrote:

> How parts of these two classes of instincts combine to fulfil the various vital functions, under what conditions such combinations grow looser or break up, to what disturbances these changes correspond and with what feelings the perceptual scale of the pleasure principle replies to them—these are problems whose elucidation would be the most rewarding achievement of psychological research. For the moment we must bow to the superiority of the forces against which we see our efforts come to nothing. Even to exert a psychical influence on simple masochism is a severe tax upon our powers [p. 243].

Anna Freud (1965) has this to say:

> Aggression becomes a menace to social adaptation only when it appears in pure culture, either unfused with libido or defused from it. The cause of this usually lies not in the aggressive drive itself but in the libidinal processes which may not have developed sufficiently for the task of toning down and binding aggression or which lose that capacity at some point during the child's development owing to disappointments in object love, imagined or real rejections, object loss, etc. A special danger point for defusion is the anal-sadistic phase during which aggression reaches a normal peak and its social usefulness is especially dependent on its close association with equal amounts of libido. Any emotional upset at this time frees the child's normal sadism of its libidinal

admixtures so that it becomes pure destructiveness and, as such, turns against animate and inanimate objects as well as against the self. What happens then is that the half-playful, provoking, self-willed attitudes of the toddler become fixed in the personality as quarrelsomeness, ruthless acquisitiveness, and a preference for hostile rather than friendly relations with fellow beings. More important still, aggression in this defused form is not controllable, either externally by the parents or internally by ego and superego. If fusion is not re-established through strengthening of the libidinal processes and new object attachments, the destructive tendencies become a major cause for delinquency and criminality [p. 180f.].

My patients had no criminal or delinquent tendencies. Their aggression was turned against the self in a savage form. If turned against the outside world, it had a strange quality to it that I can only describe as raw, not really fitting their personalities.

The fusion of the drives is considered a theoretical concept, and such it was for me until I began to study my six cases. Some of these patients showed a blatant disturbance in the integrating capacity of the ego. They had great difficulty in "taking in." Of course, the forceful and sadistic oral rape of a 3-year-old would explain further reluctance to take in anything—be it food, intellectual knowledge, or interpretations of the analyst. But this is not all. The ability of the ego to integrate, the capacity to make a whole out of fragments—if I may express it so primitively—is completely disturbed. Here I would emphasize the constant complaints of the two patients described in detail. They were fragmented, they could never feel that they were whole persons! They regarded their own aggression as dangerous and raw, whether it was turned against the self or against the outside world. They felt keenly that the traumas had caused irreparable damage.

Here a question arises: why would an early sexual trauma, arousing tremendous amounts of sexual excitement, disturb the fusion of libido and aggression? Why would not the arousal of sexual excitement, no matter how brought about, promote fusion between the two drives? Again I quote from Freud (1926):

. . . touching and physical contact are the immediate aim of the aggressive as well as the loving object-cathexes. Eros desires contact because it strives to make the ego and the loved object one, to abolish all spatial barriers between them. But destructiveness, too, which (before the invention of long-range weapons) could only take effect at close quarters, must presuppose physical contact, a coming to grips [p. 122].

Why, then, would a rape that so closely combines aggressive and libidinal contact disrupt the process of fusion instead of promoting it? [2]

Here I want to mention an experience that all child analysts, especially those who have worked in nursery schools and with parents, have stressed, and which I believe is true: fusion is greatly promoted by the warm, tender, and affectionate component of the drive. Direct sexual stimulation, with the overwhelming aggressive components inherent in the act, makes fusion extraordinarily difficult. All small children feel sex acts primarily as aggressive acts, as we well know from the study of children who have witnessed a primal scene. Yet they feel and know that there is more to this observed act than aggression; they feel the excitement that the parents feel, identifying with one or the other as the case may be. The confusion, however, is overwhelming and very characteristic of children with this experience.

There is no doubt that, with my patients, warm affection was given only sparingly to them when they were small children, compared with the aggressive sexual stimulation they encountered. At the age of 3, when some of my patients suffered this trauma, their sexual development was not delayed. They did not regress noticeably to the anal phase of development, notwithstanding the fixation points they had previously acquired. Rather, what happened could be described as a primitive leap forward in libidinal development, as described by Greenacre—one that had of course severe pathological consequences.

In these patients, regression occurred mainly in the development of aggression. Their newly acquired tentative fusion was aban-

---

[2] Although it seems quite obvious, it perhaps should be mentioned that a 3-year-old who is so tremendously overstimulated simply does not have adequate discharge channels available, with the result that the mounting excitement, which at first is pleasurable, leads to frantic efforts to get rid of it. The lack of discharge would thus be experienced as painful and stimulate aggression.

doned. As far as the development of aggression was concerned, they returned to the anal phase. Thus we see that in these cases development of libido and development of aggression do not move in the same direction, but are torn apart in opposite directions. It is this phenomenon that causes the disturbance in fusion which remains with these patients throughout their life.

BIBLIOGRAPHY

ANGEL, A. (1935), From the Analysis of a Bedwetter. *Psychoanal. Quart.*, 4:120–134.
FREUD, A. (1965), *Normality and Pathology in Childhood*. New York: International Universities Press.
FREUD, S. (1926), Inhibitions, Symptoms and Anxiety. *Standard Edition*, 20:77–175. London: Hogarth Press, 1959.
——— (1937), Analysis Terminable and Interminable. *Standard Edition*, 22:209–253. London: Hogarth Press, 1964.
FURMAN, E. (1956), An Ego Disturbance in a Young Child. *This Annual*, 11:312–335.
GREENACRE, P. (1950), The Prepuberty Trauma in Girls. In: *Trauma, Growth, and Personality*. New York: International Universities Press, 1969, pp. 204–223.
——— (1952), Some Factors Producing Different Types of Genital and Pregenital Organization. *Ibid.*, pp. 293–302.
——— (1971), *Emotional Growth*. New York: International Universities Press.
OXMAN, M. (1971), Massive Seduction, Infantile Neurosis, and Development of the Ego. Read at a meeting of the Cleveland Psychoanalytic Society.
SHENGOLD, L. (1963), The Parent As Sphinx. *J. Amer. Psychoanal. Assn.*, 11:725–751.

Changing Techniques in the Analysis of a Deaf Latency Boy

PATRICIA RADFORD, M.A.

IF THE PRIMARY ROLE OF ANALYSTS IS VIEWED AS "THE BRINGERS of understanding and the bearers of choice" (Greenson, 1958), it is possible to conceive that the analyst can fulfill these functions in the treatment of an atypical deaf boy. But it is also necessary to accept that variations and modifications in technique must arise, though these should not conflict with the ultimate goal of providing insight to the patient, so that he himself can resolve his neurotic conflicts, thus effecting permanant changes in ego, id, and superego, and thereby extending the sovereignty of his ego.

A person whose personality has been distorted by early deprivations and who, in addition, has a severe physical handicap presents a challenge to any form of treatment which aims to achieve permanent changes in the individual. The challenge is indeed magnified when psychoanalytic treatment, which essentially relies on verbalization, is undertaken with a deaf and almost dumb boy. Anna Freud has questioned by what means such a child can be

The author is on the staff of the Hampstead Child-Therapy Clinic, an organization which at present is maintained by the Field Foundation, Inc., New York; the Foundation for Research in Psychoanalysis, Beverly Hills, Calif.; the Anna Freud Foundation, New York; the Freud Centenary Fund, London; the Grant Foundation, Inc., New York; the National Institute for Mental Health, Bethesda; The New-Land Foundation, New York; the Andrew Mellon Foundation; and a number of private supporters.

influenced and what treatment methods can be found to bring about basic changes in his personality structure. Initially, there is a problem of communication between patient and analyst. Loewenstein (1958) stressed as one of the fundamental conditions of analysis that the analyst must understand the patient and be able to convey this understanding to the patient in language appropriate to that patient—a factor which Eissler (1958) considers the major tool of all analytic treatment procedures. But how can the therapist find the right language to convey his understanding to a deaf boy?

This paper will attempt to show how I tried to find such a language with David, an emotionally disturbed 9-year-old deaf boy, and how I geared my methods to his handicap and to what I perceived to be his specific needs and requirements. Laforgue (1936) commented that every rule of therapy demands an intelligent elasticity in its application. In my treatment of David I sometimes felt that this elasticity had to be stretched to infinity.

The classical technique could not be used because of David's atypical personality disturbance, and because his hearing and speech defects seriously interfered with his ability to verbalize, to change action into thinking speech, and, of course, to perceive verbal interpretations. The inability of the deaf to express dissatisfaction or anger in a normal way, that is, by emotionally toned verbalization, often leads to a physical display of such feelings. Denmark (1966) pointed out that a deaf child does not merely lack speech; he misses all the experiences and the knowledge gained from emotionally toned auditory perceptions, especially affective vocal expression. The deaf child is not only handicapped by poor language ability and intellectual retardation, but often shows such personality traits as poor emotional control and lack of tact and feeling for others.

When David was referred for treatment, he suffered not only from the personality difficulties usually found in the normal deaf, but also from the crippling results of his early experiences. At age 9, he was in danger of being excluded from his school for deaf children. He could not be contained in an environment which was well used to handling deaf children with their characteristic personality disorders. His competent stepmother was afraid that she would soon be unable to cope with his berserk physical violence, over which neither she nor he seemed to have any control. Because of his total lack of concern for others, he could not be influenced by them. He was unable to concentrate and unwilling to learn. Despite an IQ of at least 135, David could neither read nor write. His neurotic symptomatology of lying, stealing, and pathological jealousy of his brother lightened the otherwise seemingly psychopathic picture. Neurological examinations, including EEGs, had confirmed an essentially normal brain rhythm pattern and thus excluded a neurological explanation of his aggressive behavior and his inability to learn.

David had an unfortunate beginning. He was adopted by a middle-class, childless couple who 5 years earlier had adopted another child, who died 3 years later. When David came to his adoptive parents, at 4 days, he was an attractive baby, physically healthy and active, feeding and sleeping well. At 3½ months, he developed meningitis, as a result of which he became deaf. His hearing loss was considerable. A recent audiology examination again confirmed that he has only an island of hearing at about 260 decibels, with 80 percent loss in one ear and 70 percent in the other. David has to wear supplementary hearing aids.

Because he was critically ill in the hospital, his adoptive parents decided to adopt a third child. The pregnant mother came to stay in the adoptive parents' home, where John was born and immediately cared for solely by the adoptive mother. At 5½ months, David returned to his silent home, in which another baby had been given pride of place. He was put in the care of nurses, supervised by his adoptive mother, because he was so hyperactive, demanding, and difficult that she could not cope with him. He was provided with a hearing aid at 10 months, and his father took him once a week to a speech training center, but he had no speech before the age of 5. The staff of this center believed this to be due in part to a noticeable personality regression in David following the sudden death of his adoptive mother when he was 3 years, 2 months old. No explanation could, of course, be given to a deaf toddler. In addition, the father was seriously ill and absent for many months. David was looked after by a helper who dealt with all his difficult behavior by imposing no controls or restraints and frequently letting him run into danger. At 3½ years his stepmother took charge of the family, and she has remained a stable element in his life.

His behavior continued to deteriorate, however, and by age 9 he was a most disturbed boy. In her diagnostic assessment of David, Anna Freud stressed that apart from what could be attributed to his deafness, there were signs of damage in all areas of his personality: immaturity of object relatedness, uneven ego development, lack of integration and synthesis, little control over drives, and perhaps lack of secondary process thinking. His impulsive aggression seemed to ensue from the ego's inability to control strong drives, but we also considered that his aggressive behavior might be defensive and serve to ward off depressive affects linked with his poor sense of well-being and low self-esteem. The diagnostic conference concluded that if his ego development could be promoted sufficiently to obtain some object relatedness, then it might be possible to reach the neurotic conflicts at the basis of his personality disturbance and to resolve them through analytic work.

The technical problem of how to initiate treatment with a child so seriously disturbed and handicapped was monumental. No treatment alliance could be expected, nor was it possible to give David a simple explanation of the procedure. He could not read or write, he could not hear, and he would not lip-read because he would not remain still long enough to watch my mouth.[1] But, above all, he had no trust in me; he seemed to be lacking any belief that I would stay with the bad David, and he was always defensively on the attack. The initial task, therefore, was to find some means of making contact and communicating with him, with the aim of regaining or establishing some basic trust in his object. Intimacy, reassurance, and clarification were more appropriate tools at this stage than interpretation. I had constantly to bear in mind Jacobson's query (1954) of how far one should deviate from the usual practice and respond to the pathological defensive needs of the patient for active emotional and even practical help in order to promote treatment.

---

[1] His spoken vocabulary consisted of about 20 words, none of which I could distinguish until I became accustomed to his guttural, tuneless intonation.

David immediately displaced onto me the grossly disturbed behavior others could not tolerate. My fleeting impression of a sturdy, cooperative, handsome boy burdened with a cumbersome hearing apparatus was at once dispelled. In session after session he behaved like a wild animal at bay, creating havoc in the room and despair in me. He climbed on top of lockers, smashed down heavy bags of bricks, threatening me with them, his face red with fury. He tried to evoke from me the same responses he had forced from his family. He was sure that I would be so frightened of mad David, I too would put him alone in a room, which he would then wreck: then his terror of being alone and overwhelmed by uncontrollable impulses would be even more intolerable. No matter what the provocation, however, I felt it was essential I should not be overwhelmed, but function as an auxiliary ego, so that his ego might gain strength and take over internal controls. Here, I was following Kris (1951) in assuming that there is no antithesis between planning and intuition.

I sat quietly, while he hammered and screamed. I began to draw pictures, illustrating what seemed to be hidden behind his wild behavior. I drew a sad David in a room alone, crying. He stopped briefly to look; he screamed an overdetermined denial, and tore up the drawing. Gradually, a more mature defense of reversal appeared. David altered the drawings, insisting that I was the sad one, while he was smiling in his classroom. It seemed that he was asking for reassurance that I missed him. I elaborated the drawings to show David and me in different rooms, both sad and alone. David's seemingly pointless aggression temporarily abated, and to my surprise he began to show depression and despair, jealousy and signs of attachment to me—a range of affects which had not been available at home. It was possible to trace these feelings directly to incidents in treatment. After violently reproaching me that I looked after other children, he ran away, leaving me. At home and at school he became most violent. The only moments of peace were the periods during which he built a papier-mâché house to bring to me; but, as he gave it to me, he tried to destroy it. I decided to safeguard it; I wished to demonstrate that I could protect the safe place he was trying to make with me.

I had already discovered that it was essential to offset the lack of

verbal communication between us by making concrete gestures. His
behavior was so much like that of an angry, bewildered 3-year-old,
I wondered if there might be a transference element in it: a revival
of old feelings related to the death of his adoptive mother. But it was
in no way appropriate to test out such a speculation. Even in the
here-and-now supportive relationship with the therapist, his libidinal drives could not balance the aggressive impulses when he felt
overwhelmed by fears of rejection and displacement.

I preserved the house and I drew pictures of mother/me together
with her baby. I persisted in viewing his aggressive behavior, at
least in part, as an avoidance of loving feelings, which he feared
might only leave him hurt. He brought me sad pictures of empty
rooms, and then would start on his orgy of chaos. Through
drawings, I stressed that David did not want to lose me. He tried to
prove I was wrong; he made a Plasticine figure of me, bit it to
pieces, and then threw them out of the window. I would nurse my
Plasticine figure of David; he would briefly pause to look and then
renew his even more fiendish testing out of me, which always
involved incredible amounts of noise. But I did not consider his ego
sufficiently integrated to relate these torments to his handicap, nor
did I believe that at this stage he would have been listening or
speaking to me even if he had not been deaf and dumb. The
methods of torment he used with me were those which over a long
period of time he had learned were the most offensive to the people
around him; the other facets involved were not yet available for
clarification.

As sessions continued and I did not reject him, David began to
show direct affect in relation to me. For a moment, his face would
light up with pleasure when he saw me, and there would be silent
misery at the end of his hour, when he would not leave. He needed
some concrete gesture from me to insure that he would return. I
gave him tokens, but nothing I offered was any good. He always
wanted something belonging to someone else, which I would then
have to refuse him. I began to clarify his behavior; he felt sad that
others had something he did not possess. It was as well that I had
not tried to impose an outsider's view and had not linked this
directly with his deafness. His changed material brought the much

wider problem into focus: his low self-esteem in relation to other children and his angry envy of them.

His aggression became directed against the children in the Clinic. Screaming incessantly, he attempted to destroy the treatment room when he saw a doll belonging to another child in it. It was quite impossible to communicate directly with him. I got out a teddy, and sat wiping its eyes. David tried to tear it from me, but I insisted by my actions that Teddy was a sad little bear, and he needed someone for himself. David quickly drew a picture of me so he could tear it to pieces. I drew a picture of a mother, nursing her crying baby, as always identifying the figures by putting spectacles on the mother and a hearing aid on the baby. David barricaded us in the room. I drew David terrified of being pushed out by other children. He tore the paper to shreds, smashing and hammering it into the floor, but then he lay silently, letting his foot touch mine—the first positive expression of his longing for a caring object.

His despair at the end of the session was so intense that I found it difficult to stem my overwhelming feelings of guilt for not having more time for him. Technically, I had to find some means by which he could continue to feel accepted by me, while I avoided trying to take on what Eissler (1958) described as the function of the omnipotent, all-caring mother. I did this with the help of the teddy bear. I made it clear that I would look after it for David, and ended every session holding the teddy in my arms. But David needed more than this. His behavior to the other children in school became so impossible that he was excluded. The school felt that they could neither teach nor hold him. But in his acting out, David had established that he was capable of intense object relatedness, even though predominantly at a need-satisfying stage.

It is difficult to assess why this change had taken place: whether it was my tolerance of his behavior, which had been a new experience for him, or whether it was a reexperiencing of the permissive child-minder whom he had had when he was 3. It was certainly a new experience for him to have some of his preconscious affects available in consciousness. He was aware, not only of his envy of others, but also of his dissatisfaction with himself and his fears that others must be preferred. At this point we saw the reoccurrence of an old symptom, which had first appeared after his mother's death: he could not let himself go to sleep. When I drew him asleep in an empty room, he screamed in a distraught manner a sound which I had come to recognize as "Radford," and he realized he was afraid I would leave him for John.

Gradually I began to realize that I no longer treated David as quite so vulnerable and fragile. I had stopped always providing him with a token, for I knew he would not regress to the totally devastated, disintegrated cripple, unable to remain in contact with me. He as well as I could tolerate his anger.

This newly acquired ego strength was severely tested when a change of room and house occurred. This created such inappropriate intense feelings of rejection, I found myself attempting to relate his present behavior to past happenings. Any change of routine underlined the problem of communication. No matter how clearly I thought I had explained, through miming and drawings, he would inevitably misunderstand. I had told him we were moving to a permanent room, but when I tried to persuade him to take his toy box to the new house, he went completely berserk. He hammered and screamed, knocked over the furniture, threw out the teddy bear, and then, exhausted, sat on the stairs, staring, out of touch. The affective state was so overwhelming, it seemed as if he were reliving his old feelings of despair when the family had moved immediately after his mother's death. I recovered Teddy, and gradually managed to get near to David, until he could see the pictures of the new room with him and me in it. He looked at me, and he could let himself lip-read. I talked of a sad little boy who had once lost his mummy in a new house, and who felt it was going to happen again. David quietly wrapped my arms around Teddy, and then tightly holding my hand came with me to the new room, where we acted out losing and regaining the teddy on the primitive infantile level of dropping and recovering it through the window.

David's total response to the change gave clear indications of the strengthening of his ego as well as the widened range of his affects. This was illustrated in the use he made of his improved reality testing. He had angrily noted that the "chosen" nursery children stayed in their old room while he was sent away. Instead of at once attacking them and their possessions, he was not completely overwhelmed by aggressive impulses. He found substitutes for his hunger for love. He brought food, usually two large Swiss rolls, three doughnuts, and two bags of buns per session. He would sit, stuffing himself, glowering at me. I drew pictures of David hungry, while the nursery school children were fed every day. He ate these papers, too. I produced a tea service, estimating that his reality testing was sufficiently strong for him to make do with symbols. He mimed beautifully a sophisticated game in which he was enjoying waiter service. He complained about the food, the service, but, above all, about me, the waitress, who always had another customer.

The acceptance of such a constant and stable, though ambivalent, relationship to the analyst clearly had an organizing influence on his ego. The next stage of treatment required, above all, further strengthening of his ego so that he could effectively utilize interpretations. The primary task was to improve his reality testing, so that his deafness and his extremely limited guttural speech, and their impact on his external and internal worlds, could be brought into the treatment situation. We could then determine whether his lack of self-esteem was a primary or secondary consequence of his being deaf and nearly dumb, different from others of whom he was so pathologically jealous. His low frustration tolerance and poor impulse control could then be mitigated through a more economic defense structure. On the basis of identification with less damaging and damaged objects, David might be able to acquire realistic ego ideals. If these could be met, he could begin to develop some good feelings for himself and others. If he were no longer constantly threatened by feelings of disintegration, he could apply his energies to new achievements, which in turn would increase his self-esteem. Thus, my aim in the next period of treatment was to enlarge, facilitate, and make operable that part of his less damaged personality which might yield pleasure, so that eventually the more damaged areas could be approached.

I tried to achieve this aim of ego building by assiduously supporting any of David's attempts to enhance his self-esteem and by aiding his identifications such as that with me—someone of value, though handicapped (I wore glasses). David's readiness for this stage of treatment was verified when, for the first time, he used constructive, rather than destructive, methods to increase my good feeling for him and his respect for himself.

He aimed to prove he had assets denied to little children; at this time his brother was physically smaller than he. He brilliantly exhibited his acrobatic prowess, demanding my admiration and pointing out his superiority to the nursery school children. I admired his skill, accepting his ego ideal of the physically perfect athlete in the hope that it would increase his self-esteem and thereby strengthen his ego. I now doubt whether this was the most helpful way for him and if I did not underestimate the deleterious effects of such an ideal on an impulsive acting-out boy. I had fallen into the trap of assessing his handicap from the outside, rather than waiting for his material to show the meaning it had for him. Because I felt that his inability to hear and speak must create in him intense feelings of inferiority, I grasped at supporting an activity in which he experienced a reality-based pleasure in his own achievement, and I did not sufficiently consider its defensive aspect of avoidance of feelings of imperfection. Presumably, I, too, felt relieved that there was something in which he really could excel.

The inadequacy and unstable magical quality of such an ideal were quickly demonstrated when David's physical prowess failed him. Basking in my admiration, he had moved forward to oedipal strivings. He insisted he would shut me in the treatment room to keep me away from my husband; he was now calling me Mrs. Radford. Interestingly, his name for me has fluctuated throughout treatment, providing me with confirmation of the roles assigned to me. He climbed on the table to lock the windows, and then jumped. He slipped on some glue and fell heavily. It shattered his belief in his, and my, magical omnipotence. He was completely distraught; he sat on the chair crying bitterly, pointing at me, showing me he had not been able to see, and I ought to have protected him and been his eyes. He would not let me approach him, he had lost his infantile trust in my powers to protect him. He withdrew into sleep, and although there was no concussion, David slept, refusing to get out of bed during the weekend, until his next session. He regressed in treatment; he now always greeted me in the waiting room with a reproach: I should have seen for him. He then crawled upstairs, whimpering. He lay on the table, sucking at my fingers, and he went to sleep, only to wake to tell me I should have seen.

Slowly I was able to take up his disappointment in me. Technically, I went along with the regression because it seemed to me that David, as always, needed the concrete experience of feelings and situations to offset the lack of language, by which I could otherwise have interpreted and reconstructed. As it was, alongside the actual experiencing, I used a minimum of words to clarify his feelings of loss of belief in himself and his object. He could then express his longing for and his distrust in me, a real, not an idealized object.

He refused to come to the Clinic when a session time was changed; I would not be there. For his next session he insisted on coming two hours early. Although he managed to wait for most of the time, his patience eventually gave out, and he tore through the Clinic trying to find me. In his anger, he destroyed the belongings of other children, locked doors, and hid the keys. He then maintained such an innocent front when I appeared, unaware of his long wait, I did not believe the accusations flung at him, and protected him from my colleagues' justifiable wrath. David, on this somewhat unreal basis, reestablished his trust in me as the protector, and once more built a house for the baby and its mother.

This idealized picture could not withstand his improved reality testing; the nursery school children were always at the Clinic, and he was not. His intolerance of other children now emerged as part of his primitive pathology in which his low feeling of well-being, his deafness, and his envy of others formed a vicious circle. Clearly, the existence of a hearing, preferred brother, only 3 months younger than he, had left an indelible mark on his personality development. He could see himself only as the denigrated replica of John, and not as having any value himself. Only on rare occasions did he feel able to do something better than others. Aided by these occurrences, I began to steer him through the Scylla and Charybdis of his low self-esteem and his uncontrollable jealousy to approach his envy. Surprisingly, for a brief moment he became the good, helpful, cooperative boy whom he thought I would admire. It was as if he were letting me know that there was a different David who should exist rather than the imperfect one who was with us.

On this basis, I could take up the reality of his imperfections, offset as they now could be by his improved ego achievements. These were particularly noticeable in his ability to read and write, which had made him more acutely aware of the value of spoken words. Although we could write to each other, as well as draw, we could not speak as I did with others.[2] David's increased use of written words helped him to act less and thus be less frequently rejected. He certainly became more manageable when he tore up and ate my words about his envy of other children's products, rather than destroying whatever he thought belonged to them. Interestingly, this development brought with it more sophisticated forms of resistance. It was as if David recognized the possible power of words to uncover his defenses. Now, in resistance, he did not organize a physical attack, but took away all my writing materials, turned his back, and literally cut off all means of communication between us; a quite neurotic procedure, but the means chosen made it difficult to interpret anything when the patient, in one sense, was literally not there.

David was now constantly trying to offset his low feelings of self-esteem by some positive achievement, but he seemed to have to obliterate them by then embarking on some impossible task at which he must fail. For instance, he insisted he was as tall as a male colleague, who he had decided was my husband. As I verbalized this contradiction, linking it with wishes to compete, he brought in a series of fascinating masturbatory fantasies, showing his conviction that he could achieve success only if he acquired potency from others. Excitedly miming, shouting, acting, drawing, he brought vivid stories of fires burning, rockets firing, and burglars thieving. In the fires he was always in danger, but then with his great stolen strength (a fireman's helmet), he would put out the fires better than anyone else. We crawled all around the Clinic, being burglars, stealing and hiding money, under the surprised gaze of other occupants.[3] David then acted out his masturbatory wish; he

[2] His spoken vocabulary had increased to about 50 words, most of which I could understand on first hearing.

[3] I had accepted that David's need for concrete experiencing, and my need for elaboration of the material, made containment in one small room impossible at this stage of treatment.

stole from his father and hid the money. This clarified the meaning money had for him; he equated it with the power which David felt he so totally lacked. The transient identifications—typing like father, stealing father's money, painting totem poles like other patients—were always insufficient to offset his low feeling of well-being and his primitive denigrated self image. He would inevitably regress to the messing, provoking toddler, moving away from his phallic strivings as he failed to be like father.

But he was able to identify with my damaged part, presumably because it was less in conflict with his self representations. He always noted my glasses, and indicated he wanted to wear them. He bought himself a pair; he would wear them, but I must wear a hearing aid. I suggested that we had different imperfections. I could not see properly, he could not hear properly. David's immediate response was to return to his old, magical denial; he could hear and speak perfectly. I interpreted this defensive avoidance, stressing my defect to help him through identification to maintain his self-esteem as he faced the reality of his handicap. He painted a most pathetic picture of a sad ghost who inhabited a church and whom Mrs. Radford would not be able to bring back to life. This seemed to me a picture of David's psychic structure. Believing that he had now reached a stage when externalization need no longer be tolerated, I interpreted, through miming and words, that David was the ghost, wandering around looking for a lost part of himself, convinced that he could never be helped. He at once displaced his helplessness onto me; I must thread a needle, which he knew I could not do. He screamed at me that I had to be able to do it. When I sadly demonstrated that I could not and I was not perfect, he made me all-powerful. He drew a picture of me as the magical flying witch who was able to see perfectly, hear perfectly, and be so powerful that I could make David capable of doing everything. I noted the reality of my glasses and of David's hearing aid. He told me to take off the glasses and I would then be able to see; and for the first time in treatment he took off his hearing aid. As I interpreted the defensive magical thinking, he tried every possible device to avoid accepting the reality of my imperfection, which was now linked with his own imperfection. I continued to interpret the defenses; he abandoned all hope of magic in me, and looked for it in himself. I was no good; the police could simply take me to jail, but he was going to live to be 2001 and then he would be able to speak and to hear.

His ego rejected this magic formula, however, and at last the preconscious material became more available and we began to see what it meant to be deaf, to be jealous and envious of others. It would seem that we had now reached the stage where his neurotic conflict could be approached: definite themes had emerged, inappropriate affects had been witnessed, and the interpretation of defenses had unfolded a degree of internalized conflict. David's ego was sufficiently integrated to enter into a meager treatment alliance with me. It had been boosted by positive achievements; he had returned to a school for the deaf, where he was a successful, and sometimes an acceptable member. A psychological test taken at 11 years disclosed that he was functioning at a 13-year-old level; on all subtests, his achievements were beginning to catch up with his mental age. His aggressive outbursts usually arose from some misunderstanding caused by his deafness and from his jealousy. The marked pathological themes—his intense envy and jealousy of others which had persisted throughout all phases of his development, his overwhelming lack of a basic feeling of well-being which was linked with the psychic meaning of his deafness, and even the occasional appearance of guilt for his actions and fantasies—were now available for further exploration within the framework of an object relationship, constant enough to withstand some devastating separations within the next few months.

For many weeks I had a suddenly recurring virus infection, which forced me to attend sessions most irregularly. David showed an amazingly wide range of affects in response to my absences. After the first few days, he brought me a large orange which he insisted I must eat to make me better. During my second absence, he showed total disbelief, and aggressively accused his mother of trying to keep him from coming to see me. There was so much despair at my third absence—he insisted I was dead and he would never see me again—that his mother had to contact me to telephone him. His sadness and his anger were so intense and inappropriate that some transference elements were clearly involved, as if my illness had revived his desperate feelings of being abandoned by his adoptive mother, who had gone away to care for others. He told his stepmother that I was not ill, I was just looking after my baby. When I returned and mimed and verbalized the feelings of loneliness behind the anger, he cried. He enacted how he had felt abandoned by me, miming his fantasy of an accident in which he had been badly hurt and lay bleeding. I would comfort him and then I would go for help for him, but always another child would call me and I would go to that child and leave David to die.

The link with his basic needs was again underlined when once more he brought pounds of food to his sessions, and he became frantically demanding. I had to return to the old technique of drawing pictures. I drew one of a hungry baby crying for his mother who did not come. He wrote across the page: "Horrible Mrs. R.," and he added to the drawing a crocodile with a Radford in its mouth. David then proceeded to eat the paper, and he wrote me a letter that Radford was a horrible, silly baby whom David did not love. I interpreted this defensive reversal and emphasized his sadness when I, like his mother, had not been with him. He paused, shook his head, cried, and then gradually smiled with relief and proceeded to teach me the deaf language, the first word of which was "baby." He resurrected the teddy bear to help him cope with the forthcoming summer holiday. He drew a picture of a lonely Mrs. R. in tears, but as he drew it, David cried.

I used my illness to interpret David's feeling as a reliving in the transference of his sadness, loneliness, and loss over the disappearance of his mother when he was 3 years old, who he felt had left him for others more lovable than he. His ego tolerated his instinctual regression, and maintained its newly found achievements. He could admit his wish to displace all others, but then, overcome by guilt, he became worried about the disappearance of his brother to boarding school; a neurotic conflict had emerged fully.

I now aimed at helping the observing part of David's ego to look at the internalized part of his problems, the conflicts and the guilt, the intrapsychic struggle in which the deficiencies of his superego were highlighted in relation to his powerful id and his still vulnerable ego. Insofar as it was possible, the transference aspects were related back to his old conflicts so that these could be worked through and the repetition compulsion overcome.

This sounds like classical treatment: the means, however, could not be classical, not only because of his defective hearing and speech but also because of David's extremely damaged self-esteem. As treatment progressed, it became evident that the two were inextricably linked; yet the handicap itself delayed the disentangling of the strands as it posed reality problems to the process of reconstruction and working through. His lack of peripheral hearing was limiting to me as well as to David because I always had to be within the range of his vision to insure he was seeing or hearing what I said. Although there was evidence of a vast inner language and a fairly good comprehension of visually perceived spoken language, his own speech was most limited. I always found it a problem to decide whether to interrupt the flow of inarticulate speech which I was not following or to let the actions continue in the hope that I would at least understand their affective content. His increasing awareness of the handicaps which his deafness created at times also hindered the process of analysis as he would use his deafness for the type of resistance which Greenson described as the predominance of irrational fears, forces fighting against the establishment of a reasonable ego. His conscious acceptance of deafness inevitably also lowered his self-esteem. He would then fall back on earlier means of defending himself against these feelings of inadequacy, becoming once more the attacking bully. The secondary gains he obtained from his outrageous behavior also helped him to tolerate his image of himself as a hopelessly damaged person. Deaf David had the right to be treated as special, be granted privileges that no other child should have, and need not take responsibility for his actions and their consequences. His charming smiles and cajoling ways unfortunately made the environment play into the secondary gains, thus helping him to resist interpretation of the underlying conflicts.

The disappearance of his brother to boarding school aroused so much guilt that his defenses became vulnerable. On his return from the summer holiday David tried to pretend that nothing was different in the room, although some lockers had been removed. When I commented on this, he gleefully told me that his brother had gone away and it was forever. But, hurriedly, he looked for some animal pictures he had brought about a year ago. He knew just what he wanted: first, an owl which he noted smilingly had eyes just like my glasses, then an owl with her two babies; he told me they were brothers, like David and John. He quickly showed me the next picture: an insect with pinching claws; he called it Mrs. R. and reproached me for having horrible, dangerous claws which he tried to scribble out. Before I could comment he produced a picture of a fierce-looking owl, which he indignantly said pounced on little rabbits and ate them. He destroyed this picture and went back to the owl with the babies. He began to cut out one of the babies, then frantically pushed the picture away only to discard one baby. He could not make a drawing of what was left and tried to go back to the large kindly owl, but first he said he had to find the lost baby. I drew a picture of a dream of the baby owl in which the mother owl turned into a monster with claws killing her baby because that baby had got rid of his brother. David insisted I should go over the drawing again and again while he continued his fruitless search. Overcome by guilt, he wrote he would be punished, sent away forever, never be able to talk!

His material increasingly showed that he had equated the loss of speech with the loss of love and that his superego insisted that his wish to have speech, to have hearing, was at one with his "bad murderous" wish to be the only one with mother. He therefore should have nothing. He again tried to compensate for feeling worthless, trying to identify with the flick-knife boys at school, but as this failed, he returned to his magical fantasies of incorporating power. He enacted games of fellatio, through which he showed that he felt if he could magically take in the penis, he would speak. He tried to eat the all-powerful speech symbol—the telephone. Using many drawings for clarification, I interpreted this constellation of defenses, which enabled him to verbalize castration fears; deaf men were weak, they had lost their penis and could never marry.

Frantically he tried to decide where he could acquire the greatest potency as a man or as a woman. He feverishly made picture frames and built a picture gallery to be a collector like father. He learned to embroider, to be creative like mother, but the appearance of a baby in the waiting room helped him to express his dilemma graphically. Having dragged me into the waiting room to admire the baby, he crawled upstairs to climb into his locker—no mean feat for a boy 5 feet 3 inches tall—and told me to feed him. I interpreted the envy inherent in this as well as the wish; the regression lifted and his phallic wishes reappeared. He filled two balloons with water and first tried to fit them on himself as breasts. Failing this he jabbed at them with a compass, fiendishly tearing them to pieces; then he triumphantly placed the compass by his penis, miming a show about its power. When I wondered if he had wanted men to punish women, he dashed to the telephone and poured out excited denunciations of me.

Not for the first time I had to cope with the frustration of not understanding his speech and being able only to pick up the affects. I said David was sad and angry and I wondered why. He told me he could never have babies! Although there were some aspects of envy of the woman in this—disgustedly he pointed out he could not embroider as well as I could—his impotence was much more all-embracing. He equated his deafness with a lack of masculine or feminine potency and once more he became afraid to go to sleep. In his sessions he illustrated why. Like the snow he put in his pocket, parts of him melted away while he was asleep, so he must keep watch. He was so intensely depressed about his loss that I decided to approach him indirectly through his identification with my damaged part. I told him the story of a blind girl who felt she would never be grown up and acquire the things other children had. David responded with tremendous feeling, "You love John."

We could now clarify his conviction that his brother and all speaking children were preferred to him. Sadly and slowly he spoke and mimed his feelings of being inadequate; he was a boy who could never be loved, could never marry, because he was deaf. But he was deaf because he was horrible; because he was horrible, nobody could love him. But if he was not loved, he could never speak. As David had acquired some ability to give expression to his thoughts and affects, we came to see how interrelated was his inadequate self-esteem and his deafness. But how far it would be possible to disentangle his low feelings about himself from the reality of deafness could not yet be estimated.

The fact that his ego was sufficiently synthesized to acknowledge the problem and that there had been some economic realignment of his defenses made it possible to approach the conflict itself. But his punishing superego constantly insisted he was rubbish which should be thrown out. He would try to discard the contents of his locker, throwing them out the window, having attempted to steal the contents of all other lockers in his search for others' speech. His low opinion of himself was constantly reinforced by the external world. He had been delighted to belong to a scout troop. Without warning the scout master wrote that they were weary of David's inability to understand and they did not want him back in the troop. David insisted on coming to treatment in his scout uniform, but at first he said nothing of the trauma. I knew of it, but I felt he would be quite able to tell me.

He turned passive into active, going out of the room before our time was up, but then he returned to mime that he could not go back to the scouts. At the next session, still in uniform, he insisted he could build bigger and better things than the nursery children; but when I linked this with his feeling unsure of himself, he told me that our room was the warmest and brought me a card from school explaining deafness. I was astounded at the strength of his belief in my acceptance of him. He met me in the street on the way to his next session; silently he put his hand in mine and walked with me like a trusting 3-year-old. And in the session he told me he would join my scout troop, although he knew other scouts had rejected him because he could not speak or hear and that they did not want him because he could not understand, but they did want brother John. The uniform disappeared for many weeks only to be worn again on the last day of term. David was well able to recognize that separation seemed like rejection and I made the genetic link back to his dead mother. He added another dimension when he pointed sadly to his hearing aid. But his strengthened ego could tolerate the sadness, he did not have to reject me; he gave me the teddy and told me to write to him. His good feeling for his object thus had helped him maintain some good feeling about himself.

He was clearly more reality-oriented to his defect and he was trying to find ways to offset it. He would write on the board if he thought I had not understood. He would tell me to write when he was not sure what I had said. And he would turn off his hearing aid and remove pencils and chalk when he was in a phase of resistance. He had done well at school; he was at the top of his form, and did not resent it when others received prizes as well as he; and he had acquired a girlfriend.

It seems as if an increased sense of well-being enabled him to feel he could be loved even if handicapped. There was an upsurge of phallic material, renewed masturbatory fantasies, and attempts to create triangular situations between himself, his mother, and me. It was, however, difficult to estimate the extent to which this fantasied future sexual partner was predominantly a genital one or a continuation of the infantile longing to be the only one loved by mother, a longing colored by his physical maturation. Undoubtedly, in his libidinal development he had reached phallic dominance, as was shown in his oedipal strivings and resultant castration anxiety. He reversed the affect, and I, father in the transference (he had brought his father's shaving brush to shave me so I would be sure of my role), would become powerless and decrepit, while David grew richer and stronger. He kindly pushed me in my wheelchair; then, with glee, he overturned it and I was dead. His powerful motorbike would speed past my Mini, only to return to plough it down. He wrote constantly that he loved Margaret, his girlfriend, and he did not love me. But he was in angry despair when he thought I had spent the weekend with his much-admired teacher. He coped with it, however, by making very beautiful models to give the teacher to compensate him, David said, for having to put up with me, certainly a more socialized type of defensive reaction.

Although he insisted he would never marry me and told his mother he had run away from home to stop me marrying him, he was in fact quite uncertain of his ability to find any woman who would love and marry him. He held on to the fantasy that one day he would marry me because this course was safer for the maintenance of his well-being. He was sure now that I would not throw him out—basic trust had been established. But he then used this defensively; fearing rejection from others, he could not let himself give up his infantile attachments to seek new ones. Although this is a classical oedipal situation, the possibilities of resolving it are hampered by the vicious circle of the reality of the deafness and its complementary effect on his low feelings of well-being, which he tries to offset by overdetermined actions.

At this stage of treatment an increase in his self-esteem could be achieved only by helping him to uncover and work through the guilt inherent in the intrapsychic conflicts. This assumption was strengthened when David began to use his deafness to exclude himself. He insisted we should only communicate through speech, as I did with others. This created an impasse as we needed to supplement spoken words with written ones and miming. It was as if he were having to turn his handicap on himself and beat himself with it. When I interpreted this masochistic tendency, he showed me the sadistic component. He wanted to beat me. I had not given him speech and hearing because I was too busy with my other child, and with his schoolteacher, to pay enough attention to David's need. He regressed to the messing, destructive toddler. I painfully built up a verbalized reconstruction; he had to blame me, mother, to avoid feeling bad about his jealous anger with her which he thought had caused her death, punishing him by leaving him without love or speech. He grabbed the paper and ate it, and at once became much calmer as if the words had had a soothing effect. I then had occasion to speculate about the concrete manner in which primitive introjects might be incorporated when he drew a picture of David with Mrs. R. snugly tucked in his tummy and then proceeded to eat this, too.

David was now 12½ years old. He had achieved a definite stability in his ego functioning and object relatedness. On the basis of these we felt that he might benefit from attending a secondary school for deaf children as a weekly boarder. He made a good start at the school, but in his daily treatment sessions it quickly became clear that his stability and improved sense of well-being were still quite dependent on a sympathetic external environment as well as on his internal object representations, particularly when the upsurge of instinctual drives from approaching puberty was making increasing demands on his ego.

His material was dominated by the need to obtain money, always a sign he was feeling inadequate; the money was to feed babies, to help them grow. He did maintain himself on a higher level as he tried to obtain respect from the bigger boys by producing excellent models. I verbalized his anxiety about feeling small with more powerful men, but the sexual games between the big boys and girls excited and frightened him. He actively played the fireman failing to put out the fire in the girl's bedroom, as if he feared that instinctual impulses would be beyond his ego's control. He was overwhelmed with castration fear and guilt and he took on the policeman's role, punishing me and sending me to prison for my games, while at school he reported the other children's dormitory activities to the head teacher. His intellectual and exhibitionistic powers only increased the children's envy and dislike of him. For the first time in his life, David became the victim of bullying. Bewildered, his belief in his own good qualities challenged, he resorted to his old method of defense: attack. In treatment he climbed on top of the lockers as if to ward off an attack, but then he did the attacking. I tried to take up his feelings of vulnerability, but session after session he came without his hearing aid, yet another form of denial of feeling helpless and damaged. He made a telling Plasticine model of a robotlike figure standing threateningly over a smaller child, caged in an underground prison, but he would not let me comment on it.

The reality of being unwanted and unloved by the children and some of the staff overwhelmed him when even his precious physical prowess was undermined in fights. Frightened and provoked, he impulsively attacked a member of the staff and was immediately excluded. A hysterical fit a few days later confirmed his state of terror as he rigidly stood with fixed stare and clawlike hand, waiting for the attack. He had shown only too clearly the brittleness of his ego strength when he was placed in an environment that threatened his feelings of well-being.

Yet he did not regress in treatment, where we continue with the Herculean task of strengthening his ego and helping him internalize more adequate identifications. These, we expect, will expand his feelings of well-being enough to enable him to withstand external trauma. Moreover, they can aid in offsetting the effects of a denigrating self representation which now has become conscious. He was convinced he was mad as well as deaf. I had to feel the indents in his head where he had had cerebral fluid taps at the age of 4 months. He insisted I must know there was something wrong with his brain and he would never grow up. It did not take long, however, for David to realize that this was his fear, not a reality.

Technically, I felt I could continue to rely on the observing part of his ego in order to analyze his neurotic conflicts. His new symptom of running away helped us. We interpreted it as an attempt to master the anxiety engendered by instinctual and superego demands. Alone at night in the park, David was not cold and not lonely when he knew that I was not dead but sleeping safely with my husband. We clarified how, feeling destructive toward the mother figure, he punished himself. He externalized the conflict. It was my fault I had not given him speech, and I would not even try to stop him from running away. These were familiar to us as his old infantile complaints against deficient mothering.

David must learn to live with the reality of his handicap and his deprivations. The aim of our continuing work is to help him make a choice now that he has some understanding of his internalized conflicts—a choice between accepting the handicapped part of himself as an integral part of a valuable whole, or a damaging reliance on the secondary gains obtained from his uneconomic defensive structure which brings him the special recognition of being underprivileged.

Much work still needs to be done and I have asked myself whether I have been justified in trying to use analytic techniques, no matter how distorted, to help this type of problem. Has David's improvement—his trust in his object, his strengthened ego, his better reality testing, his limited insight, his increased capacity to tolerate his drives, even his slightly improved good feeling for himself which offsets a little the guilt from his punishing superego—has this improvement been obtained through my analytic understanding and the analytic process? Indeed, how far can his treatment be considered an analysis when the wide range and variations of technique were so fundamental? My constant aim was to try to make conscious what was unconscious, by means of interpretation, in the hope that this would widen the scope of David's ego functioning, undo maladaptive identifications, modify his introjects, and foster less denigrated self representations. I recognize that I was also fulfilling many other roles, but for me these were always subservient to the analytic role proper. Only further treatment will provide the answer to the question how far my present techniques can help David, deaf and traumatized, to make the choice which will bring him most happiness and fulfillment.

BIBLIOGRAPHY

DENMARK, J. (1966), Mental Illness and Early Profound Deafness. *Brit. J. Med. Psychol.*, 39:117–124.

EISSLER, K. R. (1958), Remarks on Some Variations in Psycho-Analytical Technique. *Int. J. Psycho-Anal.*, 39:222–229.

GREENSON, R. R. (1958), Variations in Classical Psycho-Analytic Technique: An Introduction. *Int. J. Psycho-Anal.*, 39:200–201.

JACOBSON, E. (1954), Transference Problems in the Psychoanalytic Treatment of Severely Depressed Patients. *J. Amer. Psychoanal. Assn.*, 12:596–606.

KRIS, E. (1951), Ego Psychology and Interpretation in Psychoanalytic Therapy. *Psychoanal. Quart.*, 20:15–30.

LAFORGUE, R. (1936), Exceptions to the Fundamental Rule. *Psychoanal. Quart.*, 5:369–374.

LOEWENSTEIN, R. M. (1958), Remarks on Some Variations in Psycho-Analytic Technique. *Int. J. Psycho-Anal*, 39:202–210.

Preventive Analysis
Following a Trauma

A 4½-Year-Old Girl Witnesses a Stillbirth

STANLEY H. SHAPIRO, M.D.

THE BRIEF BUT INTENSIVE TREATMENT OF A 4½-YEAR-OLD GIRL WILL be presented in some detail. Such close-up opportunities for the observation of the effects of a traumatic incident in a young child are not readily available. Yet the opportunity for increasing our understanding of the developmental process as well as perfecting and broadening the scope of our therapeutic approach is potentially large. For traumatic interference with development serves to bring into focus crucial elements and interacting forces which are less easy to discern and examine under conditions of smooth functioning where all the diverse elements of the psyche are merged harmoniously. The clinical material will provide the basis for a discussion of the possibilities that a brief period of analysis affords in preventing the damaging effects of trauma on the unfolding personality of the young child.

Clincial Professor, Department of Mental Health Sciences, Hahnemann Medical College and Hospital, Philadelphia, Pennsylvania.

I wish to acknowledge my indebtedness to Dr. Harold Kolansky for his invaluable help during the course of the treatment and for his comments on the initial draft of the manuscript. I am also grateful to Dr. David Sachs for discussing the manuscript with me and for providing many useful criticisms and suggestions. I especially wish to thank "Linda" and her parents for reading the manuscript and giving their permission for its publication.

249

It is surprising that there exist only few reports of analytic treatment of the preschool child following a traumatic incident. Kolansky (1960) reviewed the literature in his own account of brief intensive treatment of Ann, a 3-year-old who was suffering from stammering and an insect phobia.

Psychoanalytic investigators have noted that the immaturity of the ego of the young child increases his vulnerability to disturbance. But on the positive side there is also at this early stage of development a fluidity and susceptibility to influence providing the possibility of reversing pathological trends by appropriate methods. Dratman (quoted by Kolansky, 1960) reasoned that "if there are known traumatic events prior to the onset of the neurosis in a child during the preoedipal phases of development, and if the mother with her intimate knowledge of the child has a personality flexible enough to allow her to participate with the analyst in the child's therapeutic sessions, a relatively brief but intensive analytic treatment may be attempted" (p. 265). Solnit (in Kaplan, 1962) supports this view, noting that the consolidation and integration which take place with the resolution of the phallic phase bring with it the crystallization of defenses. Prior to this "a pathological reaction pattern . . . is plastic, and can be influenced by treatment, education, and environmental changes, depending on the degree to which the dynamics of the trauma have become internalized" (p. 573f.).

At 4½, Linda, the little girl whose treatment will be described, was approaching the upper limits of age for these principles to be applicable. Yet in many respects the crystallization process referred to does not take place to any significant degree until the actual ushering in of latency. This same contention concerning the relative flexibility of the prelatency child's psychic structure has also been made by Nagera (1966), who views the resolution of the phallic-oedipal period as a nodal point in development. It represents a synthesis and an integration of all the diverse developmental processes which have gone before.

All analytic authors stress the need for close involvement of the mother in the treatment process. B. Bornstein (1935) treated a 2-year-old girl with a severe sleep disorder in her own home, involving other members of the household where indicated.

S. Bornstein (1935) cited the importance of having the parent present to explain questions of fact, calling it "a rare opportunity." My case material amply confirms this point. Schwarz (1950) noted that the mother's presence in the consulting room provided reassurance to the child of the mother's approval of the analyst and her interpretations.

There is a sharp dichotomy between the approach of analytic therapy and the technique designed by Levy (1939) for the relief of posttraumatic conditions. Levy's "release therapy" is a purely abreactive approach. The emphasis is on the catharsis brought about by reenacting the traumatic circumstances in the child's play. The therapist controls the play situation, directing it toward the area of the child's problems. By contrast, in analytic therapy, play is used only as a *means* to verbalize with the child about his difficulties and not, as in release therapy, as an end in itself. Verbalization is given paramount importance as a tool for the child's ego to use in assimilating the traumatic experience without incurring distortion or fixation. The role of verbalization in promoting ego growth and mastery in the young child has been recognized (Hartmann, 1951; Katan, 1961; Kolansky, 1967).

CASE REPORT

THE PRECIPITATING EVENT

Linda, a 4½-year-old only child, was brought for examination approximately two weeks after she had been exposed to the precipitous birth of an 8-month stillborn.

As reported by the mother, Linda was probably awakened by her shouting to her husband downstairs that the baby was coming. He had just run down to phone for an ambulance when she began to have cramps and the "bag of waters" broke. The delivery occurred in the hall around 6:30 A.M. and there was a great deal of blood and fluid.

In the first few days while Mrs. L. was still in the hospital, Linda denied any knowledge of there having been a baby. In her daily phone conversation with her mother she never asked about the baby; she only wanted to know when was mother coming home.

This initial phase of complete denial was broken when, on the day before mother's discharge from the hospital, Linda was told about the baby having been born dead. She became hysterical and cried bitterly in response to the information that it had been too small to live. Subsequently Linda was noted to be the initiator of a new game with her playmates. It was called "dead baby," in which she always insisted on being the baby. Linda also began to complain that her stomach hurt and that her BM was hurting her. At one point she complained that she had blood on her stool, yet none was to be seen. At bedtime one night she was heard groaning. The mother suggested to her that she must have heard mommy groaning that way the day the baby was born. Linda agreed and then said she wanted to cut her stomach open to see what was inside. The perceptive mother also noted that Linda now used much more BM talk. In addition, Linda showed an increased concern about any cuts or bleeding wounds. She would react to a slight cut on her finger by exclaiming in a dramatic and exaggerated way how much blood there was. At bedtime, Linda began requesting one more story, one more glass of water, etc., in an effort to keep her mother by her bedside.

Concerned about these changes in their daughter and sophisticated enough to realize that the stillbirth might have been traumatic, Linda's parents sought a psychiatric evaluation.

DEVELOPMENTAL HISTORY SUPPLIED BY MOTHER

Linda was an only child. Her mother was 37, and her father, a salesman, was 44 at the time of referral. She was conceived after one year of marriage. Despite her birth weight of 5 pounds, Linda thrived well—the only complaint having been that she was irritable and prone to upper respiratory infection. This was still her main physical complaint. Linda was weaned at about one year and thereafter became a little finger sucker. At 3, when she was sent to nursery school, she switched to the more conventional thumb sucking. She was still a thumb sucker at the time of referral, and the role which this played in her treatment will be considered later on. Bowel and bladder training was not instituted until $2\frac{1}{2}$; both were accomplished relatively easily by the time she was 3. Mrs. L.

recalled that Linda had had to be trained in order to be accepted at nursery school and therefore could date this event rather exactly.

The adjustment at school required several days during which Linda did not want her mother to leave. The first days the teacher carried her around in her arms; thereafter Linda seemed to settle down. Both in her play at home and at school Linda showed a definite tendency to play the baby.

She often talked baby talk, but, prior to the stillbirth, this had occurred only with her parents. Mrs. L. described Linda as a friendly, petite, little girl, who liked to play with small things which could be put together and taken apart.

One year prior to the referral, Mrs. L. had had a miscarriage for which she was hospitalized two days. Linda, then $3\frac{1}{2}$, was not told the reason for mother's hospitalization. Mrs. L. became pregnant again several months later. At 4 months, when it was beginning to show, Linda was told about the baby which was to come. Coinciding roughly with the latter part of mother's pregnancy, Linda complained of frequency and burning on urination. She was found to have a urethritis with crusting. She was given antibiotics, the effect of which was followed by frequent urinalysis. The problem still persisted at the time of the referral and the pediatrician had raised the possibility of getting a catheterized specimen for culture and sensitivity studies. Mrs. L. could remember no masturbation, commenting that she seemed to be more attracted to her thumb. (More will be said about this later on.) In the next few months Linda became very interested in doll play and talked a good deal about the new baby; the parents brought home books dealing with this subject and read them to Linda.

In the course of my two initial interviews with Mrs. L. I also learned that she had been diagnosed as having ulcerative colitis 15 years ago, when she was 22. When she was 5 months pregnant with Linda, she went into psychotherapy for colitis. She continued her treatment until Linda was born, stopping only for 6 months, then resuming until Linda was about $2\frac{1}{2}$. Her illness caused Mrs. L. to suffer with bouts of diarrhea with occasional blood in her stools. Although she did not feel that her daughter knew of her condition, she noted that Linda always wanted to be in the bathroom with her, or at least to have the door kept ajar.

In summary, the development of this little girl prior to the stillbirth seemed to fall within normal limits. There was no question of a major psychiatric disturbance, even though she did show some signs of immaturity in her thumb sucking, attachment to mother, and the tendency to play the role of baby.

ASSESSMENT OF INDICATIONS FOR THERAPY

The experience of seeing her mother deliver a stillborn fetus under the conditions described certainly merits being considered a potentially traumatic event. Linda's behavior subsequent to the trauma seemed to fall into two phases:

(1) Denial (while mother was in the hospital), which lasted until she was told by her aunt that the baby was dead. Then,

(2) regressive behavior, e.g., baby talk, increased thumb sucking, and clinginess to the mother, especially at bedtime. Also noted was what might be termed a more perilous attempt at mastery by identification:

(a) with the mother by way of her groaning, claiming that her BM hurt and that there was blood;

(b) with the stillborn in the "dead baby" play.

Linda was seen within two weeks, too early to determine whether the stillbirth had acted as a trauma in the classical sense. One could speculate on the possible impingements and fixation potential that such an event and the fantasies associated with it would have on the little girl's psychosexual development, i.e., her castration complex, her feminine identity, and ultimately her attitude toward having children herself in the maternal role. Under these circumstances by what criteria is the necessity for therapeutic intervention to be decided? Had Linda displayed night terrors, refusal to eat, or inability to let her mother out of her sight, or any other gross psychopathology, there would be no doubt that prompt help was necessary. But Linda's disturbances were "manageable," and had she been born of parents less perceptive and less psychologically sophisticated, the whole situation might well have been passed over with the comment that "she'll get over it."

In addressing herself to this problem of the assessment of pathology and the need for treatment, Anna Freud (1945) emphasized the concept of interference with normal development as the prime indication for treatment. This concept evolved in her later writings (1963, 1965) into a consideration of lines of development in the total personality of the child. The progression of libidinal development from oral through anal, phallic, and genital phases would constitute one such line of development, i.e., psychosexual. Conflicts which are unresolved or poorly handled act as impediments to further development via fixations in lines of development. The child whose earlier experiences were in some way unsatisfactory due to trauma or deprivation is cumulatively handicapped in his efforts to cope with the demands of each new phase. Earlier fixations can distort subsequent efforts at mastery, causing difficulty for the child in the same way that a faulty foundation compromises the upper levels of a building under construction.

At the time Linda was seen, it appeared reasonable to assume that events of that fateful day were still relatively fresh in her mind; that the child's ego was starting to assimilate the experience; and, most important, that the affects connected with the trauma might still be accessible. Providing the child's ego with an ally at this point would serve both to facilitate an accurate evaluation and assimilation of what she had seen and to help channel the affects into an appropriate form of discharge. The aim would essentially be prophylactic.

The child analyst is in a unique position to intervene on the side of the ego to insure the child's continued development by keeping a traumatic event from becoming a stumbling block and a focus for fixation. This could be done by prompt, intensive intervention, utilizing a psychoanalytic understanding of the child to detect lines of development specifically threatened by the trauma. Unlike the usual analytic technique which is "after-the-fact," the approach here would be directed at preventing the occurrence of pathogenic repression and fixation.[1]

---

[1] There has been an upsurge of interest in the search for prophylactic social programs for the young disadvantaged child. The need for such early intervention and prevention has been given recognition in social action programs as "Get-Set" and "Head-Start." But, in order to prevent the crippling and seemingly irreversible psychological effects of cultural, emotional, and physical deprivation of the underprivileged child, there is also a desperate need for therapeutic techniques

It would seem that the case of Linda represents a most propitious choice for such an undertaking because: (1) Prior to the disturbing event she had a relatively normal developmental history. (2) She was seen by the analyst shortly after the event. (3) She had a mother who was unusually perceptive and intuitive (as the clinical material will demonstrate). (4) I had the opportunity to follow up her development 10 years after the termination of treatment. For these reasons, her case might be considered a natural starting point to assess the preventive value of an analytic approach to children known to have been subjected to potentially traumatic external events.

Course of Treatment

The entire treatment consisted of 38 play sessions. I saw Linda 5 times a week during the months of June and July; then after a month's interruption due to vacation, there were 9 more sessions in September. In many of the sessions Linda's mother was in the playroom. Early in treatment, she spent a few hours sitting in the consultation room with the door ajar.

Despite the brevity it is not feasible to present a chronological account of the entire treatment, session by session. Rather, it would seem more profitable to follow separately the evolution of various central themes as they threaded their way through the fabric of the therapy situation. However, to set the stage, the first two sessions will be described in some detail.

FIRST SESSION

Linda was, as her mother described, a petite, attractive, charming little girl. She stood shyly next to her mother in the waiting room clutching a doll in one hand and a comb in the other. She left her mother behind and followed me to the playroom where she became attracted to the family figures and the animals. She quickly elaborated a story about a baby and its father going to New York

---

solidly based on the fundamental principles of psychoanalytic developmental psychology. Hastily conceived and ill-founded approaches mounted in the service of expediency will lead only to disillusionment and hostility.

City, riding on the cow. There they stayed overnight sleeping together in the same bed. This shaded over to having all the animals ridden by all of the family figures. Then it became nighttime and the cowgirl had to stay awake to watch the sleeping men. She was joined by the mother and the baby. Their job also was to see that the cow did not run away during the night. Before giving this up, each person was assigned an animal. The baby got the calf, the mother got "tiger" (this was actually a lion). Linda then declared that she was finished and went to the blackboard.

After scribbling and drawing flowers, she drew a "choo-choo," which she later called a subway train. She talked of her subway ride to the office that day. In the choo-choo she drew women and their daughters. Some were going to New York City; some to town; but one was going to see a doctor. The little girl had a headache—no, an earache. She described the doctor giving a needle in the arm; furthermore, how a doctor uses "the thing" in your ear and also on your stomach to listen. "There's food in there," she added as an afterthought and pointed to her stomach. She played with a rubber Betsy-Wetsy doll. She asked if I gave needles. She was told that I did not, but that I helped boys and girls with worries and fears. She was incredulous that I saw boys, too. She denied having any worries or fears herself. Immediately after saying this she had to make a "duty." When she returned with her mother, it was time to stop. She told her mother what a nice doctor I was, in answer to Mrs. L.'s question, and she seemed pleased to be coming back the next day.

In this first session, through her obviously well-developed capacity for imaginative play and fantasy, Linda depicted three possible areas of conflict: (1) her oedipal attachment to the father versus a fear of him (e.g., going to New York City with father versus having to stay awake and watch the sleeping men); (2) her preoedipal tie to her mother with separation anxiety expressed in the need to prevent the cow from moving off in the night (mother's hospitalization?); (3) restitution of the dead baby (everyone gets a baby animal).

Evidently Linda perceived the reason for her seeing me to be akin to her mother's hospitalization. It is therefore significant that this theme produced in her an impulse to defecate. Was this an anxiety equivalent or a hysterical symptom expressing identification with mother by having a bloody, anal baby? I later learned from Linda's mother that the family had taken a trip to New York a year ago. However, it had been Linda and her mother who had slept together, while the father had left them to return back home. By her reversal of the facts, Linda was able to use this trip as a disguised way of representing the recent separation from mother in which she and father were left alone together. In her play, it all ended happily with everyone getting a baby, even though mother's baby was a "tiger."

During this entire session I neither probed nor attempted to direct the course of the play or fantasy. Questions were asked for amplification or clarification only. This rather inactive attitude stands in contrast to the approach in the next session.

SECOND SESSION

When Linda started with the family figures again, I asked her whether she had brothers and sisters. She answered that she was going to have a new baby, but it didn't live. She further explained that it was too small and that's why it didn't live. She then became pensive and asked for her mother. She explained that she had a secret. Linda was induced, however, to tell me the secret before telling her mother. "How does the baby get out of the tummy?" she whispered in my ear. I told her, when she claimed not to know, that the mommy had a special hole between her legs—not the tussy hole but one in front of that; that the baby comes out of that hole just like BM comes out of the tussy hole. She remained pensive in mood, reflected briefly, and then said in a hushed dramatic tone, "I saw the blood." Querying for her feelings and for more detail, I told her that it must have been very frightening. She explained that the blood came from an accident—that mommy banged her knee. She showed me on her own knee a scar which was well healed. Then, looking very sad, she said that her mother had screamed at her—told her to get back to her room. At this point we were sitting on the floor together and Linda withdrew, sliding over toward the open closet, leaning her head forlornly against the door jamb. She nodded assent when I ventured that she must have felt mommy was very angry with her. She was silent and turned her head averting my gaze. I spoke to her about how sad she looked and that I guessed she must be having some sad thoughts now about the baby and what she saw that morning. Without answering, Linda got up, went to the waiting room, and asked her mother to come in. Mrs. L. sat down on the playroom floor and Linda began to play in a distracted way with various family figures.

Suddenly, she clutched the boy figure and shoved its head under the top of her sock so that it seemed to be disappearing. Quickly she brought it out, pressed it against her abdomen, and began shouting, "Oh! Oh!—they cut my stomach open and I have a baby boy!" With this she flipped the little figure out of her grasp, letting it fall to the floor as if coming from her abdomen. Then she threw herself in her mother's arms, burrowing her head in the cleft of her mother's shoulder. A minute or so later, she recovered her composure and spent the last few minutes of the hour playing in a peripatetic way, first with a wooden sailboat whose sail she ripped off, and then with the family figures, but without an organized fantasy.

Then, interrupting this play and turning to her mother, Linda asked, "How do babies get out?" Her mother answered that they come out the vagina. Linda then said to her, "Well, tell Dr. Shapiro," in a tone of voice indicating that the mother should straighten me out. Mrs. L. and I both discussed this with Linda, explaining that the special hole that I had talked about was called the vagina. Linda announced that she had a vagina and asked if I had a penis. When I said yes, she went on that her father had a vagina. Her mother corrected her. Linda then asked if her mother had a penis. Mother said no, but Linda insisted that she did. Abruptly she said that she did not want to play anymore and, since the time was up anyway, the session ended.

BIRTH FANTASIES AND RECONSTRUCTION OF THE EVENT

At $4\frac{1}{2}$ the normal child is at the height of the phallic phase of development, struggling to master the differences between the sexes (penis envy in the girl) and to resolve the oedipal conflicts. There is as yet no firm identification with the parents of the same sex, and the superego has not achieved the consolidation which heralds the

onset of latency. There is much the child does not understand and
the gaps are filled in with fantasy, the contents of which show the
imprint of earlier experiences. Oral and anal fantasies are normally
revived in an effort to cope with phallic problems. Thus anal birth
and oral impregnation fantasies are common in the phallic child's
dream and fantasy world. Castration fears become cloaked behind
fears of death or being devoured.

Even without witnessing the stillbirth one would expect a
$4\frac{1}{2}$-year-old girl to be interested in babies—who has them and
where they come from—and to show a great deal of interest in dolls,
as the symbolic representation of these ideas. In this Linda did not
disappoint, for from the very first session she displayed a concern
about everyone possessing an animal pet; and doll playing was a
permanent feature throughout the entire treatment.

One of Linda's first communications about the stillbirth was her
"secret," which she expressed as a question: "How does the baby
get out of the tummy?" This was followed by the revelation, "I saw
the blood." At the end of the hour, after bringing mother into the
playroom, she dramatically portrayed her conception of what took
place: "They've cut my stomach open and I have a baby boy!"

While many children of this age believe that babies are born by
the mother's stomach being cut open, for Linda, the stillbirth
appeared to provide terrifying confirmation of this notion. The
added difficulty of feeling that she had also done something wrong
to make her mother yell at her that way combined with her anxiety
about the blood to make the whole experience frightening and
disrupting. For Linda, her theory about childbirth was not just an
age-appropriate sadistically tinged fantasy; it was a disturbing
reality experience. The technical problem was one of engaging the
child's ego in the task of reassessing her theory to enable her to
arrive at an accurate and nonthreatening understanding of childbirth. To accomplish this it would be necessary to explore how she
felt about the blood. The need for this was underscored by Linda's
behavior while she was at home with the measles, which occurred
after the 4th session and interrupted treatment for a week. She
became upset about needing an aspirin suppository and kept
saying, "There's blood on my tussy." She also kept asking about
rust spots on the rug and remarked to her mother about ketchup

stains on the napkin. In the office, during her first visit after she had recovered from the measles, Linda became hysterical upon getting a splinter in her finger.

To facilitate the emergence of her notions about blood, I provided a doctor kit complete with thermometer, stethoscope, syringe, and tongue blade. In addition, prominently displayed in the playroom was red paint, some of which was spilled on absorbent paper towels. There also were, of course, dolls and a plastic bottle. Her first approaches were tentative—daubing with the paint. When she asked me what it looked like, I answered, "Blood." By the end of the hour, Linda had painted a small, plastic baby with red paint, which she called "blood from a shot." She seemingly ignored my comment that the baby who died must have looked like that. Subsequently she painted the red paint on the large doll's eyes and on its belly button: she claimed this was in connection with the doll having the measles, and did not at all acknowledge that it might be related to the dead baby.

In session 11 a breakthrough occurred. Linda was messing with the red paint, getting it on her hands, her clothes, then her legs, and finally even her shoes. She was asked whether this was what mother looked like; whether her attempts to clean herself were what mother had been doing after the baby had come. She answered very quickly, "No—daddy wiped up the blood. Mommy screamed. The blood came from mommy's knee. Mommy screamed at me." When I persisted in asking where she thought the blood came from, she cut across her knee with a rubber knife. I told her she must have thought that mommy's tummy was cut open. She responded by cutting across her abdomen with the knife after first lifting up her skirt. She talked of her belly button and said, "When I grow up, I'm going to have a baby of my very own." Linda then reminisced about a pussy cat she had had; but it was given away last year. Here she was both denying the death of the baby and identifying with her mother—both had lost something dear. The denial was evidenced following clarification by Linda's mother that, indeed, the previous year Linda had briefly had a cat. But it was not kept due to the objections of her grandfather and Linda had been told that the cat was taken to a farm where it still lived.

In subsequent hours, the theme of mother's hospitalization

emerged. Linda began expressing great curiosity about what was done to mother in the hospital. This material was accessible now because reconstruction had proceeded around the idea of the blood and who cleaned it up. Linda lost her original certainty and became confused in telling me how her mother had held her knee up. When asked again how the baby comes out, she blurted out emphatically, "That's what I don't know!" Then she wanted Band-Aids, which she put on her foot and on the doll's head as if to indicate that the blood could come from anywhere but not the vagina as she had been told. (An unconscious determinant of this might have been a laceration of her forehead when she was about 2, which required a trip to the emergency room. This material was subsequently supplied by Mrs. L.)

Actually, it is not possible to determine whether Linda had prior fantasies about babies coming from the mother's stomach or whether this idea was the displacement away from the vagina as the source of all the blood; or whether it might also stem from a confusion of vagina and anus in part suggested by the observation of mother's bloody stools. Distortions in the child's knowledge of sexual matters can be due to ignorance as well as to the operations of a defense. Such allowances must also be made in the treatment of adults. The analyst is on firmer ground to suspect the presence of defensive activity if the misunderstanding persists after the correct information has been supplied. Linda's clinging to the idea that mother cut her knee was such an instance. But she also had alternative ideas about where the blood was from. These emerged from her own unique experiences and memories. In placing one Band-Aid on the forehead, Linda may have been acting out the memory of the laceration on her forehead at age 2; the reference to the foot may also have stemmed from a specific memory. This would correspond to the "germ of truth" or historical reality contained in paranoid delusions referred to by Waelder (1951).

Linda's understanding of the birth process was certainly influenced by her previous exposure to mother's colitis. At several points she erroneously claimed that the baby came out of the tussy. One of her earliest symptoms following the stillbirth was to complain that she had blood on her BM. Once at bedtime she had imitated mother's groaning and her abdominal pain and then giggled that her duty was coming out. Linda also expressed concern, both in the playroom and with her mother, about the size of the baby in the tummy and how it would hurt coming out. These anal connections thus antedated the explanation given to Linda in the second hour in which I had likened the birth process to a bowel movement.

Mrs. L. had claimed that she first had become aware of Linda after she had crawled back into bed. But from the dramatic reenactment of the stillbirth in the second hour, I suspected that Linda may actually have witnessed the birth in the hall, as well as mother pulling the fetus under the covers. The layout of Linda's home was such that her room opened on the hallway. Corroboration of this hypothesis appeared in session 14: Linda took the long end of mother's belt and wrapped it around her own waist while it was still attached to mother.

By the use of a technique of role reversal in which I became the little girl and Linda became Dr. S., Linda was enabled to play out and clarify what she had actually seen and what she had thought. The technique was successful as a means of providing distance (by reversal) and facilitating reconstruction and recall, but it was not sufficient as a method to rectify or undo distortions in her understanding. This is amply shown in more detailed accounts of the following sessions.

In the 13th hour Linda was resistive at the beginning, claiming that I was "stupid" about the baby. She was annoyed that I had said she was a baby. I explained that what I meant was that sometimes she liked to pretend she was a baby and sometimes she played that she was the doctor. I was referring to the time she and I had reversed roles in the play and she had become me. Later in the hour Linda asked to have my watch and then my sunglasses. I complied and asked her what she wanted to know since she was going to be the doctor. In a false gruff voice she replied, "Tell me about the blood and the baby—the blood-baby." I began to tell her what I thought had happened the morning of the stillbirth. I told her how I had been awakened one morning by mommy screaming in the hall and how confused and frightened I was about what was going on. Linda began to amplify my comments and correct me. She indicated exactly what mother had screamed and how she was sitting in the hall in all that blood. She told how her father tried to clean up the blood and put some in a cup and some in an ashtray.[2] I commented that I was so scared because I didn't know where all that blood came from. Linda explained that mommy had banged her knee on the table. I answered that I wanted to think that, but it really seemed that mommy must have been cut open because there was that baby outside her tummy and so much blood. I said I didn't know then about the vagina and how the baby comes out. Linda commented that it comes out the tussy; she then took off my sunglasses, saying she didn't want to play doctor anymore. This material was evidently too upsetting at this point and had to be discontinued.

But I went on saying how the worst part was when they tied mommy on the stretcher. She joined in by describing how mother was taken out of the house to the hospital. I said that mommy went away for several days, but Linda corrected me by specifying "4 days."

This same sequence was repeated in subsequent hours in a fragmentary way. One time I expressed how I (as the little girl) felt abandoned by mother when she went to the hospital. In reenacting the stillbirth Linda clarified how angry mother sounded when she screamed. In the next session she instructed me to tell her "about the baby that didn't live and tell me about when mommy hollered at me." But when I started to describe how mommy yelled, Linda interrupted. "Mommy wasn't mad. She said, 'Lovely little girl, go to your room.'" I said I wish she had said it like that, but she sounded mad as if I had done something wrong.

Talking about going to the hospital again, Linda asked me what I was worried about. I replied that mommy might not come back. Then she said that mother was lying down with her knee up in the air; she had a cut on her knee and blood was coming from it. I reiterated that I had thought that, but the blood actually came from the vagina. Linda said she would go out now and ask mother if she was cut. Joining us in the playroom, Mrs. L. explained to Linda that she had cut her knee,[3] but that was another time, after the

---

[2] An ashtray full of blood was one of the few memories still retained when Linda was seen for a follow-up 10 years later. See footnote 8.

[3] An example of a "fragment of historical truth," a real memory, used in the

hospitalization, and she confirmed to Linda in front of me that the real source of the blood was from her vagina, which was where the baby came out. Despite this explanation Linda still expressed confusion about how the baby got out, stressing how mother had had her knee up.

In the 18th hour Linda initiated a further reenactment. She took my sunglasses and asked me to tell about the baby. In this reconstruction she indicated that before the baby was born, mommy came into her room to see if she was asleep, then had father call the hospital. While he was calling, mommy had the baby out in the hall and Linda came out of her room. Linda lifted her leg to show how mommy was helping the baby to come out. I asked her where the baby came out. She took off the sunglasses. I persisted and finally she answered "the vagina," but there was no conviction in her voice. She still maintained that the blood came from mother's knee. Later she wanted mother in the playroom and immediately asked her about holding her knee up and why she had screamed at her. This gave Mrs. L. an opportunity to tell Linda explicitly that she had not been angry but merely upset and frightened herself, so that she only sounded angry.

Despite my persistent efforts to correct Linda's ideas about the source of the blood, which I felt she would need in order to grasp what she had actually witnessed, she appeared to adhere stubbornly to her theory which displaced the origin of the blood from the genitals to the knee. Even mother's support in this matter was to no avail, though there may have been some clarification and resolution regarding mother being angry at her. It should be noted that *pari passu* Linda's masturbation had come up in the treatment and being bad and feeling guilty had been discussed with her at length (see below). Linda's insistence that the blood came from anywhere but the vagina therefore seemed to have to do with her unconscious fear of damage through masturbation. This would be the underlying purpose of the defensive displacements.

However, it was right after the seemingly frustrating attempts to

---

service of maintaining a defense. See Freud (1937b). It also seems likely that right after the stillbirth itself Linda might actually have seen blood on her mother's knee which had run down her leg and dried.

educate Linda about vaginal birth that new material emerged in which the birth process itself was vividly dramatized via a repetitive play sequence.[4] Linda used as a main prop a wicker wastebasket from the playroom. She sat on it, hopped in and out of it. The first time she did this, she was telling me how mommy had told her about being cut open in the vagina—that even though it is a small hole, the vagina can stretch and the baby can get out. She referred to the basket variously as a "pee-pee" or a vagina, and showed a great deal of glee in this play. When she got stuck sitting in the basket, I helped her out, saying, "Now you're ready to be born." At this she laughed. She got her mother to "deliver" her from the basket and also tried to crawl under the mother's skirt to reenact the birth more realistically. But she also frequently squatted over the basket making toilet sounds. She never seemed to tire of this game. (Linda also played hide-and-seek in the closet, and then she would climb into the basket to be "born.") Linda was told how she must have understood that having babies was like having a "duty" come, although the baby comes out of a different hole—the vagina. She quickly followed this comment with the remark, "And the duty comes out behind that."

In one of the "deliveries," Linda suddenly shouted that the baby was dead. I was told to pretend to be asleep. From this we again reenacted the stillbirth. Linda was the doctor and I was Linda. I told her that I was frightened and asked if she was angry with me. She said, no, and I answered, "But you screamed at me. What did I do wrong?" Linda answered, "Are you guilty? Are you in jail? You're in jail." When we repeated this again, I was told in grownup tones by Linda (who was now acting the part of the mother), "No, darling, I'm not angry with you." At this point I offered the interpretation that she might not have wanted the baby and when it died she must have felt somehow that it was her fault. She interrupted me several times, asking to go home and asking what time it was.

Although the possibility of her having death wishes about the baby was approached several times, in connection with the basket

---

[4] This would be analogous to the appearance of new material following a correct interpretation.

play, no direct confirmation was ever obtained that she had such thoughts on a conscious level. Linda consented to deal with this only in the role of the mother—reassuring me (teasingly at times) when I expressed concern whether mother would love me as much as the new baby. Mrs. L. also indicated that she could remember no expression by Linda of any ambivalence toward the anticipated baby. Nonetheless, Linda was told by both her mother and me how natural and understandable such feelings were in little girls expecting a baby brother or sister.

By means of the highly excited play with the basket, Linda must have been achieving some mastery. She appeared to be working through some of her confusion about the vagina being cut or just stretched to permit the baby to emerge. Another element involved in this play was her feeling that mother was angry with her when she shouted for her to leave the room. Reenacting this scene in different ways enabled the reconstruction process to be furthered. It was noted that in her play as mother, she tried to undo the fear and guilt stirred up by having the mother tell the little girl very sweetly that she wasn't angry at her.

The great glee which accompanied this basket play in its endless repetition seemed to indicate that some disentanglement of the anxiety and conflict about birth had been achieved in the preceding hours. Previously her ideas about the birth process had been permitted expression only through the morbid "dead baby" game and through identification with her mother in the groaning and in the abdominal pain. Now Linda was able to play with pleasure even though she was dealing with previously very threatening ideas.

MASTURBATION

From her behavior in the second interview it was apparent that Linda's curiosity was aroused as to how the baby got out and where mother was cut, but it also became apparent that in her efforts to figure out what had happened more than curiosity was involved. One day early in treatment Mrs. L. had to rush a neighbor to the emergency ward because she had burned her hand. Linda was brought along because she absolutely insisted; while there she commented on the stretchers in the hall. I learned that following this, Linda several times asked her mother if Mrs. L. would like to burn her hand on the stove. Then Linda could go along and see what they did in the hospital. Subsequently this theme also emerged in the playroom. I had asked if mother had waved good-bye when she went off on the stretcher. Linda replied, "No, she couldn't because she burned her hand!"

From other material it was possible to connect the burned hand not only with mother's hospitalization but also with Linda's urethritis. The evidence pointed to the intrusion of Linda's masturbatory conflicts and guilt. One could suspect that the cause of the urethritis, which Linda developed during the latter part of mother's pregnancy, was the child's masturbation. It was highly likely that any sexual conflicts surrounding masturbation would become entangled with Linda's reaction to mother's pregnancy and particularly the stillbirth.

But it was not until the 16th session that the subject of urethritis was introduced. Linda had just been to the doctor. In her description of her condition, she had indicated that she did have "wee-wee" trouble and that mommy used to put powder on her vagina and wash it with a warm, wet rag (to remove the crusting). She readily admitted that it felt good. This piece of information made intelligible the material of the three or four preceding sessions. Linda had begun to use the baby powder I had provided and was mixing it with water, acting very silly and giggly. It is important to note that the same baby powder was used for the treatment of the urethritis and the attempt to sop up the blood from the stillbirth. Mrs. L. informed me that there was still powder in the house when she returned from the hospital.

I further learned that on the day the powder play first made its appearance, Linda had a discussion with her mother on the meaning of the word "guilty." That morning before her session she had been watching a TV drama in which someone had to go to jail. She wanted to know why and also asked who had to go to jail. She queried her mother whether only men did this or whether ladies had to go too.

Any doubt that feelings of guilt were involved in her masturbation was dispelled after the following sequence in the playroom. Linda commented that Jeffrey, a friend, had been told by his mother not to suck his thumb because it was dirty. Linda herself always made a point of washing her thumb before sucking it in the playroom. I asked her if she had ever been told to do this. Linda's mother interrupted at this point saying that she had told Linda about not touching her vagina with dirty hands.[5] She explained that she had done this because of her fear of Linda reinfecting herself. I asked Linda what this meant. In an exasperated voice she exclaimed, "That's what I don't know!" She was then told how girls often do this because it feels good, but then they are all confused and worried. She put powder on the doll at this point, saying, "I have to put it on the tussy because it's red." Why was it red? "Because she touched it." I replied that this was what mother had done for her when her wee-wee hurt her. I asked, "Why was her wee-wee red?" Linda replied, "Because she's hurt. Because she had guilt. She shouldn't touch it."

This material permitted the reconstruction that Linda had misperceived her own urethritis as punishment for masturbation. The "burning" of excitement led to touching, which made the genitals "burn" and turn red. This fantasy concerning masturbatory guilt was Linda's main fund of knowledge, which was then brought to bear on her understanding of mother's hospitalization. Mother could not wave good-bye because she burned her hand. Just as the "burning genital" was red, so was all the blood she saw that morning; and the same powder was used to get rid of both her redness and mother's red blood. Therefore, in Linda's mind, mother had to go to the hospital because she had touched her genitals and made them burn and become red.

This sequence illustrates exquisitely how the meaning ascribed to an event cannot transcend the child's own experience and understanding, and how the end result is circumscribed by any conflictual material with which it can be contaminated. Freud (1937a) spoke of "after-repression" as the mechanism by which events and impressions become drawn into the unconscious when any connections can be made with the material already repressed. Linda seems to have been in the process of interpreting illness and hospitaliza-

---

[5] Here is an example of the way in which the mother's presence in the playroom facilitated the treatment.

tion as a punishment for masturbation. An adult, with access to more realistic information, would have been in a better position to counter the intrusion of such irrational ideas associated with an unconscious conflict. Linda's ego by virtue of its immaturity was more vulnerable, and one ingredient of that immaturity is simply ignorance.

This vignette about germs and masturbation also underscores one of the advantages of having the mother in the playroom with the preschool youngster. Her confirmation of interpretations lends the stamp of approval—if mommy says it, it must be so. Following this obvious revelation of her guilt about urethritis because of her masturbation, I discussed with the mother how parents often make such a fuss about germs. She readily agreed and went on to indicate to Linda, who was listening avidly, that she now realized how she must have made Linda afraid with all that talk about germs. I pointed out how it felt good to touch, but on the other hand there was the wee-wee trouble due to germs. We all agreed that we were glad that the pills Linda took had made her wee-wee trouble all better. (I was also glad, because just prior to starting treatment, the pediatrician had begun to feel that a catheterized specimen for culture and sensitivity might be necessary. Because of the psychological situation, he agreed to hold off and in the next week or so the urine was negative for pus.)

CONCEPTION

In the 19th hour, Linda was playing at having a baby in the wastebasket. She made toilet noises over the basket. Placing a plastic watering can with a long spout between her legs, she crouched over the basket as if she were urinating. She called the watering can "beesting." Mrs. L. interjected that last summer Linda had been stung on the foot by a bee. Several sessions later while Linda was again engaged in playing at having a baby, she bit me playfully on the shoulder. Asked where else she would like to bite me, she quickly answered, "the belly button," and then added, "the tussy." At this she giggled, rushed away, and changed the subject.

In addition to rectifying distortions and reconstructing the traumatic situation of the stillbirth, I also found it necessary to educate Linda about the facts of life. Her ideas of the birth process, masturbation, anatomical differences between the sexes had all been drawn together in a tangled web around the traumatic event. This little 4½-year-old was faced with the task of mastering a gruesome experience when she was not yet in possession of the facts needed to understand, let alone assimilate it.

A few sessions later an opportunity arose to ask her if she had wondered what a daddy was for. She was playing with the powder and I wondered out loud if she had not thought that daddy might have cut mommy open in the vagina when the baby came and that that was the reason for all the blood. She got on the mother's lap obviously disturbed and wanting to go home. She began picking on a mosquito bite she saw on her mother's chest. She called it a "boo-boo." When her picking made it bleed, she said that the "boo-boo" was pregnant! She claimed to be able to see the baby inside the boo-boo. While not exactly confirming my interpretation, Linda was certainly giving evidence that becoming pregnant involved some kind of attack which hurt, swelled up, and led to blood. (In the very first session she had asked if I gave needles.)

I returned to the subject several sessions later, telling her I thought she must wonder how the babies get into the mommy's tummy. Both mother and I then talked to her about her play during the previous session when she had said that the "boo-boo" was pregnant. We pointed out that the swelling had come from the bite of a mosquito and reminded her that she had called the watering can a "beesting." She denied all this, calling the watering can at this time a "beehive." She began to crawl on all fours pretending that she was a baby that could not talk. When this was interpreted as due to her fear of what we were talking about, she took a gun and shot us both. Asked if it was a water gun she said, "Yes." Mother and I then talked how little boys were born with watering guns.

Following this rather unsatisfactory session, Linda's mother reported a discussion about a swordfish they had seen at the shore. Linda had initiated it and told her mother in a very animated way that it could "stab you right here," pointing to her abdomen.

In the next session (29) while playing with a watering can, Linda admitted wishing she had a penis and ended the hour putting cars through a narrow aperture she constructed out of blocks. As she did this she was overheard whispering softly to herself, "Penis, penis, penis." Evidently, in trying to approach the role of the penis in intercourse, we had succeeded in stirring up her penis envy. Despite Mrs. L.'s assertion that Linda had never been told about intercourse, it was quite clear from her play that she did have some fantasies about the sadistic role of the penis (water gun, watering can—beesting, swordfish). In retrospect, it would no doubt have been better not to try first to draw Linda out so much as to her own fantasies, but to have supplied her sooner with the appropriate information about the role of the penis in conception.

Linda was finally told about intercourse and conception. This was done right after she was able to verbalize again, as in the second session, her own fantasy that perhaps the doctor cuts the mother open and puts the baby in. She was very resistive, with the predominant defense of regression to baby talk, crawling, etc. Simultaneously, however, some difficulties in going to sleep cleared up. After the 31st session in which Linda was told about the penis, I made the following notation in my records:

> The material on intercourse had been pushed beyond what Linda
> is interested in at this point—but the information has been given
> which she will perhaps digest in time. Perhaps it is best to sit back
> now and see what develops.

ON THE MEANING OF SEPARATION

Caution must be exercised in applying the term separation anxiety to any reaction to an object loss. This term should be restricted to refer to problems which reflect pathology in the mother-child dyad during the separation-individuation phase. Linda's response to her mother's hospitalization did not seem to be on this primitive level with feelings of abandonment, etc. True, there was in the history a tendency to clingingness to the mother; e.g., her initial difficulty in separating at nursery school at age 3. Furthermore, a tendency to regression, playing the baby, was part of her defensive repertoire which perhaps facilitated the "dead baby" game after the stillbirth. Despite these potential preoedipal weak spots, Linda's reaction to the hospitalization occurred in terms of phallic interest. She was intensely curious about what was done to mother in the hospital. Curiosity was involved in her reactions to mother's shouting at her to get out of the room: she felt frustrated in her desire to see what happened rather than abandoned by her mother.[6] Her first "secrets" were "How does the baby get out?" and "I saw the blood." What seemed to be of imminent pathological importance about the hospitalization was that Linda interpreted mother's need to go as a punishment for masturbation, i.e., a projection of her own current masturbatory conflicts exacerbated by the urethritis.

Likewise, the material just prior to the August vacation break was strongly oedipal, with fantasies and songs of marrying me and having a baby; simultaneously she talked about mother being at the hospital and wondered what happened to her there.[7] Linda was clearly an oedipal child at the time she was seen. The last few days prior to vacation brought forth an aloofness toward me which mirrored the apparent current disinterest in her father at home. Thus, in the transference she was repeating intense interest and then defending against it by a façade of indifference.

TERMINATION

After a month's interruption due to vacation, Linda was seen for 9 visits in early September; we stopped just prior to her entering kindergarten. On the first visit she was effusive, jumped on me, and said she just wanted to "hug, and hug and hug."

---

[6] After the first follow-up visit 18 months later Linda was asked by her mother what she had done in the playroom. "You couldn't see. The door was closed," was her reply. Was Linda taking revenge on mother for sending her back to her room, frustrating her wish to know what was happening that fateful morning?

[7] Two such songs illustrating these themes are as follows:

> Dr. Shapiro I'm going to marry you
> Dr. Shapiro I'm going to marry you
> And I'm going to have a baby for my very own
> And it'll be alive—right?

> One time mommy is going to have a baby, one time
> You won't see. [Again the frustrated curiosity.]
> She'll be living, she'll be living
> You'll have the baby one day today
> You'll have the baby to the stars.

She played briefly with the wastebasket and then had to urinate. On her return I had just offered Mrs. L. a lemon drop. Linda refused at first. Her thoughts were hard to follow and she spoke of candy as "smear" and "real candy was—," and she pointed to her mouth. She abruptly asked where the milk was, answering herself by pointing to her breasts and then her genitals. She kept insisting that they were not lemon drops. The meaning of these rather confusing comments seemed to come in the next session. She was snuggling against me and sucking her thumb. Noting the hair in my nose Linda commented that her daddy had more hair, more on his stomach, and he was much bigger. She then asked for the watering can and drank out of it; she took the doll's pants off and wiped the genitals and then tried to put the pants on me. She tried to diaper the baby and asked if I wanted her to stick me with the pin. Staying with the theme that had seemed to bother her prior to vacation, I suggested that she was worried about the penis fitting into the little hole of the vagina. She said she was not thinking about this and told me: "You talk too much." But suddenly she asked mother if she was pregnant. I persisted how it must seem that the vagina is so small, but assured her that it would grow as she grows up to be a big girl. She replied rather tartly that it was not smaller than her mouth, repeating what she had said when the subject of vaginal intercourse was first introduced.

In retrospect, these interventions seem embarrassingly wide off the mark. Linda was clearly acting out an oral pregnancy fantasy. Therefore, she did not seem to be amenable at this point to discuss problems directly related to her genitals. In the last hour before terminating, there was no mistaking the oral wish for a child. She reported that she had two eggs for breakfast. Daddy's egg was put in the ashtray.[8] She reported thinking about "cutting" and then

---

[8] In reconstructing the stillbirth Linda had described how an ashtray had been used to clean up the blood. In this fantasy an ashtray is once again connected with the birth process gone amiss. Father's egg was not eaten but ended up in the ashtray. The capacity for this image to survive and be recalled as one of the few memories of the event 10 years later speaks for its importance as a symbol in Linda's unconscious. The suitability of an ashtray to become the focus of important ideas related to the stillbirth may be explained by the following speculations. By virtue of its being part of an actual memory related to the blood it is inherently

asked me to "make a baby." This was on the surface a reference to our practice of drawing on the blackboard. She acknowledged that it was her baby and the father was "daddy." I then discussed with her how much she must love her father and how little girls have these wishes, so that they cannot wait to be grown up. She averred that she would get married and have lots of babies. She grew restless, however, and began wandering around the room. Finally, she said she wanted to ask her mother something. I said, "You mean, you want to check if she's still there." She agreed and peeked several times into the waiting room. Feeling that her frank admission of her oedipal wishes had stirred up some guilt about her mother, I ventured to speak to Linda about this. I told her that there seemed to be two Linda's; one wanted a baby from father and wanted to have him all to herself; the other Linda loved mommy and wanted to be with her all the time. With some feeling she responded, "But I love them both!" I pushed further and likened this to how she must have felt when mother was away in the hospital and she was home with daddy; she then elaborated the fantasy of mother going first to the supermarket and then to the hospital. Through this fantasy she made oral restitution to the mother, equating food with the lost child. (This recalls her play in the very first session where each animal and the mother were supplied with a baby.) I reassured Linda that her mother surely would not mind her having these thoughts about daddy. There seemed no doubt now that Linda had firmly in her mind that she had to have a father to have a baby, even though the fantasy was being expressed in oral terms.

FOLLOW-UP

Only 2 months after termination Mrs. L. had to be hospitalized again for a week. There was no time to prepare Linda, who, in addition, had to go to stay with Mrs. L.'s sister in another city.

---

part of the traumatic event. In addition, through association with the idea of burning, it is connected with Linda's urethritis and masturbation conflicts in the same manner as the neighbor's burned hand. The ashtray would thus appear to symbolize the damaged female genital incapable of having a child because it had burned (i.e., because of masturbation).

There appeared to be no difficulty and the mother spoke to Linda on the phone every day. There was no problem upon mother's return and a few weeks later Linda wanted to go back to her aunt's for another visit.

Eighteen months later Linda was seen for one visit on my request. She appeared amnesic for her original reasons for seeing me. I reminded her about the baby, and she then spontaneously told me what had happened.

> There was a lot of blood in the hall. The baby died and mother went to the hospital. Grandmother came and cleaned up the blood. She stayed there while mother was away.

Linda denied any worries about it; nor did she remember discussing any of the questions she had had. She remembered that I used to write on the blackboard, but then she changed it, saying that she was the one who wrote her name on the blackboard. This seemed to be a reference to school and a wish to impress me with her progress. Then followed a stream of thoughts about pets that were given away or were pregnant, neighbors who had been pregnant and how many children they have. She also spoke of wanting a baby and announced that she was going to marry a boy in her class and would be Mrs. Z., the boy's last name. I took this as a sign of progression in displacing her oedipal wishes; that is, she was beginning to accept substitutes for father.

I reminded Linda of the question she used to have about how the baby gets out. She could not remember. But her next thought was of swallowing a penny. She had to go to the hospital and take some bitter medicine, revealing again the prevalent oral theme.

A letter from Mrs. L. about this visit revealed great anticipation about playing with my toys. But Linda insisted to mother that the doll she had painted red had been given to her by me. Mrs. L. also wrote that one day she caught herself telling Linda to wash her hands before sucking her thumb. She then reminded Linda that Dr. Shapiro used to say that mothers worry too much about that. Linda denied any memory of this. She then told mother that I was a trouble doctor. She recalled she had talked about where the baby came from and all the blood.

More important, word was received 3 months later that Linda's mother had to be hospitalized again, this time for acute appendicitis. She took Linda to school, went to the doctor, and from there had to go directly to the hospital. Her father explained to Linda about the operation, but the child was already familiar with it because one of her favorite books since she was 3 was the Bemelman story of Madeleine, the little girl who has to have her appendix out in the middle of the night. Linda had no apparent difficulty, keeping to her usual routine in school and going to her dancing and swimming lessons. She spent one weekend with an aunt and wanted to go back there the next weekend, even though her mother had just come home. Her main interest was in seeing the scar and showing it to her friends.

I was at first discouraged that there was so much amnesia for the concerns which had occupied Linda 8 to 9 months earlier. Yet her psychosexual development had evidently progressed, and the wish for a baby was still there. What was missing were the kinds of concerns which the pregnancy and then the stillbirth had stirred up; namely, damaging her genitals through masturbation and the urethritis, anxiety as to how the baby gets out, and confusion about what happens to cause all the blood. If these ideas and all the attendant sadistic fantasies had become nodal points for fixation, one would expect some signs of perseveration and preoccupation with derivatives of attack, etc. On the other hand, Linda's amnesia was itself developmentally appropriate, for successful repression leaves no trace. Only when there is unresolved conflict does the repression barrier give way requiring new efforts by the ego to bring about compromise formations with the repressed. From the evidence of a 1½-year follow-up which included two emergency hospitalizations of the mother, it would seem that the effects of the trauma had been nullified. Linda was doing very well in school. There was no sleep disturbance or continuation or eruption of the kinds of symptoms she had shown immediately following the trauma. However, her preference for playing the baby did persist, and she was still a thumb sucker, both elements of her personality which were well established prior to the trauma.

A further follow-up was arranged, this time 10 years later. Linda, now an attractive 15-year-old high school sophomore, came on her own to my office. She indicated that she remembered an ashtray full of blood, going to mother's room and being told to get out. She recalled going back to her room and closing the door. Linda told me that mother had had many hospitalizations in the intervening years mostly in connection with exacerbation of her ulcerative colitis.

She recalled a few dreams. In a recent one a roach and a spider came out of her school locker. She was afraid of all insects. From childhood she recalled two dreams: (1) Mother forgets to put her to bed and she is sitting on the floor. (2) Mother is on a stretcher. She was not sure whether these were dreams or daydreams.

In view of the extent to which role reversal and dramatization was used in her treatment it was interesting to learn that Linda's main interest has been drama. She has taken acting lessons, appeared in children's theater, and participates in the school drama club.

Linda's parents consider her to be a normal adolescent, somewhat rebellious and antagonistic to authority, especially to her mother. She can be quite outspoken in her criticism of her mother or mother's friends, but the relationship with father is good. Linda has gone to overnight camp since she was 10.

As far as could be ascertained, Linda's development seems to have proceeded along usual lines showing no evidence of interference traceable to the traumatic event when she was 4½. This meager information concerning Linda's adolescence was tantalizing because of possible connections with and implications regarding the unconscious effects of the stillbirth 10 years earlier. For example, in view of the importance played by blood, how did Linda react to her menarche? Did her fear of insects represent a residue of the beesting which played a pivotal role in her ideas about impregnation? The answers to these and other questions must unfortunately remain beyond reach. For Linda consented reluctantly to come only for one visit. She was quite guarded, as if not sure of my motives, treating me with the same reserve and suspicion which most young adolescents display in consultation. This comprised a barrier to any efforts to probe about her current emotional life. She focused her comments mostly on the "safe area" of what she remembered of the stillbirth. She had no recollections, whatever, of her treatment.

DISCUSSION

The presentation of the rich material provided by this young patient required some screening and organizing under the rubric of central themes. While this may have given the appearance of a therapy characterized by orderly clearly demarcated sequences, it must be recognized that this was in large part an artifact necessary for the purposes of clarity and communication. If the material were presented adhering to a chronological sequence alone, the reader would soon be inundated with the complexities even in this relatively brief therapy. In addition, in a single hour there would be overlapping references to various themes. For example, the very first time that Linda began the reenactment of the birth, using the wastebasket, she also patted the crotch of the baby doll and admitted that the baby liked to be touched there a lot; in addition, this was the same hour she referred to a watering can between her legs as a "beesting."

In retrospect, a general trend might be discerned; but here too, the influence of my interventions in creating this trend cannot be discounted. First, there was the concern about Linda seeing so much blood. Then, when this was sufficiently clarified and the traumatic effect reduced, further questions and problems about sex began to emerge.

In approaching this material, I tried to focus on areas where sexual conflicts and/or misinformation could be seen directly intertwined with the traumatic event. My aim was to disentangle ongoing developmental processes from the disrupting effect of the trauma. I originally made the assumption that the material to be dealt with would consist of fresh impressions which would essentially be conscious and available. I expected not to have to deal with the unconscious as such, and therefore saw my treatment as being extraterritorial to the domain of child analysis. However, it proved impossible to accomplish my task without operating within a psychoanalytic paradigm. For only by avoiding content altogether, as Levy (1939) recommended in his "release therapy," could one avoid dealing with derivatives of the unconscious as they emerged. To mitigate the effects of internal conflicts they must be delineated and understood.

Indeed, it is only because of the attachment which develops between ongoing conscious and unconscious processes and the impressions created by the disrupting episode that the event acquires its pathogenic (i.e., traumatic) importance. Otherwise, whatever the child (or adult) experiences is transiently frightening, shocking, stirring, exciting, etc., but not traumatic. For example, two young children see a horror movie; both scream and are frightened by the ghoulish events of the film, which is designed exactly for that purpose. One child develops a sleep disturbance which persists for several weeks and becomes frightened to go into a darkened room. He refuses to watch any more such films and will not even listen to any talk about ghosts, mummies, or monsters. The other child may have trouble going to sleep that night, but there are no other sequelae. He is eager for the next monster film to be offered. Descriptively, the first child has been traumatized by his experience; the second one has not.

Dynamically, this would mean that the content of the horror film had become the vehicle for the expression of the first child's own unconscious sadistic fantasies.[9] Thus provided with a pathway for externalization, the unconscious drives connected with the fantasy can achieve some discharge. It is also the means by which an internal danger situation becomes converted to an external danger which can then be avoided as in the phobias.

After a link between internal developmental conflicts and external event has been established, the traumatic effect of the event is further enhanced by the child's being compelled to form and retain an erroneous view of reality. The understanding of an external event, be it stillbirth or horror film, has thus been subverted to serve the purposes of the Dybbuk of the unconscious and its aims.[10] A young child, such as Linda, lacking in the basic

[9] Horror tales often deal with the mind of an innocent victim being taken over by an alien force, converting him to an evil person despite himself. It is interesting to note how this process, attributed to the actions of a vampire, Dybbuk, or creature from space, actually conforms to the psychoanalytic conception of the unconscious itself.

[10] In her discussion of Robertson's (1956) account of her child's hospitalization for a tonsillectomy, Anna Freud made similar comments concerning the pathway by which an external danger situation becomes transformed into a traumatic

information and experience to maintain reality, is much more vulnerable than the adult. This is one meaning of the statement that the ego in the young child is relatively weaker than the drives.

It was seen how several aspects of what Linda experienced appeared to have this traumatic potential. Two weeks after the event Linda's understanding of the stillbirth, including mother's hospitalization, was already becoming organized in terms of her own guilt about masturbation. The child's statement that mother could not wave good-bye because she burned her hand was one derivative which indicated how she had made the connection. Taken together with the other fantasy material about burning, touching, and punishment, the unconscious belief that mother had been hospitalized because she masturbated could be inferred. Even though no interpretation concerning this equation was given to Linda, it served as a guide for the direction of the therapeutic work. This method does not differ from our usual procedure of gradually building up our understanding of analytic patients in preparation for making an appropriate interpretation. It is applicable in the treatment of both child and adult, and would hold whether the interpretation is to be a reconstruction or the elucidation of a particular drive-defense complex manifested in current behavior.

Much of what Linda had to say about impregnation was expressed in oral terms. Her excitement when she talked about biting me on the belly button or tussy betrayed the erotic quality. Another time, after being told that the vagina is not too small for the penis even though it may seem that way, Linda commented that her mouth was not too small. Playing with the hypodermic syringe full of water, she enjoyed squirting it in her mouth. This interest in the oral would be expected from a little girl who was a finger sucker from infancy. But it seemed quite clear that Linda's conflicts and her main sexual interests were strongly phallic-oedipal. Her orality was a form of expression not a level of functioning to which she had regressed.

---

event. She noted that there was "a constant urge to distort and magnify external danger situations and use them as representations of internal threats." These external events remain manageable "unless they touch on and merge with id material which transforms them into experiences of being assaulted, emptied out, castrated or condemned" (p. 431).

In the approach to her masturbation, the interpretative work focused on Linda's conflict between the wish to touch her genitals and the fear of hurting herself because of germs, a conflict which was reinforced by her mother's prohibition. The struggle was thus between the id and the nascent superego, partially internalized, though still buttressed by mother's warnings. The analytic work consisted of delineating the conflict this created both intrapsychically and with mother; then, aided by the mother's recanting of her overstrict attitude about germs and touching, the harshness of the prohibition was mitigated. If masturbation no longer entailed the threat of punishment, then the stillbirth and hospitalization would lose their foothold in Linda's unconscious as a possible form of inevitable punishment. With this accomplished, the child could begin to understand what really had happened. Her resistance to doing this at first was shown by her insistence that the blood came, not from the vagina, but from the knee. That her anxiety concerned damage to the vagina was confirmed by the basket play which followed and which was a reenactment of the birth process.

In a similar way, the essentials of Linda's oedipus complex were delineated. Through her verbalizations and play she had made it abundantly clear that she wanted a baby from me and then from her father. In the approach to her wish for a child, emphasis was placed on the conflict with her feelings about her mother that this wish engendered. This was communicated to her in terms of there being two Lindas: one, wanting a baby from father and having him to herself; the other, loving mommy and wanting to be with her all the time. Linda's understanding of this dilemma was graphically revealed by her plaintive response, "But I love them both." No claim can be made that this bit of analysis resolved Linda's oedipal conflicts. It was not intended to do so. Rather, it was of greater concern to maintain Linda's development at a phase-appropriate level, thus safeguarding her continued development toward a feminine identity by helping her resolve her ambivalence to her mother.

Linda's identification with her mother, a normal progressive step for the oedipal girl toward the achievement of a stable sexual identification, was placed in peril by the trauma. For it appeared from her response to the stillbirth that she felt she either could be a baby or become like mother with pain, blood, and suffering. This idea would receive further reinforcement from Linda's previous exposure to her mother's bloody diarrhea during colitis attacks. Linda had to be helped to continue to grow up (give up infantile wishes) and accept her femininity. The awesome difficulties that being a woman seemed to require would no longer have any hold on her, once Linda was able to understand accurately what the stillbirth was all about. She could then proceed to form a viable feminine identity. Otherwise, there was the distinct danger that in response to the trauma, Linda would have evolved a pathological "solution" by a regression and a fixation at the preoedipal level of being mother's little baby. Premonitions of this eventuality could be seen from the outset in Linda's initial reaction such as the "dead baby" play, and, during the therapy, when she would regress to crawling on all fours and drooling in response to anxiety situations.

Essentially, the backbone of the treatment with Linda was the analytic reconstruction of how she had perceived and experienced the traumatic episode. The stillbirth was traumatic since it had placed in jeopardy the crucial developmental task of achieving gender identity by appearing to give external reality confirmation to sadomasochistic trends and to Linda's guilt over masturbation. It became clear that the obstacles to her understanding of the event stemmed on the one hand from lack of factual knowledge, which then facilitated the intrusion of masturbatory conflicts and sadistically tinged fantasies about procreation and birth. These were responsible for persistent distortions and misinterpretations of what she had seen. Only analytic work on these conflicts could free this child's cognitive and perceptual faculties from interference. Without treatment her psychosexual development would no doubt have been marred by serious fixations and distortions. The reconstruction foundered momentarily on her refusal to accept the vagina as the source of the blood. The anxiety about vaginal birth was then worked through in the repetitive basket play. Further clarification was then accomplished with regard to both her masturbation concerns and her confused but sadistic ideas about procreation. In addition to analytic work on conflicts stirred up by the stillbirth, Linda had to be supplied with correct sexual information to help reduce her vulnerability to the continued pressure of sadistic fantasies which interfered with her perception of reality. This interference actually comprised a further pathological aspect of the trauma, in addition to the exacerbation of developmental conflicts due to the breech of the "stimulus barrier."

This treatment then represents a fragment of a child analysis. It was incomplete, to be sure, but so are all analyses in some respect or another. What is of importance is that conflicts which periled development were modified so that the child could continue her personality growth, despite the intrusion of fate in the form of the tragic stillbirth.

SUMMARY

An account of the treatment of a 4½-year-old girl has been presented. The goal of therapy was to prevent the traumatic effects of having witnessed a stillbirth at home. The rationale for a prompt brief psychoanalytic treatment prior to the resolution of the child's oedipal phase was discussed. The methodology of such an approach relied upon analytic insights into the developmental process. The necessity for close cooperation and involvement of the mother of the preschool child in the treatment process was amply corroborated.

The technique aimed at fostering verbalization and identification of affects to facilitate ego mastery over the traumatic events. The traumatic episode was reconstructed and connections between masturbation guilt and hospitalization were disrupted. Sexual information was given about the birth process and procreation to help Linda assimilate appropriately what she had seen. Through the dual approach of rectifying distortions demanded by her unconscious (analysis), and supplying appropriate information (education), Linda's ego was strengthened.

The apparent successful outcome, as seen in a 10-year follow-up, encourages the use of such an approach as an example of an abbreviated psychoanalytic therapy suitable for use in preventing the effects of trauma on the developing personality.

BIBLIOGRAPHY

BORNSTEIN, B. (1935), Phobia in a Two-and-a-Half-Year-Old Child. *Psychoanal. Quart.*, 4:93–119.

BORNSTEIN, S. (1935), A Child Analysis. *Psychoanal. Quart.*, 4:190–225.

FREUD, A. (1945), Indications for Child Analysis. *This Annual*, 1:127–149.

——— (1963), The Concept of Developmental Lines. *This Annual*, 18:245–265.

——— (1965), *Normality and Pathology in Childhood*. New York: International Universities Press.

FREUD, S. (1937a) Analysis Terminable and Interminable. *Standard Edition*, 23:209–253. London: Hogarth Press, 1964.

——— (1937b), Constructions in Analysis. *Standard Edition*, 23:255–269. London: Hogarth Press, 1964.

HARTMANN, H. (1951), Technical Implications of Ego Psychology. In: *Essays on Ego Psychology*. New York: International Universities Press, 1964, pp. 142–154.

KAPLAN, E. B. (1962), Panel Report: Classical Forms of Neurosis in Infancy and Early Childhood. *J. Amer. Psychoanal. Assn.*, 10:571–578.

KATAN, A. (1961), Some Thoughts About the Role of Verbalization in Early Childhood. *This Annual*, 16: 184–188.

KOLANSKY, H. (1960), Treatment of a Three-Year-Old Girl's Severe Infantile Neurosis. *This Annual*, 15:261–285.

——— (1967), Some Psychoanalytic Considerations on Speech in Normal Development and Psychopathology. *This Annual*, 22:274–295.

LEVY, D. M. (1939) Trends in Therapy: III Release Therapy. *Amer. J. Orthopsychiat.*, 9:713–736.

NAGERA, H. (1966), *Early Childhood Disturbances, the Infantile Neurosis, and the Adulthood Disturbances*. New York: International Universities Press, p. 57.

ROBERTSON, J. (1956), A Mother's Observations on the Tonsillectomy of Her 4-Year-Old Daughter. With Comments by Anna Freud. *This Annual*, 11:410–433.

SCHWARZ, H. (1950), The Mother in the Consulting Room. *This Annual*, 5:343–357.

WAELDER, R. (1951), The Structure of Paranoid Ideas. *Int. J. Psycho-Anal.*, 32:167–177.

Ego Strengthening Prior to Analysis

ANNEMARIE P. WEIL, M.D.

WE GENERALLY ENCOUNTER FEW DIFFICULTIES IN DECIDING WHETHER analysis is indicated or contraindicated when we see children who have clearly circumscribed neurotic or psychotic symptomatology. But many children about whom we are consulted today do not fall in these clearly defined categories. Rather, we see increasingly large numbers of disturbances that do not lend themselves to such simple classifications. We find a whole spectrum, at one end of which are children who have a clear-cut neurotic disorder and whose basic ego development is age-adequate, even though it shows some inhibitions and distortions brought about by their neuroses. At the other end are children with *basic* disturbances of ego development that are not the result of neurotic conflicts. On the contrary, the deficient ego development may even have precluded neurotic symptom formation. Most of the children who come to our offices, however, are somewhere between these end points of the spectrum.

This spectrum represents the various degrees of basic structuralization of the ego, ranging from balance and minor variations to gross defects and imbalances. Usually, however, the ego defects are amalgamated with some neurotic or preneurotic symptomatology.

The group of children I wish to focus on belong in the middle of

Read at the Panel on "Indications and Contra-Indications for Child Analysis," Fall Meeting of the American Psychoanalytic Association, December, 1972.

Faculty, New York Psychoanalytic Institute; Senior Psychiatrist, Child Development Center.

the spectrum. In this paper I shall further limit myself to young, essentially prelatency children. I shall single out those considerations that have a direct bearing on our diagnostic thinking and recommendations.

The difficulties of arriving at a diagnosis are also reflected by the fact that we have a number of different labels for these disturbances: ego deficient, ego disturbed, deviational, and borderline. Many of us feel that some of these children are analyzable. It is my opinion, however, that with some of these children we should not frame the question in terms of whether or not they are analyzable, but rather ask: *when* is such a child ready for an analysis that does not require the introduction of many parameters? We may find that *initially* some of these children will derive great benefit from other procedures—e.g., mother guidance, therapeutic education—that are more commensurate with their predominant disturbances at the time.

It may help our diagnostic thinking and therapy planning if we conceptualize their disturbances in metapsychological terms. The most prominent features are intersystemic and intrasystemic imbalances:

Imbalance between ego and drives;

Imbalance within the ego;

Imbalance between libido and aggression, with aggression prevailing;

Imbalance between nonhostile and hostile aggression.

As the word imbalance implies, these children show disturbances in the integrative function. Often this imbalance in its rudimentary form already is evident in infancy when sensitivity threshold and tension discharge or excitability and soothability are out of kilter, and when the ordinary devoted mother—and sometimes even the more than ordinarily devoted mother—cannot relieve her infant's tension. Hence an initial regulatory stability (Sander, 1962) between mother and infant cannot be achieved. The further vicissitudes of the mother-child interaction will then determine the extent and the quality of disturbance that arises from the initial vulnerability.

I want to expand on the specific imbalances outlined above.

Imbalance between ego and drives may be due either to variations in drive endowment and/or variations in the ego as was described by Alpert et al. (1956).

Imbalance within the ego covers a variety of manifestations. There may be a discrepancy between excellent autonomous ego apparatuses and the development of the ego as a structure with its various functions. For example, a child may show high intelligence, advanced motor skills, and highly sensitive perceptivity, in sharp contrast to unusual defects in basic structuralizations such as object relatedness, reality testing, acceptance of and adjustment to the reality principle. In some, different functions may have developed at very different rates. Or the defect may manifest itself primarily in the child's defense organization. He may lack age-adequate defenses or use certain age-appropriate defenses excessively or rely solely on one type of primitive defense.

With regard to object relatedness, these children often have remained in the various subphases of the separation-individuation process. This arrest may at the same time be associated with intense struggles with all types of anxieties. Possibly in connection with distress experienced as a result of their vulnerability in infancy, many of these children give clear signs of a predisposition to anxiety (Greenacre, 1941) and will to a considerable degree continue to experience the automatic anxiety of helplessness. In their case, the accumulation of early presignal anxiety experiences (Tolpin, 1971) has not led to the development of genuine signal anxiety. These children then are left with a chronic anxiety readiness, their ever-present fears attaching themselves sometimes directly to many different and constantly changing objects. While the choice of these "feared objects" may reflect the gradual progress in cognitive development and the acquisition of some symbolic thinking, the process by which these children's fears become attached to objects differs markedly from that in neurotic development. The "phobic object" of the neurotic child is the result of complicated conflict-associated processes, but the pathway via conflict is absent in these anxiety-ridden children.

With regard to the *libido-aggression balance*, we have become increasingly aware that in some children aggressive drive expressions outweigh the libidinal ones, often it seems from a very early age on. This happens when early tensions cannot be successfully relieved; hence, the first libidinal interaction with mother and the turning of libido to the outside world are interfered with.

In addition to the prevalence of aggression over libido, there is also a disturbance in the balance between *hostile and nonhostile aggression* (see Weil, 1970). Normally, as the child grows older, the usual phase-specific aspects of the aggressive drive become increasingly channelized and in this form contribute to his personality. In these disturbed children the negative aspects of the sequence often predominate over the positive, constructive, assertive ones. Negative moods, angry insistence, lurid fantasies, and hostile aggressiveness may prevail over constructive assertiveness, persistence, and mastery, i.e., over the neutralized manifestations of the aggressive drive.[1] This hostile aggression may be directed to both self and objects, and the degree of sadomasochistic tendencies that these children may develop will no doubt be codetermined by maternal handling.

Having outlined the nature of these basic defects and imbalances on which we should focus, I now want to emphasize the need to consider their causes: whether ego dysfunctions are secondary to neurotic symptomatology; whether they are a consequence of disturbing fantasies (anxieties, defenses) or whether they preceded, amalgamated with, or possibly even precluded neurotic development; and in which way the earliest and subsequent child-environment interaction has contributed to the defects.

Whenever we assess a child, we know that each facet of his functioning represents the end result of a complementary series of interactions, which are determined by the child's original makeup and by the mother's makeup. The mother's handling will influence the unfolding of the child's potentials in different areas of his functioning; yet, the way in which he responds will in turn evoke specific responses from the mother. Thus, each piece of behavior or specific trait reflects the history of innumerable and multifaceted interactions, with each characteristic in turn interacting with and organizing the other traits.

I want to suggest that we scrutinize and deduce as exactly as possible the different facets of imbalances and distorted develop-

---

[1] In psychotic children the balance is often even more disturbed.

ment in order to reach meaningful conclusions with regard to our therapeutic recommendations. I further want to suggest that we broaden our view and think not merely in terms of whether analysis is indicated or contraindicated, but consider which analytically informed method might be instituted at the outset. All disturbed children benefit from analytic understanding, but not all children benefit directly from analysis proper. The fact that we understand how a particular child's clinical picture has come about does not mean that we can relieve it by interpretation, especially since so many of these disturbances are so massively rooted in preverbal times.

I have seen many of these children in prelatency and early latency and have often been consulted after such children had had an unsuccessful analysis. On the basis of these experiences I have reached the conclusion that initially analysis is not indicated for many of these children. In the past such a statement has often meant that the idea of analysis is then completely abandoned. It is my belief, however, that appropriate educational-therapeutic methods will often help such children to achieve considerable ego consolidation and a better balance of internal forces. After such educational help child analysis may not only be possible but actually indicated and be carried out successfully.

It is of course true that such educational measures can be carried out within the frame of an "analysis," and we all know of treatments in which the first years were used predominantly for such educational help with a view toward furthering ego growth. To my mind, however, this procedure raises a number of questions.

Should such early educational activities really be carried out by the same person who later conducts the analysis proper? I believe they should not, because these nonanalytic interventions may later interfere with the analytic process and the development of the transference—especially if the child's mother was included in the educational work. On the other hand, such educational work may have little chance of succeeding if the mother is excluded to the point of being only an informant.

There is also a practical consideration. Such attempts at combining techniques seem to me to be doing analysis a disfavor because it leaves people in the child's environment with the impression that "analysis" has been extended over so many years.

Finally, we should ask whether an analyst who gives 50 minutes a day is really the best person to achieve the educational goals. For a variety of reasons I do not think so. I believe that a specially trained teacher working under the supervision of a child analyst is in a much better position to help such children because she can give more time than the analyst and make full use of her educational training. Moreover, working with young children, a teacher can go to the child's home, thereby directly including the mother, who in this way is given an opportunity to identify with the teacher.

Occasionally we also encounter highly motivated and modifiable mothers with whom we can work directly in mother guidance. Such mothers as well as such teachers will often enable a child to achieve the degree of ego consolidation which is necessary for an analysis. And then an analysis proper may indeed be indicated.

Having introduced a new dimension in our thinking about indications for both analysis and education, I return once more to the problem of assessing the special group of children I am concentrating on in this paper.

The single behavioral manifestations that these children present are neither novel nor very unusual. Rather, the clinical picture is determined by their intensity and timing, by the arrested, slowed, and uneven progression of various facets of ego development. And since, normally, the ego in the beginning grows via the mother, via the one-to-one relationship over long stretches of time, one can try with preanalytic help to induce this ego to grow, though somewhat belatedly, to catch up in some of its important functions, and to reach greater age- and phase-appropriateness.

By developmentally tracing back how and where interaction failed and by supplementing and reinforcing in this area of failure, we can often help the arrested development to a considerable degree.

The sources of interaction failures (Winnicott, 1958; James, 1962) are manifold. Minor innate, neurophysiological imbalances, which could possibly have been alleviated by especially empathic, skillful mothering, become aggravated when this mutual adaptation has not been achieved. On the other hand, neither the mother nor later the enlarged environment may have been able to reduce existing vulnerabilities.

One must not underrate the effect of the unusual, distorted feedback that parents of such children sometimes receive and which increases the maternal-parental task considerably. Referring to comments made earlier by Hartmann (1950) and Benjamin (1961) (that congenital equipment and innate differences may help determine experiences and self-experiences), Korner (1964) made the apt statement that "genetic differences in the biological sense may help create genetic differences in the psychoanalytic sense" (p. 59). The range of potential parental attitudes to a child is extensive and includes the unconscious ones. It is the infant himself who determines which ones will become operative, thereby creating the specific outcome.

A parent's inability to modify aspects of pathological functioning in the child may have different reasons. Some parents tolerate it, are unable to change it, are genuinely puzzled, and feel helpless about their so different child; others scotomatize and deny the disturbance; some aggravate it because of their own psychological problems or because they themselves suffer from biological-genetic disturbances in the same sphere as the child.

I have previously referred to the "multifaceted complementary series of interactions," on which I now wish to elaborate.

A somewhat less responsive infant may do poorly with a mother who has a similar makeup and who may be inclined to capitalize on his "independence." Yet the same infant will develop rather differently with a warm and empathic mother. On the other hand, an outward-directed infant may succeed in extracting more emotional supply even from the same unresponsive mother and induce her to some greater outgoingness. An originally neurophysiologically hypersensitive, tense, potentially anxious infant may nevertheless thrive when he has a mother who succeeds in cuing, in toning down tension, and generally creating a calm atmosphere. Such a mother will later introduce the child to empathically gauged small doses of anxiety-producing experiences. How different the development of the same infant would be with a mother who reacts with anxiety herself or one who creates panic by forcing anxiety-producing situations.

If a mother eventually succeeds in calming a tension-ridden infant, and if a fairly successful symbiotic period is associated with those important, initial fragmentary introjections, much is gained for the development of confidence, trust, a positive basic mood, self-esteem, and, I think, for fusion of drives, which then again may facilitate neutralization.

On the other hand, if a mother, because she is unpredictably available or ambivalent herself, does not succeed in calming such an infant, he will develop into a tense, demanding toddler who shows basic mistrust, is unwilling to renounce omnipotence, and who in the rapprochement phase will be dominated by the anger and negativism components of his ambivalence strivings. At that time it will be even harder for the mother—the environment—to remedy the situation.

As a matter of fact, much of the slowed progression of ego structuring that we see in children of all ages goes back to arrest in rapprochement difficulties. The child with the brittle basic core, who has not experienced a satisfactory symbiotic phase, does not weather well the rapprochement crisis, as Mahler (1971, 1972) has shown. At this time the demands of individuation-separation intertwine with symbolic representational thinking that gives rise to fantasies and conflicts. It is in this period that the original automatic anxiety of helplessness changes to signal anxiety. Moreover, during this period the basic anxieties of childhood coincide: fear of object loss becomes associated with fear of loss of love; and under the impact of further psychosexual development, toilet training, and of increased castration awareness, castration anxiety is added. For these reasons this is a particularly difficult period for the child with the brittle core. As Mahler elaborated, such a child who has faltered, is then trapped without a good internalized object. Not having experienced the state of well-being (Sandler and Joffe, 1965), he cannot strive for it again and he emerges with less trust and without a good, and often only with a markedly ambivalent, relationship to the object. In brief, he has not attained object constancy.

Subsequently, many of these children with inadequate progression (Weil, 1953) experience the phallic-oedipal phase in a distorted way. Their uncertain identity and their need for identification may create the impression that they have entered oedipal development when actually they are still engaged in yet another dyad. These children merely show "as if" oedipal tendencies, which, in some cases, are promoted by the parent's seductiveness. Hence, the real nucleus for neurotic conflicts of the oedipal phase may be missing or weak.

From the rapprochement period on, developmental lacks and lags become even more obvious and the environmental contribution to them even more distinct. The deficiencies are still preoedipal, many dating to preverbal times, and affecting primarily ego structuring. The resulting imbalances and ego defects relate to form—to attitudes and behavior rather than to content. They become part of a child's basic personality characteristics, although they also color his fantasies, especially since they seem to become more organized (Mahler, 1971).

For instance, we encounter the not well-related child who also is reality-estranged, and who also shows unfocused aggression, or who shows diffuse, ever-changing fearfulness. Again, whatever aspect is more in the foreground is partly dependent on the innate, neurophysiological equipment, the earliest interaction, the vicissitudes of individuation-separation, later genetically determined changes, and ongoing experiential factors. Some children can make the most of very little. Some children reach out and find resources with which to cope even with psychotic parents (Anthony, 1973). However, many a child's ego fails to grow with a mother who is unpredictably available and who creates a longing for something that is there sometimes and missing at other times. The children to whom I am here referring would have needed an especially well-related, empathically available, and predictable mother.

Yet, many such children for whom the early interactions went wrong and whose ego integration and consolidation did not proceed adequately can be helped. Provided their biological equipment permits it, they can be modified even after toddlerhood if belatedly they are offered the stable availability and the specific stimulation through which ego growth would have been fostered in the first place.[2]

---

[2] The tense, potentially angry toddler will develop differently if the mother, or someone else, can still remedy the situation with libidinal infusion (A. Freud, 1949,

Some modifications in the child's behavior may at times be facilitated by changes in the parents' attitudes. We have learned from the Yale study that parents react differently to their child in different stages of his development (Coleman et al., 1953). Some mothers who could not adapt to their child's special needs in infancy may still do so once he is a toddler, particularly when they are given help. If the mother cannot do it with some guidance, this is what a special teacher can do, and sometimes the mother herself can then change in identification with the teacher.

Teachers are of course especially trained in the area of developing autonomous skills, and they may be quite resourceful in other areas as well, e.g., in dealing with the pathological manifestations of the aggressive drive.

The child who is less inclined to externalize the aggressive drive, who is underimpulsive, underactive, has little zest, and often is only mildly related can be improved by someone who will invest him and his budding ego functions. This will help him to achieve pleasure in functioning and will stimulate him to turn toward objects, animate and inanimate. This type of child needs much educational therapeutic help.

We encounter pathology of the aggressive drive in other clinical pictures, not only in the group of children I am focusing on. Both types of children tend to channelize aggression into lurid aggressive fantasies by "introjection" (a kind of keeping in) and by projection. A very wild, unfocusedly aggressive little boy said: "Do insects kill, step him dead." All such children raise the issue whether they should first have a period of therapeutic education before analysis is indicated and the decision rests in part on the degree and nature of the pathology. Yet, unfocused, nonobject-directed aggression is, in my experience, more accessible to an initial period of therapeutic education than it is to analysis. It thus becomes a matter of timing when analysis is indicated.

The same considerations apply with respect to anxiety. The more

---

1951), by offering a good introject, by toning down his difficulty in delaying; by helping him relinquish omnipotence, by being available, unangrily limiting, distracting, avoiding targets of negativism and redirecting aggressive strivings into the growing autonomous skills toward mastery, hence, toward neutralization.

a child's anxiety is focused, the more conflict he experiences, the more symbolic displacement has led to organized symptomatology —in short, the more signs of structure formation he shows, the sooner I think of analysis. However, if a child's anxiety is diffuse, unfocused, and he also has poor object relationships, he will initially benefit more from a relationship to a teacher or from the educational influences of a therapeutic nursery school. I am thinking of the diffusely anxious child whose phobias persist beyond toddlerhood, whose fears are ever-present but continuously changing, one fear following the other in rapid sequence: e.g., the neighbor with a cast on his leg, the nun with the long robe, the child with a Band-Aid, etc. In these children the anxiety is attached directly to something that arouses their castration anxiety. It is not the result of conflict, as it is in the neurotic phobias, and the symbolic content is much more transparent. Moreover, outside the area of the specific phobia, the neurotic child's reality testing is relatively intact, whereas the diffusely anxious child often shows striking defects in reality testing.

Disturbances in reality testing become particularly conspicuous in and after toddlerhood when the maturation of autonomous apparatuses permits the child to have more reality experiences. The attainment of upright locomotion brings about a changed relationship to the outside world. In the course of the practicing period temporal-spatial schemata are established; subsequently symbolic representational thinking leads to better understanding of causal relationships; and, relying more and more on secondary process thinking, the child greatly increases his knowledge of reality. In this gradual development he will be enormously helped by a mother who not only provides for new experiences at the appropriate time but who also verbalizes what is happening, explains connections, and points to feelings about them (A. Katan, 1961). This type of verbalization helps the child to integrate experiences and promotes adequate development toward reality. Nursery schools and later primary school continue to strengthen this development.

Again, a mother who is not quite available or one who herself has a disturbance in relation to reality, or one who is not willing to extend herself will often fail her child in this development, especially if the child has some initial weaknesses in this sphere. A mother preoccupied with her own personal life once said to me: "Who has time to answer so many questions?" It is no surprise that her somewhat vulnerable toddler maintained a considerable tendency to primary process talk and confused thinking. Some such children (and their parents) live in two worlds, one of reality and one of fantasy.

Some parents will further the "imaginativeness" of their child to a pathological degree. A mother of a very intelligent dyslectic child, who lived predominantly in a narcissistic fantasy world, so enjoyed her child's "imagination" that in a way she supported the girl's inability to learn to read. This mother said to me: "Does she really have to learn to read?"

Of course, the reality-estranged, withdrawn child who has neither a good inner nor a good outer object will have fantasies that support his estrangement. But I think that a good new outer object can create a climate of warmth and stimulation that may still be able to foster ego growth in such a prelatency child by directing his energies toward the outside world. While such a climate should of course have been experienced earlier, I believe that such a child can still be rescued. In fact, I consider this the optimal period for instituting therapeutic educational measures. With older children even these will frequently not succeed to the same degree.

In other words, deficient experiences in the past can still be made up for by therapeutic educational work, especially before latency. On the other hand, psychoanalytic interpretation and reconstruction of past deficient experiences may make such a child feel more in contact with himself, but they may be less helpful in actually promoting ego growth. After preparatory educational help, however, interpretation is frequently more effective.

The relative proportion of ego defect and neurotic development should help us decide whether to recommend therapeutic educational work or analysis. As already stated, analysis preceded by educational therapeutic measures often seems to be the best solution. Some of these children can then maintain a sufficient degree of creative fluidity, in which they are helped by their great sensitivity and perceptivity—traits which are so frequently found in these somewhat brittle, but often highly gifted children.

I usually think of preliminary educational help first when I am dealing with younger children, in whom ego deficiencies and structural imbalances are in the foreground and whose clinical picture is related to early adaptive failures (Winnicott, 1958). Obviously, with the older child whose development went predominantly out of kilter in relation to situations experienced in the verbal period, and whose clinical picture is dominated by internalized conflicts and neurotic symptomatology (Anna Freud, 1965), I believe that analysis is indicated.

Summary

All children benefit from analytic developmental and dynamic understanding, but not all children who come to us benefit from analysis at that time.

I have singled out a group of young children in whom imbalances and ego defects prevail, although they often are amalgamated with and shape neurotic or preneurotic development. For these young children analysis may often not be as effective as other measures at that time. I suggested that such children may become analyzable when given preparatory educational therapeutic help which aims at making up for early interactional failures and at stimulating ego growth and better integration. Some such children show considerable modifiability by such educational therapeutic management. Subsequently, with their more clearly emerging neurotic symptomatology, these children can be more successfully treated with psychoanalysis.

The practical advantages of therapeutic educational work in the beginning is that its influence is extended beyond 50 minutes daily and can be extended over longer stretches of time. These are needed because we know that the ego grows via continuity of relationship. Moreover, it can reach the mother and often give her a better opportunity for identification.

I trust I have made it clear that this ego-growth-promoting work should be done and supervised by someone other than the person who later conducts the analysis.[3]

---

[3] Since it included work with the mother—the parents—specific advice and other interventions.

Our decision and planning should be determined by tracing the facets of failure in interaction and development in each child.

A considerable number of children who have failed in attempted analyses or who used to be considered unanalyzable can be helped by such preliminary work to such marked degree that analysis is possible at a later date.

BIBLIOGRAPHY

ALPERT, A., NEUBAUER, P. B., & WEIL, A. P. (1956), Unusual Variations in Drive Endowment. *This Annual*, 11:125–163.

ANTHONY, E. J. (1973), How Children Cope in Families with a Psychotic Parent. *J. Amer. Acad. Child Psychiat.* (in press).

BENJAMIN, J. D. (1961), The Innate and the Experiential in Development. In: *Lectures on Experimental Psychiatry*, ed. H. W. Brosin. Pittsburgh: University of Pittsburgh Press, pp. 19–42.

COLEMAN, R. W., KRIS, E., & PROVENCE, S. (1953), The Study of Variations of Early Parental Attitudes. *This Annual*, 8:20–47.

FREUD, A. (1949), Aggression in Relation to Emotional Development: Normal and Pathological. *This Annual*, 3/4:37–42.

———— (1951), Observations on Child Development. *This Annual*, 6:18–30.

———— (1965), *Normality and Pathology in Childhood*. New York: International Universities Press.

GREENACRE, P. (1941), The Predisposition to Anxiety. In: *Trauma, Growth, and Personality*. New York: International Universities Press, 1969, pp. 27–82.

HARTMANN, H. (1950), Comments on the Psychoanalytic Theory of the Ego. *This Annual*, 5:74–96.

JAMES, M. (1962), Infantile Narcissistic Trauma. *Int. J. Psycho-Anal.*, 43:69–79.

KATAN, A. (1961), Some Thoughts about the Role of Verbalization in Early Childhood. *This Annual*, 16:184–188.

KORNER, A. F. (1964), Some Hypotheses Regarding the Significance of Individual Differences at Birth for Later Development. *This Annual*, 19:58–72.

MAHLER, M. S. (1971), A Study of the Separation-Individuation Process. *This Annual*, 26:403–424.

———— (1972), Rapprochement Subphase of the Separation-Individuation Process. *Psychoanal. Quart.*, 41:487–506.

SANDER, L. W. (1962), Issues in Early Mother-Child Interaction. *J. Amer. Acad. Child Psychiat.*, 1:141–166.

SANDLER, J. & JOFFE, W. G. (1965), Notes on Childhood Depression. *Int. J. Psycho-Anal.*, 46:88–96.

TOLPIN, M. (1971), On the Beginnings of a Cohesive Self. *This Annual*, 26:316–352.

WEIL, A. P. (1953), Clinical Data and Dynamic Considerations in Certain Cases of Childhood Schizophrenia. *Amer. J. Orthopsychiat.*, 23:518–529.
——— (1970), The Basic Core. *This Annual*, 25:442–460.
WINNICOTT, D. W. (1958). *Collected Papers*. New York: Basic Books.

CONTRIBUTIONS TO PSYCHOANALYTIC THEORY

Psychoanalytic Interpretation

STANLEY A. LEAVY, M.D.

INTERPRETATION IS THE FOUNDATION OF PSYCHOANALYSIS. THEORY OF whatever degree of abstraction can be tested only by reference to some kind of data, and in psychoanalysis the data follow from the act of interpretation. We have been interpreting so long, and have for so long depended on the basic interpretations made by Freud and his followers, that we often interpret without knowing we are doing so; it is otiose to have to go through a series of steps of thought when we know by experience what the outcome will be. All the same even the simplest psychoanalytic account we can give has in it must be salutary to reexamine this fundamental process from time to time.

The question "what is interpretation?" admits of several kinds of answer. In the first place there would be an empirical answer, coming down to a detailed scrutiny of the operations involved in making an interpretation, without deliberately offering any theoretical explanation, although theoretical ideas already learned would undoubtedly influence any such enterprise. A second answer would be historical, showing the origins and development of the concept and its connections with other concepts. Related to the historical approach would be a theoretical one, in which the theory of explanation is restricted to psychoanalysis itself. That has the plain limitation of being circular, since it must draw upon inferences from the very act of interpretation which we are trying to explain. For

Clinical Professor of Psychiatry, Yale University Medical School, New Haven, Connecticut.

example, to account for psychoanalytic interpretation in terms of the theory of psychic structure—the theory of ego, id, and superego—would be to beg the question how, but for interpretations already made, do we know anything at all about psychic structure? One very good thing that can be said for this kind of answer is that the psychoanalyst is used to making it so that his errors would therefore be least excusable. Here alone he is the expert; when he goes outside psychoanalysis, his success in being convincing may require that his reader be as naïve as himself. All the same it seems to me that anyone who tries to tell what a method of interpretation is ought to do so without sole recourse to a system and a language which are the result of repeated acts of interpretation. He ought instead introduce openly and judiciously concepts originating elsewhere than in the theory to which he owes his professional allegiance.

To do this is not substantially new; from Freud's time to ours experimental, psychological, neurophysiological, and general biological concepts have been introduced for the purpose of explaining psychoanalytic ones and even of buttressing their theoretical validity. We cannot draw upon any of these disciplines in studying the act of psychoanalytic interpretation, but those on which we might be able to draw are not any further than they from the subject we are trying to understand.

I propose to try to answer my question from only two points of view—the empirical, and what for the moment I shall only call the "critical" point of view, leaving the details of what I mean by that for later on.[1] For the present let me discuss interpretation as one himself a psychoanalyst and teacher who makes interpretations every day out of the necessities of the psychoanalytic situation, interpretations which may be right or wrong, good or bad, true or false, properly or improperly worded, but essentially like the interpretations made by most other psychoanalysts, whose training and experience have by now become conventionalized.

---

[1] I hope to be able to review the subject of interpretation historically and theoretically in a more comprehensive work to which this study is an introduction. The literature is a large one, and my references here are only to the most directly pertinent sources.

While my main source of information about the empirical nature of interpretation is myself, I can supplement this source and maybe relieve it of a solipsistic trend by reference to the interpretive work of the analysts whom I have supervised, as well as those who supervised me in the past, and those contemporaries and friends who have shared their ideas with me in their writings or their clinical presentations and discussions. I shall make no attempt at theoretical consistency, preferring rather to try to hit the mark by the shotgun approach of description. I also want to say in advance that the "critical" scrutiny which I am reserving for later may undermine some of the assumptions which I am now making without question.

I parcel out the interpretive process for the purpose of description into five overlapping steps: preparation, attention, disturbance, imagining, translation. It is not that I consider any of these steps to be elementary or irreducible, but I think that they do exist in some form or another in all interpretation. By preparation I mean here the preparation of the interpreter, the psychoanalyst who has been "programmed," so to speak, not only by the earlier words of the patient and all his other patients, but by a lot of other things. In this connection the analogy of the analyst's mind with the mirror is as inappropriate as that of the *tabula rasa* with the infant's mind, but it is nevertheless useful to hold that the analyst reflects to his patient the very thoughts that the patient has expressed unreflectively, so that now the patient pays attention to his utterances and himself draws inferences from them. The process of reflection is, however, more like a system of mirrors than just one, so placed to reflect one another to a theoretical infinity. That too is a static analogy, making no allowances for changes taking place in time.

The preparation of the analyst is the product of his personal experience and his acceptance of the constraining influences of psychoanalytic theory. Let us assume that he has personally verified the theory, meaning that he has come to grant recognition to discernible constants in mental processes, not themselves immediately apparent in the discourse of his patient. The oedipus complex, for example: our interpreter need not be literalistic or dogmatic and demand that Freud's original scheme emerge in every case from what he hears of its latent presence in the patient's discourse. He may merely expect that some persistent mental formation will appear in every patient, revealing patterns, persistent through time, of unconscious affective ties to his parents, ties which might indeed be more conspicuously preoedipal than oedipal. The oedipus complex is here reduced almost to the level of common sense ("so long as he loves his mother") since everyone knows that he has affective ties to his parents or to his memories of them; the Freudian contribution lies in the recognition that the ties are mainly unconscious and that they unconsciously influence current personal relations, often in quite mysterious ways. But however far one might go to liberalize the analyst's assumptions, they cannot be expunged without making him into something other than an analyst. The most important technical resource of psychoanalysis, the transference, is of operational value because it stands for the parent-child dyad and triad.

So, beginning with this example of the oedipus complex as a predisposing element in the analyst's readiness to interpret, we come out with the more general concept of the unconscious survival of the past in the present. Theoretical elements precede any contact at all with patients. I might say "objective" elements, since they have no bearing on the subjective experience of any one person. I can expect that the patient with whom I intend to begin a psychoanalysis next month will make known to me, by a variety of means, evidences of the persistence of earlier experiences into the present, and I shall further expect that these vestiges exert a determinative influence on his present character and symptoms. I expect this, and a lot more, because the sphere of my own mental activity engaged in psychoanalysis is animated by concepts of that sort; to operate without them would require an amnesia or an aphasia. They are cognitive categories, backed by masses of what I take for adequate evidence.

Since the Freudian system, however liberalized, animates and even dominates the mind of the analyst, it might seem that our interpretations are made in advance, the analysis consisting of a process of indexing, finding appropriate slots for entries as they arise. To the extent that psychoanalysis is a technology that is the case, but to that extent only. A class of students of analysis listening to a case report will react as individuals to what they hear, several observers of the same data offering different interpretations.[2] One might be prepared to hear unconscious fantasies; another might be struck by the defensive operations; a third, by autonomous ego functions. We recognize that some interpretations are correct and some incorrect, regardless of the predisposition of the analyst, and also that even when several correct interpretations existed, it might be consistent to offer one, and erratic to offer another. Be that as it may, the mind of the analyst has been systematically prepared to make certain types of observation and to infer certain types of meaning, but only as they uniquely appear in individual patients.

Technical and theoretical preparation of this sort—to accomplish which is one of the tasks of our training institutes—is only a single part of the whole preparation for interpreting, although it is also the easiest to define. The personal history of the analyst, lifelong and contemporaneous, is a more diffuse and intangible influence. Through the personal analysis of the analyst the influence is supposed to become more efficiently and less prejudicially instrumental in the work of analyzing. Training analysis ought to free analysts of unconscious autisms. It cannot homogenize analysts. If they manifest class conformities, as they do when observed collectively, these are conformities representative of the bourgeois estate rather than those of psychoanalytic education. Far from deploring the idiosyncrasies young analysts show in their personalities, we have to attribute to them the possibility of our ever learning anything new, since while only the prepared mind can observe the laws of nature, only the perplexed mind will take the trouble to look for them. However all-encompassing the theoretical system might be, or become, the psychoanalytic task falls short of its commission if the analyst's interpretations are not fresh variations on familiar themes, and he needs to be able to fall back "flexibly," as we say, on the variability within himself to grasp the variability outside.

All the same it makes a difference in the type and timing of an interpretation if one has suffered a recent loss or been rewarded by the admiration of colleagues or if one anticipates a vacation, or a joyful or dreaded reunion. More significant in the long run are the

[2] For a persuasive illustration of this theme see Abrams (1972).

events and conditions of the past: having been an only child, having emigrated early or late from one's native land, or simply one's stature, health and physique, ethnic origin and religious priorities, all influences exerting a constant pressure on the interpreter. It might be protested that idiosyncrasies are responsible for the errors and distortions rather than for positive contributions to understanding. As blind spots, they ought to have been corrected by training analysis. Leaving out of further consideration that training analysts might themselves have to use imperfectly standardized equipment, I repeat that far from being handicaps to good interpreting I look on individual peculiarities as part of the endowment of the analyst, sensitizing him to the infinite nuances of personality and indispensable to the researcher. They need to be distinguished from obsessional preoccupations, and that may not be an easy task.

The analyst must reckon with another kind of preparation, his experience with patients, earlier patients and the present one. Even the formation of special points of view, special interests, is based in part on earlier experience with patients. Happy is the analyst who has been able to make the same new (to him) observation on two patients, but he is in mortal peril of making the same observation again and again. Still, it is the accumulation of impressions that ordinarily leads to the analyst's awareness of a mental formation in himself that he can communicate to his patients, and this process is intricately interrelated with all the other mental events involved in his preparation.

We refer often to the special kind of attention with which the analyst listens and observes. A great deal of preparation for this too has taken place in his life and training. Freud's "free-floating" attention, distributed evenly to the whole range of his patient's communications, remains the desideratum, particularly useful like all such recommendations as a standard against which to judge a deviation. A precondition is our intention to begin every day's hour afresh, quite deliberately not taking up where we left off, and not trying to preserve the illusion that a prevailing mental trend need continue long without interruption. Such attention demands a trust in the method not likely to be present early in the career of a psychoanalyst. The avid notetakers, the prodigies of memory and recall of details are such not only out of fear of their supervisors.

They have not yet learned at first hand that for all the waves and eddies and currents, all the erratic puffs of wind, the distortions, inhibitions, obsessions, and anxieties that must interrupt the course of communication so that no one could hope to remember all he hears, one thing is predictable: the spontaneous return of unconscious structures within the patient's discourse, as inevitably but not as regularly as the tide.

Attention is inseparable from disturbance. It has been said that all learning is a matter of disturbance: we take note and begin to reflect on our notations only when discontinuities appear in the sensory background. A continuous flow of language, while it may be interesting as good conversation or a good lecture is interesting, is not a favorable source of psychoanalytic interpretations, although in retrospect any hour may turn out to have been more revealing than was apparent at the moment. To have access to unconscious meaning, we need to be startled, surprised by an incongruity, the illogical white crow in the black flock, to arouse us from our state of free-floating attention to one of inquiry. The illogic may not be momentous: a mere oddity of speech, such as the young mother's word "consternation" at seeing how quickly her child was growing up, said instead of a more usual word like "amazement," disturbs the listener and fixes his attention.

In emphasizing the disturbance I do not mean to underestimate resistance, especially when it takes the form of such "armor" as the constricted discourse of obsessionals provides, or the entertaining wit of other personalities, or the difficultly analyzable performance of patients who narcissistically adorn their speech, like birds preening their feathers, before permitting utterance. These forms of speech also require interpretation, often at the deepest levels of character analysis. But there too we can interpret only as we are surprised out of our free-floating attention into recognizing the anomaly. A series of lapses into periods of obsessional rumination, for example, may signalize the isolation of a specific theme. Ordinary discourse becomes interpretable psychoanalytically only when it becomes monstrously ordinary.

The illogical, incongruous, and excessive point to hidden meaning. So do all forms of *double entendre,* vivid metaphor, all kinds of unintentional literalness, wherein hidden meaning is identical with the ostensible mask. "I was only speaking figuratively" may be true enough, but it is still an evasion by disavowal. All other figures of speech which we associate with literary creation and literary analysis are possible windows to unconscious meaning. I shall have more to say about this in my discussion of interpretation from what I have called the "critical" point of view. Here I want to emphasize that Freud's invention, so to speak, of free association as the basic analytic technique has led to the discovery of the psychological importance of these properties of speech. Without intending to do so, and in fact without a primary concern for language as such, Freud recognized the fact, always open to inspection in poetry, that communication of meaning is not simple or linear or exclusively logical, but plural, with complex internal relations. Free association and poetic language are not the only representatives of this fact. As far as I know, mathematical language alone is nonmetaphorical, nonallusive, and quite lacking in regard for feeling. Aside from mathematical statements (and scientific statements in general to the degree to which they approach mathematical purity), all expressions in words are only approximations of meaning, and ambiguity is an essential property of speech. In direct logical discourse we ordinarily try to ignore latent meaning even when it crops up unexpectedly in stylistic use, or in slips of the tongue, but we know latent meaning is there all the same. Free association may or may not be attainable by our patients, but it is indispensable for analysts, since it is the inner process whereby we pass from "free-floating" attention to the dissolution of verbal statements and the resynthesis of their imaginal fragments that discloses unconscious meaning—as in both dreaming *and* dream interpretation. The capacity for this is a test of the analyst's competence. In consequence we listen for and are disturbed by all manner of trifles that only disagreeable pedants and carpers usually notice at all. As Jones (1930) said, "De minimis curat psychoanalysis" (unlike the law), but it is the selection of the "minima" that makes all the difference in what we have to do.

While I emphasize the vocal, the verbal, the grammatical, the semantic as the primary data of interpretation, I would not slight those nonverbal statements of which Feldman (1959) and Mahl (1967) have written. Gestures and other bodily movements, facial expressions, as far as the analyst is able to see them from his usual position behind the patient on the couch, also communicate something. However, while they are generally unconscious from the beginning, in the sense that the patient is not only unaware of the meaning, but does not even know they occur, they are of value as data for interpretation to the patient only so far as they are open to translation into words. They are anticipatory cues, but the ensuing words are required to verify the gestures. As an archaeologist working in the historical period once reminded me: one word may be worth a thousand pictures.

What is the intrapsychic fate of the analyst's reactions to his patient? In the first place, they may be what might be called "micropathological" reactions. If his response to what he hears and sees is a strong affect of anxiety, anger, indignation, rage, desire, impatience, compassion, admiration, envy, affection, to name a few possibilities, his imagination is dominated by the affects and their accompanying fantasies. They vitiate the analytic process at this point because the analyst cannot define the extent to which they reflect the contemporaneous mental state of his patient; he is preoccupied with himself. When he recovers from the shock of such intense feeling, and from the fascination of the fantasies, he may be able to use the experience to good purpose, since he is prepared to look on it as an effect unconsciously intended by his patient. But this is still at the maladaptive extreme of affective responses, even when the situation can be redeemed. The desirable response is not the opposite extreme of indifference. Affective temperaments of analysts cover a fairly wide range, and optimal temperaments cannot be established, but everyone reacts affectively to any disturbance. A relatively low-keyed affective response of nonscopophilic curiosity is said to be the most desirable one, but any of the feelings which I have diagnosed as micropathological when they are dominating may under controlled conditions—that is, subjected to the demands of scientific curiosity—favor the interpretative process.

Psychoanalytic empathy is the psychoanalyst's form of creative imagination and is an essential part of his capacity to interpret. Like the imagination of the scientist and artist—or the historian— the empathic state, which I have merely sketched so far, is one in which the resynthesis of the analyst's associations to his patient's words takes place, to produce something new. It is a joint effort, this re-creation, which makes it different from other forms of creative imagination, the other person involved being a constant source of new impressions and a constant critic of the truth of their new synthesis. Empathy of this kind is a recognition within one's own mind of affectively toned imaginative states which can be related with some probability to similar and simultaneous states in another person. In psychoanalysis empathy depends as a rule on discernible cues. In fact, it may be the predictive use of cues that confirms our opinion that we have achieved an empathic state. For example, a few comments not manifestly related to one another taken together remind the analyst of a personal memory which is like a symbolic resynthesis of them. If he makes the prediction that further seemingly unrelated comments by his patient will elaborate his own personal memory, and if this prediction is fulfilled, he can be convinced that he is listening "on the same wave length."

The act of interpretation is imagination in a very complex sense. Let us consider its more literal sense first: images appear in the analyst's mind, claiming special attention, having been instigated in the first place by some discontinuity in the patient's discourse. Secondly, these images are rooted in the private memories of the analyst. At any time the images may be elaborate, fluctuating, evanescent, but interpretation becomes possible when the images persist and demand to be noticed. If, as I have suggested, they are not one-sidedly personal, their tincture by the private memories of the analyst yields to responses to the patient's memories as the analyst has appropriated them. Spontaneously emerging in the analyst, images serve as indices to memories which acquire preconscious significance at this moment of the analysis (that is, under the influences of transferences, etc.).

All this leads up to the act of interpretation which I have called translation. I do not mean that at this point, or anywhere else along the way, an interpretation is something told to the patient, although that is what it may be, and what in the long run the analysis is all about. I mean here as before the analyst's discovery of the unconscious meaning of his patient's communications to him. As for "translation," that is not how the dictionary defines "interpretation." According to the Oxford English Dictionary (1935), "interpretation" is "explanation"; its meaning as "translation" is obsolete, surviving only in the related noun "interpreter" when the latter refers to the person specializing in "translating the communications between persons speaking different languages." "Translation" in turn is defined as "the action or process of turning from one language into another." It is obvious that there are differences between the work of the interpreter of languages and that of the interpreter of unconscious communications. I think that the difference is more easily grasped through the use of the linguistic differentiation between "language" and "speech," the former being the particular national language in use, the latter referring to the speaker's actual performance of it. Even when the interpreter is literally translating different national languages, he needs also to translate nuances of meaning peculiar to the speaker of the moment. But the interpreter of unconscious communications works, ordinarily, within the structure of one national language, and his translations are limited to operations on private meanings of words within that language. All the same, he is translating, since he offers to the patient words and sentences different from the ones originally used, and in substitution for them. He is translating an unconscious language into a conscious one.

Freud's concept of the interpretation of dreams as a decoding process gave the starting point to this way of thinking:

> The dream-thoughts and the dream-content are presented to us like two versions of the same subject-matter in two different languages. Or, more properly, the dream-content seems like a transcript of the dream-thoughts into another mode of expression, whose characters and syntactic laws it is our business to discover by comparing the original and the translation [1900, p. 277].

By way of digression I want to state that I do not look on Freud's view of interpretation as a form of translation from one language to another as only an analogy. Whoever has tried an extended bit of literary translation—from one written language into another—knows that the cliché *traduttore-traditore* is true, and not only for bad translators. Translation even of languages closely cognate with English at many points can only be approximated, because subjective experience cannot be expressed in universally applicable verbal forms; perceptions and apperceptions, privately established within the primary family, are validated by a linguistic community which exists in partial isolation from all others. Meanings are held in common only within the community, including affective as well as cognitive significances. Words like "simpático," "menschlich," "chutzpah," "mores majorum," are difficult to translate because they belong to metaphoric and metonymic series and contexts foreign to their English partial equivalents. If one says one of them, he automatically drags in those series and contexts, and these cannot be replaced by any amount of English elaboration. So too with syntactic structures: the impenetrability of some German sentences, for example, and the rude dynamism of Biblical Hebrew syntax.

Translation of a literary work demands an attitude like that of the psychoanalytic interpreter. The book must "speak" and the reader must "listen." The reader allows the words to create inner perceptual forms and syntheses, and it is these that he rewrites in his own language, faithfully to the extent that he has mastered the meanings of the foreign language within its own system, and also has mastered the meanings of his own language, but also to the extent that the languages possess overlapping sets of meanings. In the psychoanalytic interpretation all this takes place within the language of one community, one lexical, phonetic, and syntactic system, and the differences of meaning are provided by the experience of the individual within the community.

There is a distinction to be made between "decoding," a process initially appropriate to work on a rebus or on an unknown script (like Minoan Linear B) or on artificially composed ciphers for military use, and on the other hand "translation" as "turning from one language into another." It is only a specific item that is decoded, while an interpretation is part of an ever-developing context. What I wish to insist on is that the similarities are greater than the differences, because for both decoding and translating and for interpretation in general, an objective reality does not take the place of words. The analyst interpreting the verbal structures of his patient only gives him other verbal structures—which of course does not prevent the patient from wanting something else. He does indeed give attention, respect, time, pleasing surroundings, and above all his own knowledge and wisdom—but attention, time, and the rest are not interpretations, and even they become specific properties of the analyst only when they accompany the words which the analyst speaks to this particular person. Just as he does not offer a book as a substitute for the word "book," neither does he offer love as an interpretation of the word "love"—whatever his personal feelings might be. Psychoanalysis is not "symbolic realization" (Sechehaye, 1947), even though the latter, deriving its theoretical justification from psychoanalysis, might be a therapeutically effective way of offering objective substitutes for essential elements missing in earlier relationships.

This fundamental matter corresponds with the problem of the traumatic event. There too, the essence is not in the objective reality, meaning here the historical event as an outsider might have seen it and noted it down. Traumatic events exist, to be sure, in the sense that symptoms and memories and mental structures can be shown to be genetically derived from them, but, as Freud discovered so early, and as later generations of analysts need to rediscover, the relation of the event to the memory or to the present pathological experience is not one of mechanistic cause and effect. Events, including traumatic events, are symbolized; they are given significances by the subjectivity of the experiencing person of whatever age, significance which may change repeatedly in retrospect. Interpretations in the form of reconstructions follow the model: "The structure x of ideas which you and I observe in what you have told me is a transformation of the structure y of such-and-such date."

While not every interpretation is a reconstruction, reconstructions too partake of the inescapably verbal character of all interpretations. The model for interpretation in general is like that for reconstructions, minus the temporal clause: "The structure x which you and I observe is a transformation of the structure y," in both cases x being a preconscious formation and y an unconscious one. Incidentally, I mean nothing by "structure" here that would not be covered just as well by "Gestalt," "pattern," "form," "cluster," or, in Freud's German, *Gebild*; structuralist theory is related to such ideas, but it is not their source. Briefly, then, the consciously intended structure of the patient's language during "free association" includes structures which the analyst detects and decodes, or translates, and connects with other memories and other interpretations under the conditions I have described.

If the new forms are included unconsciously within the old conscious structures from which they emerge through interpretation, what can we say about their existence before interpretation? How is it possible to know for certain that the discovered structures are inherent in the speech in a way that an indeterminate number of other structures are not? According to the theory of a dynamic unconscious, prior to interpretation or any other analytic procedure definite and concrete mental formations operate, of which the consciously intended ideas of the subject are only the superstructure. But the age-old criticism of psychoanalysis, that our interpretations are cut to fit preestablished theoretical patterns, may also take the form, elaborated by Karl Popper (1957), that our data cannot be falsified; that is, that we cannot discriminate between true and false interpretations, since any one declared false might with equal assurance be claimed to have unrecognized antecedents. I have already dwelt a little on this problem discussing the preparation, and hence the predilections, of the analyst. We do not draw very strong support for our contention that such discriminations can be made through recourse to objective confirmation: for example, the confirmation of the recovered image by external testimony. These are rarely obtainable, and more rarely unequivocal, but even if they were commonplace, they could not tell us anything about the meaning of the recalled event to the person who had experienced it. We can have more confidence in confirmatory parapraxias, which repeat the preconscious clusters in a different form, such as in the case of the patient whose associations bore witness to his passive oedipal rebellion, and who then described himself parapraxically as a "carbon cop-out" of his father! We could not rest too heavy a case on such accidents, however, but what we seem to depend on is the sheer weight of the positive evidence, the summating effect of a series of clusters, fleshing out the original bare supposition about unconscious motivation.

We do not quite get off the hook of uncertainty about truth and falsity in interpretation by saying the magic word "transference." It is through transference interpretations that we make our most confident assertions, since in the transference we have a here and now, but that is no guarantee that we interpret the transference correctly, and criteria for correctness, when they exist, often seem to belong to the personal style of the analyst, or to the "school" to which he belongs. The most obvious example is the still serious controversy over Kleinian interpretations, which—unlike Jungian, for example—purport to be based on the same kind of data as other Freudian interpretations. The crux of the matter seems to be this: how do we arrange the clustered data of association so as to read their unconscious intention? Without criteria our interpretations differ from reading tea leaves only in their greater intellectual sophistication. It is a little odd to hear Kleinian views dismissed with the same readiness that has traditionally faced all Freudian interpretations and interpreters, that is, as unscientific. Kleinian interpretations are a challenge not just because they are derived from or lead to a theory of development which we cannot accept, but because they imply that the truth criterion may not be available at certain points where it is urgently desired, and that we have no way *within the system* of discriminating between true and false interpretations. The customary recourse is to drag in a criterion from biology: since Kleinian interpretations are presumptive reconstructions of the fantasied experiences of the first weeks and months of life, they cannot be true, for lack of myelination of the neurones on which the persistence of fantasies as mnemic traces depends. Similarly, observations of early childhood are said to provide objective correlates for interpretations made in the analysis of adults.

By now I hope that I have made it clear that my view of psychoanalytic interpretations precludes any recourse to means of validation drawn from sources not available within the psychoanalytic process. It is quite illegitimate to confirm an interpretation of a patient's primary dependent need for the analyst by reference to a history of maternal deprivation, unless what we are so stating in a kind of shorthand form is that the present demand is related to a demand for maternal caring, and complaint about its insufficiency in the past. The "actual facts"—did the mother deprive or did she not?—are not at the heart of interpretation. Of even less value is

reference to Spitz's emotionally starved babies, or Harlow's deprived monkeys, which are obviously only analogies, useful for
fostering the convergence of different theoretical approaches, but
still only analogies.

This point of view, if its implications are followed, is at variance
with much that is important and influential in psychoanalytic
thought. Even with the concept of empathy we do not entirely
depart from our attempt at *objectivity* about psychic processes, an
objectivity that seems to be necessary for the scientific respectability
of psychoanalysis. We maintain the ideal—admittedly unattainable
in practice—of observation of natural phenomena with the use of a
standardized, calibrated instrument itself neither modifying the
data nor being modified by them. Conceivably, a computerized
manipulation of a program of recorded and consensually validated
objective data would represent the fulfillment of this ideal. To the
extent that psychoanalytic interpretation is performed in accord
with this ideal we assume, however covertly, the interaction of an
ego as a standardized instrument with objective data obtained in a
manner as free of arbitrariness as though consensual validation
(other than dyadic, when analyst and analysand are in agreement)
were possible. This is something like the traditional psychoanalytic
position, and the claim of psychoanalysis to scientific status—as a
process, let alone as a theory—seems to depend on it. Empathic
communication is theoretically no less definable according to this
model than the interpretation of the symbols of dreams, since
empathy in interpretation seems to suppose the presence of the
standardized ego on one side and concrete data on the other, even
where the latter are only the words and images aroused in the mind
of an analyst by the stimulation of his patient's words. Intrapsychic
objectivity is not necessarily a contradiction in terms.

There is an alternative approach that simply avoids any
assumptions at all about the objectivization of psychic processes—
except perhaps in naming them and thus making them discussable
in the first place. It assumes to the contrary the irreducible nature
of subjectivity, and *not* by dichotomizing the mind-body unity. The
model for study is no longer that of the observer confronting dead
tissues or live animals, but of the encounter between persons. The

ground of the operations between patient and analyst is "inter-subjectivity,"[3] to which all objective demonstration is subordinate and not explicative. Psychoanalytic interaction—and *a fortiori* interpretation—is only a specialized variety of person-to-person encounter, the fundamental nature of which can be realized only through the interchange of meanings between the persons involved.

One of Jacques Lacan's (1955) illustrative analogies is to be found in his analysis (not psychoanalysis in any usual sense) of Poe's story "The Purloined Letter." The story has to do with the problem of locating and recovering a stolen letter, the publication of which would be embarrassing to the French royal court. The method of Dupin, the detective, consists of imagining not only the motives of the thief, but also the thief's conception of what would be going on in the minds of the rightful possessors of the letter, and of anyone undertaking its recovery. Dupin puts himself in the place of a thief who is putting himself in the place of his pursuers. The analogy with interpretation is clear: there are no objective data, since every statement of the patient is directed to the analyst, whose intentions toward him are assumed even before the analysis begins. The theory of transference—and therefore of the transference interpreta-tion—has to be reviewed in the light of the position of intersubjec-tivity. While we have always allowed for the existence of transfer-ences outside the psychoanalytic situation, what we may have failed to recognize is that these and all transferences are also special cases of intersubjective relations generally. No interaction between persons is possible in isolation from the inferences which they constantly draw from one another's speech and behavior. These inferences are meanings, mainly given unconsciously through verbal and other cues, themselves unconsciously uttered, but the process of interaction is always one of mutual interpretation.

At this point a clinical example may be informative. An exhaustive example, one in which all the elements of interpretation were clearly illustrated, would perhaps be most convincing, but it would also tend toward infinity. This instance is one which I obtained from a colleague in another connection, but which may be the more significant in that it had no immediate bearing on my present thesis.

[3] For further discussion of this term the reader is referred to Ricoeur (1970).

My colleague told me about this bit of psychoanalysis as an example of the way in which a particular maneuver of resistance concealed an unconscious fantasy. His patient, a young woman, told him a dream, but refused outright to tell him any associations to the dream. She excused this refusal to cooperate with the analytic rule on the grounds that she knew quite well what he, the analyst, had in mind, and so would not say anything about it. She did allude, however, to the idea that the thought she attributed to the analyst concerned "phallic symbols." The analyst had noticed an unusual irritability in himself earlier in the session; at that time his patient had told him that she had a totally different picture of him when she lay on the couch, from the one she had when she looked at him directly. Seen face to face he didn't look at all like someone who might want to harm her. On the other hand she would not say what he did look like when she lay on the couch, but remarked perversely that it was *he* that must change at that time. The analyst found himself thinking: "Damn it, why can't you and I look at this idea of yours?" with emphasis on the word "look." When the young woman refused to examine the "phallic symbols" of the dream, he remembered that she had told him in the past of her having as a little girl witnessed a man's exposure of his genital. He reminded the patient of this idea. She said she was astonished at the connection, but she admitted that she often thought about that man, and whenever she did so she thought the phrase "I hate you!" which, as it happened, was the way in which she very often greeted the analyst, and with equal lack of conviction.

I submit that this little episode illustrates some of my main points—the verbal allusions to images which taken together constitute a new whole, the influence of the analyst's affect and his recollection of the patient's previously acknowledged "traumatic" memory, but above all the intersubjective phenomenon: once more we see that the steps toward interpretation (and in this instance only steps were taken) were contingent on a series of guesses that a pair of persons made about one another's state of mind. It would be easy, and sound properly objective, to limit the analysis to only one of the minds taking part in the dialogue—to see the patient's "projections" is not difficult. But simultaneous with her imputation of her own images to him, and equally essential to the work of interpretation, was his frustrated wish to join her in "looking," which awakened in him *his* memory of *her* memory. It was also the cluster of certain highly significant words—"symbols," "picture," "look"—that attracted the attention of both patient and analyst; the associates in the analytic process have moved further toward community of meaning.[4]

Speech is by far the most elaborate and flexible means of human communication. Speech is in effect the externalization of subjectivity, and is inseparable from subjective experience after earliest infancy—the obvious exception of the deaf-mute child notwithstanding, since as far as we know the deaf-mute only learns to communicate with others through techniques of artificial forms of speech invented by persons who can speak, and who are able to translate (once again!) the categories of speech into other modalities. Speech also arises only within a context of interaction and intersubjectivity. It is the basic symbolizing action of people, and all of its components are traditional and learned (even if Chomsky [1968] is right in his claim that basic grammars are innate). Speech is also ambiguous, and, above all, it is addressed to a listener.

Up to this point we have been on more familiar territory not too far from the accustomed domain of psychoanalysis, although I have tried to examine it from a personal position. I have acknowledged sharing the traditional psychoanalytic methods of interpretation, and I have more or less tacitly acknowledged sharing the traditional explanation of interpretation. Now I should like to take a closer and critical look at it, and to do so I find myself using language that does not sound very much like the language of psychoanalytic theory. Analysts have not always recognized the point of view which their language betrays: the position as if the data of interpretation were concrete external data—even when they spoke of them in abstractions like "affect," "memory," "drive," "trauma," "defense," as in the dictum "interpret the defense before interpreting the drive." Every communication between patient and analyst takes place within the coordinates of a common symbolic universe. In a way the work of analysis consists of a persistent effort

[4] Permission to include this fragment of a case history was granted to me by the late D. Clint Smith, M.D.

to differentiate between the symbolic nuances of the patient and those of the analyst, nuances occurring within a general lexical community but deriving also from the private experience of individuals. Which is to say also, as any reader of poetry knows, that every person has a private symbolic treasury. To try to differentiate between the symbolism of the analyst and that of the patient is not another objectification. We cannot reach a point at which analyst and patient are in accord because they have got out of the symbolic net and reached an external reality with which their symbols now correspond. There is no such reality in human experience, that is, no reality (no trauma, for example) which is apprehended other than within the symbolic and symbolizing net and made to conform to it (while also deforming it).[5]

Interpreting, we explore the range of meanings given to words, including the meanings imputed to the analyst's actual or imagined words. We avoid attempts at objectification, at getting to the thing-in-itself behind the word, when we see that such an achievement is an illusion, since the elements of experience including the most primitive ones exist for us only inside the world of meanings. That goes for "object relations" as fully as for any of the other theoretical elementary structures of personality. We may know through biological research, or through experimental psychology, or with less certainty through direct observation of the development of children, that some patterns of mothering provide optimal conditions for what we consider to be desirable development, but such patterns and the deviations from them are recoverable through psychoanalysis itself only as they are transformed into idiosyncratic symbolic interpretations, and no less so when we infer them in making transference interpretations. Between the symbolic world that we know by interpretation and the objective event that we know by external observation there is a gulf that psychoanalysis cannot cross.

Before trying to define still more closely what I consider a psychoanalytic interpretation to be, I must say a little more about what I consider it not to be. In the first place, and summarizing much of what has gone before, it is not a statement of some

---

[5] See in illustration of this point Kris (1956).

condition existing in the patient in isolation from his symbolic world. Second, it is not a statement existing in the patient in isolation from the special meanings he has imaginatively attributed to the analyst's symbolic world. Third, an interpretation does not present to the patient a historic event "as it actually happened." Fourth, it is not a translation of the patient's words into a language in which the meanings are universal, the language, that is, of the standard dictionary.

Positively, an interpretation can be made when the symbolic interaction between analyst and analysand has reached a point at which the analyst entertains in his imagination persistent structures the origins of which he imputes to the analysand's unconscious intentions. Speech having been the medium of symbolic interaction, the apperception of such structures depends on the properties of speech. Lacan (1957), following the linguistic line from F. de Saussure to Roman Jakobson, holds that metaphor and metonymy are the principal forms of speech which permit the transmission of unconsciously intended imaginal structures. Metaphor does so by offering a series (potentially infinite) of interchangeable indicators of meaning: in psychoanalysis we are most familiar with metaphor in our use of the symbolic significance of words—here in the narrow sense of the word "symbol," where, for example, "house" is a substitute for "woman." In metonymy the signifiers are not interchangeable, and allusion is made by contiguity, or by substituting an attribute or other suggestive word for the name of the thing. Freud's great discovery lay not far from here: when he showed that symptoms had a sense, and dreams a meaning, he did so by getting patients to express the words—the metaphors and metonymies—that reflection on symptoms and dreams stimulated.

I do not believe that all psychoanalytic interpretations can be boiled down to the recognition of metaphoric and metonymic elements in speech, but the principle might be correct that our intuition of unconscious mental structures is effected through the perception of grammatical structures hidden in patients' speech and in our own verbal (spoken or not) responses to them.

It might seem that this places too heavy a burden of significance on words. It is one thing for Breuer's patient to call the treatment the "talking cure" and quite another for us to take the term in such earnest. But an unspoken objection may exist in the notion that the word is merely ideational, and how can we look exclusively at words when it is the recognition of affects that really defines the psychoanalytic project? The distinction "idea" and "affect" is where the trouble lies. Affectless ideas may indeed exist, but in full purity only in mathematics. I suppose that this is what Edna Millay had in mind in her line "Euclid alone has looked on beauty bare." Another writer on the subject—I assume a mathematician and not a poet (Adler, 1972)—writes: "Mathematics . . . is unique among languages in its ability to provide precise expression for any thought or concept that can be formulated in its terms." That precision is obtainable only in the absence of affective value, and the language of persons is inescapably affective and hence impure and imprecise. Freud (1950) thought that language was only a safety-valve for affect, part of the ego's effort to modify external reality for the most efficient satisfaction of instinctual needs. That is a possible psycho-biological explanation of the origin of language, but it is from another universe of discourse than the one with which I am dealing. Within the universe of intersubjective meaning, we can only make the observation that psychic organization, the formation of structures of meaning congruent with the structures of meaning in other persons, is at the same time an organization of affect.

When we interpret, the data of interpretation are found in metaphoric contexts which are both ideational and affective. Images are entertained with feeling. We interpret when we have been able to extend the series of metaphors available to our analysand's consciousness, to include those for which other metaphors have been instituted. Both the original process and the later reinstatement of metaphors take place in affective fields. The question of primacy between idea and affect comes up when we push a dichotomy too far: when we come to believe that ideas and affects, being logically separable, are therefore distinct elements in subjective experience, which they are not. Displacement, so often taken to be the proof of the separation of ideas and affects, really only confirms the relation of metaphoric and metonymic change to symbol formation and distortion. In the course of personal history subjective experience may be modified in the interest of interpersonal relations through the substitution of one member of a metaphoric series for another. The affective coloring is determined by the fact that a metaphoric item exists in many series at once, so that when it is introduced into a present context it brings along the affective value it held in another series. The phenomenon of euphemism is at least analogous, if not fully representative: a functioning euphemism abolishes the unpleasant values of the substituted expression by introducing the affective and aesthetic value it has in its other uses. People cannot stand saying or hearing the word "shit" because it is part of the vocabulary of hostility, or because it conveys too intensely the memory of unacceptable smells, whereas Latinisms like "excrement" or even "feces" convey affective and aesthetic derivatives proper to libraries, where quiet prevails and the odor is inorganic.

By the very fact that this way of thinking prescribes that interpretation discloses meaning, and that meaning is verbal, it is clear that there cannot be a rock-bottom interpretation exhausting the meaning of a psychic structure. The thing signified by any signifying word is another signifying word, in all the dignity of its private, personal, historical, affective value. Even though its ultimate antecedents may be too primitive for words, they can become conscious only through the medium of words. When we believe that we have got through the ego's defense to reach nuclear complexes, we know that every psychic structure now disclosed has antecedents, and it is a speculative question to ask which are the most primitive possible structures. The early memories which we recover through reconstructions are not rudimentary: their own form has been historically controlled by still earlier structures.

We cannot do without the concept of preverbal psychic structures, since such parsimony is forbidden by our observations. True, the unity of words and ideas is of extremely early origin in the child, so that words and wordlike expression and the use of primitive sentences mediate experience long before the oedipal period. Yet the psychoanalysis of oral phenomena interprets sensations related to the mouth and tongue within a metaphoric series. The words of the series belong to specific chronological epochs, including the preverbal. Transference interpretations establish the contextual relations of the metaphors: the fantasied presence in the mouth of nipple, or food, or penis, or magical power, or knowledge. Sensation in the mouth, and also images, including fantasies in the visual modality, existed before any words could have designated them. Theoretically, then, interpretation points to memories of ideas that could not have had verbal representation to begin with. All the same, the interpretable in unconscious experience is that for which some verbal reference is possible: interpretations of the earliest experiences are per se anachronistic, because they must be made into words, which are of later appearance than the memory. It is not so very different, perhaps, from the way that chemists "handle" substances through the use of formulae which exist in another world of reality than the substances themselves.

A criticism often leveled at Kleinian interpretation is that the analyst is engaged in *Rückphantasierung:* that he is attributing to a very early period of life a fantasy appropriate to a more mature one. The trouble with the criticism is that it probably expresses equally rightly charges against *any* interpretations, including those of the verbal period, but especially those involving any kind of preverbal or nonverbal experiences. The interpretation uses the imagery and the language of a later period, the present, in fact. For the patient with whom we are speaking now, subjective experience and language are separable as logical categories, but are really inseparable as psychic reality.

Breuer and Freud (1893–1895) explained the efficacy of their early treatment of hysterical patients in a way that deserves to be reexamined in the light of these ideas. Assuming that symptoms are caused by energies dammed up through the repressive action of the ego, they explained the relief of symptoms as the result of the discharge of the dammed-up energy, through the elaboration provided by new access to thought via speech. In fact, it was the failure of such elaboration to take place that signalized repression. From the patient's point of view it was a "talking cure"; but from the analyst's, a "thinking cure," the talk being regarded as a behavioral cue to the significant experience, thought. The repressed is not that which cannot be spoken, but that which cannot be thought or felt. But exactly as in the case of preverbal experience, when we try to imagine thought that cannot be put into words, that is in fact ineffable, we see that we are unable to proceed. Language is not just the tool of thought, but is at once the organ, organizer, and organization of thought. Interpretation consists of the disclosing of unconscious mental processes through the exposure of the underlying language that dominates them, and secondly, its translation into the language of consciousness.

Taking language as the focus of analytic interpretation inevitably leads to important questions to which I have only barely alluded. For example, what kinds of interpretation do we make, and what are the rules for making them? For it is plain that the qualifier "psychoanalytic" itself indicates not every possible kind of interpretation, but those which it is the business of psychoanalytic interaction to reveal. Whether they be of unconscious content, or of unconscious aspects of the form of presentation, interpretations are usually categorized as species of universal types. We interpret defenses, resistances, transferences, or the oedipus complex, or pregenitality, or the castration complex, latent homosexuality, latent anxiety, etc., the list being long enough that interpretation need never be monotonous, but it is a finite list. The act of interpretation designates the category to which a mental structure can be assigned. The categories themselves represent theoretical hypotheses closest to the direct experience of psychoanalytic interaction, and are of a different order from the metapsychological categories, or from structural theory and other higher explanatory concepts.

Our classification of types of interpretation nevertheless may be incomplete. Since they are abstractions they are not themselves intersubjective events. Might not an increasingly refined investigation of the language of those events expose to the prepared mind instances of unconscious structure that do not fit into our present concepts? [6] Preparation for this undertaking requires a capacity to entertain new meanings in the presence of old words, to be alerted to new metaphors. In a sense it is trying to repeat some of Freud's work, under changed conditions, and with new emphasis, but it is a continuation of the thrust of psychoanalysis toward the discovery of meaning. Dilthey's principle is appropriate to our science: "The single moment derives its meaning from its connection with the

---

[6] Edelson (1972) has begun such an undertaking in his linguistic study of dream theory.

whole." While we cannot with the best psychoanalysis and the longest reveal the "whole" of a lived experience, we think it is possible to reveal more of it by our method than by any other, and that is a substantial claim.

BIBLIOGRAPHY

ABRAMS, S. (1972), Freudian Models and Clinical Stance. *Psychoanal. Quart.*, 41:50–57.

ADLER, A. (1972), in: *The New Yorker*, February 19, pp. 39–45.

BREUER, J. & FREUD, S. (1893–1895), Studies on Hysteria. *Standard Edition*, 2. London: Hogarth Press, 1966.

CHOMSKY, N. (1968), *Language and Mind*. New York: Harcourt, Brace & World.

EDELSON, M. (1972), Language and Dreams. *This Annual*, 27:203–282.

FELDMAN, S. S. (1959), *Mannerisms of Speech and Gestures in Everyday Life*. New York: International Universities Press.

FREUD, S. (1900), The Interpretation of Dreams. *Standard Edition*, 4 & 5. London: Hogarth Press, 1953.

——— (1950 [1895]), Project for a Scientific Psychology. *Standard Edition*, 1:283–397. London: Hogarth Press, 1966.

JONES, E. (1930), An Over-Determined Remark. *Int. J. Psycho-Anal.*, 11:344–345.

KRIS, E. (1956), The Recovery of Childhood Memories in Psychoanalysis. *This Annual*, 11:54–88.

LACAN, J. (1955), Le séminaire sur "La lettre volée." *Écrits*. Paris: Editions du seuil, 1966, pp. 11–64.

——— (1957), The Insistence of the Letter in the Unconscious. In: *Structuralism*, ed. J. Ehrmann. New York: Doubleday, 1970, pp. 103–136.

MAHL, G. (1967), Some Clinical Observations on Nonverbal Behavior in Interviews. *J. Nerv. Ment. Dis.*, 144:492–505.

POPPER, K. (1957), Philosophy of Science: A Personal Report. In: *British Philosophy in Mid-Century*, ed. C. A. Mace. London: Allen & Unwin.

RICOEUR, P. (1970), *Freud and Philosophy*. New Haven: Yale University Press.

SECHEHAYE, M. (1947), *Symbolic Realization*. New York: International Universities Press, 1951.

On the Concept of Aggression

JOSEPH H. SMITH, M.D.,

PING-NIE PAO, M.D.,

AND NOEL A. SCHWEIG, M.D.

IT IS OUR INTENTION TO PRESENT AGGRESSION AS A GENERAL MOTI-
vational concept and to define the nature of behavior which we
believe could most usefully be designated as the referent of such a
concept. We believe that the question of a unitary versus a dualistic
drive theory ordinarily rests on an unnoted reification of the
concept of instinct or instinctual drive and is to that extent itself a
false question. Rather than addressing ourselves to that question,
we shall attempt to consider the conditions under which and the
extent to which behavior displays a unitary motivational aspect and
the ways in which the actual plurality of motivational determinants
of behavior nevertheless lend themselves to a dualistic conceptual
strategy—a *conceptual* dualism which need not be simplistic.

On the assumption that all behavior is directional, we suggest
that the motivational aspects of all behavior may be conceptualized
in terms of tendencies to approach an object of positive valence or of
tendencies to distance or destroy an object of negative valence and
that these tendencies may be taken as the referents of libido and

Dr. Smith is Chairman, Forum on Psychiatry and the Humanities, Washington
School of Psychiatry; Faculty, Washington Psychoanalytic Institute; Consultant,
Adolescent Section, Adult Psychiatry Branch, N.I.M.H. Dr. Pao is Director of
Psychotherapy, Chestnut Lodge, Rockville, Maryland; Faculty, Washington
Psychoanalytic Institute. Dr. Schweig, Faculty, Washington Psychoanalytic Insti-
tute; Assistant Clinical Professor of Psychiatry, University of Maryland, School of
Medicine.

aggression. We shall attempt to trace, from primitive modes of approach and withdrawal, the derivation of behavior reflecting advanced forms of these tendencies.

We approach the topic of aggression by considering mind as an aspect of the biological; instinct as an aspect of mind; danger and desire as equiprimordial coordinates of motivation; and, finally, libido and aggression as general motivational concepts.

MIND AS AN ASPECT OF THE BIOLOGICAL

From the time following his "Project for a Scientific Psychology" [1895], Freud put aside his own efforts to explain psychological phenomena in terms of their neurophysiological correlates. He chose to remain on an expanded psychological ground—expanded by virtue of his concept of a psychic unconscious which permitted sufficient explanatory leeway to account in psychological terms for the gaps in conscious phenomena (Freud, 1940, p. 159)—leaving the establishment of the assumed neurophysiological correlations to later workers. However, he was guided by the assumption of such a correlation so that his psychological concepts tended to reflect or conform with his picture of neurophysiological function in particular and with biological development and function in general. Thus the central dynamic of his model of the mental apparatus conformed with the idea of phylogenetically internalized reflex activity (Freud, 1900, p. 565; Schur, 1966, p. 138).

Although many of his concepts were biologically rooted, Freud's insight, we believe, was that the surest ultimate correlation of biological and psychological phenomena depends on thoroughgoing explanation at each level and of each in its own terms. Even though a biological event can cause a psychological response and vice versa, explanation in either realm requires more than knowledge of initiating cause. We can legitimately settle for cause as explanation only when there is a consensus of understanding about ongoing continuities of the realm in which the cause intervenes.[1]

---

[1] The importance of explanation in this sense became clearer in retrospect to psychoanalysts through the example of the deeper understanding of id motivation which resulted from greater knowledge of ego psychology (Hartmann, 1948, p. 80; 1952, p. 156).

Since reliable correlations between different levels of functioning depend on knowledge of each level, Freud's earlier project of explaining psychological phenomena in neurophysiological terms was, at best, premature and could have resulted only in reductionism. Schafer (1970) believes that even the biological orientation which Freud retained, and which was later systematized by Hartmann, was a conceptual strategy of undue costliness. However, the problem of pseudoexplanation which Schafer discusses may be attributable to the general tendency to reify concepts and models[2] rather than specifically to Freud's (and Hartmann's) biological orientation.

Our understanding of Freud's work following the "Project" is not that he was reducing psychology to biology. We believe that he was involved instead in the continuing search for the kind of conceptualization proper to the unity of body and mind, but from a standpoint of remaining on psychological ground. The task he set himself was to explore the psychological in its own terms as a realm of functioning which had become differentiated within the biological sphere during the course of phylogenetic and ontogenetic development.

A pervasive assumption in accord with this task was that mind, as that aspect of the broadly biological which enables a creature to be aware of and modify itself and its world, arises or differentiates from its matrix in such a way as to be partially modeled on elements of its matrix. His choice and definition of concepts were guided by this assumption. In relation to the biological in the narrow sense, repression, for example, and even high-level acts of repudiation by judgment were seen as deriving from neurophysiological automatic avoidance of noxious stimuli.

---

[2] Even physicists must struggle with whether and how they reify concepts like energy or electrical field and they too can inappropriately rely on mechanical models as explanatory. Bridgman (1927) wrote, "I believe many will discover in themselves a longing for mechanical explanation which has all the tenacity of original sin. The discovery of such a desire need not occasion any particular alarm, because it is easy to see how the demand for this sort of explanation has had its origin in the enormous preponderance of the mechanical in our physical experience. But nevertheless, just as the old monks struggled to subdue the flesh, so must the physicist struggle to subdue this sometimes nearly irresistable, but perfectly unjustifiable desire" (p. 47).

It would, of course, have been permissible to borrow concepts from any realm, provided only that they be adaptable to and useful in conceptualizing psychological phenomena. Freud, however, was guided specifically by biological analogues as the context and, in some measure, model of psychological processes. He saw the pleasure principle, for instance, as a principle of animate functioning and thus felt justified in forming his speculations on the beginnings of mind as analogous in certain ways to the beginnings of life (Freud, 1920).

Of course, some of his concepts (like energy, absolute psychic determinism, and perhaps the pleasure principle itself) reach through biology to dynamic aspects of inanimate nature by which the biological itself was shaped. He mentioned such an extension in the case of Eros and the destructive instinct: "The analogy of our two basic instincts extends from the sphere of living things to the pair of opposing forces—attraction and repulsion—which rule in the inorganic world" (1940, p. 149).

INSTINCT AS AN ASPECT OF MIND

The assumption that psychological processes will bear some resemblance to neurophysiological ones is quite different from assuming that knowledge of the neurophysiological explains the psychological. To conceptualize the psychological as a differentiated realm requires knowledge not only of how it is similar to, but also of how it is different from, the biological matrix.

We understand Hartmann's (1939) and Erikson's (1950) interpretations as well as ethological studies of imprinting by Lorenz (1935, 1937) and others, and, finally, recent studies by Loewald (1970, 1971, 1972) as pertaining to another aspect of the Freudian assumption mentioned above: psychological processes arise within and are shaped by not only physiological functions but also by the nonhuman and especially the human environment. This truism, properly understood, need not blur the distinction between inner impulse and external stimulus which Freud (1915, p. 118) and later Rapaport (1960a; see also 1957 and 1959, 2:255–262) and others stressed. It does, however, confront the prior question of how internality and externality become established. As a result, the concept of instinct as an autochthonous given, radically independent of experience, is modified in the direction of a concept of instinct as not only released but also partially constituted by experience in the world (Hartmann, 1952, p. 159; Rapaport, 1960b, p. 835; Olinick, 1970, p. 664; Loewald, 1971, p. 101; 1972, p. 242).[3]

Loewwald (1971) wrote:

> It is by interaction with them [for the observer, surrounding or environmental psychic systems] that motivational forces of various order of complexity and integration, and stable motivational structures of any kind, come into being within the newly emerging psychic unit, the child. On that basis, but never without maintaining further interaction with psychic forces of the environment, interactional processes within the new psychic system can be built into various forms of structured organization, whereby higher levels of motivation come about [p. 101].

Another way of formulating how environmental influence mediates the derivation of higher-order motivational forces is in terms of the object. Rapaport wrote that "the defining characteristic *object* is the outstanding conceptual invention in Freud's theory of the instinctual drive" (1960a, p. 877). It seems to us that it is precisely this defining characteristic which makes Freud's concept of instinct a psychological one. However, it must be understood that at every level of mentation we speak of objects, including the objects of the infant's primitive perception and memory, regardless of how these are represented in the mind of the infant.

The objects (in the sense just mentioned) of early perception and memory provide the content which is organized as primitive anticipatory thought (memories of prior gratification experienced

[3] The acknowledgment that instincts are partially constituted by experience highlights the intricacy implied in Freud's concept of the complemental series. The several pairs which Freud used as polar terms to convey the idea of a complemental series (1940–1941, p. 148f.; 1895, pp. 122, 138; 1905, p. 239f.; 1912, p. 99; 1914, p. 18; 1916–1917, pp. 346f., 364) refer, in the main, to constitutional-maturational factors, on the one hand, and environmental-experiential factors on the other (Rapaport, 1959, p. 804). However, early life experience combines with inherited constitution to form the subsequent dispositional factor (Freud, 1905, p. 240; 1916–1917, p. 362; Monod, 1971, p. 118f.).

as present need). This striving to make present a future in terms of the past, to paraphrase Freud (1900, p. 620), is the primordial temporality of behavior. As such, it cannot itself become even a tool or means of thought—let alone an object of thought—until the establishment of reflective self-awareness. Nevertheless, the conceptually "timeless" primitive organization of perception and memory as primarily drive-determined anticipatory thought begins hierarchical development as introjection and identification.

Explanation of development tends to focus on frustration at various turning points. Indeed, the organism is first of all awakened to some sort of awareness by reason of tension as a psychological correlate of somatic disequilibrium. The directionality of behavior is simply there as tending away from tension, the means provided by phylogenetic givens and the average expectable environment. Behavior is polarized as away from the source of tension and toward gratification, the experience of which achieves some kind of representation with its first occurrence. Subsequently, need evokes not merely tension or random percept, but an image of the experience or object of satisfaction. The relationship between need and object has been in some primitive fashion internalized; need can be experienced as wish or desire.[4]

DANGER AND DESIRE AS EQUIPRIMORDIAL COORDINATES OF MOTIVATION

Perhaps Freud's use of dualistic concepts was at times simplistic as Schafer (1970) has suggested. It was Freud's way of being consistently faithful, in any event, to the fact that man is a creature of conflict, the latter a truism but not a simplism. However, we understand Schafer's meaning (and also Freud's) to be that conflict is multiply assured and is not ultimately dependent on Eros and destructiveness as separate and autochthonously given drives, forever at odds.

It may be that conflict is ultimately assured by reason of behavior being directional—polarized to the extent that it always manifests

[4] Desire, though a synonym of wish, may more directly convey the distinction between need and wish made by Freud (1900, p. 565f.). Cf. Ricoeur (1970, p. 370).

tendencies away from (the primary source of tension) and toward (the object of satisfaction). Conflict proper, in any event, presupposes directionality, together with obstacles. But simply directionality and obstacles would codetermine only low-level conflict. The essence of human conflict is anchored in the leeway which allows an object or pole of positive valence to become negative.[5] It is this possibility which founds ambivalence. Moreover, the establishment of change in the dominant valency of an object necessitates the search for new objects of positive valence. Thus, while the infant's world is enlarged and multidirectional possibilities for behavior open up (Rapaport, 1951, p. 722; Hartmann, 1955, p. 219), conflict and the necessity of choice in a determined, though more complex world are simultaneously established.

Presumably, the first instance of an object assuming a negative valence is in the experience of the absent (or present only as hallucinated) object. At this point in primitive object relatedness it becomes useful to group tendencies toward an object of positive valence under the concept libido, and to conceptualize tendencies toward an object of negative valence as aggressive. The behaviors determined by these tendencies are initially passive, *ad hoc* responses of approach or avoidance. However, to understand the significance and power of either libido or aggression, it is necessary to extrapolate backward to the unidirectionality of even more primitive object relatedness. There the mode of away from (the source of tension) can be conceptualized as the prototype of aggression and the mode of toward (the object) as the prototype of libido. The ascription of discrete drive aspects at such a level may seem to do violence to a unitary phenomenon and also to the principle that on the horizons of the knowable concepts tend to "lose their individuality, fuse together, and become fewer in number" (Bridgman, 1927, p. 24; see also pp. 22, 42, 51, 78, 105, 146, 194, 223). However, it is one thing to permit a "fusion" of concepts at a point where the phenomena actually become simpler or unitary, and quite another to reify concepts like libido and aggression and hold that they exist as fused in primitive response (Schafer, 1970, p. 441).

---

[5] As will become clear below, the positive to negative change of valency does not imply a frustration theory of aggression.

The latter fosters the tendency to think of two kinds of energy associated with two basic drives, present but fused from the beginning, which defuse or differentiate in experience—a variety of reductionism from which Freud (1926) was trying to move away.[6]

That all behavior is directional denotes an inevitable degree of polarity—usually multiple polarities—which need not be ultimately accounted for by a simplistic instinctual dualism. In 1926, Freud put the emphasis on the situation—for purposes of explicating anxiety, on the danger situation and the individual response to it. Development proceeds to a point where the avoidance of danger can sometimes lead to missing or delaying a desired experience of satisfaction. However, in the original state of relative adaptedness, behavior which avoids danger is largely identical with the behavior which approaches satisfaction. The crucial satisfactions resolve needs which unresolved are the crucial dangers. It seems awkward in the extreme to conceptualize such early behavior in terms of the infant dealing with a certain quota of libido and a certain quota of aggression which are fused in motivating the identical behavior. That such early behavior can be conceptualized in terms of approach and avoidance aspects and that later on it becomes useful to conceptualize all approach behaviors as one kind of motivation (libido) and all avoidance (flight-fight or distance-destroy) as another (aggression) seems a way of retaining an emphasis on the situation proper to both internal and external sources of stimulation. At the same time such a conceptualization might avoid the pitfalls of the popular concept of aggression as only a response to frustration, the latter also narrowly conceived (Hartmann, Kris, and Loewenstein, 1949, p. 28). While we assume that aggression

---

[6] Of course, Freud reverted to heavy reliance on Eros and Thanatos in his later thought. According to Loewald (1972, p. 238), this may have been an effort to overcome the overly rigid division of the psyche into id, ego, and supergo—we would say the hypostatization of those concepts. That Eros and Thanatos, in turn, became subject to the hypostatization fallacy is clearly evidenced in the notion of fusion and defusion of instincts. Regarding the latter, Ricoeur (1970, p. 297) wrote, "fusion and defusion are simply the correlates, in energy language, of phenomena discovered by the work of interpretation when it focuses on the area of the instinctual representatives." In a comparable passage Schafer (1968, p. 214) defines fusion and defusion in terms of compatibility or synthesis (or the lack thereof) of specific libidinal and aggressive aims.

first becomes manifest as *ad hoc* response in the event of frustration, we also assume the same for libido or even awareness.

But frustration in this broad sense is primitively the psychological correlate of physiological disequilibrium. It is the basis for behavior as directional; i.e., frustration initiates behavior which proceeds in accordance with the pleasure principle. The latter regulatory principle conceptualizes a basic dynamic operative within such structural givens that attention is directed outward from a central psychological source of disequilibirum and met, in the average expectable environment, by the object of satisfaction. The movement away from a central psychological source of disequilibrium toward an object of satisfaction is one movement. There is no need to think here of approach as a striving toward the object and of avoidance as a movement away from the source of disequilibrium. However, this unity underlines that the ultimate power of libido and the ultimate power of aggression are also one (Bibring, 1941, p. 298; Jacobson, 1964, p. 13ff.; Applegarth, 1971, p. 413), employed in early development as movement toward a changing sequence of objects of satisfaction and as movement away from a changing sequence of danger situations.

The task of genetic psychology is, of course, not to explain all behavior by reduction to primitive "automatic" modes of approach and avoidance, but to account for how the complexity of adult behavior evolves from such primitive modes. There is not only a changing sequence of satisfactions and of dangers, but also a changing sequence of approach and avoidance modalities. Approach and avoidance in the narrow sense of referring purely to the directionality of immediate behavior become insufficient at higher levels and are subordinated to (i.e., superseded by but included within) libido and aggression, motivational concepts of greater generality. The relatively simple directionality of primitive approach and avoidance behavior yields to various levels of intentionality which are based on assimilative and accommodative learning (Klein, 1967, p. 126), i.e., on the established internalization of prior relationships with both objects of satisfaction and sources of danger. Both approach and avoidance can be less automatic and less peremptory.

Libido and Aggression As
General Motivational Concepts

Heeding the danger itself is a step beyond primitive pleasure-principle regulation and beyond what used to be called the purified pleasure ego (Freud, 1915, p. 136) to the reality principle and the reality ego. Just as the scope of reference of the pleasure principle includes, but is not limited to, the phenomenon of pleasure-seeking (Rapaport, 1960a, p. 875; see also Freud, 1950, p. 371), libido as a general motivational concept includes, but is not limited to, primitive approach behavior "automatically" directed toward the object of satisfaction. Similarly, aggression as a general motivational concept is not limited to "automatic" avoidance of noxious stimuli.

Libido may be defined as a concept referring to the motivational aspect of behavior which aims to resolve tension[7] by dependent interaction with objects of satisfaction and of interest. It encompasses the motivational aspect of primitive approach and consummatory action and whatever is involved in the integration of such experience, including the derivative motivations thus established.[8]

Aggression may be defined as a concept referring to the motivational aspect of behavior which aims to resolve tension by eliminative, independent action in relation to the source of tension or whatever comes to represent the source of tension. Aggression proper derives from primal aggression. The latter we define as the motivational aspect of the primitive automatic flight response. Primal aggression, understood as automatically veering away from a source of tension, is itself objectless. Aggression proper, by virtue of attention being paid to whatever represents a source of tension, can either put at a distance or destroy (Freud, 1915, p. 137) a thus constituted object of aggression. In addition, and in series with the above, distancing can be repudiation by an act of judgment. In

---

[7] Although the dynamic of motivation is from high tension to low, there could be no tension without structure, i.e., tension maintenance. Learning amounts to the establishment of new-order tension-maintaining structures. The direction of overall development is thus toward higher tension tolerance.

[8] Cf. Kurt Lewin's "quasi-needs" in Rapaport (1951, p. 123).

terms of a dualistic conceptual strategy, we would include such high-level forms of distancing as referents of aggression, just as libido would refer to the motivational aspect of derivative and high-level forms of love and interested approach.

The extreme instance and meaning of dependency is that without interaction with the object of satisfaction, the individual would die. The extreme instance and meaning of eliminative, independent action is that without such action death would ensue by continued exposure to a source of tension or by continued interaction with an object of danger. The phylogenetically established means of dealing with these contingencies is assumed to be first of all the automatic psychological flight response from a source of tension. Danger (the primary source of tension) would thus seem to be temporally prior to desire (the wish).

However, it is assumed that the very nature of the primitive flight response is that attention is directed away from the primary source of tension (Rapaport, 1960a, p. 902).[9] It is in that sense as much a flight toward the object of satisfaction as a flight from the source of tension. Regularly, but never without delay, the flight is met by the object of satisfaction. The object of satisfaction, experienced subsequently as wish or desire, achieves primitive ideational definition prior to the source of tension. Danger, as first of all a source of tension, comes to be consciously or unconsciously defined or interpreted through experiences of release from tension by the intervention of the need-satisfying object. Danger and desire can thus each claim a kind of temporal priority; danger institutes desire and desire implies danger. However, desire leads to the experience of satisfaction through which danger is defined. The question of temporal priority is subordinate to their being mutually constitutive and in that sense equiprimordial.

A previously satisfying object can become an object of danger, in which case the libidinal motivation will be replaced by aggressive motivation. Or, beyond absolute splitting, an object of satisfaction

[9] Piaget (1965) said that "conscious realization starts from the peripheral result of actions before turning to their inner mechanism, which, moreover, it never completely attains" (p. 47; see also pp. 135, 160). The correlative Freudian passages are in Chapter 7 of *The Interpretation of Dreams* (1900, pp. 574, 611, 615).

can become partly an object representing tension, and thus an object of ambivalence. Neither sadism nor masochism is "pure-culture" aggression; both are object-dependent, complex expressions of partially denied ambivalence (Hartmann, Kris, Loewenstein, 1949, p. 27). However, even aside from the obvious ambivalence of sadism and masochism, there may be no pure-culture aggression proper. On the model of moving away from the perceptually identical object of primitive ideation, all objects of aggression probably represent to some extent erstwhile objects of satisfaction. Such a factor could modify any actual flight or fight in various ways. It might account for a component of retaliatory intensity on the basis of an interpretation of having been betrayed. The same factor, on the other hand, might be a basis for identification with the aggressor (A. Freud, 1936; Schafer, 1968, p. 210) wherein the object is eliminated as an object of danger by a merging similar to that which on prior occasions had occurred with the object of satisfaction, transiently in moments of consummation and more enduringly in periods of absence of the object.

The psychoanalytic literature contains many references to the difficulty of conceptualizing an object of aggression on a par with the object of libido. According to our formulation, the objects of aggression and libido are not on a par. Thus we mention two forms of aggression, primal aggression and aggression proper, and do not do so in the case of libidinal motivation. The reason for this difference is that we assume objects are initially constituted as peremptory or nonperemptory objects of satisfaction or interest, encountered in the process of attention being directed away from a central psychological source of disequilibrium—in Klein's terms (1967, p. 90), a primary region of imbalance. In analogy with the Jamesian theory of affect (1890, pp. 449–454), whatever knowledge one has of the source of imbalance derives not from consciously directing attention to it, but by virtue of the automatic flight from it. At such a primitive level, the concepts of primal aggression, primal repression, and the pleasure principle merge. All refer to such automatic flight (see Freud, 1900, p. 600). However, the memory of tension resolved allows for ideational and affective signal anticipation of both objects of satisfaction and sources of danger. Such learning is the basis for going beyond knowing that there is a danger by reason of flight, and, in departure from the Jamesian affect analogy, allows for a decision to flee (or fight) because a danger has been recognized. At such a level, primal aggression as flight can become aggression proper—the eliminative intention to distance or destroy.

Primal aggression has no object in the sense of the libidinal object. Its "object" could only be its own source from which flight occurs—hardly an object as ordinarily defined. Aggression proper can be directed toward erstwhile objects of satisfaction or any other object experienced as a threat.

The primal objectlessness of aggression, the fact that movement away from threat is primitively identical with the movement toward satisfaction, i.e., that primitive aggression and libido are one, is the source of a power in aggression proper beyond simply a response to external frustration. Objectless aggression founds the possibility of unprovoked attack, which is the essence of aggression proper. Aggression and libido are in the service of a given directionality and developed intentionality to live out a life plan. Obviously, the satisfaction of an integrative intention differs from the satisfaction of an eliminative intention, as does the object relationship involved. However, that one is eliminative and the other integrative does not mean that one aims for death (even silently) and the other for life; both are involved in living out a life plan which eventuates in death. The idea of one instinctual drive aiming for death and another for life grew out of initial reification of the concept libido and later reification of the concept of a destructive drive counterpart. In our opinion, however, the gist of Freud's concept of the death instinct cannot be relegated only to the realm of the biological, as Hartmann, Kris, and Loewenstein suggested (1949, p. 10), anymore than the pleasure principle itself. It is necessary, though, to think of it not as a wish to die, in the narrow sense, but as a general motivational principle on a level with the pleasure principle. Indeed, the pleasure principle as explicated by Rapaport (1960a, p. 875), together with the structural concepts which have evolved, means that the unpleasure principle (Schur, 1966), the constancy principle, the Nirvana principle, the repetition compulsion as originally conceived, and the death instinct are all superfluous concepts. Nevertheless, that which Freud formulated under the name of the death instinct as a silent instinctual drive was perhaps, in a series of attempts, his most far-reaching effort to conceptualize the depth, power, and steadiness of man's potentialities for aggression and of the place of aggression in carrying through the life plan.

SUMMARY

We have suggested that aggression can be defined as the motivational aspect of behavior directed or intended to distance or destroy by modes of flight, fight, or reasoned repudiation. We assume that these modes all derive from a primitive "automatic" flight mechanism which is a part of the primary mental endowment.

Primitive flight responses as attention directed away from a primary region of imbalance are recurrently met, in the average expectable environment, by an object of satisfaction. The memory of this experience (however represented) and the anticipation of its recurrence establish the possibility of approach responses. The interaction, that is, allows the primitive flight response to find a goal and subsequently to become an approach aiming to resolve tension by dependent interaction with an object of satisfaction; the possibility of motivation we conceptualize as libidinal is thus founded.

We have discussed several implications of considering the libidinal and aggressive drives to be both derived from a primitively "blind" flight mechanism and constituted as such through interaction with the environment. We have attempted to show how such a conceptualization might account for convergent and divergent motivation in more adequate fashion than the concepts of instinctual fusion and defusion.

Finally, we have suggested that the actual plurality of motivation in human behavior can nevertheless lend itself to a dualistic conceptual strategy.

BIBLIOGRAPHY

APPLEGARTH, A. (1971), Comments on Aspects of the Theory of Psychic Energy. *J. Amer. Psychoanal. Assn.*, 19:379–416.

BIBRING, E. (1941), The Development and Problems of the Theory of the Instincts. [Reprinted:] *Int. J. Psycho-Anal.*, 50:293–308, 1969.

BRIDGMAN, P. W. (1927), *The Logic of Modern Physics*. New York: Macmillan.

ERIKSON, E. H. (1950), *Childhood and Society*. New York: Norton.

FREUD, A. (1936), *The Ego and the Mechanisms of Defense*. New York: International Universities Press, rev. ed., 1966.

FREUD, S. (1895), A Reply to Criticisms of My Paper on Anxiety Neurosis. *Standard Edition*, 3:121–139. London: Hogarth Press, 1953.

——— (1900), The Interpretation of Dreams. *Standard Edition*, 4 & 5. London: Hogarth Press, 1953.

——— (1905), Three Essays on the Theory of Sexuality. *Standard Edition*, 7:125–243. London: Hogarth Press, 1953.

——— (1912), The Dynamics of Transference. *Standard Edition*, 12:97–108. London: Hogarth Press, 1958.

——— (1914), On the History of the Psycho-Analytic Movement. *Standard Edition*, 14:3–66. London: Hogarth Press, 1957.

——— (1915), Instincts and Their Vicissitudes. *Standard Edition*, 14:111–140. London: Hogarth Press, 1957.

——— (1916–1917), Introductory Lectures on Psycho-Analysis. *Standard Edition*, 15 & 16. London: Hogarth Press, 1963.

——— (1920), Beyond the Pleasure Principle. *Standard Edition*, 18:3–64. London: Hogarth Press, 1955.

——— (1924), The Economic Problem of Masochism. *Standard Edition*, 19:157–170. London: Hogarth Press, 1961.

——— (1926), Inhibitions, Symptoms and Anxiety. *Standard Edition*, 20:77–175. London: Hogarth Press, 1959.

——— (1940), An Outline of Psycho-Analysis. *Standard Edition*, 23:141–207. London: Hogarth Press, 1964.

——— (1940–1941 [1892]) Sketches for the Preliminary Communication of 1893. *Standard Edition*, 1:146–154. London: Hogarth Press, 1966.

——— (1950 [1895]), Project for a Scientific Psychology. *Standard Edition*, 1:283–397. London: Hogarth Press, 1966.

HARTMANN, H. (1939), *Ego Psychology and the Problem of Adaptation*. New York: International Universities Press, 1958.

——— (1948), Comments on the Psychoanalytic Theory of Instinctual Drives. In: *Essays on Ego Psychology*. New York: International Universities Press, 1964, pp. 69–89.

——— (1952), The Mutual Influences in the Development of Ego and Id. *Ibid.*, pp. 155–181.

——— (1955), Notes on the Theory of Sublimation. *Ibid.*, pp. 215–240.

——— KRIS, E., & LOEWENSTEIN, R. M. (1949), Notes on the Theory of Aggression. *This Annual*, 3/4:9–36.

JACOBSON, E. (1964), *The Self and the Object World*. New York: International Universities Press.

JAMES, W. (1890), *The Principles of Psychology*, Vol. 2. New York: Henry Holt.

KLEIN, G. S. (1967), Peremptory Ideation. In: *Motives and Thought*, ed. R. R. Holt [*Psychological Issues*, Monogr. 18/19]. New York: International Universities Press, pp. 78–128.

LORENZ, K. (1935), Companionship in Bird Life. In: *Instinctive Behavior*, ed. & tr. C. Schiller. New York: International Universities Press, 1957, pp. 83–128.

—— (1937), The Companion in the Bird's World. *Auk*, 54:245–273.

LOEWALD, H. W. (1970), Psychoanalytic Theory and the Psychoanalytic Process. *This Annual*, 25:45–68.

—— (1971), On Motivation and Instinct Theory. *This Annual*, 26:91–128.

—— (1972), Freud's Conception of the Negative Therapeutic Reaction, with Comments on Instinct Theory. *J. Amer. Psychoanal. Assn.*, 20:235–245.

MONOD, J. (1971), *Chance and Necessity*. New York: Knopf.

OLINICK, S. L. (1970), Negative Therapeutic Reaction. *J. Amer. Psychoanal. Assn.*, 18:655–672.

PIAGET, J. (1965), *Insights and Illusions of Philosophy*. New York: World Publishing, 1971.

RAPAPORT, D., ed. & tr. (1951), *Organization and Pathology of Thought*. New York: Columbia University Press.

—— (1957), The Theory of Ego Autonomy. In: *The Collected Papers of David Rapaport*, ed. M. M. Gill. New York: Basic Books, 1967, pp. 722–744.

—— (1957 & 1959), Seminars on Elementary Metapsychology. Mimeographed Copies of Seminars held at Austen Riggs Center, ed. S. C. Miller et. al.

—— (1960a), On the Psychoanalytic Theory of Motivation. In: *The Collected Papers of David Rapaport*, ed. M. M. Gill. New York: Basic Books, 1967, pp. 853–915.

—— (1960b), Psychoanalysis As a Developmental Psychology. *Ibid.*, pp. 820–852.

—— & GILL, M. M. (1959), The Points of View and Assumptions of Metapsychology. *Ibid.* pp. 795–811.

—— & WEBER, A. O. (1941), Teleology and the Emotions. *Ibid.*, pp. 80–90.

RICOEUR, P. (1970), *Freud and Philosophy*. New Haven: Yale University Press.

SCHAFER, R. (1968), *Aspects of Internalization*. New York: International Universities Press.

—— (1970), An Overview of Heinz Hartmann's Contributions to Psychoanalysis. *Int. J. Psycho-Anal.*, 51:425–446.

SCHUR, M. (1966), *The Id and the Regulatory Principles of Mental Functioning*. New York: International Universities Press.

Acting Out As a Character Trait

Its Relation to the Transference

MARTIN H. STEIN, M.D.

FEW TERMS IN OUR FIELD OF INQUIRY HAVE BEEN SUBJECTED TO more abuse than has the expression "acting out." For the most part it has been interpreted so broadly as to include any behavior which is assumed to be irrational. As a reaction to this trend, there has been a move to confine it narrowly to the status of a transference phenomenon.

Even analysts are by no means unanimous about what acting out is, in whom it occurs, and how it should be treated. Some have suggested that we do away with the term altogether, but I am inclined to agree with those (e.g., Greenacre, 1968) who feel that we should be in no hurry to do so. It is my thesis that acting out, adequately defined, is the prototype of complex human behavior and that a thorough study of the phenomenon can teach us a good deal about the nature of human activity on a wide scale, including something about the nature of social and political forces.

One attempt to resolve the confusion which has beset the term was that of Anna Freud (1968). At the 1967 Copenhagen symposium she advanced the thesis that in the neurotic patient, acting out occurred only in the analytic situation, thus: "Unlike the neurotic, the delinquent, the addict, and the psychotic act out habitually, i.e. also without the releasing benefits of the analytic technique" (p. 168).

An earlier version of this paper was presented at the Regional Psychoanalytic Meeting, Mohonk Mountain House, June 3, 1972.

This idea, which is held by others as well (e.g., Rangell, 1968; Vanggaard, 1968), is based on the proposition that the adult neurotic acts out to a significant degree *only* in connection with the analytic situation, while in a state of resistance stimulated by the transference.

Such a thesis was perhaps necessary to reduce the intolerable diffusion of the term which had overtaken Freud's original definition in "Remembering, Repeating and Working-Through" (1914): "we may say that the patient does not *remember* anything of what he has forgotten and repressed, but *acts* it out. He reproduces it not as a memory but as an action; he *repeats* it, without, of course, knowing that he is repeating it" (p. 150).[1]

We could indeed adhere to Anna Freud's use of the term "acting out," so long as we confined ourselves to the analysis of the "ideal neurotic," i.e., that elusive patient whose analysis consists only of the resolution of neurotic symptoms—obsessional thoughts, phobias, and the like. With such patients we might treat the analytic situation as if it were a closed system, with due regard for the other 23 hours and 10 minutes of the patient's life, and view that residue of the day as a period during which the patient undergoes a set of experiences for the sake of his 50-minute analytic sessions.

This is of course a caricature, as Freud learned when he attempted the analysis of Dora. His patient's character structure and the vicissitudes of daily life made the analysis a highly complex and fluid situation, although—this cannot be repeated too often—it need not threaten the essential intactness of the analytic method for analysts and patients who are willing and able to use it. I have discussed this at length in a previous paper (1969).

I propose that Freud's relatively restricted definition, as restated by Anna Freud, be made more broadly applicable, without at the same time encouraging the overuse to which it has been subjected. It is regrettable that the term "acting out" has been applied to a very wide range of behavior, including the impulsive behavior of

---

[1] In the preface to this work the Editor of the *Standard Edition* stated: "This paper is noteworthy, apart from its technical interest, for containing the first appearance of the concepts of the 'compulsion to repeat' (p. 150) and of 'working-through' (p. 155)" (p. 146).

delinquents and criminals, the actions of political extremists, sexual promiscuity, extended even to defiant or merely mischievous behavior by which patients succeed in provoking their analysts.

This has created a clinical and theoretical confusion which needs to be resolved, as Anna Freud suggested, but not, I propose, at the cost of leaving out of our description a highly interesting series of characteristics manifested by adult neurotic patients, not only during, but *before* analysis has begun. These are best denoted as a distinct character trait: "the tendency to act out." Such patients give a history marked by repetitive, complexly patterned behavior, generally precipitated by frustration. This pattern offers a contrast to their usual mode of life; it has certain features distinctly at variance with what appear to be the dominant modes of the personality.

When such patients enter analysis, the acting-out pattern continues as before and it may, for a time, become more flamboyant, a development which is likely to be disconcerting even to the most unflappable of analysts. Nevertheless, in the more favorable cases, this situation changes with the development of a transference neurosis. We are likely to see an increasing control of the repetitive behavior pattern outside the analysis, followed sooner or later by the occurrence of some equivalent behavior within or in clear relation to the analytic situation. In other words, acting out in life is replaced by acting out in the transference.[2]

This is analogous to the classical development of the transference neurosis in the predominantly "symptomatic" patient, whose character problems are less prominent in the pathological structure, and in whom symptom formation rather than "acting-out" behavior recurs in a transference setting.

"Acting out in the transference" would be defined now very much as Freud defined it in 1914. But the *tendency* to act out, regarded as a character trait, implies that the patient has been "acting out" for much of his adult life; and, further, that the acting out in the transference which occurs during analysis is a secondary development—and, as I shall try to demonstrate, a crucial one for

---

[2] This is reminiscent of Aichhorn, but we are not dealing with delinquents, nor are we departing from the usual analytic technique.

the success of the analytic method.[3]

I am in agreement with those authors who maintain that the character trait, "the tendency to act out," need not be considered pathognomonic of delinquency, addiction, or psychosis.[4] On the contrary, it may be seen in its purest form in a group of neurotic patients, otherwise fairly well-integrated, sometimes talented and distinguished people, who may have achieved considerable personal success and even prominence in fields in which a dramatic way of life has some advantages.

It is true that we observe in delinquency, addiction, and psychosis, as well as in adolescence, a great deal of impulsive, grossly irrational, even violent behavior which is likely to be chaotic and unpredictable. I maintain that such chaotic behavior, often referred to, all too loosely, as "acting out," should not be so classified, for it is in essence quite different.

"Acting out," whether in preanalytic daily life or during analysis, is irrational and may indeed be impulsive and violent. It is, however, neither chaotic nor unpredictable. On the contrary, it is highly organized, requiring a well-structured ego, though it may not be fully adequate in some important respects. The phenomenon of acting out includes a number of constant features, which allow us to establish a distinct category and in turn to describe a recognizable character trait. None of this is new to the literature of acting out, yet it is worth summarizing here. (Cf. Bird, 1957; Fenichel, 1945; Greenacre, 1950, 1963, 1968; Spiegel, 1954.)

The term should be restricted to actions which are complex and are repeatedly carried out over extended periods of time—not merely a series of symptomatic acts which are in themselves trivial and relatively simple.

Acting out is repetitive in the strict sense, not merely recurrent, and it is often predictable by the individual's friends and family

---

[3] In a discussion of an early version of this paper Burness E. Moore emphasized the usefulness of the distinctions between "acting in," "acting out," and "living out." Although these are useful distinctions descriptively, I wish in this paper to emphasize the continuity of these various phenomena and therefore employed the rubric "the tendency to act out" as a character trait.

[4] See "Reports of Discussions of Acting Out" (Klauber, 1968; Calef, 1968; Gonzalez, 1968; Heilbrun, 1968; Laplanche, 1968).

and, ultimately, his analyst. When such an action has occurred, there are plenty of people ready to say, "He (or she) has done it again." Only the patient is likely to be surprised—or, more often, chagrined. Distinct episodes are related to a particular type of frustration to which the individual responds in a characteristic way.

A constant feature is the disturbance of reality testing, which is temporary and confined to the area that is under control of the dominant fantasy. Judgment, otherwise excellent, is ignored, impaired, or largely suspended. In this respect it differs from the disturbances in reality functions which characterize the psychotic and delinquent, in whom these defects are likely to be widespread and fixed. Although not immediately evident, the progress of the analysis reveals the extent of magical thinking. Here again its prominence is temporary, and is confined to the area controlled by the fantasy.

At the time the action occurs, it is usually completely rationalized. It is, so to speak, ego-syntonic, so that it is carried on free of criticism, and generally is not immediately subjected to moral disapproval.

A really well-developed piece of acting out will soon reveal a distinct element of drama in the act itself. It occurs most often and most distinctly in individuals with some ambition or flair for drama—or melodrama. Prominent narcissistic and exhibitionistic features are observed or readily inferred.

The state of mind in which acting out occurs is comparable to the person's normal alert wakefulness. In a few cases, often associated with perverse activity, or alcohol, rather complex acts may be carried out in a dissociated, almost fuguelike state. Not typical of the neurotic acting out, such a state occurs now and then in this group of patients.

The tendency to act out is in my experience more likely to be associated with so-called "hysterical" characters—at least it seems to be less frequent in obsessional and phobic patients. When it occurs in borderline and psychotic patients, or addicts, it is less well defined, more chaotic and impulsive—and more likely to be associated with disturbances of consciousness—and must be understood and treated rather differently.

When acting out is subjected to analysis, it *may* take only a few weeks or months to give some idea of the unconscious fantasy which underlies the phenomenon, and which is being quite literally "acted out." Very often, the patient's behavior may best be described as a dramatic performance in a play which he has written, and in which he plays the chief role and often others as well. The play is acted over and over again. Except for the (usually tragic) hero or heroine, the cast changes from time to time, but the script remains the same, and the ending is anticipated by the audience—but not by the author-director-actor, who each time looks for a happy ending which is never to occur. And so it goes, again and again. This dramatic element has been described by Anna Freud (1949) and Greenacre (1963), yet even now its dynamic and genetic significance and implications for technique are not sufficiently explored.

Usually late in the analysis we discover that the underlying fantasy is highly organized and condensed, and that it represents both the direct derivatives of, and the defense against, the conflicts engendered by an early traumatic experience or set of experiences. While such fantasies are highly charged with erotic elements, they do not lack aggressive features, often of a castrating type, but which may be even more primitive, e.g., cannibalistic.

The acting out, although related often to one predominant fantasy and one traumatic experience or a series, nevertheless carries when fully developed a large group of meanings. It constitutes an ideal illustration for the principle of multiple function, as I have discussed it elsewhere (Stein, 1969).

Greenacre has suggested that the significant traumatic experiences are likely to date from that special period during which speech development is particularly rapid, viz., the age of 2 or 3 or so. While such a speculation is difficult to establish as a general rule, it makes very good sense theoretically, accounting for the predilection for action rather than thought and verbalization. Now and then one comes across some striking clinical evidence which tends to support it.

For some months a young woman patient, well advanced in analysis, had been voicing the most intense admiration for me, my skill as an analyst, my standing in the profession, and the like, a phenomenon akin to if not identical with the "idealizing transference" described by Kohut (1971), of which more below. Meanwhile, her pronounced tendencies to act out seemed to have disappeared entirely. She became, for the time, a "perfect" analysand.

When, after some thought, I indicated, as gently as I might, the need to subject this development to analytic scrutiny, she reacted with intense anger and threatened to resume her formerly well-established pattern of behavior.

These threats were not carried out, but a few days later, she told me at the beginning of a session that she would refuse to leave my office at the end of the session. Perhaps she would stay all day! If I wanted her out, I should have to remove her forcibly. At the appropriate time, I indicated the end of the session. She stood up, gave me a somewhat wry smile, and left without further incident.

The following session revealed this episode to have been a reenactment, in the transference, of a distinctive childhood experience. At the age of 2, she had been sent off to a nursery school, but she cried so uncontrollably that she had to be removed, and the attempt abandoned for the time. Two years later a sibling was born, and she was again sent to school.

Now she tried to remain home by complaining of illness, but after being pronounced fit on several occasions by the family pediatrician, she was carried out of the house and to the nearby school, kicking and screaming. It may have been the doctor himself who took her on several occasions. Once at school, she was transformed into a model student, a bright and well-behaved little girl. But each morning, for some time, the "act" would be repeated, until it finally disappeared.

The little girl had in fact been neglected by her elegant and narcissistic parents, who, professing the highest ideals of child rearing (according to Freud and other authorities), flouted these ideals in practice and ignored the child, except when they could show her off to advantage.

This young woman demonstrated discrepancies between verbalized thought and behavior to an extent which permitted self-destructive acting out to occur in an atmosphere of apparent rationality—or rationalization. Throughout life, she provoked rejections and desertions, each time being disappointed when the inevitable occurred. It was a pattern entirely predictable by close friends and regarded with chagrin by the patient when the episode was over.

Interestingly and not at all atypically (for this type of patient), the acting out affected her personal life most severely. In contrast to a long series of self-induced setbacks in her attempts to establish a gratifying homelife, her very complicated professional career remained virtually free of the tendency to reenact the traumatically determined fantasy, thus permitting considerable occupational success and gratification.

In another patient, acting out in the transference was persistent, taking the form of breaking away from the analysis psychologically, while remaining in it physically. This behavior seemed to have been influenced by a period of physical restraint in childhood, a situation in which only the mind could roam freely while the body was literally bound. The resistance to analysis reenacted what must have been an early acceptance of physical restraint, while rejecting any psychic bonds.

The adult life of this patient was marked by a pattern of repetitive responses to stress which consisted of complex and futile attempts at solution of conflicts that appeared to be current, but which represented on a deeper level the process of being restrained and trying to escape. Highly articulate, he used speech for manipulation and, as is so often the case, quite successfully; but its employment to advance thought, particularly in the quest of self-understanding, was far less successful.

Originally, the capacity for expressing, for enthusiasm, for charm, even for a certain degree of impulsivity, had provided crucially valuable techniques for preserving individuality and effectiveness. Now they had become grossly inadequate to deal with important aspects of adult life.

A convincing memory of traumatic experience in early childhood may be recovered and worked through, but this is a development that occurs late in the analysis. Usually the memory is screened by massive conflicts dating from the oedipal phase and relived in adolescence. While episodes of "acting-out" behavior may occur in adolescence as an effective mode of reality testing (Blos, 1963), the drama in the group I am describing continues to be reenacted throughout adult life, while little effective reality testing occurs and nothing is resolved.

The specific acting out sooner or later makes clear the patient's attachment to a past object, usually a parent or parent surrogate. The lovers who are chosen, for example, may look quite different at first; but we soon discover that they are all the same and that they represent a highly idealized infantile object—idealized negatively, very often, under a cover of worshipful admiration of the parent's remembered image. These and other related narcissistic phenomena are very much part of the clinical picture.

Ultimately, the intense ambivalence of attitudes toward the parents appears in the transference, creating a complicated and stormy analytic situation which places enormous demands on the analyst's understanding, self-discipline, and technical skill (see Bird, 1957). The analyst is particularly subject to attempts at seduction by the most subtle means—and not necessarily at all in the conventional erotic mode. Much more often he is idealized as being beyond such unworthy feelings, and is regarded as truly godlike in his wisdom and self-control. By some patients, he is treated as if he were a powerful protector against destructive impulses, and a totally perfect and benign parent—in complete contrast to the all-too-imperfect parents in reality.

During this phase of the analysis, patients who previously acted out a good deal may become model analysands, entirely happy with their analyses, and behave as if they were totally and miraculously cured. At this point their love for the analyst seems entirely desexualized, and they appear to be in love with analysis itself, as in one of the patients described above.

While this phenomenon bears a close resemblance to what Kohut (1971) has termed "the idealizing transference," I am not sure that the patients I have considered would warrant classification as "narcissistic personality disorders." Narcissistic problems are evident enough, but the essential structure of the personality is not very different from that originally described as "transference neurosis," and there is every reason to adhere to standard psychoanalytic technique.

Kohut's emphasis on special consideration, tact, and careful timing is of course altogether warranted and should be part of any analysis. But in these cases we find little justification for long delays in confronting the analysand with the need to subject his transference attitudes and fantasies to analytic scrutiny.

This does not at all imply an early *interpretation* of transference, but it does assume that the analysand is capable of a degree of critical self-scrutiny, including an awareness of his narcissistic conflicts and their role in distorting his views of reality (see Greenacre, 1950), including the image of the analyst.

Failing to convey this until late in analysis exposes the analyst to the risk of being cast in a role as the sharer or even the accomplice of the most regressive elements in the personality of the analysand, a tricky if not untenable (i.e., unanalyzable) transference position. In patients like these, with a fair capacity for reality testing and high perceptivity, such modifications are rarely necessary and generally undesirable, however indicated they may be in the narcissistic disorders described by Kohut.

It is too bad to introduce trouble into paradise, but it is a task which cannot be too long delayed in the quest for understanding. The patient may, of course, react to such confrontation rather violently, threatening resumption of the more distressing features of old behavior patterns. But this is often followed by a flood of new memories and associations, revealing a history of attempts to be an ideal child who, in the act of overcoming the more violent erotism of the oedipal phase, seduced his parents by his delightful behavior and intellectual accomplishments.

Seductive attempts by these complex and often very intelligent people may therefore consist of playing on the analyst's therapeutic zeal and his narcissistic investment in his work. It is so easy to be off one's guard with a patient who seems to be (and perhaps really is) working very hard at analysis and showing important signs of improvement, and fail to realize the erotism and violence which are so carefully concealed.

More familiar, of course, are hostile attempts to provoke the analyst into activity, to induce him to intervene in such a way as to make further analysis complicated or frankly impossible. Anxiety in the analyst may induce him to prohibit, to warn, or to interpret unnecessarily and prematurely. He may even be impelled to intervene in more massive ways, making ultimate analysis of the transference futile. Rather than destroying the analysis themselves, these patients are more likely to manipulate the analyst into doing so—a victory of sorts, which preserves the self-esteem of the patient and convinces him of the uselessness of analysis. It may convince the analyst, too, but that is another matter.

In these patients, therefore, the hostile transference is most likely to take the form of an attack on the analyst by destroying his work, a self-destructive phenomenon which is sometimes regarded as a manifestation of the negative therapeutic reaction. Whether or not it is so classified, it offers a difficult technical problem. (See also Bird, 1972.)

Fortunately, in this group, reality testing is reasonably intact in most areas, and the problem can usually be brought within the scope of analysis, although by no means is it easy to recognize, understand, and interpret. Nevertheless, the capacity to bring the acting-out pattern into the analytic situation in the form of a transference resistance is a great step forward, if it is accompanied by some degree of self-imposed control of behavior outside the analysis. It is only then, probably, that the patient can understand it in the immediate and vivid (i.e., the "analytic") sense with the analyst as object.

Difficult as this procedure is for the analyst, it is incomparably more distressing for the patient, who must tolerate frustration and anxiety to an extent previously unfamiliar to him. Not only is this extraordinarily painful, but the memories which are invoked and reexperienced are likely to be even more distressing. The situation described in the brief vignettes I presented included extreme suffering, requiring all the resources of the patient to tolerate analysis without resuming self-destructive behavior. Self-control and attempts at renunciation often gave rise to panicky feelings of identity confusion, and even to brief attacks of depersonalization, as if to say, "If I do not act, who am I? Do I exist?"—phenomena which in these patients are generally no more severe than they are in reasonably healthy adolescents in time of stress.

These people are often articulate and may even have chosen careers in which speech plays a crucial role. Their use of words presents us with a fascinating and often exasperating problem.

They are experts at what might be called "pseudocommunication" in analysis, using speech to charm, to attack, to confuse, and much less often to reveal, explore, and inform. The analyst's "best" interpretations (i.e., those of which he is most proud) are taken by the patient and related back as proofs of good behavior, as magical incantations, as intellectual resistances, all without being allowed to touch the core of conflict and memory (Greenacre, 1950, 1963, 1968; Loewenstein, 1956).

In some patients, the memories evoked are those of serious and prolonged illness during the very early years. Sometimes only the later period of an illness is remembered, its earliest symptoms having developed during the first year or two of life. Part of the history consists of the tales told by the parents, especially of their sacrifices for the sick child. The illness also leaves its traces in the form of somatic patterns, in both voluntary and involuntary muscular systems.

Psychically, the experience of forced inactivity during childhood may leave its mark in the need to resist any constraints, including those imposed by the analysis. The analytic principle of thought before action, implied if not spelled out, the regularity of sessions, the use of the couch and the like, may all be treated as if they were revivals of the discipline of the sickroom, with the analyst cast as the oversolicitous or neglectful parent. What more natural than that the child should want to go out and play with his friends, regardless of his illness? And the patient to act, regardless of his neurosis? And to be forbidden and protected?

Here, analysis of the acting out is more difficult, and sometimes limited in scope. But with some adequate structure, it may be possible for the patient to accomplish a good deal, in the way of substituting more for less appropriate defenses, and to derive the substantial benefits of a more efficient reality testing function. Some material may remain intellectualized, partly out of the need to hypothesize early events, rather than reconstruct them; sometimes the memories of infantile disease or neglect are simply too painful to allow extensive reconstruction and recall. Even so, much of the self-destructive quality of the acting out comes under control, and the need for fantasy-bound action is less urgent. The life pattern may follow the same general outline as before, but on a more gratifying, less destructive level.

All of this group demonstrate what might be called "neurotic character," in that their conflicts are expressed in the form of fantasy-bound complex actions, rather than primarily in the form of phobias, conversion symptoms, or obsessions. Aside from the important predilection for repetitive dramatic and maladaptive action in response to special stresses, they do not differ so much in other respects from the symptom neurotics.

Many of our patients who begin analysis as phobic or obsessional lose their symptoms within a few months, leaving us with the task of analyzing the underlying character structure; in a number of cases this contains the tendency to act out as a prominent trait, a fact which may be clearly recognized only after some months or even years of analysis. It is this problem of character which furnishes the essential indication for analysis, even though it may never have appeared as an original complaint.

We know little about those constitutional factors which predispose to acting out, but it would be wise to postulate the existence of early, perhaps biologically classifiable determinants, e.g., the presence of hyperactivity at birth, as well as very early experiential factors, such as those noted by Greenacre (1941). Sociocultural factors are also of the greatest importance in facilitating certain modes of action which are more or less acceptable to the particular society in which one lives, furnishing what Hartmann, Kris, and Loewenstein (1951) called "pathways of discharge." The latter may not predispose to acting out, but they do make one or another form of it more likely. (For examples, see Gans, 1962; Becker, 1964.) This, however, deserves a separate discussion beyond the scope of this paper.

The ego functions which control action are unstable, and there are serious, if temporary lapses in reality testing and judgment. But the disturbance of function is limited in scope and duration, and occurs generally only during the course of the performance, so to speak. Defects there may be, but they are fluid and subject to attempts at repair, often successful.

This group does not correspond precisely to what Helene Deutsch

(1930) described as "fate neurosis," a term with overtones of Wagnerian doom. Her cases occupy a place at the lower end of the scale, with the more severely masochistic, self-destructive character disorders. A similar qualification applies to Greenacre's classic descriptions of "the predisposition to anxiety" (1941), a group of cases which occupy perhaps the lowest level of what might still be called neurotic.

There is some overlapping as well with the borderline and "narcissistic" patients described in some detail by Kohut (1968, 1971) and Kernberg (1970). It is particularly difficult to fit the group I am concentrating on precisely into one or another of Kernberg's categories, which may be too restrictive for the purpose. Generally, my patients would be considered under his "Higher Level of Organization of Character Pathology"—yet the predilection for impelled action would place them in an "Intermediate Level," as would the evidence of pregenitally determined conflicts. At the same time their general level of functioning in many aspects of life gives one the impression of a relatively highly structured and efficient ego and superego functioning—with qualifications.

Such categories as Kernberg's and Kohut's are valuable in allowing us to communicate more freely with others who are investigating the same general questions. But there is the danger that even applying the terms "narcissistic" or "pregenitally determined" may influence the analyst to decide too readily to dispense with the usual psychoanalytic method. As long ago as 1926, Glover concerned himself with this temptation, citing the efforts of Ferenczi, Wilhelm Reich, Waelder, and Aichhorn. He concluded: "we can say definitely concerning the treatment of neurotic character that the ultimate success of any treatment depends on classical psycho-analytic methods which do not shrink from subjecting the seemingly banal routine of everyday life to detailed scrutiny" (p. 30).

His statement still stands. If the patient is analyzable at all, major therapeutic modifications are generally undesirable in that they consist of maneuvers which render the subsequent analysis of transference impossible—or, at the very least, hellishly difficult.

In this group of patients, the development of the transference neurosis is signaled by episodes of acting out in relation to the analyst. If these constitute vital threats to the analysis itself and cannot be dealt with by analytic methods, it becomes obvious sooner or later that the analyst will be forced to break off the analysis and recommend another approach. It should be a reluctant decision, but openly recognized by analyst and patient alike. It may require terminating the treatment, perhaps a transfer to another analyst, in order to avoid stalemates, those analyses which are neither psychoanalysis nor good psychotherapy, but which may go on for years with no benefit to anyone. Some patients with well-developed tendencies to acting out are simply not analyzable, and the sooner this is recognized the better (Bak, 1970), so that other means may be employed for their benefit.

Ideally, however, and fairly often, the acting out in the transference, which has replaced the acting-out pattern in life, need not bring about modification or destruction of the analysis. Given a patient who has the capacity to control action sufficiently to continue the analysis, and an analyst who can tolerate and understand the threats of destructive action, the analysis can maintain its course.

The neurotic character disorders are particularly suited to analytic study and treatment, whether they appear as character problems from the start or are screened by one or another of the classical symptoms of neurosis (e.g., "Dora"). Even though analysis is not invariably effective, it remains the procedure of choice. I do have the impression that it is not given an adequate trial nearly often enough, with an open understanding by both analyst and patient of the goals and limitations of the method and the need for periodic evaluation of its effectiveness.

The importance of the tendency to act out one's fantasies in a recurrent and compelled fashion extends far beyond the small group of cases discussed here. In other neurotic patients, perhaps the majority who request analysis, acting out does not play a prominent role in preanalytic life, but some form of it appears sooner or later with the development of the transference neurosis. Such "acting out in the transference" differs only in degree from the "characteristic" acting out I have described. It is likely to occur later in the analysis, to be less flagrant in its appearance and less threatening to the analytic situation.

In its fundamental quality and genesis, however, it is much the same as in our prototypical group. All the criteria are there, although more difficult to find, including evidence of a previously established repetitive pattern of behavior. At first sight, this would seem to have been well integrated and adaptive, quite unlike "characteristic" acting out. Yet when such an episode of acting out in the transference is carefully analyzed, we find that it and the previously established pattern may be traced to unconscious fantasies and their infantile sources.

Unless this behavior plays a major role in the personality, it is not justified to describe it as a character trait. But the wide occurrence and reenactment of romantic fantasies, of rashly conceived rescues, are the stuff of everyday life. They serve on the one hand to make it tolerable in the face of crushing burdens, but they also act as carriers of anachronistic and irrational elements. We may even postulate such manifestations in the lives of so-called normal individuals, in whom they appear as regressive phenomena without frank symptom formation. They are like the lunatic fringes in stable societies, active and dangerous during periods of severe stress, but fading out of sight with the return of stability.

We may therefore hypothesize a continuum of individual tendencies to act out, from those in whom such patterned behavior becomes evident only under unusual circumstances, such as serious object loss, to those whose lives are dominated by the need to reenact the same pattern of destructive behavior over and over again.

Returning to my central argument, the tendency to act out may be regarded as a universal human characteristic, which in some individuals is sufficiently marked to be considered a character trait of some pathological significance, in that it affects seriously and adversely the course of the individual's life, while in other individuals it is of only minor significance.

In neurotic patients of the type described here, acting out in the transference does not develop *de novo*; it occurs rather as an irresistible shift into the analytic situation, of a previously well-established and clearly outlined pattern of pathological behavior, evoked by the pressure and opportunity offered by the transference. It is in these patients a signal of the development of a transference neurosis and a development essential to the advance of the analytic process.

BIBLIOGRAPHY

BAK, R. C. (1970), Psychoanalysis Today. *J. Amer. Psychoanal. Assn.*, 18:3–21.

BECKER, H. S. (1964), *The Other Side.* New York: Free Press.

BIRD, B. (1957), A Specific Peculiarity of Acting Out. *J. Amer. Psychoanal. Assn.*, 5:630–647.

―――― (1972), Notes on Transference: Universal Phenomenon and Hardest Part of Analysis. *J. Amer. Psychoanal. Assn.*, 20:267–301.

BLOS, P. (1963), The Concept of Acting Out in Relation to the Adolescent Process. *J. Amer. Acad. Child Psychiat.*, 2:118–143.

CALEF, V. (1968), Reports of Discussions of Acting Out. *Int. J. Psycho-Anal.*, 49:225–227.

DEUTSCH, H. (1930), Hysterical Fate Neurosis. In: *Neuroses and Character Types.* New York: International Universities Press, 1965, pp. 14–28.

FENICHEL, O. (1945), Neurotic Acting Out. *Collected Papers*, 2:296–304. New York: Norton, 1954.

FREUD, A. (1949), Certain Types and Stages of Social Maladjustment. In: *Searchlights on Delinquency*, ed. K. R. Eissler. New York: International Universities Press, pp. 193–204.

―――― (1968), Acting Out. *Int. J. Psycho-Anal.*, 49:165–170.

FREUD, S. (1914), Remembering, Repeating and Working-Through. *Standard Edition*, 12:145–156. London: Hogarth Press, 1958.

GANS, H. J. (1962), *The Urban Villagers.* New York: Free Press.

GLOVER, E. (1926), The Neurotic Character. *Int. J. Psycho-Anal.*, 7:11–30.

GONZALEZ, A. (1968), Reports of Discussions of Acting Out. *Int. J. Psycho-Anal.*, 49:227–228.

GREENACRE, P. (1941), The Predisposition to Anxiety. In: *Trauma, Growth and Personality.* New York: International Universities Press, 1969, pp. 17–82.

―――― (1950), General Problems of Acting Out. *Psychoanal. Quart.*, 19:455–467.

―――― (1963), Problems of Acting Out in the Transference Relationship. In: *Emotional Growth.* New York: International Universities Press, 1971, pp. 695–712.

―――― (1968), The Psychoanalytic Process, Transference, and Acting Out. *Int. J. Psycho-Anal.*, 49:211–218.

HARTMANN, H., KRIS, E., & LOEWENSTEIN, R. M. (1951), Some Psychoanalytic Comments on "Culture and Personality." In: *Psychoanalysis and Culture*, ed. G. B. Wilbur & W. Muensterberger. New York: International Universities Press, pp. 3–31.

HEILBRUN, E. (1968), Reports of Discussions of Acting Out. *Int. J. Psycho-Anal.*, 49:228.

KERNBERG, O. F. (1970), A Psychoanalytic Classification of Character Pathology. *J. Amer. Psychoanal. Assn.*, 18:800–822.

KLAUBER, J. (1968), Reports of Discussions of Acting Out. *Int. J. Psycho-Anal.*, 49:224–225.

KOHUT, H. (1968), The Psychoanalytic Treatment of Narcissistic Personality Disorders: Outline of a Symptomatic Approach. *This Annual*, 23:86–113.

—— (1971), *The Analysis of the Self.* New York: International Universities Press.

LAPLANCHE, J. (1968), Reports of Discussions of Acting Out. *Int. J. Psychoanal.*, 49:228–230.

LOEWENSTEIN, R. M. (1956), Some Remarks on the Role of Speech in Psycho-Analytic Technique. *Int. J. Psycho-Anal.*, 37:460–468.

RANGELL, L. (1968), A Point of View on Acting Out. *Int. J. Psycho-Anal.*, 49:195–201.

SPIEGEL, L. A. (1954), Acting Out and Instinctual Gratification. *J. Amer. Psychoanal. Assn.*, 2:107–119.

STEIN, M. H. (1969), The Problem of Character Theory. *J. Amer. Psychoanal. Assn.*, 17:675–701.

VANGGAARD, T. (1968), Contribution to Symposium on Acting Out. *Int. J. Psycho-Anal.*, 49:206–210.

On Attachment to Painful Feelings and the Negative Therapeutic Reaction

ARTHUR F. VALENSTEIN, M.D.

IN THE COURSE OF A FAIRLY CONSIDERABLE EXPERIENCE WITH A number of difficult patients who tend to be refractory to psychoanalytic treatment—and even more so to psychoanalysis in its standard form—it has become evident that many of them have the propensity to be deeply attached to pain. For the most part this is psychic pain, although such patients do not emotionally neglect the possibility of fulfilling themselves with physically occasioned pain, should it present itself. Such individuals, unlike the usual neurotic patient, are also apt to react in a negative therapeutic fashion to what would ordinarily seem appropriate and well-timed interpretations made in the course of the treatment, especially as the transference deepens.[1] They do so to the point where this negation

---

A slightly different version of this paper was presented to the Philadelphia Association for Psychoanalysis, April, 1972, to the Cleveland Psychoanalytic Society, June, 1972, to a joint meeting of the Boston and Western New England Psychoanalytic Societies, October, 1972, and to the San Francisco Psychoanalytic Society, the Denver Psychoanalytic Society, and the Topeka Psychoanalytic Society, November, 1972.

Associate Clinical Professor of Psychiatry, Harvard Medical School, Boston.

[1] By appropriate and well-timed interpretations is meant verbal interventions of an explanatory nature which in timing, form, and specificity seem correct in the context of the analytic data as they have been evolving—and presumably would have been so in the case of a "good" neurotic patient; that is to say, a patient who is capable of substantive recognitions and responses to the content and transference context of the interpretations, who establishes a well-defined transference neurosis, but who is reasonably consistent in grasping what originates from within and what from without, what is fantasy and what is real, and what is past and what is present.

of the potential therapeutic efficacy of the treatment is clearly characteristic of their neuroses or, as is usually the case, their "more than neuroses." In other words, in the course of treatment the transference neurosis becomes the very site of the patient's predilection to exact a singular quality of pain from human relationships, as a consequence of which we see the negative therapeutic effect as it was described by Freud.

I propose to develop the thesis that the core of the negative therapeutic reaction in these instances comes from the patient's attachment to pain. Affects of a painful quality refer to experiential circumstances or events occurring very early in the lives of such patients. Such experience takes place in the setting of the primary object tie as it develops out of the "objectless" stage of primary narcissism (Spitz, 1965), i.e., that time immediately after birth when self and object are in no sense differentiated, being still fused into the limitless self-object, and continuing on into the self-object symbiotic phase of anaclitic love.

THEORETICAL CONSIDERATIONS

A DEFINITION OF PAIN

Since this communication deals predominantly with the maladaptive use of pain and affects connoting pain as a way of relating to the self and others, a limited discussion of the term pain is in order. When it comes to specifying pain of mental origin, i.e., psychic pain in contradistinction to its physical correlate, pain of physical origin, it becomes clear that this distinction is no more valid than the so-called mind-body dichotomy. Psychoanalytic contributions to the subject of pain, starting with Freud's original dynamic formulation in his "Project for a Scientific Psychology" [1895], underscore the borderland nature of the concept and phenomenon as something which developmentally and functionally is between the biological (physiological) and the psychological.[2]

For all its omnipresence as the watchdog alarm guarding life,

---

[2] For a more extensive consideration of pain in general and pain of mental origin as an affect see Ramzy and Wallerstein (1958) and Spiegel (1966).

pain is nonetheless extraordinarily difficult to define succinctly. Webster defines pain as "a state of physical or mental lack of well-being or physical or mental uneasiness that ranges from mild discomfort or dull distress to acute, often unbearable agony; may be generalized or localized, and is the consequence of being injured or hurt physically or mentally or of some derangement of or lack of equilibrium in the physical or mental functions (as through disease) and that usually produces a reaction of wanting to avoid, escape, or destroy the causative factors and its effects."

At the experiential level, in response to either inner or outer stimuli, pain implies sensations, more often discrete, and/or diffuse emotional states of an uncomfortable, unpleasurable, and distressful nature. Qualitatively, the contemplation of pain calls forth such synonyms as pang, ache, and suffering; or misery and agony; or anxiety, disquiet, insecurity, and worry; or irritation, bitterness, and discontent; or unhappiness, depression, grief, anguish, and wretchedness. Coordinately, fear or anxiety, rage, whether directly expressed at others or frustrated and possibly turned back upon the self as guilt and depression, longing and frustration, or loss and grief, or helplessness and hopelessness, or somatic distress associated with *Unlust* at the psychic level—all these constitute painful affects.

Briefly then, for purposes of this communication, I shall use the term *pain* broadly within the context of these considerations. The term encompasses pain and affects associated with it, whether the pain is initiated physiologically and has psychic concomitants, or whether the pain is predominantly psychic in origin in consequence of interpersonal or intrapsychic unconscious conflict and has physiological concomitants. The connotation will be a specific affect (*Schmerz*) or related affect within the psychoanalytic concept of unpleasure (*Unlust*).

THE NEGATIVE THERAPEUTIC REACTION

Not surprisingly, the earliest reference to the negative therapeutic reaction[3] comes from Freud (1918) who, in reporting his experience

---

[3] The validity of the term "negative therapeutic reaction" has been questioned by several discussants. No doubt, the historical issues which led to the concept, as well as its current clinical and theoretical value, could be critically reconsidered.

with the Wolf-Man, referred to the patient's "habit of producing transitory 'negative reactions'; every time something had been conclusively cleared up, he attempted to contradict the effect for a short while by an aggravation of the symptom which had been cleared up" (p. 69). He compared it to the tendency of children to respond negativistically to prohibitions when they are first invoked.

However, in *The Ego and the Id*, Freud (1923) raised such negative reactions, if they are sustained and refractory, to the level of a recognizable syndrome, the "negative therapeutic reaction," of which he wrote: "Every partial solution that ought to result, and in other people does result, in an improvement or a temporary suspension of symptoms produces in them for the time being an exacerbation of their illness; they get worse during the treatment instead of getting better. They exhibit what is known as a 'negative therapeutic reaction.' There is no doubt that there is something in these people that sets itself against their recovery, and its approach is dreaded as though it were a danger. We are accustomed to say that the need for illness has got the upper hand in them over the desire for recovery" (p. 49).

A thorough review of the subject would be redundant, especially since there is a comprehensive report by Olinick (1970) of a panel discussion of the negative therapeutic reaction. However, I would like to mention a few of the historical links which broadened the concept and its etiology subsequent to Freud's introduction of the syndrome, largely to exemplify the potential intransigence of the superego and the aggression embodied in an unconscious sense of guilt and in "masochism immanent in so many people" (Freud, 1937, p. 243).

Later contributions brought out that the negative therapeutic reaction is more than the expression of a relentless superego exacting its "pound of flesh" or suffering, or exerting an "unanalyzable" resistance to the process of "cure." Karen Horney (1936) took up ego and technical aspects in emphasizing that negative therapeutic reactions develop out of a masochistic character structure, are pervasively narcissistic, and are characterized by

---

Perhaps this should be done, but I have not undertaken to do so at this time as it is beyond the scope of this paper.

negative transference reactions with essential competitiveness to the analyst and to his interpretive efforts. Such patients are exceedingly vulnerable in their self-esteem and are afraid of success, which to them connotes the destruction of others. As she put it, "*The negative therapeutic reaction is a special form of the fear of success.* . . . [W]here Freud stresses feelings of guilt I have emphasized anxiety" (p. 38f.).

Joan Riviere (1936) applied the Kleinian point of view of internalized objects and the manic defense against a depressive position to a consideration of the problem of the negative therapeutic reaction. Her major emphasis was on the extent to which ambivalence exists unconsciously in the extremes of love and hate for the internalized object. Of such patients she wrote:

> The true aggressive character of their love, and their unconscious guilt of that, is still denied [p. 320]. There is an even greater fear, . . . over and above this anxiety of accepting analysis on false pretenses and deceiving and betraying his good objects again by it. . . . This is the dread that if he were cured by analysis, faithfully and truly, and made at last able to compass the reparation needed by all those he loved and injured, that the magnitude of the task would then absorb his whole self with every atom of all its resources, his whole physical and mental powers as long as he lives, every breath, every heartbeat, drop of blood, every thought, every moment of time, every possession, all money, every vestige of any capacity he has—an extremity of slavery and self-immolation which passes conscious imagination. This is what cure means to him from his unconscious depressive standpoint, and his uncured *status quo* in an unending analysis is clearly preferable to such a conception of cure—however grandiose and magnificent in one sense its appeal may be [p. 318].

Stanley Olinick (1964) suggested that "those people who display the negative therapeutic reaction were endowed from birth with greater than average funds of aggressive orality and anality. This in turn made the mothering relationship stressful (as it may later the analytic), by investing it with realistic anxieties about filling an assigned role with these masterful infants and children" (p. 544). Both in this paper and in an updated recapitulation (1970), Olinick emphasized that "The negative therapeutic reaction is an acute, recurrent, negativistic emotional crisis in a sadomasochistic person who is prone to depression; it represents a category of superego resistance . . . denotable also as a phase of transference resistance" (p. 666). The negativism, which he sees as highly characteristic, is oppositionally defensive against "the regressive pull towards fusion with an early, depressive, maternal object" (p. 657).

Anna Freud (1952), in a contribution to states of negativism and emotional surrender, said:

> Such persons see the relation to a love object exclusively in passive terms. . . . The passive surrender may signify a return from object love proper to its forerunner in the emotional development of the infant, i.e., primary identification with the love object. This is a regressive step which implies a threat to the intactness of the ego, i.e., a loss of personal characteristics which are merged with the characteristics of the love object. The individual fears this regression in terms of dissolution of the personality, loss of sanity, and defends himself against it by a complete rejection of all objects (negativism) [p. 258f.].

THE DEVELOPMENT OF AFFECTS
IN RELATION TO OBJECTS

Since the topic I have chosen centers on affects and their form and specificity with respect to self and object and the progressively evolving relationship between the two, ideally it calls for a comprehensive theory of affects and a coordinate theory of object relations. Unfortunately, one of the major deficits of psychoanalytic theory is the lack of just such an adequate theory of affects. Possibly we are better off when it comes to a theory of object relations, but even here when we consider the preverbal period and especially the first few months after birth, we are in a highly speculative realm.

Lacking such elegance of theory, I shall offer some hypothetical formulations and speculations that bear upon the early development of affects before I narrow my discussion to the question of pain. A general theory of affects, it seems to me, rests not only on formulations of early development derived from reconstructions retroactively extrapolated from psychoanalytic data, but also on certain assumptions which to some extent are supported by direct observations of the neonate and infantile development, and the extension of modern neurophysiological research into subcortical centers and pathways of the central nervous system associated with what I call "primal affects." [4] There is an accumulating, though rather inconclusive body of phylogenetic and ontogenetic data in this regard.[5]

Consistent with psychoanalysis being paramountly drive-oriented in its earlier phase, the manifestations of affectivity were placed "essentially in motor (secretory and vasomotor) discharge resulting in an (internal) alteration of the subject's own body without reference to the external world" (Freud, 1915b, p. 179). However,

[4] In 1962 I wrote of the theoretical necessity and empirical justification for a concept of *primal affects*, really proto-affects, which developmentally anticipate primitive affects. I acknowledged that the concept of primal affects is necessarily somewhat indefinite because we do not know with any exactitude either the phenomenology or conditions of psychic function at the earliest and most primitive level of life. In this regard, though, we are no worse off than we are with respect to early thought process, or early perception, or any other function during a phase of development when primary process is dominant, and adaptive functional capacities are in a precursor form prior to the differentiation of an increasingly coherent ego. In due course, as a matter of maturation, primitive affects are modified through the process of "taming" (Fenichel, 1941) and modulation, differentiating into a whole variety of socially conditioned affects.

[5] Various observers of the neonate have noted not only evidence of what Spitz (1965) calls *reception* of stimuli, but even the more evolved *awareness* of stimuli (perceptions) much earlier than had heretofore been thought possible. During this earlier, preponderantly physiologically adapted state, before the indices for psychological development begin to differentiate out of the psychophysiological nondifferentiated condition, there are reflexlike physiognomic and bodily responses coincident with feeding, excreting, fondling and caretaking by the mother, which might well be the precursor elements of what later emerges as discernible affects. Spitz (1965) wrote of "primitive prototypes of affective responses."

P. H. Wolff (1966) cautioned "that we must distinguish between an affect expression [in the infant] and the emotional significance which the adult observer may attribute to it." He made an explicit distinction between congenital affect expressions (i.e., *structural attributes*) which are observable in the neonate and their inferred functional significance. There is reasonable consensus that "crying is part of a global experience of discomfort from which more discrete feelings of discomfort will differentiate. . . . [T]here is some evidence that the smile of the infant may be initiated by primitive psychological as well as physiological causes, and that affective meanings are gradually subsumed under the smile as it becomes a means for social interchange with the mother. . . . But when it comes to other affect expressions there is no such consensus about the structural-functional continuity from birth to that time when symbolic behavior makes possible direct inferences about the significance of the expressive behavior" (p. 76).

with the introduction of a systematic ego psychology (Freud, 1923), and even more so after the integration of an explicit adaptational point of view into psychoanalysis (Hartmann, 1939), affects took on an added significance as signals internally (within the self) and as communications externally (with regard to objects). By this time what amounted to an earlier id theory of affects had been supplemented by an ego theory of affects (see Jacobson, 1953, 1971; Rapaport, 1953).

Importantly, this gave theoretical recognition to the clinical observations that "Very early in life, motor responses reflecting affective distress begin to have communicational meaning for adaptation. In general, a whole range of affects, whether affection, anger, guilt and remorse, sadness, despair, etc., convey meaningful action—reaction mobilizing information to the self, as well as to others; often with the implicit or explicit intention of promoting adaptively helpful environmental intervention" (Valenstein, 1962, p. 316). Implicitly this also interdigitates a developmental theory of affects into a developmental theory of object relations. Of course, empirically, the arousal and specificity of affects and the nature of object experience are mutually interactive.

At this point, I should like to call attention to the pleasure principle which suggests in effect that drive discharge or drive satisfaction is associated with affects of a pleasurable variety,[6] whereas impediments to or complications in the fulfillment of inner needs are likely to stimulate painful affects, i.e., anxiety, tension due to frustration, anger which might have to be contained, sadness if not depression. Crucial to the maintenance of optimal levels of psychophysiological equilibrium in the very young child and to the satisfaction or lack of satisfaction of his needs are the ministrations of the mother or mother surrogates (Ritvo and Solnit, 1958).

---

[6] Freud (1915a), in considering the genesis of *love* and *hate*, and their antithesis, suggested that the "relation of *unpleasure* seems to be the sole decisive one. The ego hates, abhors and pursues with intent to destroy all objects which are a source of unpleasurable feeling . . . , [whereas] Love is derived from the capacity of the ego . . . [to obtain] organ-pleasure" (p. 138). "[T]he word 'to love' moves further and further into the sphere of the pure pleasure-relation of the ego to the object and finally becomes fixed to sexual objects in the narrower sense and to those which satisfy the needs of sublimated sexual instincts" (p. 137).

The functional evolution of a good mother-child fit coincident with appropriate and increasingly sensitive mothering responses guarantees to the infant not only survival but the fulfillment of his essential instinctual needs with their components of pleasure. However, if we concede that there is a lability and fluidity of response to objects in the beginning and that affects representing object experience could equally much crystallize in the direction of pain (*Unlust* rather than *Lust*), then it follows that the nature of the object tie during the earliest period of life is critical for the qualitative structuralization of affects out of "primal" and primitive affects.

Another way of phrasing it might be that the predilection toward particular affect responses, i.e., the quality of the affects, may very well reflect the nature of the early object tie as well as, in a superimposed sense, later object experience. My impression from a number of cases which exemplify the negative therapeutic reaction is that the attachment to pain—I might even say, in terms of masochism as well as the instinctual drives,[7] the fixation to pain—generally suggests a major problem in object tie from the first year of life and thereafter. As a matter of fact, well before there can be much differentiation of self and object; a good deal impinges upon the infant from within, viscerally and autonomically in terms of his own physiological functioning; and from without in direct or indirect consequence of the (mother) caretaking surround. It follows that the earliest prototypes of affectivity are responsive just as much to inner events as to outer ones. Thus, a colicky infant may be inclined toward "pain" and *Unlust* in the same way as an infant in whom pain was induced from the outside. If a mother of a discomforted and restless infant then adds to the mother-child misfit, either because of her own incompetency or because of

---

[7] For a consideration of masochism as the outcome of having introjected "the pain-giving object because of an oral need for its love," see Berliner (1947, p. 461). See Loewald (1972) for an extended examination of Freud's conception of the negative therapeutic reaction in terms of a reformulated concept of the instinctual drives. Loewald suggests that "In its more intractable forms the negative therapeutic reaction is rooted in preoedipal, primitive distortions of instinctual and ego development and is thus hardly amenable to interpretations in terms of guilt, conscience, and need for punishment" (p. 244).

reciprocal difficulties, an increasing structuralization of a set toward pain as the predominant affect connoting self and object is likely to emerge in the child.

It seems to me that during this earliest phase of development object representation and self representation coalesce more around the affective correlates of experience than around its cognitive potential. I would suggest, speculatively, that initially affectivity leads cognition, as it were; or at least sets the stage for cognitive realization. To follow Spitz,[8] self and objects are first coenesthetically sensed; later, after having been emotionally "received," they are perceived with added increments of cognitive awareness. In this regard, it may well be that it is the affect coordinate as it takes on a systematic quality of pleasure or unpleasure which provides the experiential substance to object recognition and an increasingly stable object representation bringing about object constancy. If the affects, especially those primal and primitive affects associated with the early self and self-object experience, take a predominantly painful direction, then a set is established wherein pain, i.e., painful affect, connotes the original self-object, and more succinctly later, the self and/or object. Primal and then primitive affects, as I conceive them, appear to serve phenomenologically as transitional experience toward the definition of self and object awareness.

Since preverbally, memory traces are not laid down in a cognitive recoverable form (concretistic experience intersecting with primary process then being the mode of mental functioning), it appears that motor and affect referents of experience serve some equivalence for discrete memory traces in the cognitive sense. Primitive affect states occurring during periods of marked regression are likely to be as far as it is possible to go therapeutically

---

[8] Spitz (1965) called the system present at birth "the *coenesthetic organization*. Here, sensing is extensive, primarily visceral, centered in the autonomic nervous system, and manifests itself in the form of emotions. Accordingly, I prefer to speak of this form of 'perception,' which differs so fundamentally from sensory perception, as *reception*. . . . In contrast to this stands the later development of what I have called *diacritic* organization, where perception takes place through peripheral sense organs and is localized, circumscribed, and intensive; its centers are in the cortex, its manifestations are cognitive processes, among them the conscious thought processes" (p. 44).

toward the recovery of the events or circumstances of the preverbal period. And such primitive affect states appear to be consequent to the propensity of such individuals to relive in later life and in the intense transference recrudescence what they cannot cognitively remember, namely, the aura of early experience including the *sense* of self and self-object. This is especially so if, as is usually the case, they are strongly fixated to early trauma associated with pain; then they readily regress to primitive affect states characteristic of such trauma.[9]

What is more, as development proceeds apace for such individuals, later conflicts originating postverbally and increasingly subject to secondary process functioning and cognitive organization are laid down as distinct memories, the cognitive and affective qualities of which are recoverable through the analytic instrument of free association. This would refer particularly to the oedipal phase, but not exclusive of preoedipal, phallic, anal, and even in certain respects oral loci for conflict. All these developmental phases, though, offer a potential lodgement for *Unlust* that has been carried forward from the preverbal period if an opportunity is needed for realizing a previously acquired taste for pain. Individuals who are markedly fixated to early self and object experience in terms of painful affect maladaptively exploit the *Unlust* of conflicts of a developmentally more advanced phase, condensing into them their underlying earlier requirement for suffering as a matter of facility and overdetermination.

The domain of analysis proper as a therapeutic procedure is in conflicts of the oedipal phase and those preoedipal conflicts which originated postverbally and which are thus recoverable through free association, and made accessible to secondary process consideration and interpretation. What appears to happen in persons such as I am describing is that even though these later conflicts[10] are brought

[9] Trauma is defined as an event (or events), whether originating endogenously or exogenously or both, which occasions overwhelming stimuli, the psychic consequence of which is the arousal of substantial painful affect (Freud, 1926). As Strachey in his introduction to *Inhibitions, Symptoms and Anxiety* pointed out, trauma is in essence "an experience of helplessness on the part of the ego in the face of an accumulation of excitation, whether of external or of internal origin, which cannot be dealt with" (p. 81).

[10] Among these conflicts I include not only those of the oedipal situation, but also

forward and analyzed appropriately, the expected improvement and recovery does not take place. Such patients appear to react refractorily to correct interpretation with regression to primitive negativistic states. They become immersed in painful affects to which they appear to cling.

I believe that such affects are emphatically held to because they represent the early self and self-object. Giving up such affects, coincident with mostly correct, but insufficiently deep interpretations would be equivalent to relinquishing a part of the self and/or self-object at the level which those affects represent. Paradoxically, even if given in that depth, such interpretations would be nevertheless nonmutative because they would aim at preverbal states and trauma antedating cognitive recoverability, and hence unavailable cognitively or verbally at the paradigm level of the latent affect. It would be like asking the patient to change the sense of his early self and self-objects, almost before he could have become really perceptively aware of their form. And this is asking a "bit" much of any patient.

CASE REPORT

This clinical report which of necessity is selective is intended to illustrate the preceding theoretical discussion. One qualification, though, must be made explicit. Clearly, a person who has a considerable proclivity for pain is certain to be significantly masochistic in his character structure and sadomasochistic in his libidinal organization and erotic life. I will not, however, directly address myself to this issue, nor will I expressly include a discussion of the narcissistic elements on this instance, even though they were clearly evident, since I wish to focus primarily upon early affects of a painful quality as potential developmental organizers of the sense of self and/or objects.

My patient, with whom I worked intensively for some five years, was 21 years old when he was referred to me because of a growing decompensation in his adjustment during the latter part of his final

---

the preoedipal ones which are within the range of cognitive recoverability and specificity.

year at college. His disturbance became acute in the months immediately preceding and following his graduation. What precipitated his pervasive anxiety and fear of loss of control, even to the point of going crazy, was the dread that he might be inducted into the army, and his inability even to contemplate this eventuality.

As he put it shortly after we started treatment, "The thought of going into the army, the total male environment, the discipline of it . . . being thrown in with all those men I can't stand, having to move your bowels in the first five minutes of the morning. I just couldn't do it, . . . to be completely at the mercy of all those men. I knew I couldn't face it. This is what brought it to the fore really, that and the dreams I have been having all that time; dreams of sexual perversion and dreams of erupting in my family, erupting at my mother which kept coming back and back. . . . The mind is funny, destroying me, and I am mad at being like this."

He was really on the verge of a homosexual panic and practically recognized it, even though he could hardly bear the realization because it verged so much on the real for him. In fact, throughout much of the treatment, especially the first half, he was taxed greatly by his near conviction that wishes, i.e., feelings and thoughts, were tantamount to action. He was intensely afraid that he would be seen as a homosexual, or at least that such compulsive homosexual thoughts would get the best of him.

However, lest the initial precipitating homosexual threat to his stability be mistaken for the major source of his difficulties, let me add at this point that it soon became evident in treatment that his uncertain sense of self and his conflictual, pain-ridden tie to objects were on a much deeper and fundamental level of basic distrust-trust, with a strong paranoid coloring and an ambivalent struggle to free himself from an anaclitic tie to his primary objects.

After a series of vis-à-vis interviews during which the patient gave considerable evidence of an introspective gift and of good potential for objectivity and insight, we agreed to the use of the couch, with the hope of carrying through an analysis in a relatively standard form. However, before very long it became evident that the patient was too disturbed for this procedure. So we returned to a vis-à-vis arrangement, although still on an intensive basis. Thus he regained the opportunity of observing me directly, and of having much more feedback and responsiveness from me than would be the case in a standard analysis.

In describing his symptoms early in the course of treatment he spoke of having spells or attacks when he would become aware of very disconcerting tingling sensations in and about his anus, which then spread out toward the inner thighs, testicles, and scrotum. The scrotum would then contract, pulling his testes close in toward the body. With it would come a sense of movement in the lower bowel, with a movement of its fecal contents and a discomfort, not exactly like a cramp but perhaps more like gas. At such times he would become very upset and tremble agitatedly. His feeling was that there must be some connection between the anus, defecation, and sex.

At a more general level, he often somatized anxiety and was highly sensitive to changes in temperature, tactile stimuli, and noise. Throughout his treatment he complained of being uncomfortably hot, and under circumstances of physical closeness to others he sometimes felt such literal revulsion that it might be experienced as nausea. The separation between affects and physiological effects was quite fluid in him, and in this respect his psychophysiological responsivity was unusually labile and like that of an infant or small child.

After a year or more in treatment he finally acknowledged one of his secret dreads. He confessed that as a small child he had habitually engaged in a really awkward masturbatory practice which he was fully convinced had permanently damaged him. While he held this conviction in a delusional way, it also might have been true that there was a minor asymmetry of his genitals. In reality though it did not appear to create a functional handicap and should have been relatively inconsequential. However, through much of the treatment he clung desperately to this "fixed idea" of an irrefutable and irreversible defect, which fragmented his sense of intactness as a person and destroyed his adequacy as a man. And through it, in expectation of derision and humiliation should he expose himself, he validated his essentially paranoid distrust of others.

As a genetic paradigm for the future it is highly significant that his childhood masturbation was more anxiety- and pain-provoking than pleasure-yielding, thus fixating pain into autoerotic experience. Developmentally, this anticipated his adolescent and adult expectations that sexual intimacy would be inevitably shaming and painful, putting it in the service of distrust and alienation from others rather than trust and closeness and pleasurable intimacy.

Not until approximately three years later did we turn to the use of the couch in a more systematic psychoanalytic free-associative procedure. By then we had done a great deal of therapeutic work with regard to the facultative delusions regarding his body, and toward the diminution in the transference of the considerable homosexualized distrust, replacing it with a more abiding and sustained quality of trust. He really was afraid at a deeper level that he would lose his integrity and individuality. It was not that the intense attraction-repulsion nature of the transference totally disappeared in the course of time, but gradually it took a more neurotic form. Even though the patient might become substantially regressed, he did not necessarily believe that fantasy would become fact.

To give something of the personal history of this handsome and highly intelligent man, he was the third in a family of four boys. He was apparently his mother's favorite and should have been the daughter that she wanted. He also resembled her physically and in manner more than any of his brothers.

The mother, the only girl in her family of several brusque, athletically burly older brothers, a distant father, and a thoroughly controlling, overwhelming mother, had grown up to be more comfortable riding horses and looking after them than caring for small children. She was an attractive woman and could be pretty when she gave herself a chance, but she apparently inhibited realizing and expressing her femininity, even though she was not really masculine. There was much to suggest a strong defensive identification with the phallic aggressor in her character structure. She was not without interest in or love for her children, but basically shy and inhibited; she was inconstant in her ability to express warmth. It was clearly there, but mostly hidden behind jittery doubting and indecision which alternated with argumentativeness and a potential for explosive anger, especially when my patient was younger and she was taxed by her lively masculine brood.

An incident which occurred relatively late in his treatment was described by him as characteristic of his mother, and how it must have been when he was small. He had gone home for a Thanksgiving reunion. An older married brother was there with his family, the youngest of whom, a little girl, was taken on her grandmother's lap to be loved. However, the grandmother, that is, the patient's mother, apparently could not allow herself to be maternally warm and loving, which is clearly how she felt toward her granddaughter, but instead expressed her affection in a clumsy, typically aggressive way. "She was sort of gruff, she didn't talk to the child nicely, but made noises, almost as though she was going to eat it." She jiggled the child in a way that should have been uncomfortable for the baby, being insensitively abrupt and aggressive, so it seemed to my patient. Looking on, he felt as though it were familiar to him, as if she might have been like that at pivotal times when he was little.

Yet, during a Christmas visit home a few weeks later, when pictures from childhood were being shown to the family, including some of his mother playing with or holding her children when they were small, she did not look all that unmaternal. This impression or recollection of her connected with other memories, from the positive side of his ambivalent tie to her, of the years when he was very small and so dependently attached to her. He recalled how nice she could be when he was sick and how she might sit by the bed and read to him. Once he started nursery school, continuing into kindergarten, he looked forward eagerly to her coming to take him home, desperately fearing though that she might not come.

He added, however, that he was now conscious that his mother had an "oral" way of loving, speaking of a little child as being "good enough to eat," or a real sweetie, or something like that. And he made a connection to his own orality in his lovemaking with women, of how much closeness he wanted while becoming distinctly uncomfortable if the closeness was perpetuated too long.

To return to the family background, his father, a driving, self-made, successful industrialist, with perfectionistic standards, had little time for his family. He was moralistically strict and brusque, and apparently unable to make much of a friendly approach to any of his children, especially when they were small.

In one of the early interviews the patient spoke of his father as follows: "I am told that I didn't see my father for over a year, and then when I did he was in uniform. I'm scared of people in uniform. Yet I admire them; there is something upright and strong about a man in uniform, but I am scared of authority. The attraction which older men have for a boy is not unnatural, but I seem to have gotten it mixed up. . . . I don't think as a little boy my father ever picked me up at all. I can remember only once sitting on his lap."

Two other figures stood out as crucially important in his childhood. One was his grandmother, mother's mother, a controlling overwhelming woman who quite early became very important to him as a mother figure. Until he was 6 they lived in a cottage near the home of his maternal grandparents and there was much visiting back and forth. In fact, his grandmother was apparently more than generous in advising the patient's mother how to raise her family. His grandmother, an obese woman, could be warm and affectionate and comforting if you were in her favor, and he was. He wondered whether she did not pick him up and cuddle him sometimes, possibly enveloping him in her bountifulness. However, she was arbitrary in her revulsion of little boys' active and mischievous ways, or their playing in the mud, and certainly anything connected with masturbation. He remembered vividly her telling him once: "Never, never to touch that thing, ever again!" when she saw him as a small boy fingering his penis. Practically fanatical in her literal Protestant religiosity and in her churchgoing, she filled him with dread of fire and brimstone and with awe of the glory of God. Her hope was that he might grow up to become a minister. When he came to see me, he was still torturing himself with religious fantasies and virtually a conviction that God sees all, and that his grandmother, not long dead, must be hovering over him watching every transgression. Desire was not to be tolerated, and there was even a moralistic rightness and sense of honor in suffering almost constantly the pangs of the flesh. This "pain" of the mind and body additionally signified the grace of God and the presence of his grandmother.

The other especially important figure in his childhood was his

3-year-older brother. This brother, much more aggressive and boyishly provocative than he, was the bane of the mother's existence. She disliked and often abruptly struck out punitively at this son. It would seem that she had transferred to this son the negative side of her competitive, hostile, ambivalent tie to her older brother, who probably had victimized her during her childhood. At the same time she so clearly preferred the rather delicate and sensitive next younger child, the patient. This must have added greatly to the inevitable competitiveness between them, and this older brother lost no opportunity to make life miserable for the patient. In fact, there was little overt or reliable warmth in this overmasculine family. As a matter of tradition strength was signified by restraint of positive feelings in favor of the verbal or physical expression of aggression. The patient, being the fourth down the masculine ladder, including the intensely striving father, and intended to have been the girl, recalled his childhood as having been one long series of incidents of ridicule, torment, and criticism.

There is one very important element in relationship to this older brother whom he very much hated and yet idealized. In one early interview he said quite directly that he would like to be the brother sexually, not have him, but to be him. Hence he was attracted to this brother who seemed to personify effective masculinity.

Later, after about two years of treatment when he revealed another secret, it became clear that it was this brother's penis in particular that he wanted. In fact, he felt that it was the only thing that might "cure" him, to have the brother's penis in place of his own. This explained his fatalistic pessimism about the treatment with me. Obviously, I could not give him a normal penis, therefore the treatment was bound to fail. In this connection it is highly significant that during puberty and early adolescence there was something of a homosexual relationship between the two brothers, in which the patient played the seductive feminine part. Their mutual loneliness and need for overt affection drew them together too, despite their antagonism. For their occasional physical closeness was marked by explicit tenderness, which, however, did not negate an immediate return to their customary competitiveness and combat, verbal and physical, after each briefly affectionate encounter.

This involvement with the brother, the only one ever really carried out by the patient that had homosexual overtones, added to the strength of his conviction throughout the strenuous early years of the treatment that he was irretrievably different and beyond psychoanalytic help.

And now, a few words of our impression of his early development. We had reason to reconstruct that the patient had been a colicky baby and had cried a great deal from the first months of life on. His nurses, so far as we could reconstruct, were coldly efficient "nanny" types. We conjectured that as an infant he had experienced much physical discomfort and had been a feeding problem; furthermore, he had had the misfortune not to find a mother or mother surrogates who might extend a perceptive and sensitive maternalism for an uncomplicated baby, much less a restless, hyperactive, and internally overstimulated infant such as he must have been. We also gained the impression that he had been subjected to elaborate scheduling for feeding, napping, and a vigorous toilet training, which imbued him with an overready, excessive sense of shame, and highly polarized reaction formations of clean and dirty, right and wrong. In due course he became fastidious like his mother and something of a prejudiced social and intellectual snob.

Although he was psychologically sensitive and insightful, at the same time he was massively crippled in the therapeutic situation by reason of a basic paranoid distrust and a conviction that he could never confide in me or anyone else in depth. He often felt that he was "all head," imprisoned within his ceaselessly obsessing and doubting mind. Although he had acquired the social amenities (in fact, they were mandatory within the family tradition), and was very successful scholastically, anyone outside of himself was suspect and regarded as a likely intruder into his inner self, located as the inside of his mind. Yet he was far from totally isolated; he had many good friends, for he was quite genuinely likable and had considerable charm except when he was overly anxious. He could be cleverly and humorously responsive so long as the talk remained relatively superficial. The major inhibition was his inability to allow any relationship to become singular in scope or depth. He then had to turn all that might be positive and pleasurable into something which would be exceedingly painful and disrupting.

With devaluation of himself or the object, trust became distrust, approbation became criticism, and anxiety replaced ease to a tormenting extent. With it all there was an enormous depressive feeling that he was doomed. By himself he was safe but ineffably lonely and depressed; with me, he obsessively tormented himself with doubts, "rucktioning" his thoughts back and forth like an internalized stammer, while constantly chewing at his fingers.

In due course, we mutually appreciated that starved as he was for an object tie, his object experience from his early years on, especially with his inconstant mother and paradoxical grandmother, connoted pain. Painful affects apparently had come to signify object proximity or object loss. We also conjectured that having started as a colicky baby, he later construed his cramping gut and what he called spasms of his genitals as torments, which were readily equated with external objects as if they were persecutory tormentors. Those persons to whom he wished to be close, he could not trust lest they be equivalent to those internal parts and systems of himself which gave him pain and anxiety. It was as if his mother experientially came to signify not only the somatic distress which so often had been unassuageable, but she was also the primary object, or came to stand for the primary object who could be "so good" or "so bad." Marked ambivalence apparently qualified his feelings about her from early on, and in retrospect it appeared that "when she was good," he felt her to be "so very, very good," but, "when she was bad," she must have seemed "horrid." For when she was there and more relaxedly giving, she apparently imparted some sense of love and comfort, but then she could be so erratically tense and abrupt, or not there at all, that her inconstancy promoted anxiety and depression in him. This later led to his conviction that she could not be trusted to understand his needs. Long before I saw him he was already certain that he was "special" and beyond being understood by anyone: and since "to be understood is to be loved," he could not expect to be loved, or at least not with any consistency or constancy.

It is highly significant that as a small child, possibly as an infant, he was a head banger and a rocker. In an early interview he said, "I used to get up on my knees and smash my head against the headboard of the bed before going to sleep. Another thing, I used to rock myself and still do. I couldn't go to sleep without rocking myself and I still do it a little bit, and I love being rocked. Trains and cars too; I love particularly sleeping on a train. When it is moving it rocks just right."

Yet a few hours later he said, "Auto accidents used to make me sick to my stomach. So many things did make me sick to my stomach when I was small. I was a very difficult young child, crying all the time for the first year. Something was supposed to have been wrong." (Did he have pylorospasm, or some such disturbance?)

Some years later in treatment he returned to the same theme recalling that not only had he been a head banger, but he had rocked himself whenever he was uncomfortable or unhappy in order to go to sleep. "When I went to boarding school I remember saying that I just had to stop this, this rocking myself to sleep—masturbating and living in dreams—and saying my prayers. It went on, you know, into my first year of analysis."

This raises the question of head banging and rocking representing transitional object activities. The pillow was not enough. It seems as if he had to engage in rhythmic, noisy, and even painful experiences in order to stimulate both somatic and emotionally charged perceptions. Perhaps such an activity is within the psychophysiological matrix of experience—preverbal and yet going on into the verbal phase, affirming both the primary object and the self.[11] Are the hard slats of the bed, which can hurt, the mother, or the part-mother who hurts, yet also the self who hurts and is hurt? Is it an activity which at one and the same time repetitively establishes merging and separation in a pain-organized, rhythmic, rockinglike, rocking-connected way?

Analysis as such not having been possible, the intensive psychoanalytic psychotherapy which we continued vis-à-vis became a

---

[11] In 1954, Greenacre spoke of "head knocking which had to do with a need, in some peculiar way, to establish a body reality in that particular area" (p. 38). And Anna Freud (1954) described rocking as "the most archaic of all autoerotic activities . . . as a regressive, and therefore unwelcome, unpropitious activity. . . . [R]ocking as the lulling, repetitive activity par excellence, has no legitimate place at all in extrauterine life but belongs to the intrauterine existence, its last legitimate offshoot being the passive experience of being rocked in the cradle or in the mother's arms" (p. 28).

long-drawn-out experience for him in distrusting-trusting me and gradually, although intermittently, taking hold of the potential for trust, affection, and pleasure in relationships, rather than the inevitable literal pain and unpleasure which he associated with ultimate object experience. What started as a long, distrustful, regressed, depressive, and anxiety-ridden transference gradually gave way to a more mature realization of other ways of being close. Fortunately, we could count on the availability, sooner or later, of his keen analytically insightful perspective and a leavening sense of humor. But these characteristics did not minimize the "obstipated," sadistic quality of his paranoid, sullen, negativistic, anhedonic position when he markedly regressed following correct interpretations or external or internal frustration. The problem was to bring him to take chances in life and with people, and with women for affection and erotic satisfaction, even though this would promote temporary anxiety and possible frustration.

During these regressed phases he would obsessively ruminate about how much he hated his mother, and later his father. Both with regard to his mother and within his own self he evidently organized viscerally a sense of pain and unpleasure into the functional psychosomatic substratum of his bowels and genitalia. Concomitantly he would justify his feeling of rage and depression and make the most of painful affects, obviously seething with antagonism at himself, at me, in a pent-up, negativistic, pessimistic way. He alternated withholding through silence and irritable recriminations, which he knew by then were unrealistic. The basic affect would be pain, connoting the turn toward the negative side of his ambivalently intense tie to his mother or toward the internalized mother within himself; his internalized mother against himself in this constant, obsessive, disjunctive way of going about things.

He said once, "When I get like this, I feel colicky and cross as if my snowsuit were too tight. . . . I am cross and I am kind of disappointed in myself. It hasn't taken me long to fall back into this position. I knew I might, but it was just that I didn't expect it to happen so abruptly. I thought it might be somewhat distant and happen very gradually."

In the next interview he said of his piqued sulky mood and discomfort, "It feels like raw diapers. It goes back before memories, but the feeling is there. It feels like before I could talk." This approximates clinically what I speculated on in my previous theoretical discussion; namely, the qualities of ill-defined, diffuse affect experience—memories which possibly anticipate and set the stage for later perceptions and cognitively organized memories.

Late in his treatment the patient was for an interval in a regressed mood, precipitated mostly by having been disappointed by a young woman who was indeed inconstant and frustrating. During his treatment hours at this time he was withdrawn and infantile. At one point he commented with respect to the living out of his pain and rage in the transference: "I do feel in a cocoon of grumpy loneliness which gets stronger and stronger the closer I get to coming here."

A week or so later as he began to emerge from this position he said, "When I get regressed, I say anything to keep that painful mood going. It is as if I go about a relationship assuming in advance that there is no harmony to be expected, and then I get mad when there isn't any, like with this girl." He was referring to another girl whom he had met subsequent to the more justified disappointment.

In an interview or two further along he commented, "I think this mood will probably pass. But what will I have to put in its place? I don't know." I would suggest that "mood" refers to the affect state which equals the missing object, and that the "what" refers to the who, namely, the object and the affect states particular to the object.

A "bad mood" would often be referred to as if he were the passive victim of his moods. For example, "I woke up in a bad mood" is in my opinion the symbolic affect referent used primitively, almost concretistically as the mother. In this regard the negative affect state represents the primary object, i.e., the mother. By attributing the bad mood to waking up alone, I believe he confirmed this formulation. The aloneness then is evocative of the negative mood state, the "bad mood," i.e., the lonely mood, the negative affect state representing the missing or pain-provoking primary object.

I close this case report with an account of a particularly revealing and moving interview which took place at a time when the frequency of visits had been much reduced and the patient knew that the treatment was in a closing phase; that we had "analyzed" about as much as we could of the main issues. Although he understood that he still was under the impact of unrealizable transference wishes for a good father and fusion with a consistently to be trusted and lovable mother, he felt that I had failed him nonetheless.

As had been the patient's mien lately, he presented himself in a heavy, depressive, regressive mood, a position which was characteristic of him and which signified his unhappiness and disillusionment with the treatment and with life. He started the hour in this withdrawn, rather disgruntled, uncomfortable, sullen way, being silent for a period and then complaining overly much about life. He was sure his discomfort must be more than the hangover that he thought he had.

However, during the latter part of the hour he went on to speak incisively about the nature of his problem and his current position. He started to talk about sensuality—that it is hard for him to accept it as a natural and necessary part of life and as a reservoir of feeling which brings people together, not necessarily in a degraded way. But he explained that he had to see it as negative and painful: "This discomfort in my body, roiling about all the time, cramping and pains—everything hurts and is uncomfortable; it is as if I hold on to it as the only thing I have ever known, the familiar, and I go back to it, uncomfortable though it is. It goes way back, as long as I can remember.

"I didn't expect this to come out of the analysis and it is not an answer in any of the books. But it's why I always fought against the analysis, not wanting to know about my closeness to my mother and my caring for her or my homosexual attachment to my father. And it isn't an oedipal problem, although I have that too [smiled for the first time], but something much earlier which I have always had, something which I expect I have always known and know how to feel about it and how to respond. I don't know how to do without it—this constant pain. Without it I would have nothing, and if I gave it up it would be like being different and like falling off a chair into space and being terrifyingly alone. It is as if I don't know how to be sensual in any other way and it does comfort me."

At this point he paused briefly, and then after asking whether I was familiar with Harlow's experiment of raising monkeys in total isolation, removed from the mother at birth and given only a cloth-covered wire-rack crude substitute for her, he continued with a certain poignancy, "I am reminded of Harlow's monkeys, raised on that wire rack—horrible!—crouched into themselves, rocking back and forth. I know how they must feel."

SUMMARY

This patient, as well as others of a similar type whom I have treated, is illustrative of those individuals whose attachment to pain signifies an original attachment to painfully perceived objects and inconstant objects at that. It appears that in the development of such individuals, instead of the early pleasurable object experiences being consolidated into love and a sense of trust, the opposite occurs. Early affects are predominantly painful and as such recur consistently, crystallizing in the direction of attachment to pain and distrust of objects. The painful affects are then held to, both as a defense and as an instinctually charged concomitant of object experience.

On this fundamentally pregenital base may be grafted more sophisticated object-oriented experience deriving from beyond the oral level; that is to say, from the anal and phallic levels. Thus, object experience moves progressively not only from "who eats whom," but also to "who controls whom," "who shreds whom," "who dumps on whom," "who pierces whom," "who shafts whom," and "who screws whom," whether heterosexually or homosexually. The amalgam of all three levels condensed as they are into specific current experience adds up to the pain and degradation of the transference neurosis or transference psychosis.

In this context then, the obsessive isolation and mental discord and conflictual turbulence serve to set the self off from the anaclitically needed object and represent integrity and strength, especially in the light of the essential passivity which so often coexists. Within it all a paranoid outlook declares the persecutory nature of the object tie, while it also establishes the defense. Altogether this constitutes a formidable and miserable situation for such neurotic patients, who, as I have pointed out, are also more than neurotic.

Furthermore, as I see it, the nuclear determinant of the "negative therapeutic reaction" is located developmentally much earlier than definitive superego formation. It originates in the very young child's failure to establish constancy in relation to a positively valued object, without which increments of pleasurable affect are neither consolidated out of object experience, nor reliably anticipated thereafter. In fact, the opposite prevails, namely, the development of an affinity for painful affect, the painful affect states connoting the inconsistently pleasure-unpleasure-yielding object.

The case report also exemplifies the technical difficulties encountered in the treatment of such conditions, and the limitations of psychoanalysis as such. Since the major disturbance in self and object relations constitutes an early developmental defect in ego structure, psychoanalytic interpretations, which after all cannot really reach the preverbal-earliest verbal level of development, are nonmutative and relatively ineffective. Such disturbances are even strongly resistant to interpersonal, experiential, nonverbal therapeutic measures. However, if the therapist persists in working toward the possibility that the patient can and will progressively and adaptively use both what is recapitulated and articulately remembered, and what is behaviorally recapitulated and reconstructed from the time when it cannot be literally remembered, then the outcome might be the achievement of a significant measure of corrective experiential reeducation supplemented by cognitive understanding. And through it the patient may gain increasing leverage on the way in which he has habitually abused relationships to realize an *Erlebnis* (i.e., an inner emotional experience) which was paradoxically fulfilling even though not pleasurably or harmoniously satisfying.

BIBLIOGRAPHY

BERLINER, B. (1927), On Some Psychodynamics of Masochism. *Psychoanal. Quart.*, 16:459–471.

FENICHEL, O. (1941), The Ego and the Affects. *Psychoanal. Rev.*, 28:47–60.

FREUD, A. (1952), Notes on a Connection between the States of Negativism and of Emotional Surrender (*Hörigkeit*). *The Writings of Anna Freud*, 4:256–259. New York: International Universities Press, 1968.

——— (1954), In: Problems of Infantile Neurosis: A Discussion. *This Annual*, 9:28.

FREUD, S. (1915a), Instincts and Their Vicissitudes. *Standard Edition*, 14:109–140. London: Hogarth Press, 1957.

——— (1915b), The Unconscious. *Standard Edition*, 14:159–215. London: Hogarth Press, 1957.

——— (1918), From the History of an Infantile Neurosis. *Standard Edition*, 17:3–123. London: Hogarth Press, 1955.

——— (1923), The Ego and the Id. *Standard Edition*, 19:3–66. London: Hogarth Press, 1961.

——— (1926), Inhibitions, Symptoms and Anxiety. *Standard Edition*, 20:77–175. London: Hogarth Press, 1959.

——— (1937), Analysis Terminable and Interminable. *Standard Edition*, 23:209–253. London: Hogarth Press, 1964.

——— (1950 [1895]), Project for a Scientific Psychology. *Standard Edition*, 1:283–397. London: Hogarth Press, 1966.

GREENACRE, P. (1954), In: Problems of Infantile Neurosis: A Discussion. *This Annual*, 9:38.

HARTMANN, H. (1939), *Ego Psychology and the Problem of Adaptation*. New York: International Universities Press, 1958.

HORNEY, K. (1936), The Problem of the Negative Therapeutic Reaction. *Psychoanal. Quart.*, 5:29–44.

JACOBSON, E. (1953), The Affects and Their Pleasure-Unpleasure Qualities in Relation to the Psychic Discharge Processes. In: *Drives, Affects, Behavior*, Vol. 1, ed. R. M. Loewenstein. New York: International Universities Press, pp. 38–66.

——— (1971), *Depression*. New York: International Universities Press.

LOEWALD, H. W. (1972), Freud's Conception of the Negative Therapeutic Reaction, with Comments on Instinct Theory. *J. Amer. Psychoanal. Assn.*, 20:235–245.

OLINICK, S. L. (1964), The Negative Therapeutic Reaction. *Int. J. Psycho-Anal.*, 45:540–548.

——— (1970), Panel Report: Negative Therapeutic Reaction. *J. Amer. Psychoanal. Assn.*, 18:665–672.

RAMZY, I. & WALLERSTEIN, R. S. (1958), Pain, Fear, and Anxiety. *This Annual*, 13:147–189.

RAPAPORT, D. (1953), On the Psycho-Analytic Theory of Affects. *Int. J. Psycho-Anal.*, 34:177–198.

RITVO, S. & SOLNIT, A. J. (1958), Influences of Early Mother-Child Interaction on Identification Processes. *This Annual*, 13:64–85.

RIVIERE, J. (1936), A Contribution to the Analysis of the Negative Therapeutic Reaction. *Int. J. Psycho-Anal.*, 17:304–320.

SPIEGEL, L. A. (1966), Affects in Relation to Self and Object. *This Annual*, 21:69–92.

SPITZ, R. A. (1965), *The First Year of Life*. New York: International Universities Press.

VALENSTEIN, A. F. (1962), The Psycho-Analytic Situation: Affects, Emotional Reliving, and Insight in the Psycho-Analytic Process. *Int. J. Psycho-Anal.*, 43:315–324.

WEBSTER'S *Third New International Dictionary* (1961). Springfield, Mass.: Merriam.

WOLFF, P. H. (1966), *The Causes, Controls, and Organization of Behavior in the Neonate* [*Psychological Issues*, Monogr. 17]. New York: International Universities Press.

APPLICATIONS OF PSYCHOANALYSIS

Psychoanalytic Research and Intellectual Functioning of Ghetto-Reared, Black Children

DALE R. MEERS

PSYCHOANALYSIS HAS BEEN CRITICIZED AS A THERAPY FOR THE RICH and as a psychological system that is at best irrelevant to the profound sociocultural distress of our time. Rhetoric tends to obscure a measure of truth. Critics appear, however, rather ill informed as to why analysts have not introduced themselves as experts in matters of social change. Our knowledge of psychopathology, for example, remains far from complete and our understanding of that which is normal, and that which is not, is even less clear (A. Freud, 1965). As clinicians, moreover, psychoanalytic expertise is clearly limited to a small spectrum of psychopathology, and psychoanalytic experience even with the transference neuroses is conducive to considerable humility. Psychoanalytic contributions to man's knowledge of the sociocultural "structures" that shape his

Presented at the Eighth Annual Symposium, "The Disadvantaged Child," sponsored by the Milwaukee Psychiatric Hospital and Milwaukee Children's Hospital in cooperation with the Medical College of Wisconsin, November 5, 1971.

Co-principal investigator, with Reginald S. Lourie, of "Culturally Determined Retardation: Clinical Explorations of Variability and Etiology." Research support is gratefully acknowledged from the Foundation for Research in Psychoanalysis, California; the van Ameringen Foundation, New York; and the Eugene and Agnes E. Meyer Foundation, Washington, D.C. Professional sponsorship of the research is provided by the Children's Hospital of Washington, D.C. and the Baltimore-District of Columbia Institute for Psychoanalysis.

superego, his conflicts, and his humanity extend beyond the profession's clinical base and necessarily become speculative.

In matters of social relevance, one hardly needs to be a psychoanalyst to recognize bias and injustice. Where appropriate social change is imperative, the analyst's clinical knowledgeability is largely irrelevant; i.e., he too is more a student than an expert. The introspective, deliberative, and relatively passive characteristics of psychoanalytic work, and the self-selection procedures of individuals who elect analytic training and careers appear antithetic to social activism. Moreover, a point most frequently missed in the nonanalytic community, the very anonymity which provides the psychoanalyst with his most effective therapeutic tool (i.e., the transference) is undermined by his social or political notoriety. In recognition of this range of limitations, analysts from Freud onward (Jones, 1957), have reflected that their greatest contributions to social change might be in the selection of particular patients who find in their own analyses the potency and drive to engage in meaningful social and political action.

Most psychoanalysts, I am convinced, are reasonably persuaded (from their clinical practice) that variations in both cultural values and social institutions have particular relevance to the types of psychopathology that ultimately emerge in any given time and place. Transcultural psychiatric research has been limited by two interrelated problems. First, the concerned professions (psychiatry, social psychology, and cultural anthropology) have been unable, conceptually and clinically, to distinguish between behaviors and affective states that are (a) psychopathological, and (b) that are culturally "normal," *vide* ritual murder (Devereux, 1970). Second, the *macroscopic* methods of social research do not permit the study of the psychological processes of an individual's mind so that distinctions between "cultural deviance" and psychopathology can be made. Psychoanalytic microscopy of the life history of any one person provides data on the interchange of culture, social structure, and the dynamics of personality development. In this sense, analysis offers a method of studying the manner by which cultures and societies perpetuate themselves via the individual's selective acceptance or rejection of particular values and modes of functioning. Since the psychoanalytic profession holds a monopoly on this method of intensive and extended psychological research, it is my conviction that the profession carries a corresponding collective responsibility for the initiation of relevant research.

My own research has derived from such convictions. The study of man's intellect has an extended history, but one that is colored by profound narcissistic prejudices that are particularly evident in the assessment of American blacks (see Thomas and Sillen, 1972, pp. 1–44). This paper starts with issues of intelligence and extends to clinical and social issues that have been highlighted by the research on which it is based.

With few exceptions,[1] psychoanalytic literature has viewed "intelligence"[2] as *an* "ego function" that is more genetically than culturally derived. This is particularly anomalous since psychoanalytic theory of ego development is conceptualized as a maturational progression in which the *interchange* of nurture and drives is quite explicit. Two early studies have illuminated the interrelatedness of nurture and intelligence: the sociological research on institutionalized pseudodefective children (Skeels and Dye, 1939; Skeels, 1964), and the psychiatric studies of the brilliance of autistic children (Kanner, 1949). Psychoanalytic experience is fully consonant with Skeels's and Kanner's findings: namely, failures in early nurture can give rise to a range of anomalies of ego development in which either defectiveness or brilliance may be a consequence. The technique of psychoanalysis extends such psychiatric and social research in facilitating discriminations between developmental *defects,* developmental *arrests,* and neurotic *inhibitions* of ego functions.

---

[1] David Rapaport's (1952) "Toward a Theory of Thinking" is the most outstanding and overlooked contribution to the conceptualization of "intelligence."

[2] The analytic literature concerned with "intelligence" typically refers to the dynamics of ego inhibitions or to developmental ego restrictions. Usually, however, there is the assumption that the characteristics of ego functions subserving intelligence are based on genetic limits. That is a plausible assumption, relative to cortical structure and metabolic functions. But it is also an oversimplification. Nongenetic, constitutional impediments to maturation of both cell mass and myelination of the cortex have been demonstrated in experimental animals. Research on the impact of failures of early childhood nurture are embryonic (Meers, 1971), yet it appears most plausible that the best of genetics cannot overcome the worst of early deprivations.

In making such discriminations, the analytic method also elucidates ontogenetic data as to *cultural* differences ("normal deviance") that contribute to nonpathological variations in ego functions.

The young child is especially vulnerable to severe psychological damage. Psychopathological trauma always impairs transiently or permanently some ego functions; the earlier the trauma, the more critical are the biopsychological adaptations. I suspect that sociocultural exposures of children to early and chronic distress are indeed traumatic and that this contributes to particular deformations and inhibitions of ego functions, and thereby to subsequent symptoms (that are conventionally understood as defining mental illness). Since one of my topics is that of *intellect* and impediments to ego functions, it is essential to state the obvious, namely, that the relationship between mental illness and defects or inhibitions of ego functions is anything but simple. Some psychotics, for example, remain intellectually brilliant and other patients who suffer with severe obsessional neuroses are frequently most gifted in their intellectual, defensive accommodation.

Given the obvious disadvantage and distress of ghetto-reared black children, and given their very well-documented lower academic functioning, I have continued to be puzzled that few clinical researchers have related these children's academic and intellectual difficulties to their demonstrable potential for psychological damage. To state this as a question: could the pervasive, limited intellectual functioning of the disadvantaged black child be a psychiatric symptom that derives from the extended disadvantages of his early years?

SOCIAL AND SCIENTIFIC RAMIFICATIONS OF THE PROBLEM

Many thousands of black children in our community, and perhaps several million in the nation, continue to manifest a comparative intellectual dysfunctioning. This has often been referred to as "culturally determined retardation." The problem of academic retardation is massive, and the condition has proved relatively immutable to a vast range of Head Start type inventions. The omnibus conceptualization of differences in intellectual functions, as is evident in the term "culturally determined retardation," implies a common and oversimplified etiology. Too frequently treated as a homogeneous problem, children who are intellectually impaired suffer from a range of quite different types of dysfunctions. Some children, for example, are undereducated, some are miseducated, and some are readily educable given modifications in either a school system or a child's maturational level. While millions of black children function somewhat lower on academic and IQ tests, an indeterminate number of black children function at relatively severely retarded levels, i.e., IQ's of 60 to 80. It is the latter population that has been my predominant concern. In the early days of my research, I was impressed with the consonance of my clinical experience with that of a New York legislative survey that concluded that $30,000,000 spent in 1967 in that state was for academic baby-sitting with approximately 10,000 children, who appeared to the researchers as more disturbed than retarded (see *New York Times*).

Many academic problems are tragic, and some schools are simply poor. These types of problems are readily identifiable and give rise to appropriate concern for their earliest modification. Yet institutional failures only account for the fact that our children may be miseducated or undereducated. If psychologically free to learn, then children could use remedial programs to fill in the gaps in their education at a later time. It has become clear, however, that arguments on the ease of remediation entail much wishful thinking, and too often grossly oversimplify very complex social-psychological processes. Even our better inner-city schools find a relatively large percentage of children, perhaps up to 40 percent (Passow, 1967; Coleman, et al., 1966), who cannot or will not make use of remedial options. Studies continue to confirm that the inner-city black child is not only behind national norms in his early years, but that his disadvantage increases with each successive year of school attendance (Coleman, 1966). Because of genetic preconceptions of inheritable intelligence, the lower academic level of black children has been invidiously interpreted by many as derivative of "racial" inferiority. The massiveness and pervasiveness of depressed scoring of black children has lent credence to such arguments. Jensen's (1969) resynthesis of preexisting data is the latest, conceptually most sophisticated statistical effort.

Genetic speculations on "race" and intelligence defy, in my view, efforts at logical rationalization (Erlich and Holm, 1964; Penrose, 1952; UNESCO, 1950). Since some scientists, even at the level of the National Academy of Sciences, are prepared to revive a controversy that lacks scientific definition of either *race* or *intelligence,* it seems probable that such interests reflect emotional, prejudicial preconceptions. Central to "racial" contentions, and lacking any meaningful genetic or chromosomal evidence that I am aware of, an assumption is offered that all relevant variables can be held statistically constant in comparisons of intelligence test functioning of populations such that any variations between "races" are then inferentially attributable to some genetic, "racial" attribute.[3] Jensen's readiness to ignore the limitations of a null hypothesis has led him to extend statistical inference to speculative conclusions that are a testimonial to nonempirical, ivory-tower views of ghetto realities. Jensen, among others, has denied that child rearing in the black ghetto includes deprivations that are beyond statistical control. He concludes, moreover, that only *severe* deprivations, such as occurred in Skeels's population, could account for significant variations in intellectual functioning. This view reflects the considerable clinical ignorance of many academicians of the range of developmental, environmental insults that children survive with clearly demonstrable severe impediments to both physical and psychological normalcy even where the environment is *not* overtly, severely deprivational (Ribble, 1944; Kanner, 1949; Silver and Finkelstein, 1967; Powell et al., 1967). Parenthetically, I would add that the black population makes a small but meaningful contribution to the white social scientists' and educators' ignorance. Few blacks share their experiences and feelings even with their closest white friends—and even more rarely with researchers. Children of the ghetto, as I have learned, are close-mouthed with almost all adults, including their parents. The most sorrowful and tragic of

---

[3] Crow (1970) offers an excellent evaluation of Jensen's impressive, if misguided paper.

family experiences go unreported and unrecognized outside of a very few family or street intimates.

Many people have disputed the Jensen-type statistical arguments by derision of IQ tests as irrelevant and culture-bound. In my view, this is a logical error. Benet, the father of psychometrics, knew full well that the tests he designed were culturally biased—as do all knowledgeable psychometricians of our day, including Jensen. IQ tests remain, whether one likes it or not, our most reliable instruments in making effective predictions about our educational systems. I have heard professionals, whom I consider romantically misguided, argue for another form of test that would demonstrate the ghetto's exemplary education in practical survival. But we do not—and I suggest we *should* not—train or test for "survival quotients" in the very ghettos that the residents would like to escape. Genetic theoreticians should, I conclude, be disputed where they are the most ignorant, namely, on their too-ready assumption that conditions of the poor black and the poor white are separate but statistically equal.

Psychotherapists across the nation are readily prepared to conceive of "educational retardation" by reference to terms such as underachievement, poor motivation, pseudoretardation, school phobias, reactive depression. These are all familiar, descriptive labels that we find associated with the "exceptional child," as we euphemistically describe the retarded, middle-class, atypical white child. The massiveness of underfunctioning of the black child, I am persuaded, has covertly prejudiced the conceptual imagination of the white professional. Is it possible, I would repeat, that the epidemic proportions of intractable, severe retardation of black children may be symptomatic of psychiatric dysfunctions that only selectively impair a relatively few of our white children?

Psychoanalytic clinicians share with many educators a particular awareness of the acute sensitivity of children to modifications in their life circumstances. Injuries, separations, deaths in the family, fear and loneliness can all produce striking consequences in both the child's latent mental endowment and in the motivation that is essential to his exploitation of his potentialities. The disadvantaged black child has been chronically exposed to undue risks from conception onward, e.g., intrauterine damage, postnatal nutritional deficits, maternal deprivation, and traumatic psychological damage (Ainsworth, 1962; Blodgett, 1963; Chess, 1969; Pasamanick, 1946; Winnicott, 1965), all of which may impair intellectual capability. Yet, the psychiatrist, the psychoanalyst, and the child development researcher have had scant experience from which to consider the specific impact of particular environments on any one individual's intellectual functioning. Where social, cultural, and "racial" factors compound our ignorance, both researchers and social planners lack such simple and basic data as: in the context of the black ghetto, what constitutes psychologically "normal" behavior at different chronological ages? Behavioral differences of ghetto children are frequently understood pejoratively, as if *difference* (from some sociocultural norm) were evidence of moral deviance. Indeed, there is evidence that some cultural characteristics of the black, e.g., physical expressions of heterosexual conflicts, are invidiously considered as *prima facie* evidence of psychopathology. Alternatively, a reverse prejudice appears evident in underdiagnosis, in which severe pathologies, such as schizophrenia, are misdiagnosed as "cultural retardation" (Grier and Cobbs, 1968).

PSYCHOANALYTIC RESEARCH

Our research has been described more extensively elsewhere (Meers, 1970). It began in 1966 with an observational study of ghetto school classes that continued for two years. As a psychiatric consultant to particular schools, I had the opportunity of observing classes. In return I provided advice and liaison for psychiatric referrals of those children whose teachers were concerned with them. Thirty percent of one school's first grade had been designated as too retarded for a normal curriculum, and they had been assigned to two special remedial classes. I had elected to study first grade classes because I had hoped to see children *before* they were exposed to any circular repetitions of difficulty within a school that might then obscure indigenous characteristics of their mental functioning. My interest has been to look at the influence of environment and "culture" on mental functioning. In fact, however, the first grade remedial classes already included children who had two and sometimes three years of unsuccessful previous experience. My first patient, then 6 years old, was selected from one such class. Since circular, repetitious difficulties had already developed for many in the first grade, I subsequently studied kindergartens and selected my second patient from one such class.

Of the particular classes I am discussing here, all of the children and three of four teachers were black. Because of the overt hostility between one class of students and their black teacher, where the latter was chronically, manifestly angry and dramatically controlling of her class, it was impossible to see much of the children's spontaneous modes of speech or thinking. The class from which I chose my first psychoanalytic subject was conducted by a warm and engaging, enthusiastic and powerfully built woman. Even within this class of academically "retarded" children, the range of dysfunction was marked, and the teacher had logically separated the children into three performance groups. Relating herself to their considerable differences in skills and involvement, the teacher consented to a controlled bedlam. In the absence of the teacher's direct attention, in the midst of organized confusion, some children would stare into space, others would poke and joke with each other, and a few put their heads on their desks to doze. The preponderance of the children were singularly uninvolved in their own education. Over time, the various children were discussed in private, particularly where it was apparent that one child or another was in need of medical attention, of possible protection from beatings at home, when a child had arrived from out-of-state without parents and had no place to go directly after school, etc. There was scant evidence of any observable psychopathological symptoms among children who were known to have been physically traumatized. Absenteeism, however, was so extended for some children that school phobias appeared as a possible symptom choice. Most remarkable, from my vantage, was the inhibition of aggression and the relative gentleness of the children. In the years of my observation, both in class and on the playground, I did not personally witness one serious, intentional assault of one child on another, though this was common among older children.

Contrary to psychiatric descriptions of low frustration tolerance, impulsivity, and acting out of lower-class children, black or white, those that I observed appeared at this age as remarkably controlled.

My observer status, however, failed to give me meaningful psychological data on the questions that interested me most. I proposed, therefore, to take two children from remedial classes into treatment who were "representative" in terms of academic difficulties and sociocultural factors. I offered the teachers the idea that since conventional, remedial efforts were not successful, I would provide treatment on a 5-day-a-week basis. Parental support came quickly, and has continued most positively even under extremely trying family circumstances.

QUESTIONS OF COLOR

There is a broad clinical and educational consensus that the total effect of color prejudice impairs the black child's sense of self-respect, and contributes to an unconscious set of expectations and defensiveness toward the predominantly white world (that is at best indifferent about him as a person). Kindergarten children, as I was reminded by a black teacher who was pleased to have me on exhibit, see white men in police cars, at hospitals when the children are hurt, as bill collectors, as supervisors of black work crews, and as the "envied others" portrayed in luxury on national TV. Exposed to riots, National Guard confrontations, and incipient black racism, the black child manages some sense of perspective for himself. I found it quite awesome to have three 5-year-old boys question me in a kindergarten class one day as to *what* I was. In as serious a manner as I have seen in a child, one of the more open boys asked me if I wasn't white. I asked him why he asked, i.e., what did I look like to him? He intensely repeated the question twice more, providing no clues as to his motivation in asking. I then responded that I was called white, as he was called black, and the child nervously blurted out: "Man! They're gonna kill you!"

I tend to agree with the black view that whites probably never fully understand what it is like to be black in this country. What may be missed in this generalization, however, is the fact that color perception is highly subjective. The fact that I am neither white nor my patients black is not the issue. The question is one of emotions rather than gradations of discernible color. Depending on the status of my patients' fears and injuries, I am sometimes very tan and at other times an albino honkey. As a subjective impression, I am persuaded that black parents are prepared to have a white clinician see their child because of habituation, because there is little choice available, and possibly because they harbor convictions that continued association may help their child and themselves with the white establishment. I have found the parents and grandparents of my patients prepared to test my sincerity and commitment with cautious optimism. With each family, I have had an increasing acceptance which has extended each year, so that privileged information not shared with close friends or relatives has become available. Yet, I am still also surprised to find particular types of information that have been withheld for over four years; I am still learning simple but important facts that I would have expected to be open from the early days of analytic work. Trust is conditional and my apparent color is not an irrelevant variable.

The relative ease of my working relationships with black children has interested some black psychoanalysts, and I have heard some interesting speculations. One black analyst suggested that black patients have a very striking, very early negative transference with black therapists. Butts (1970) suggested that this negative reaction appears to be precipitated by the evidence of the black professional's apparent freedom from the prejudice that plagues the lower-class black. The completeness with which the black patient initially disassociates himself from the white therapist limits, in this view, the black patient's direct envy. With black children, however, I suspect the problem is more elemental. The pain and sorrow of the black child may be a consequence of white exclusions, denigrations, or indifference. But in his early formative years, the black child is only indirectly exposed to whites. For the very young child—and it is in the young that unconscious defenses are consolidated—if one hurts, it is because one's parents have failed to protect and nurture. The black child is exposed to deprivations by black parents, and color discrimination of the black may begin with the child's conclusion that if one were white it would be different. Analytic experience with children who have survived Nazi death camps provides an object lesson in this regard. Observing that authority, the power to punish or kill, lies with the uniformed guards and that it is the parents and the child who are behind bars, such children evolved

convictions of their own badness, despite the most patent evidence
of the sadism of their persecutors (A. Freud and Dann, 1951;
Gyomroi, 1963).

PSYCHOANALYTIC CRITERIA FOR TREATMENT

The criteria for assessing the analyzability of patients usually
includes the following: The patient should be (1) consciously
motivated for treatment by the painfulness of his symptoms; (2) he
should be verbal; (3) psychologically insightful; (4) intelligent; and
(5) have sufficient control over impulses so that anxieties can be
scrutinized rather than relieved by acting out. These are undoubtedly desirable characteristics for any psychotherapeutic patient. In
private discussions, yet not too frequently encountered in the
literature, one hears such criteria cited to sustain pessimistic views
of the use of insight therapies with black children. Most briefly, I
would like to comment on each of these criteria.

1. Patients who are not in pain, who do not conceive of their pain
as symptomatic, clearly work less purposefully in psychotherapy.
This is particularly true where patients believe that the only source
of their discomfort is the world about them. In this respect, most
children, white or black, respond to analysis much like adult
patients with character disorders where the effectiveness of analysis
is often very slow. This problem is characteristic of *all* child analysis
and distinguishes it from most analytic work with adults.

2. It is simply incorrect to conclude that black children are not
verbal. While there are vernacular and syntactical differences
between the ghetto-reared black child's verbal skills and my own, I
have never found significant differences between the volume of
output of black and white, rich or poor children. Some problems in
communication are cultural, but most derive from dynamic considerations. All children communicate something, even when they are
relatively silent, and most children talk fairly readily with a
therapist who is responsive to the child's moods and his immediate
needs.

3. Psychological insight involves ego processes that can be
damaged by defensive inhibitions. Such inhibitions are the very
subject of analytic exploration and treatment. That is, if there is an

impediment to "insight," this is a reason for analysis and not an argument against it. My young patients became very experienced practicing psychologists in their tender years, and long before I introduced them to the notion that their psychological skills could be extended to solve their own difficulties.

4. It is probable that brain damage, cortical dysfunctions, or severe deprivation in early childhood may affect intellect sufficiently to preclude psychoanalytic therapy. Analysis does not, however, concern itself with esoteric problems of higher mathematics or physics. The subjects that must be intellectually grasped are those of immediate, emotional importance. My patients are, in fact, intellectually impaired. If our research hypotheses are correct, however, then even this limitation to the use of analysis should modify with therapeutic change as defenses and impairments in ego functions became less necessary.

5. The last criterion concerns the child patient's capacity for sufficient control of tension and anxiety so that these can be explored analytically. This problem is also general to all child analysis, and to particular forms of adult neurosis. It is diagnostically relevant in assessing, quantitatively, the child's potential for modification of a form of drive discharge that is *normal* to childhood. Analysis of children from cultural backgrounds where drive discharge is encouraged presents a particular technical problem. But I would defer this point at this moment since it also bears on special problems of differential diagnosis.

In almost every scientific meeting in which I have discussed this research, one or more analysts or psychiatrists have raised the question of ethics. I have heard it contended that it is a psychiatric disservice to analyze the severely disadvantaged child since he will necessarily continue to live in circumstances beyond his control; greater psychological awareness can only leave him more vulnerable to acute emotional injury from which his defenses, prior to analysis, had protected him.

Freud's views of the eventual extension of analytic treatment for the poor have been indirectly referred to in this context. In 1919, Freud offered a conservative and pessimistic commentary on the social structure of his day: "We shall probably discover that the poor are even less ready to part with their neuroses than the rich, because the hard life that awaits them if they recover offers them no attraction, and illness gives them one more claim to social help" (p. 167). Freud could not have anticipated that the caste system of the U.S. today would permit our black families to send a higher proportion of their children to college than the present white working class of Great Britain. But the ethical justification of psychoanalytic treatment of disadvantaged children is more elemental and should not be restricted to considerations of relative class mobility within a static caste system. Few things in reality are as damaging as a lifelong, psychopathological impairment and exhaustion that derive from neurotic conflict or clinical depression. My patients' neurotic conflicts, particularly their defenses against their own unconscious sadism, have led to severe impediments in reality testing. They have suffered chronically from accident proneness, psychosomatic illnesses, and not infrequently from their own masochistic invitations to the environment to injure or punish them. However provisional my conclusions on the first successes of their treatment, I am most impressed with their tentative retreat from masochistic tendencies. However difficult life in the ghetto can be, the ghetto is *not* homogeneous and with increasing discrimination children prove able to take more from their milieu when they are less psychologically constricted. If our black families are to modify their environment effectively or escape from the bias with which they live, they need insight and not distortions of reality that derive from psychopathology (or drugs).

Another theoretical issue has been raised: whether the treatment of my patients is "truly" psychoanalytic or merely an intensive form of psychotherapy. Does this therapy become an effective vehicle for transference interpretation, which is the core of psychoanalytic modification of psychoneurotic pathology? The question is important in considering the choice of therapy for given types of psychopathology. I would like to note my impressions on the frequency of treatment for severely disadvantaged children. It is the experience of many psychiatrists that once weekly therapy is met by a profound resistance, particularly manifest in failed appointments. In the cases of nonintensive therapy that I have seen, supervised, or consulted on, vague stirrings of hope seem to elicit expectations of bitter disappointment that would be sure to follow. The loosening of defenses in once weekly therapy, which is preparatory to better modes of adaptation, leaves children to cope without therapeutic relief for a time span that seems interminable. Where therapy is made available daily, however, it becomes possible to sustain the child's therapeutic work and to clarify and resolve fears of disappointment and rage that are common to attachment and unreliability of adults.

QUESTIONS OF DIAGNOSIS

Freud concluded, as have most analysts since him, that man's susceptibility to psychological distress can be best understood in terms of *origins* of conflict. Nonanalysts readily accept that psychological conflict arises continuously from demands made upon an individual by others *external* to himself. While there have been some dissensions in the profession, most psychoanalysts appear to concur with Freud that mankind is genetically heir to *internal* conflicts that derive from opposites within himself that are mutually incompatible. Freud saw these internal conflicts as deriving from man's bisexual and passive-active potentialities. The primary interests, however, of psychoanalytic clinical practice have been with a third form of conflict, that which we term *internalized*. Such intrapsychic conflicts derive from the child's internalization of sociocultural views that require particular renunciations or displacements of his elemental instinctual drives. Such internalized conflicts become manifest by their resolutions in the structure of one's superego, character, or symptoms.

External conflicts arise from the object world that makes demands on the ego for accommodation. When external conflicts are sufficiently trying that the individual cannot readily master his distress, as is not uncommon in childhood illness, we are accustomed to seeing a range of consequent symptoms. Regressive emergence of night terrors, tics, stuttering, phobias, psychosomatic complaints, etc., are relatively common in the face of acute childhood distress. But the transience of such symptoms and the earlier developmental history of a patient provide diagnostic evidence when such symptoms are *not* psychoneurotic, i.e., that such symptomatology is only a response to *external* conflict.

Analysts have typically treated individuals who have a large measure of autonomy in the ordering of their daily lives. Particular maturational and social conditions, however, may severely limit one's autonomy and control of one's person or relationships. For example, such diverse phenomena as pregnancy and military service are both conditions that are conducive to regressions and particularly acute symptoms that carry psychiatric labels of post-partum psychoses and combat neuroses. Both psychiatric conditions tend to improve dramatically when the individual is no longer a captive of his or her status.

In the inexhaustible reservoir of one's narcissism, one wants to believe that one's own ego is relatively immune to the intrusions of bizarre, instinctual, primary process ideas and feelings. Miller's paper "Ego Autonomy and Sensory Deprivation, Isolation and Stress" (1962) provides a fascinating review of literature concerning persons (1) who have involuntarily lost control of their autonomy via accident or imprisonment; and (2) who volunteered for immersion-tank experiments that limit external stimuli. His findings document that the relative strength and stability of ego functions are partially determined by man's capacity to insure a continuous feedback of sensory and social data that will reaffirm his expectations. Involuntary, solitary confinement of prolonged duration contributes to chronic fears of insanity and obsessive efforts to keep one's mind doing some form of busy work. Sensory deprivation provides extremely rapid inundation of the ego with feelings and ideation that are profoundly distressing even to normal subjects.

Chronic external conflict and distress appear to me to be a condition of ghetto life in which the child is threatened by a flood of unpredictable stimuli. If we are to assess diagnostically the nature of the ghetto child's mental health, then we must be prepared to distinguish between (1) symptoms and regressive, adaptive behaviors that are situationally reactive to *external* conflicts, and (2) those symptoms that derive from *internalized* conflicts (that remain intractable in the face of environmental change). The following two illustrations are intended to clarify this distinction.

Genie was a responsive and alert 5-year-old; she was not one of my patients. Her kindergarten teachers were distressed with a precipitous change in which Genie's manner became vacant, her mood depressed, tense, and frightened; her understanding of conventional class activities dissolved. Clarification with the child's mother, who was even more distressed, provided an immediate, probable answer to Genie's symptomatic change. She had been raped by an adult in her home. Psychobiological trauma does not necessarily lead to neurotic, internalized psychopathology—that outcome is based both on the child' pretraumatized mental status and her subsequent adaptation to the trauma. I use this particular tragedy to illustrate that Genie's psychological symptoms represent accommodations to external trauma. We should be even more concerned, after the fact, if a 5-year-old was *not* emotionally affected by such an event.

Virgil, who was one of my patients, was a most self-possessed 5-year-old. He was adamant about taking directions that did not suit him, and efforts to obtain his compliance led to Virgil's walking out of kindergarten or to physical struggles with any teacher who tried to stop him. Virgil was chronically inattentive, wanting to return home whenever his anxieties emerged. His subsequent analysis documented that his upsets were more or less concurrent with his mother's beginning deterioration on heroin, when she would disappear for days while "hustling" to finance her drugs. Given Virgil's chronic worries about his mother's absences and disorientation, one might diagnostically conjecture that Virgil's symptomatic behavior was also reactive and only situational. As Virgil's analysis has continued to document, however, the situational traumas of everyday life merely obscure his neurosis. Virgil suffers from chronic anxiety irrespective of external events. The realities of his life compound his intrapsychic conflicts and even in the absence of adult controls or recriminations, he turns his aggression back on himself in a range of accidents and provoked punishments that have seemed unending. Virgil's masculinity has a profound sadistic base, and his compensatory defenses have led to regressive, passive, effeminate accommodation. Virgil's dominant fears are of his painful emerging fantasies and dreams of being a girl. Such passivity and effeminate inclinations, however, outrage his self-esteem, and his acting out appears as a chronic need to reestablish his sense of masculinity.

In the course of my analytic work, I became most curious about the realities of violence in the neighborhoods in which my patients lived. It was my wish to identify the type and incidence of crime that might have an *immediate* impact on my patients. With the help of the District of Columbia's Police Department,[4] data were identified for 1970 for each street within an area seven blocks square around the homes of my patients. The number of blocks was a compromise between police reporting methods and what I conjectured might be a child's view of his own neighborhood, i.e., about three blocks in each direction. "Crime profiles" of the child's neighborhood, coded by type of crime, were particularly dramatic. The following data are for the area contiguous to Virgil's home. They include the total reported crime for the year 1970:

Homicide	17	Prostitution	30
Rape	16	Sex Crimes	4
Aggravated Assault	320	Larceny	1037
Robbery	568	Auto Theft	251
Burglary	794	Vandalism	118
Weapons	117	Other	453
Drugs	371	Arson	11
		Total:	4107

These police data are a conservative statement of criminal activity. Estimates on the underreporting of crime vary from 30 to 70 percent. Moreover, most crimes against or by children are unreported even to their parents. Ghetto convictions concerning bias, disinterest, or impotence of the police contribute to such underreporting. But the pride of ghetto families also restricts reports of manifestly criminal behavior within families. Thefts, beatings, and rape have been reported to me by almost every family I have known clinically, i.e., without police reports having been made. Whatever the exposure of the ghetto child to the trauma of the streets, his vulnerability appears greatest in his earliest years when distress and overexcitation occur in the relative privacy of his own home. Rorschachs of many black mothers of the inner city look like those of psychotics or patients who have been in analysis for some

[4] Captain Herbert F. Miller, Operations Planning Branch, Metropolitan Department of Police, was particularly helpful in making these data available.

time (Layman, 1971).[5] It is my suspicion that this type of Rorschach response reflects accommodation to the overinstinctualization of ghetto life. It is my further conviction that the failure of society to provide minimal family security and protection have direct and serious regressive effects on ego capacities.

Differential diagnosis of psychopathology in black children is further complicated by the subculture's tolerance of behavior that is "deviant" from the diagnostician's conceptualization of "normalcy." Different cultures value or disparage quite different attributes in their children. If a particular mode of childhood adaptation that is psychologically determined, such as crying or clinging, is rejected within a culture, these adaptations do not easily survive. In conventional psychoanalytic practice, we are impressed with the fact that an instinctual regression from heterosexual potentials may lead to anal, sadomasochistic adaptations. Depending upon the structure of a patient's morality, anal expressions of symptoms may then be profoundly distressing to both the patient and his parents. In such instances, we are accustomed to seeing yet another regression in which, in this example, anal symptomatology may be displaced and become manifest in oral terms. While all children throughout the world may have common genetic potentials for particular sequences of adaptation or regressions, the culture will partially determine which of these expressions will be acceptable or rejected. I am reminded of a vastly experienced pediatric psychiatrist's account of a particular hospital's cure of enuresis. If consultation did not bring about a transference cure, a preliminary study was begun with a small catheter. If wetting persisted, a more extended examination followed with a larger catheter. Few children's enuresis appeared to survive this regime, which one might characterize as the child's symptomatic accommodation to a medical culture.

Life has been hard for the ghetto parents I have come to know. Their own education is hard knocks leaves them little prepared to spare their own children. And current hardships and frequent

[5] Layman's study included "normal" mothers, mothers with children in psychiatric treatment, and mothers of pica children. The Rorschachs were more striking for their similarities than for their differences.

emotional distress, endemic with adults, leave parents little emotional freedom to sustain their own youngsters. When childhood symptoms emerge that are offensive, such as transvestism, anal masturbation, anxiety hysterias, they are very short-lived in the face of profound parental interdiction. Cultural values of the ghetto resident black family are more apt to sustain other forms of symptomatic adaptation, particularly discharge of anxiety or tension by action. We are familiar with particular types of drive displacement in the defense of "identification with the aggressor." Isolation of affect also appears culturally syntonic and common to many children. Since I have noted the relative passivity of younger children, and now refer to their discharge of anxiety by action and sadistic acting out in later years, I add that this transition appears to me to be a change in defensive adaptation (Meers, 1971; Meers and Gordon, 1971).

If my diagnostic speculations are more or less true, then it is probable that symptoms that customarily define the neurosis of the middle-class white child will not be the same for the ghetto-reared black child. These black children, in my experience, manifest symptoms indicative of impulse disorders, reactive depressions, isolation of affect, etc. If these symptoms are a secondary response that follows the primary emergence of symptoms, then meticulous developmental histories should disclose the basic *neurotic* nature of the psychopathology (that is masked by symptoms culturally sustained in the milieu). Psychoanalysis is an enormously costly form of research and therapy. Yet it provides the only clinical method that can effectively discriminate between symptoms that are situational (external) and those that are psychoneurotic (internalized).

Conclusions

My own research is quite limited, both by my research objectives and by the number of patients I can see. From my vantage, one of the appropriate professional contributions of psychoanalysis to social action is in this type of selection of a socially significant problem where the analyst's unique technical opportunities, rather than his prestige, may realistically contribute scientific knowledge of the consequences of social action or inaction. While my provisional findings have been reported elsewhere (1970), I would note here that my patients' worst apprehensions have been continuously confirmed by the experience of their most tender years. They have consolidated views of themselves as less than beautiful, less than adequate, as marginal children of marginal families in an ambivalent "racial" community. The psychological microscopy of our work has outlined severe ego impediments which include both subtle and gross distortions of perception and memory, and extend to chronic self-devaluations that affect motivation.

As previously stated, the initial selection of children was based on their apparent representativeness; they did not manifest observable evidence of psychopathology. If these children, Virgil and Genie, are representative, the evidence from the children's treatment suggests that both they and their families pay a horrendous price for society's indifference and the subculture's incapacity to protect them. If my sample is representative, then the very best of analytic, psychiatric, or educational help will never begin to compensate for the lack of effective community action. If further research should substantiate my tentative conclusions, i.e., that retardation of the ghetto child is a culture-specific expression of psychopathology— one of the contentions of many genetic determinists will also have been rebutted. More significantly, however, extensive documentation of the psychiatric injury of these children might serve as a further, dramatic stimulus to direct social and political action.

BIBLIOGRAPHY

AINSWORTH, M. (1962), The Effects of Maternal Deprivation. *Deprivation of Maternal Care.* Geneva: World Health Organization, Public Health Papers 14, pp. 97–159.

BLODGETT, F. M. (1963), Growth Retardation Related to Maternal Deprivation. In: *Modern Perspectives in Child Development*, ed. A. J. Solnit & S. Provence. New York: International Universities Press, pp. 83–93.

BUTTS, H. (1970), Personal Communication.

CHESS, S. (1969), Disadvantages of "The Disadvantaged Child." *Amer. J. Orthopsychiat.*, 39:4–6.

COLEMAN, J. S. (1966), Equal Schools for Equal Students. *Publ. Interest*, 4:70–75.

———— & CAMPELL, E. Q., HOBSON, C. J., McPARTLAND, J., MOOD, A. M.,

WEINGELD, F. D., & YORK, R. L. (1966), *Equality of Educational Opportunity.* Washington, D.C.: Department of Health, Education and Welfare.

CROW, J. F. (1970), Genetic Theories and Influences: Comments on the Value of Diversity. *Harvard Ed. Rev.*, 39:301–309.

DEVEREUX, G. (1970), Normal and Abnormal: The Key Concepts in Ethnopsychiatry. In: *Man and His Culture*, ed. W. Muensterberger. New York: Taplinger Publishing Co., pp. 113–138.

ERLICH, P. R. & HOLM, R. W. (1964), A Biological View of Race. In: *The concept of Race*, ed. A. Montague. New York: Collier-Macmillan, pp. 177–178.

FREUD, A. (1965), *Normality and Pathology in Childhood.* New York: International Universities Press.

——— & DANN, S. (1951), An Experiment in Group Upbringing. *This Annual,* 6:127–169.

FREUD, S. (1919), Lines of Advance of Psycho-Analytic Therapy. *Standard Edition*, 17:157–168. London: Hogarth Press, 1955.

GRIER, W. H. & COBBS, P. M. (1968), *Black Rage.* New York: Basic Books.

GYOMROI, E. L. (1963), The Analysis of a Young Concentration Camp Victim. *This Annual*, 18:484–510.

JENSEN, A. R. (1969), How Much Can We Boost I.Q. and Scholastic Achievement. *Harvard Ed. Rev.*, 39:1–123.

JONES, E. (1957), *The Life and Work of Sigmund Freud*, Vol. 2. New York: Basic Books.

KANNER, L. (1949), Problems of Nosology and Psychodynamics of Early Infantile Autism. *Amer. J. Orthopsychiat.*, 19:416–426.

LAYMAN, E. (1971), Rorschach Studies of Mothers. *Pica and Lead Poisoning*, ed. F. K. Millican & R. S. Lourie (unpublished manuscript).

MEERS, D. R. (1970), Contributions of a Ghetto Culture to Symptom Formation. *This Annual*, 25:209–230.

——— (1971), International Day Care: A Selective Review and Psychoanalytic Critique. In: *Day Care: Resources for Decisions*, ed. E. H. Grotberg. Washington, D.C.: Office of Economic Opportunity, pp. 4–26.

——— (1972), Crucible of Ambivalence: Sexual Identity in the Ghetto. *The Psychoanalytic Study of Society*, 5:109–135. New York: International Universities Press.

——— & GORDON, G. (1971), Aggression and the Psychoanalysis of Ghetto-Reared American Negro Children. Presented at the 27th International Psycho-Analytical Congress, Vienna.

MILLER, S. C. (1962), Ego-Autonomy in Sensory Deprivation, Isolation, and Stress. *Int. J. Psycho-Anal.*, 43:1–20.

New York Times: Disturbed Pupils Held Neglected, March 26, p. 37, 1967.

PASAMANICK, B. (1946), A Comparative Study of the Behavioral Development of Negro Infants. *J. Genet. Psychol.*, 69:3–44.

PASSOW, A. H. (1967), Summary of Findings and Recommendations of a Study of the Washington, D.C. Schools. Teachers College, Columbia University (mimeographed).

PENROSE, L. S. (1952), *The Race Concept, Results of an Inquiry.* Paris: UNESCO.

POWELL, G. F., BRASEL, J. A., RAITI, S., & BLIZZARD, R. M. (1967), Emotional Deprivation and Growth Retardation Simulating Idiopathic Hypopituitarism. *New Engl. J. Med.*, 276:1279–1283.

RAPAPORT, D. (1952), Toward a Theory of Thinking. In: *Organization and Pathology of Thought.* New York: Columbia University Press, pp. 689–730.

RIBBLE, M. A. (1944), Infantile Experience in Relation to Personality Development. In: *Personality and the Behavior Disorders*, ed. J. McV. Hunt. New York: Ronald Press, Vol. II, pp. 621–651.

SILVER, H. K. & FINKELSTEIN, M. (1967), Deprivation Dwarfism. *J. Pediat.*, 70:317–324.

SKEELS, H. M. (1964), An Interim Brief on the NIMH-Iowa Follow-up Studies Relative to Mental Retardation, Dependency and Maternal Deprivation (mimeographed).

—— & DYE, H. B. (1939), A Study of the Effects of Differential Stimulation on Mentally Retarded Children. *Proc. Amer. Assn. Ment. Def.*, 44:114–136.

THOMAS, A. & SILLEN, S. (1972), *Racism and Psychiatry.* New York: Brunner/Mazel.

UNESCO Citation (1950), *The Race Concept.* Paris.

WINNICOTT, D. W. (1965), *The Maturational Processes and the Facilitating Environment.* New York: International Universities Press.

The Jinx Game

A Ritualized Expression of
Separation-Individuation

JEROME D. OREMLAND, M.D.

Play and Games

AS EARLY AS 1900, FREUD RECOGNIZED THAT CHILDREN'S PLAY served important functions. He emphasized that what had been passively experienced often becomes the theme of the play, with the important shift from passive to active. This was seen as providing a sense of mastery and, often, integration. In this regard, the similarity of play to fantasy life, dreaming, and neurosis has been extensively explored (Freud, 1920; Greenacre, 1959; Waelder, 1932).

Peller (1954) makes a useful distinction between primary and secondary play gains. Among the primary gains of play, she describes its role in giving expression to and achieving control and mastery over the phase-specific sequential instinctual concerns as well as its role in developing object relatedness. Secondary play gains include those many capabilities which to varying degrees

Faculty, San Francisco Psychoanalytic Institute.

I wish to express my appreciation to Dr. Anna Maenchen for her encouragement and suggestions, and to Cici, Noah, and Annalisa, and their many friends for letting me in on their secrets.

I am especially indebted to Drs. Calvin Settlage and Albert J. Solnit for many specific suggestions which significantly enlarged and improved the theoretical understanding of these observations.

develop autonomously and which are exercised and perfected in play, including such ego functions as memory, perception, motor-coordination skills, and the like.

Anna Freud (1965) schematically draws a developmental line "from the body to the toy and from play to work" (p. 79). In this complex progression, a number of play activities of the infant-toddler period, when studied analytically, seem especially associated with the delineation of the self and the differentiation from objects.

Mahler and McDevitt (1968) have pointed to the importance of molding and stiffening behaviors of the lap baby. They see these as facilitations of the libidinizations of the surface of the baby's body in the service of delimiting the body-self. This behavior may be formalized as a lap game in which the external object, the mother, holds on to the baby's hands, helping him to stand in her lap (a separation), and then lets the baby collapse in her lap amid shared delight and laughter, often with the mother completely enveloping the baby in a hug to her body (a dedifferentiation). Typically, the game is repeated again and again, portraying and mastering both the regressive tendencies and the progressive developmental pulls.

Kleeman (1967) studied "peek-a-boo" from the standpoint of experimenting with objects, exercising control over them, and establishing object constancy. Elaborating on Bühler's (1930) observations, he emphasized the developmental importance of the shift from the passive (object-induced) experience to the child's actively initiating the making and breaking of contact with the object.

"This little pig" has been interpreted as an experience in the establishment and integration of the self concept (Kohut, 1971). In this game an external object, generally the mother, first isolates various body parts (This little pig went to the market; this little pig stayed home . . .). The game is climaxed by bringing back together the individual body parts into a whole as the mother rubs the child's body "all over" with shared enjoyment and laughter by mother and child ("all the way home") (p. 119).

The toddler's block tower play, among other things, is related to his newly won mastery of the standing position and his continuing exploration of his place in space. He carefully places one block on top of the other, building a shaky tower. With glee, he knocks it over so that he can rebuild it and repeat the exercise. Presumably, he is actively doing what he so incessantly experienced in his own attempts to gain the upright position (Erikson, 1937).

The play and games of latency children have been extensively studied by anthropologists and psychologists (Opie and Opie, 1959, 1969; Piaget, 1945; Stone and Church, 1968). Analytic observers often note various compulsive, ritualistic defenses against impulse break-through in simple latency play, such as "Step on a crack, break your mother's back." Erikson (1937, 1951) described the importance of latency and preadolescent play configurations in establishing and reinforcing sexual identity. Kaplan (1965) details the variety of libidinal-aggressive and ego needs that find satisfaction, in a sublimated form, in such typical latency motor play as skipping and jumping rope.

Peller (1954, 1955) underscored the developmental importance of games in the establishment and maintenance of object relationships as well as many other ego capabilities. In latency, competitive peer activities, which may be formalized as sports or table games, such as Monopoly, become increasingly important. In these activities, Peller identified an attempt to gain mastery over competitive relationships reflecting both oedipal and sibling conflicts.

Two games regarded as specific to the latency period have been subject to analytic scrutiny. Simmel (1926) extensively elaborated on Freud's interpretation of "the doctor game"; and more recently, Ross (1965) described and interpreted a play activity of schoolchildren, "the teacher game."

This paper describes a sophisticated, stereotyped ritual playfully entered into by older latency and preadolescent children, which for the purposes of this discussion is called the Jinx game.[1]

THE JINX GAME

When several children are talking and playing, and two children happen to say the same word or the same phrase at the same time, one will immediately exclaim: "Jinx." [2] The child who does this

---

[1] Jinx comes from the Greek *Iynx*, the wryneck, a bird used in incantations and charms. The dictionary defines jinx as slang, meaning to cause bad luck to.

[2] Though the Game is played in a remarkably identical manner in various

first is in control, and the other must remain mute until the jinxer or another child calls the name of the one jinxed. He is then free to resume his normal position and activities with the group.

Stone and Church (1968) describe an important variation of the Jinx game.

> A sense of fraternitylike membership is well demonstrated when two children catch themselves saying the same thing at the same time and instantly fall into the ritual of hooking their little fingers together, making a silent wish . . . and remain mute until a third person speaks to one of them and so breaks the spell. If they forget and speak without this release, the wish is lost. All the other children are aware of their role in the rite and of their power to enforce silence until they choose to free the main participants. . . .
> One assumption of the game is that the principals should not be liberated too quickly, and if anyone speaks too soon, this is felt as a gratuitous and offensive destruction of a *magical moment* to be greeted by the indignant and almost equally ritual cry of "No fair!" [p. 375f.; my italics].

These ceremonies are especially appealing to late latency and preadolescent children, apparently having little interest to pubertal adolescents. However, Opie and Opie (1959) describe related ceremonies in many lands among older adolescents and even among unsophisticated adults (p. 310ff.). Apparently the ritualized response of some children and nearly all older adolescents to the "saying the same thing at once" coincidence emphasizes the joining with someone in order to have a wish granted, rather than the muteness-oneness with release through pronouncing the name (the Jinx game in its "pure" form) which characteristically is seen in late latency.

Children as young as 5 participate in the game, but their interest is more of a mimicking type. They participate mainly in order to be included in a game of older children and do not show the vehemence and intensity which seem to appear about the age of 7 and continue until about 10 to 11.

---

geographical areas, the word used to induce the spell varies widely, e.g., Israeli children shout, *Ain,* the Arabic word for ghost or evil eye. (I am indebted to Millie Maas, M.S.W. at Hebrew University, Jerusalem, for this information.)

The ritual is joyful, playful, exciting, highly stereotyped, and tends to occur in spurts. Often after the first occurrence, there follows a series of incidents, one after the next, where one or another of the children will find himself saying the same word or the same phrase in unison with another.

DISCUSSION

If, as Settlage (1971) has suggested, separation-individuation is a prototypical issue which is reworked at each successive developmental stage, it would seem that these latency children, because they have a relatively well-established self-object differentiation, can enjoy ritualistic playing out of a fusion-separation experience. Having gained a feeling of control over and distance from such fusion experiences, they can participate in a regressive expression, recapitulation, and ritualistic repetition, which further enhances their developmental achievement—the new-won sense of autonomy.

In the game, the children play out the fusion-separation experience in remarkable detail. The chance happening of the two individuals saying the identical phrase stimulates the wish for return to fusion with the lost symbiotic partner. Each struggles to establish who is to be the surviving one, achieving this by being the one who first says the magic word "Jinx." This renders the other mute, cementing the union. Where there had been two, now there is but one, sometimes symbolized by linking the little fingers. This continues until the survivor or some rescuer says the name of the one so bound. By the magic of the pronouncement of his badge of identity and self, his name, he is freed from the union and may resume the role of a separate and equal participant. This is all done with laughter, excitement, and enjoyment. Often, however, the intensity betrays the presence of unconsciously wished-for and feared processes which the ritual permits and at the same time keeps from awareness.

RULES IN GAMES AND RITUALS

Piaget (1945) presents interesting observations on the development of rules in children's play, distinguishing between rules which are "handed down . . . passed on [from] one generation" to the next and rules which arise "spontaneously" (p. 143). He observes that rules rarely appear before the age of 4 and that they become very conspicuous between 7 and 11, rather categorically setting age 7 as the time when play "really becomes make-believe in contrast to 'reflective belief'"(p. 168). He sees the institution of rules as part of the socialization process which becomes the central characteristic of adult play and as part of the link between play and work (p. 146).

Metapsychologically, the function of rules is an important distinguishing characteristic between games and rituals. In ritual, the "rules" must closely fit the unconscious needs so that the individual has a feeling of obeying outer directives and at the same time is to varying degrees aware of an inner syntonicity. There is little room for flexibility and modification. In games, the rules are agreed-upon external regulations which comprise the format, assuring repeatable structure. However, there can be considerable negotiation, alteration, and modification.

In this regard, it is interesting to observe the children in the process of establishing each element of the Jinx game. In general, it appears to be "handed down" in that a child who previously has played the game introduces the rules. However, the striking fact that the rules are relatively invariable and never questioned or debated when they are imposed, suggests that they also correspond to inner needs. Metapsychologically, they are overdetermined, thus establishing the game as a true ritual. It can be argued, though, that for some children, the Jinx game is more a game and less a ritual, and for others, more a ritual and less a game, depending on the developmental level they have reached and their susceptibility to regressive pulls.

It is fascinating to study a particular rule, really a safeguard, built into the ceremony. This rule provides that the jinxer *or* another child can break the spell. It would seem that the terrifying potential of actually being merged with another (the regressive wished-for state) requires that the jinxed not totally depend on the jinxer for his release. This provision that a third person, by stating the name of the jinxed child, can also separate the fused pair limits the power of the jinxer. In other words, the oedipal configuration with the third person as an interrupter of the mother-infant dyad is also represented in the ceremony.

SADOMASOCHISTIC CONSIDERATIONS

Another clearly observable element of the game is the sadomasochistic interplay between the children. Here Berta Bornstein's (1951) observations on latency children are highly relevant. She stresses the vulnerability of newly acquired accomplishments, the most important of which is the establishment of the superego. While she distinguishes "at least two major divisions, . . . the element common to both is the strictness of the superego."

She describes the first period of latency, from 5½ to 8 years:

> The ego, still buffeted by the surging impulses, is threatened by the new superego which is not only harsh and rigid but still a foreign body. The first phase . . . is complicated because of the intermingling of two different sets of defenses: the defense against genital and the defense against pregenital impulses. . . . In the second period of latency [from 8 until about 10 years] the situation is different: The ego is exposed to less severe conflicts by virtue of the facts that, on the one hand, the sexual demands have become less exerting and, on the other, the superego has become less rigid. The ego now can devote itself to a greater extent to coping with reality. The average eight-year-old is ready to be influenced by the children around him and by adults other than his parents [p. 280f.].

The concurrence of Piaget's observation and Bornstein's description is striking. Piaget, emphasizing the increasing significance of rules, and Bornstein, emphasizing significant modifications within the superego, both describe important changes taking place in children of about 7 to 8. It is around this age that the child's behavior more closely approximates Freud's *ideal of latency* (1905).

The Jinx game is most commonly played by children in Bornstein's second stage of latency, who have considerable control over pregenital impulses. However, derivatives of aggressive drive components or direct instinctual breakthroughs can regularly be observed in the play and games of these late latency children. Their play is characterized by bumping, shoving, pulling, and pushing, with frequent accidental and intentional hurting of each other. Sudden breakthroughs of aggression in the form of temper outbursts frequently occur even in such highly organized games as tag, the various competitive sports, and the table games.

In the Jinx game, the aggressive drive derivatives are easily detected as the jinxer's sadism is titrated against the jinxed's ability or desire to submit, his masochism. They are closely regulated, dosed, and mastered by simultaneous ego and, especially, superego influences. However, understanding the game solely from the viewpoint of controlled expression and mastery of drive derivatives ignores many specific elements of the ritual. Likewise, understanding the game solely from the standpoint of victim and victimizer introduces a conceptualization on a higher, more object-differentiated level than the differentiation-dedifferentiation experience which, I believe, the Jinx game more perfectly serves.

To illustrate this difference, it is instructive to contrast the Jinx game with some other latency and preadolescent games which are clearly object-differentiated and play out a true victim-victimizer situation. For example, "Mother, may I?" and the various "Slave" games can be understood as direct exercises in surrender of control to others. I suggest that these games are predominantly object-differentiated sadomasochistic enactments and represent essential developmental differences from the Jinx game's portrayal of merger and redifferentiation.

THE FATE OF THE JINX GAME

Interest in the Jinx game tends to decline as the child approaches puberty. The ritual loses meaning for the youngster, often is seen as childish, and occasions considerable resentment when a younger child attempts to engage the older one in it.

Geleerd (1961) described "a partial regression to the undifferentiated phase of object relationship" in adolescence (p. 396). Blos (1967) referred to the "catastrophic danger of the regressive loss of self, of a return of the undifferentiated state, or of merger" (p. 171f.), emphasizing that "the ego weakness of adolescence is not only due to the increasing strength of the drives but . . . to the disengagement from the parental ego support" (p. 164).

If adolescence is viewed as a second individuation process, with the differentiation of self and object again being imperiled by regressive pulls, it would seem that the Jinx game may be too real and too threatening for the young adolescent, who must therefore depreciate and avoid it. However, later in adolescence, with increased consolidation of personality structure, the game may again be enjoyed—now, as a momentary, symbolic mother-infant reunion, with illusionary omnipotence, a feeling of magical control, and a special potential for wish fulfillment.

WISH FULFILLMENT AND MERGER

An important variant of the game involves the linking of little fingers after coincidentally having said the same thing at the same time. Opie and Opie (1959) and Stone and Church (1968) note the nearly universal importance of wishing in these linking ceremonies, *especially* of older adolescents and some unsophisticated adults.

In these situations, it is hypothesized that the "magic moment" which brings about the feeling that a wish can be granted is an unconscious acknowledgment that "saying the same thing at once" represents a symbolic reunion with the mother (the wish-fulfilling object). The momentary unconscious experience of the return of the illusionary omnipotent mother-infant state finds expression in the half-play, half-fantasy feeling that a wish can be granted.

These linking ceremonies with wishing, though developmentally related, differ from the Jinx game. In these linking ceremonies there is little emphasis on the mutism-oneness and reestablishment of separateness by the pronouncement of the individual's name. The major emphasis, rather, is on illusionary omnipotence through linking. Perhaps, in this can be seen an important developmental shift from wished-for fusion with the mother to wished-for reunion with the mother as a wish-fulfilling object.[3]

THE MAGIC OF THREE

Opie and Opie (1959) note that "There seems to be some connexion between . . . the practices associated with unexpectedly

---

[3] I am grateful to Dr. Calvin Settlage for clarifying this distinction.

finding a thing in duplicate [such as two kernels in an almond], and those associated with accidentally duplicating the same words" (p. 312). These incidents of unexpectedly finding a thing in duplicate, which are closely related to wish fulfillment, commonly are associated with a ritualized need to do something or say something in threes. Apparently, the merger fears and/or the omnipotent fantasies associated with the coincidence of doubles can be mitigated by emphasizing a triadic relationship. The fortuitous identicalness activating the feared and wished-for (mother-infant) fusion frequently must be counteracted by a ritualistic symbolic representation of the oedipal triangle. This seems in accord with the view that preoedipally, the father (the third person) facilitates the child's struggles to emerge from the symbiosis with the mother. The father continues to offset the child's regressive tendencies until, with the child's further development, more pressing age-relevant concerns of the oedipal period predominate (Abelin, 1971; Loewald, 1951; Mahler and Gosliner, 1955).

This magical power of the triad to undo fusion is, as previously described, an important component of the safeguard that in addition to the jinxer, another person can release the jinxed one. However, saying or doing something in threes (counting to three, making three wishes, naming three poets, and the like) is a more sophisticated (symbolic) activity than actual intercession by a third person as seen in the Jinx game.

SOME GROUP RESPONSES

The group interaction in the Jinx game, especially the individual responses of the other children to the linked pair, is of particular interest.

As stated, it is often a third child who terminates the spell. If he accurately responds to minimal clues, the optimal dosing of the tension and its release result in much gaiety and satisfaction in the group. Some children, however, intervene prematurely, either in competition with the jinxer or because they are overly concerned with the "state" of the victim. Whatever their motivation, they spoil the fun. Depending on the spoiler's position in the group, the reaction to his intercession may be playful derision or complete exclusion from the group's activities.[4]

Another curious group response is manifested in the tendency of the Jinx game to occur in spurts. Apparently, once a sense of identity in the group has been undone through the coincidence of two children spontaneously and simultaneously saying the identical phrase, the barriers which keep self and object representations separate temporarily decrease in the other members. The tendency toward such dedifferentiation phenomena "epidemically" increases (much like slips of the tongue or punning) and more and more children "spontaneously" say the same phrases and then playfully "merge" and "free" each other.[5] After several repetitions, the activity loses its enchantment—sometimes if it becomes too real, more often, as there is extinction through mastery. It is then forgotten until some later time when there is again an unexpected coincidence of two children saying the same word or phrase and the ritual begins anew.

Summary

The psychoanalytic study of the Jinx game is presented as an observational study of the development of object relations. The game is initiated by the coincidence of two children spontaneously saying the same word or phrase and is terminated by pronouncing

[4] In "The Teacher Game" Ross (1965) describes very similar group phenomena in response to the titration of the "teacher's" authoritarianism against the "pupils'" disobedience. If the "teacher" is too punishing, or too repressive, she is excluded from the game, and sometimes, depending on her position in the group, from the subsequent activities. Likewise, a "pupil" can become too provocative and bring about the group's derision and/or his expulsion. It is fascinating to observe the preciseness of the ego and superego functioning which is necessary in order for a game to continue as a game. When the titrations fail, there is severe denouncement, punishment, at times even banishment of the offending group member, or total disruption of the activity.

[5] It is interesting to compare this pleasurable, excited, playful merging with a psychoanalytic experience with a borderline patient who rigidly insisted on the analyst's responding to her only in terms identical to her own. Her insistence on identicalness *protected* her from intensely feared merger feelings (Oremland and Windholz, 1970).

the name of the child who has been jinxed. Its rigidly adhered to rules, each reflecting, among other things, recently acquired ego and superego components, ritualize differentiation and subsequent redifferentiation. The game is viewed as a formalized latency and preadolescent recapitulation of aspects of the separation-individuation process, aiding the maintenance of self-object differentiation and the consolidation of the sense of autonomy.

Although participating in the expression of and control over aggressive impulses and sadomasochistic and omnipotent fantasies, the Jinx game specifically portrays merger issues rather than control of separate object issues, which are seen in pure form in such victim-victimizer games as "Slave" and "Mother, may I?"

I have suggested that pubertal children may lose interest in and depreciate the game because their sense of identity is again imperiled by regressive processes which make the threat of merger too real. However, with maturity, the game may again be enjoyed with a shift in emphasis to momentary, illusionary omnipotence and a feeling of potential wish fulfillment associated with unconscious primary merger processes.

BIBLIOGRAPHY

ABELIN, E. L. (1971), The Role of the Father in the Separation-Individuation Process. In: *Separation-Individuation*, ed. J. B. McDevitt & C. F. Settlage. New York: International Universities Press, pp. 229–252.

BLOS, P. (1967), The Second Individuation Process of Adolescence. *This Annual*, 22:162–186.

BORNSTEIN, B. (1951), On Latency. *This Annual*, 6:279–285.

BÜHLER, C. (1930), *The First Year of Life*. New York: John Day.

ERIKSON, E. H. (1937), Configurations in Play. *Psychoanal. Quart.*, 6:139–214.

———— (1951), Sex Differences in the Play Configurations of Pre-adolescents. *Amer. J. Orthopsychiat.*, 21:667–692.

FREUD, A. (1965), *Normality and Pathology in Childhood*. New York: International Universities Press.

FREUD, S. (1900), The Interpretation of Dreams. *Standard Edition*, 4 & 5. London: Hogarth Press, 1953.

———— (1905), Three Essays on the Theory of Sexuality. *Standard Edition*, 7:125–234. London: Hogarth Press, 1953.

———— (1920), Beyond the Pleasure Principle. *Standard Edition*, 18:7–64. London: Hogarth Press, 1955.

GELEERD, E. R. (1961), Some Aspects of Ego Vicissitudes in Adolescence. *J. Amer. Psa. Assn.*, 9:394–405.

GREENACRE, P. (1959), Play in Relation to Creative Imagination. *This Annual*, 14:61–80.

KAPLAN, E. B. (1965), Reflections Regarding Psychomotor Activities During the Latency Period. *This Annual*, 20:220–238.

KLEEMAN, J. A. (1967), The Peek-a-Boo Game. *This Annual*, 22:239–273.

KOHUT, H. (1971), *The Analysis of the Self*. New York: International Universities Press.

LOEWALD, H. W. (1951), Ego and Reality. *Int. J. Psycho-Anal.*, 32:10–18.

MAHLER, M. S. (1963), Subphases of the Separation-Individuation Process. Paper and film presented at the Annual Meeting of the American Psychoanalytic Association, St. Louis.

——— & FURER, M. (1963), Certain Aspects of the Separation-Individuation Phase. *Psychoanal. Quart.*, 32:1–14.

——— & GOSLINER, B. J. (1955), On Symbiotic Child Psychosis. *This Annual*, 10:195–211.

——— & McDEVITT, J. B. (1968), Observations on Adaptation and Defense in Statu Nascendi: Developmental Precursors in the First Two Years of Life, with film illustrations. Presented at the San Francisco Psychoanalytic Society.

OPIE, I. & OPIE, P. (1959), *The Lore and Language of Schoolchildren*. London: Oxford University Press.

——— ——— (1969), *Children's Games in Street and Playground*. London: Oxford University Press.

OREMLAND, J. D. & WINDHOLZ, E. (1970), Some Specific Transference, Counter-transference and Supervisory Problems in the Analysis of a Narcissistic Personality. *Int. J. Psycho-Anal.*, 52:267–275.

PELLER, L. E. (1954), Libidinal Phases, Ego Development, and Play. *This Annual*, 9:178–198.

——— (1955), Libidinal Development As Reflected in Play. *Psychoanalysis*, 3(3):3–11.

PIAGET, J. (1945), *Play, Dreams and Imitation in Childhood*. New York: Norton, 1951.

ROSS, H. (1965), The Teacher Game. *This Annual*, 20:288–297.

SETTLAGE, C. F. (1971), Discussion of the Experience of Separation-Individuation and Its Reverberations Throughout the Course of Life. Panel of meetings of American Psychoanalytic Association, December.

SIMMEL, E. (1926), The "Doctor Game," Illness and the Profession of Medicine. *Int. J. Psycho-Anal.*, 7:470–483.

STONE, L. J. & CHURCH, J. (1968), *Childhood and Adolescence*, 2nd. ed. New York: Random House.

WAELDER, R. (1932), The Psychoanalytic Theory of Play. *Psychoanal. Quart.*, 2:208–224, 1933.

WEBSTER'S *New World Dictionary* (1970), 2nd Coll. Ed. New York & Cleveland: World Publishing.

The Image of the Lost Parent

MARTHA WOLFENSTEIN, Ph.D.

LOVE IMPLIES A STABLE ATTACHMENT TO THE IMAGE OF THE BELOVED person in his absence. While the infant experiences the object only as an immediately present source of pleasure, the growing child forms an image of the object that remains intensely cathected in the interludes of the object's comings and goings. The attachment to the images of the first love objects, the parents, attains a great tenacity. We know with what travail the adolescent, under the stress of developmental circumstances, achieves a partial decathexis of his parents, in order to free libidinal energies for a mature sexual life.

The loss of a parent by death while the child is still in the process of growing up presents an extreme emotional exigency. Clinical studies suggest that the child is developmentally unprepared for what Freud (1917) calls the "work of mourning," the gradual, painful decathexis of the image of the lost object. I have put forward the hypothesis (1966) that mourning becomes possible only after adolescence has been passed through. Adolescence serves as a trial mourning, an initiation into the way of decathecting a major love object. Children who have lost a parent at an earlier age tend to retain their intense cathexis of the image of the parent. At the same time they acknowledge superficially the fact of the parent's death. Thus they maintain a dual and contradictory attitude toward a major reality of their lives. There is a splitting of the ego insofar as the two opposing views of the lost parent are not mutually confronted.

Associate Clinical Professor of Psychiatry, Albert Einstein College of Medicine.

Freud in a late paper (1927) recorded his observation of such a division of the mind in respect to a parent lost in childhood:

> In the analysis of two young men I learned that each—one when he was two years old and the other when he was ten—had failed to take cognizance of the death of his beloved father—had 'scoto-mized' it—and yet neither of them had developed a psychosis. Thus a piece of reality which was undoubtedly important had been disavowed by the ego. . . . I also began to suspect that similar occurrences in childhood are by no means rare. . . . It turned out that the two young men had no more 'scotomized' their father's death than a fetishist does the castration of women. It was only one current in their mental life that had not recognized their father's death; there was another current which took full account of that fact. The attitude which fitted in with the wish and the attitude which fitted in with reality existed side by side [p. 155f.].

I have attempted to explore elsewhere (1969) some of the consequences of this inability to renounce a lost object, as well as the possibility for a child, under favorable circumstances, to achieve some detachment from a lost parent in a way which differs from adult mourning. What I wish to do in the present paper is to look at some examples of the image of a parent lost in childhood, an image which persists over time and which reveals that dual aspect of near and far, present and absent, lost and inalienable, living and dead. I shall illustrate this imagery from the work of a poet and a painter, each of whom lost his mother in boyhood.

I

A. E. Housman (1859–1936) was an eminent classical scholar and also the author of two short books of poems, *A Shropshire Lad* (1896) and *Last Poems* (1922).[1] In his poetry, Housman assumes the role of a simple rustic, exiled in London, pining for his home countryside, which is vividly evoked before the mind's eye. He recalls nostalgi-cally the lost comradeship of friends with whom he used to share the

[1] Information on Housman's life is drawn from memoirs by Laurence Housman (1938, 1967), Katharine E. Symons (1937), A. S. F. Gow (1936), Grant Richards (1942), and Percy Withers (1940).

bounties of the spring landscape and the country fair. The pleasures and hopes of youth being brief and deceptive, the poet offers to all young men compassion for the inevitable disappointments of life which they, no less than he, are bound to suffer. The assumed simplicity and kindly fellow feeling of Housman the poet were at marked variance with the posture of Housman the scholar. In the latter capacity he was noted for his haughtiness and his devastating critiques of the errors of fellow scholars. In life he was aloof and solitary, not finding in the generations of his students the counterparts of the beloved lads of his poems.

The son of a provincial solicitor, Housman had been the eldest of seven children, with four brothers and two sisters. His mother had died on his 12th birthday. Housman had been away from home at the time, staying with friends of the family for his Easter holiday. He was told of his mother's death in a letter from his father. There is evidence from his adolescent verse that the young Housman turned longingly toward his widowed father (Wolfenstein, 1956). However, the father soon married again. Housman then attached himself with strong feeling to his younger siblings, especially his brothers. For these younger children he was an admired leader and master of the games. He initiated collaborative production of poems, stories, and plays, in which there was a sharing of fantasy life. Comradeship with his brothers replaced his earlier envy and resentment of them. They, who had appeared in turn to deprive him of his mother's love, had become together with him all equally deprived through her death.

From schoolboy days, Housman had been a brilliant student, and as an undergraduate at Oxford gave evidence of the quality which was to mark his eventual distinguished career. However, he suffered a devastating reverse when he failed his final examinations at Oxford. The prospects for an academic career seemed closed to him. He studied for the civil service and took a modest position in Her Majesty's Patent Office, remaining in this servitude for some 10 years. In every spare moment he continued to pursue his classical researches, and published several papers which began to make his reputation. He obtained a professorship in Latin at University College, London, and after 19 more years attained his due place with a professorship in Latin at Cambridge. His examination failure had cost him some 30 years of wandering off course. It also had vitiated the comradely relations with his brothers, whom he could not face as a fallen leader, from whom he turned away in bitter pride.

Housman's examination failure has remained a puzzle to his biographers. Without here reviewing the various interpretations which have been offered, I shall indicate briefly what I consider to have caused it. At the time Housman's father had fallen seriously ill. His stepmother was advised by the family doctor to alert the eldest son that his father was not expected to live. This then was the news that Housman received on the eve of the fateful examination. The family was in straitened financial circumstances, and there were the four younger brothers to be seen through school. No doubt they looked to Housman, assured, as they thought, of an excellent career, to become head of the family and to provide much-needed support. To pass his examinations would have meant for Housman taking his father's place. Academic triumph became fraught with unconscious connotations of parricide. Housman suffered a kind of paralysis and could write almost nothing on his examination papers. It was an added irony that his father did not die at that time, but lived on for more than a decade.

At Oxford Housman had met his greatest friend, a fellow student named Moses Jackson, to whom he remained intensely attached. When he moved to London, he shared rooms for a time with Jackson and Jackson's younger brother. This comradeship was interrupted when Jackson went off to pursue a career in India. He returned to England to marry, and later settled in another outpost of empire, in Canada. There is little doubt that Housman was deeply bound to Jackson and that he suffered a painful sense of loss from Jackson's leaving him. After Housman's death, when his brother Laurence published a memoir of him, together with a collection of posthumously published poems which spoke of a thwarted love for a man, there was considerable speculation as to whether Housman had been an overt homosexual. Without here sifting the relevant evidence, I will simply state the conclusion to which I have come, namely, that there was no overt homosexual relation between Housman and Jackson. Nevertheless Housman suffered deeply the pangs of disprized love in relation to his friend.

It was a second edition of what he had felt for his father in his adolescence. The Epithalamium which Housman wrote for Jackson's wedding could have served equally for the occasion of his father's second marriage. "Friend and comrade yield you o'er/ To her that hardly loves you more" (1922, XXIV).

It was when Housman was in his 36th year, while he was a professor at University College, London, that he experienced the one intensive and protracted episode of poetic inspiration in his long life. Out of it emerged *A Shropshire Lad*. The onset of what was, from Housman's later accounts, a profoundly agitating as well as productive state, followed on the death of his father. I would suppose that this loss served to stir up latent feelings for all previous losses, and especially to release emotions related to his mother's death which were probably inhibited at the time, as they generally tend to be in childhood.

The persisting image of the lost parent finds expression in Housman's poetry particularly in the way in which he deals with time. In some earlier verse he had mused about the remote past, about gods whose altars are deserted, and kings whose kingdom is done.

> Their arms the rust hath eaten,
>   Their statutes none regard:
> Arabia shall not sweeten
>   Their dust, with all her nard [1936, III].

This imagery of a finished and irrevocable past did not accord with Housman's more complicated feelings of loss and unassuaged protest against it. The device which he found in *A Shropshire Lad* was that of evoking something longed-for and absent but still existing. The image is that of his home countryside from which he is exiled in London, and which he imagines flowering anew each spring though he cannot be there. Housman followed in the tradition of many poets who have identified mother with nature. The distinctive aspect of his evocation of nature consists in his envisioning it always from a distance. It is the beloved, intimately known home landscape from which he is always absent, for which he is pining from afar. Something from time past is transformed into something remote in space. It is an essential difference between time and space that time is irreversible, while in space we can travel back and forth. By translating time into space, Housman expressed his dual attitude toward his lost mother as removed from him but never renounced. Here is an archetypal exemplification of this basic theme:

> Into my heart an air that kills
> From yon far country blows:
> What are those blue remembered hills,
> What spires, what farms are those?
>
> That is the land of lost content,
> I see it shining plain,
> The happy highways where I went
> And cannot come again [1896, XL].

Time past is transformed into a far place; the possibility of return, explicitly denied, is implicitly retained. The dual effect of something lost but still enduring pervades Housman's poetry. If we compare the poem just cited with an unpublished variant of it, we see how important this dual effect was for Housman, how he rejected a more unambiguous view of the past. The alternative version begins: "The farms of home lie lost in even,/ I see far off the steeple stand. . . ." Its leitmotiv is: "The land is still."

> The land is still by farm and steeple,
> And still for me the land may stay:
> There I was friends with perished people,
> And there lie they [1936, XIV].

In this discarded variant the finality of death is acknowledged. The lost beloved lies buried and the landscape becomes a graveyard. In the preferred version a human warmth still seems to linger about "the land of lost content." The countryside is infused with the quality of the lost beloved, the source of childhood pleasures. The highways where the poet cannot come again are figuratively the past. Yet the word "highways" retains the literal connotation of one's being able to travel back the way one came. There is the further ambiguity of that which is lost having been internalized (through the killing air which has entered his heart) and remaining external ("I see it"). It is both past and present, remembered and directly seen. There is an ambivalent view of the dead as both vengeful and good. The dead beloved has entered into the poet through respiratory incorporation (a recurrent theme of Housman's), becoming a bad internal object that kills. Yet she is also remembered as benign, as having given content. The poet has become one with the dead mother by internalizing her, yet she lives on in him; he preserves and immortalizes her. Thus opposite feelings of despair and hope, loss and return, separation and union, killing and preserving are simultaneously evoked.

The effect at which Housman aimed was one in which there is an endless alternation of a sense of loss and denial of loss. In some of his discarded poems hope and despair appeared too discretely and disjoined to produce this effect. An extreme denial of loss—"No star is lost"—had been followed by a deeply pessimistic statement of the world's being irremediably flawed (1936, VII). A poem about the restoration of the fallen campanile in Venice (1936, XLIV) had ended with the poet's saying a last farewell to that lovely city. In the poems which suited Housman better there was a more continual counterpoint of such opposing feelings, of loss and restoration, departure and return. One of many examples is the poem beginning: "White in the moon the long road lies . . . That leads me from my love." There follows a description of the still moonlit landscape in which the departing lover pursues his ceaseless way. While the stillness suggests the finality of death, an assurance of return is offered:

> The world is round, so travellers tell,
>   And straight though reach the track,
> Trudge on, trudge on, 'twill all be well,
>   The way will guide one back [1896, XXXVI].

The ironical tone mocks the hope of return, which nevertheless persists. The protractedness of separation evokes a further protest: "But ere the circle homeward hies/ Far, far must it remove. . . ." Though there is a sense of deep affliction, irretrievable loss is still denied. Time is translated into space, and loss becomes separation. However far the poet is removed from the lost beloved, it remains possible to return: "The way will guide one back."

The beloved countryside is seen under the aspect of mortality and as perennially renewed. Since Housman's mother had died at Eastertime, spring recurrently evoked in him feelings of transience, of "the Lenten lily/ That has not long to stay/ And dies on Easter day" (1896, XXIX). His regret for being absent from the home countryside is compounded with a sense of the transitoriness of its spring flowering and a restitutive wish to stay the withering of its blooms: "Lie long, high snowdrifts in the hedge/ That will not shower on me" (1896, XXXIX). That his mother had died on his birthday produced a lasting impression that when one expects the best one is likely to get the worst. A "spoilt spring" (manifestly from incessant rain) provokes a bitter reproach against frustrating fate:

> It is in truth iniquity on high
>   To cheat our sentenced souls of aught they crave,
> And mar the merriment as you and I
>   Fare on our long fool's-errand to the grave [1922, IX].

His birthday evoked in him recurrently thoughts of his own death. In a poem ironically titled "The Immortal Part," he condenses birth and death in the grim fantasy that dying means giving birth to the enduring part concealed within: ". . . every mother's son/ Travails with a skeleton./ Lie down in the bed of dust;/ Bear the fruit that bear you must . . ." (1896, XLIII). For all this forcing on himself (and us) of the reality of death, the identification of dying with giving birth has something of the ambiguity of Eliot's "Death is life, and life is death."

Housman's associations of nature with transience and moribundity alternated with images of nature as ever-renewed and enjoyed by successive generations of youths. In the recollections mingled with fantasy in his poems, Housman pictured himself a young rustic who together with beloved comrades had shared the pleasures of the spring landscape and of the country fair. Ludlow Fair is a recurrent image, a counterpart of bounteous nature, where the boon companions drank their fill. The sense of regret for a lost past is pervasive, at the same time that new generations of young men are envisaged, repeating the same pattern, with whom the poet feels identified, though at a distance.

> Between the trees in flower
> New friends at fairtime tread

> The way where Ludlow tower
> 　Stands planted on the dead.
> Our thoughts, a long while after,
> 　They think, our words they say;
> Theirs now's the laughter,
> 　The fair, the first of May [1922, **XXXIV**].

The successive generations who enjoyed what Housman had once possessed had been in the first instance his brothers, who in turn supplanted him in his mother's arms. At first bitterly resented, they had become the objects of strong, compassionate fellow feeling when they had all been equally dispossessed of the mother through her death. It was then that the comradeship of the brother band had been forged. There had been the sharing of many imaginative games, with the brilliant eldest brother as leader. This close affiliation had been severed after Housman's examination failure, when he felt he had fallen in his brothers' eyes and withdrew from them in frozen aloofness. Subsequently a second brother band had been established, when Housman lived in London with his friend Jackson and Jackson's younger brother. At the time of Housman's writing *A Shropshire Lad*, Jackson had been for many years away in India and Jackson's brother had died. The intense, though restricted fellowship that Housman had known had receded into the past. The poems evoke the comradeship of those two brother bands, fused together, in the setting of the lost countryside.

Housman's capacity to form new love relations had come to an end in early manhood. Too many losses and disappointments had left him unwilling to commit himself again. From very early in life he had lost his mother repeatedly to a rapid succession of siblings, so that her death confirmed an already chronic sense of loss. His adolescent longing for his widowed father had been thwarted; his comradeship with his brothers, vitiated. The persistent and embittered attachment to the friend who left him stood for all the disappointed early loves from which he never detached himself. As he wrote in one of the poems apostrophizing his friend:

> But this unlucky love should last
> 　When answered passions thin to air;
> Eternal fate so deep has cast
> 　Its sure foundation of despair [1936, **XII**].

Another motive for Housman's nostalgia for his youth was a longing to recapture the time before his examination failure. Several poems suggest that that disgrace gave rise to thoughts of suicide or the wish he might have died before it happened. We see this in the lines "To An Athlete Dying Young":

> Now you will not swell the rout
> Of lads that wore their honours out,
> Runners whom renown outran
> And the name died before the man [1896, XIX].

Among the painful losses of his youth had been the loss of the good image of himself. His need to vaunt his own excellence as a scholar may be seen as an effort to reconstitute that image.

The simple rustics toward whom Housman expressed such strong fellow feeling in his poems found their counterparts in the fellow scholars whom Housman considered simple-minded, and toward whom he expressed quite opposite sentiments. Housman the scholar had a reputation for arrogance and for considering himself infallible. He tended to regard only a few great classicists from the past as his peers. Though the exceptionally high level of his scholarship could not be denied, the scathing satire with which he plied his contemporaries often provoked hurt feelings and sputtering protests. In Housman's conception of his field of study, very few were worthy to enter it, and he was chronically indignant at the intrusion of those he thought inadequately qualified. A recurrent theme in his critiques was that the scholars he considered incompetent were like infants. Typical strictures were that they "comprehend neither Latin nor any other language" (1903, p. xliv), produce "gibberish, not human speech" (1926, p. xxiv), and frequently "mistake the meaning of simple words and phrases" (1907, p. 63). The work of one of his colleagues gave him the feeling of being "in perpetual contact with the intellect of an idiot child" (1930, p. xxiii). In the context of scholarly dispute these are obviously exaggerated statements. As applied to his first rivals, his infant brothers, they would have been literally true. Housman's resentment of their intrusion on his domain, unworthy as they seemed compared with him, persisted and found expression in his unsparing critiques of fellow scholars. His poetry, in marked contrast, celebrated the prized moments of mastery over this contemptuous rage, the hard-won goodwill toward those poor fellows, his brothers.

Not all poets who celebrate the beauties of nature assume, as Housman did, the role of simple rustic. Nor was this role for Housman anything but a poetic fiction. From his school days aloof and studious, he had never got drunk with farm lads at country fairs. I would see as a motive for Housman's assuming this role in his poetry a need to humble himself to the level of his brothers, to recapture the good feelings of the brother band of his youth. This humility also served to mask the grandiosity which was more overt, though moderated with irony, in Housman the scholar. In the final poem of *A Shropshire Lad*, the poet, still in his rustic guise, becomes the protagonist of the parable of the sower. The seeds he sows, his poems, are thus likened to the words of the savior.

> Some seed the birds devour,
>   And some the season mars,
> But here and there will flower
>   The solitary stars,
>
> And fields will yearly bear them
>   As light-leaved spring comes on,
> And luckless lads will wear them
>   When I am dead and gone [1896, LXIII].

Housman explicitly offered his poems as a solace to all young men whose high hopes are doomed to disappointment. Implicitly he makes a larger claim: he has come to save. And his followers will be legion, for the luckless lads we have always with us. From his adolescence, Housman had renounced the religious faith in which he had been reared, but its imagery stayed with him. As the Christian savior had assumed the form of a common mortal to fulfill his destiny, so Housman the poet put off his grandiosity in the hope that all unhappy youths of successive generations might identify with him. Thus it was also his own immortality he sought.

The opening poem of *A Shropshire Lad*, commemorating Queen Victoria's golden jubilee, celebrates the reign of a long-lived queen.

The second last poem pays tribute to a long-lived king, Mithridates, who knew how to outwit death. These glorified parent figures, endowed with great power to endure, are an expression of the poet's wish to immortalize his parents, and especially to deny the early death of his mother.

More than a quarter century after the publication of *A Shropshire Lad*, Housman brought out his *Last Poems*. He was then 63 years old. While many of the poems in the latter volume had been written or begun earlier, Housman seems to have experienced a brief upsurge of poetic inspiration in that year. Housman's father had died at the age of 63, and Housman, having reached that age himself, probably had revived in him some of the same feelings which had given rise to *A Shropshire Lad*. In *Last Poems*, youthful comrades still range the country roads, and the home landscape flowers, evanescent and ever-renewed. There is the pervasive sense of transience and of the ever-living past.

II

René Magritte (1898–1967) was a Belgian surrealist painter, whose works have a baffling and haunting quality.[2] In a deceptively simple manner, Magritte presents us with ordinary, everyday objects, but they appear in unexpected combinations, in altered relative size, or in process of turning one into another. His pictures, painted in a naturalistic style, produce a strong illusion of reality, at the same time that the situation he presents appears impossible. He produces an effect of the familiar becoming strange. Magritte developed his distinctive style in the latter 1920s, and continued for the rest of his life to produce works in this manner, which have the cumulative effect of constituting a mythical world of great integrity. In life Magritte was sober and unostentatious, with nothing of the bohemian about him. He resembled, intentionally, the tightly buttoned-up man in the bowler hat who appears in many of his paintings. Living with his wife in a modest suburb of Brussels, he

---

[2] Information on Magritte's life is drawn from Magritte's *Esquisse Auto-biographique* (1954) and *La Ligne de Vie* (1938); and writings about Magritte by Scutenaire (1945), Soby (1965), Waldberg (1965), Sylvester (1969), and Gablik (1970).

walked his dog, played chess in the café, and rarely traveled abroad. As his emissaries to the world his paintings traveled to New York and London, to Paris and Hollywood, to Rome and Basle, to Houston, Cologne, Stockholm. His images have become a part of the furnishings of the mind of many of his contemporaries.

The son of a provincial businessman, Magritte was the eldest of three boys. When he was 13 years old, his mother committed suicide. The circumstances as later recalled by Magritte and told to a close friend were as follows:

> [The mother] shared the room of the youngest son, who, in the middle of the night realizing that he was alone, aroused the family. They searched throughout the house in vain, then noticing footsteps on the threshold and on the path, they followed them to a bridge over the Sambre, the local river. The mother of the painter had thrown herself in the water, and when they recovered her corpse, her face was concealed by her nightgown. They never knew if she had covered her eyes not to see the death she had chosen or if the movement of the water had veiled her in this way [Scutenaire, p. 47].

The impact on the young Magritte of his mother's death was complicated by the circumstances of that strange and terrible night scene: his mother's body, her nightgown having been washed up over her head, was exposed naked to his guilty and avid gaze.

Magritte in later years (1938) recalled a major memory of his boyhood, which I would take to be a screen memory, in which a wealth of fantasy is condensed. According to his recollection, he used to play with a little girl in an old, deserted cemetery where the children would descend into the underground tombs. One day, coming up from the darkness into the light, they saw an artist amid the broken monuments and fallen leaves, painting the picturesque view. This was the first artist Magritte had ever seen, and art seemed to him then endowed with a magical aura (p. 3f.). This memory of Magritte's has a mythical quality, combining the themes of love, death, and art. The scene in the sunlit cemetery masks the nighttime scene in which his mother's body was carried up from the river. In the screen memory the tragedy is undone: the young Magritte, like Orpheus, brings a beloved girl back from the underground tomb. The artist in the cemetery appears as a forerunner, prefiguring what Magritte is to become. As a detached onlooker, he is also an alterego, exemplifying Magritte's estrangement from himself, a tendency which was to find expression in his art in his creating a *Doppelgänger*, the man in the bowler hat. In Magritte's memory the artist appears oblivious of the children and their forbidden games as he occupies himself with painting stones and leaves. Here too he is the counterpart of Magritte, who often substituted nonhuman for human subjects, among which leaves and stones were favored leitmotivs.

There are so many images in Magritte's work which may be taken as relating to his mother, and to the circumstances of her death, that I can here give only a summary and selective account of them. In an early appearance of the man in the bowler hat, *Les Rêveries du Promeneur Solitaire*, we see this alterego of the artist walking beside a river at night. Behind his back, floating horizontally in air, appears the naked corpse of a woman. This haunting image pursues the artist, however much he may try to put it behind him. Women in Magritte's paintings frequently have the aspect of being both alive and dead, there and not there. *L'Inondation*, for example, shows a nude woman standing beside a river; the upper part of her body fades out and her head is invisible. The dead mother's head covered by the nightgown is recalled in *L'Histoire Centrale* where a clothed woman appears with a suitcase as if about to depart, and with her head wrapped in a white cloth. In *Les Amants*, a man and woman, both of whose heads are wrapped in white cloths, exchange a muffled, necrophiliac kiss. This is like a fantasied reunion of the parents in death, as if the son addressed the father in bitter mockery: "Embrace her now if you dare." *La Philosophie dans la Boudoir* shows a nightgown, neatly hung up, from which two luminous, rosy breasts emerge. This is a condensed image of the garment which should have concealed and that which it failed to conceal. The gown endowed with breasts is also a fusion of the animate and inanimate. Beautiful women are often statue women. Frequently appearing with the sea in the background, they stand in lifelike postures, but their eyes are blank; body, lips, eyes, hair are of a uniform color (e.g., *Les Fleurs du Mal*). *La Memoire* shows a marble head which bleeds from the temple. A painful memory is like a never-healing wound, and in Magritte's pictures as in dreams, such a simile is rendered as a concrete visual image. The wound is condensed with the woman turned to stone who caused it, or is vindictively inflicted on her in turn. Yet, this dead woman still shows signs of life in the fresh red blood flowing from her marble brow.

The forbidden vision of the mother's naked corpse gave rise to denial of having looked, pretended mistakes as to what was seen, and overscrupulous covering up. Magritte painted a picture of a nude woman framed by an inscription: "*Je ne vois pas la* [picture of female nude] *cachée dans la forêt.*" This was one of a series of paintings in which a visual image and a written inscription appear mutually contradictory. At the time of painting "*Je ne vois pas . . .* " Magritte was a member of the surrealist group in Paris. A collage was made with this painting in the center, and as a frame a series of photographs of members of the group, each with his eyes shut tight. The effect of these grown men, all artists, simulating a childish innocence adds a further absurdity to that of the painting itself.

In *Le Viol*, Magritte makes us see a female torso as a face. The breasts are eyes, the navel a nose, and the pubic hair a mouth. This torso-face is surrounded by a mass of hair and set on a long sinuous neck. The impact of this image is both disturbing and comic. As Waldberg (1965) puts it, we are moved to "panic laughter" (p. 180). Magritte's torso-face is a variant of the Medusa head, evoking the frightening castratedness of woman. *Qua* torso this woman lacks a head; *qua* face, her eyes are sightless, her nose an indentation instead of a protuberance, her mouth incapable of speech. On one level it is a cynical view of woman as a mindless body. On another level it preserves a very archaic image of the human form, what we see in a child's first drawing in which head and body are one, a single circle containing facial features, with rudimentary limbs extending from it. In relation to Magritte's life, his last view of his mother was one in which he should have seen her face, but it was covered; he should not have seen her body, but it was bared. His painting of the torso-face seems to present a grimly humorous alibi: "Was that her body? It looked like a face to me."

In a revision which Magritte painted of David's Mme. Récamier, the setting is preserved in all details, but the lovely lady on the couch is ensconced in an elegant pink coffin, nicely accommodated to her seated posture (Fig. 1). Magritte pretends to mistake the image for the object, and it is as if he were saying: "Do you really want to look at a lady long dead?" In his typical mocking way, he demonstrates his superior sense of propriety by enclosing her decorously in a coffin. If we have before our mind's eye David's portrait of the ever-fresh and rosy young woman, we may get from looking at Magritte's revision an impression of her being alternately alive and dead, or perhaps an apprehension of premature burial. Magritte applied a similar treatment to the Balcony of Manet, where, in that ephemeral and enduring glimpse of life, coffins enclose the elegant ladies and gentleman, seated and standing. In a variant on this theme, a coffin appears to enclose a seated figure, resting on a low wall by the side of a road. The title *La Belle Heretique* seems an allusion to the mother's suicide and the question to which it may have given rise as to whether she could be buried in holy ground.

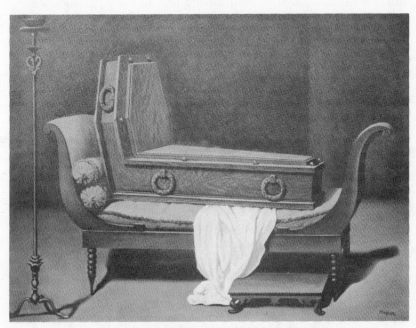

Figure 1. *Perspective: Mme. Récamier de David* (1950)
Oil on canvas, 24¾ x 31½". Private collection

In a haunting dead-alive image, *Le Thérapeute*, we see a wayfarer who appears to have paused to rest on his journey. Firmly grasping his staff and his sack, he is prepared to set out again. Yet without his being aware of it, he has come to his journey's end, for his torso has turned into a large birdcage-ribcage. There are two white doves, one on the outer ledge of the cage, one still inside, like the soul about to take flight, like the still fluttering heart. The man's capacious cloak is draped over the cage and his broad-brimmed hat set on top of it. Though he is headless and hollow, the firm outlines of the seated figure together with the sturdy arms and legs produce a strong effect of unvanquished humanity. As he often does, Magritte here condenses different moments in time, from the midst of life and after death. The condensed image produces an effect of comic pathos: this is the predicament of all dead men, who have been brought to a stop while still preparing for the morrow.

In a series of pictures men, animals, the interiors of rooms with all their furnishings have turned to stone. Two men in business suits have stopped as it seems on their way to work; one of them is trying to remove a speck from the other's eye. In the midst of this trivial action they have turned to stone (*Journal Intime*). In another picture, the same two men are walking away from each other, and in that moment have become ossified (*Le Chant de la Violette*). The interior of a room reveals a dignified man in frock coat, holding a top hat, with a lion couchant at his feet. These figures seem to have been displaced from a monument in the park to a modest setting of everyday life. The man, the lion, the walls and furnishings of the room are all of worn and aging stone. As a paradoxical indication of inextinguishable life, the stone flame of a stone candle casts a strong illumination on the scene (*Souvenir de Voyage*). Magritte's ossified rooms and men turned to stone in postures of everyday life have something of the aura of Pompeii, of things long dead, preserved forever (Fig. 2).

Fantasies and parodies of resurrection abound in Magritte's work. He had been reared in the Catholic faith and had been intensely pious in boyhood, but in adolescence had become a mocker and an unbeliever. As he said later (1938), speaking of the displacements and transformations of objects in his pictures: "The body of a woman floating above a city replaced to advantage the angels which have never appeared to me; I found it useful to see the seamy side of the Virgin Mary" (p. 11). We may suppose that the profound impact of having seen his mother's drowned corpse destroyed the credibility of the angels in the stained-glass windows and of the image of the pure and asexual Mother. The pitiful and pitilessly exposed body was incompatible with previously cherished ideas of resurrection. Mockery of the myth of resurrection may be seen as one determinant of Magritte's penchant for placing all kinds of objects in the sky: rocks, horsebells, chairs, tubas, loaves of bread,

Figure 2. *Souvenir de Voyage* (1955)
Oil on canvas, 63⅞ x 51¼". Collection, The Museum of
Modern Art, New York. Gift of Dominique and John de Menil

bowler-hatted men. It is as if he were saying: "This is no more implausible than what they taught us, that the dead would rise to heaven."

The myth of resurrection nevertheless retained a strong hold on Magritte's imagination. We see it in his pictures translated into imagery akin to that of classical mythology, in metamorphoses. A favored image of Magritte's, which he painted many times, shows large leaves springing out of the dead ground, and becoming transformed into birds (e.g., *L'Ile au Trésor, Les Compagnons de la Peur, Les Graces Naturelles*). In some instances a bird, already fully formed, is taking flight, while others are still emerging from the leaves (*La Clairière*). A variant shows a bird-leaf with closed eye and drooping head, its body being eaten by worms (*La Saveur des Larmes*). Here the apprehension of inevitable decay breaks through. Belief in immortality contends with doubt in Magritte's image of the leaves turning into birds. The mocking thought seems to be implicit: "If the dead are supposed to arise out of the earth and take flight into heaven, this might be a way of doing the trick." Yet the imagery also suggests a deep longing for revival and return of what has been lost. Green shoots emerging from the dead ground in spring have been from ancient times the occasion of celebrations of renewal, associated with the return of the dead to life, with gods who died and rose again. Superimposed on these older myths was that of the Christian god who died and was resurrected in the spring. The bird, from early Christian times, has been a symbol of the soul. Metamorphoses in ancient mythology often occurred in the context of loss of a beloved, of whom a transformed vestige was retained. To take one of many instances, the nymph Syrinx, fleeing from the god Pan who had become enamored of her, was changed into a reed. Of the reed Pan made the pipes on which he played his haunting melodies. The sense of something preserved along with a desperate sense of loss is perpetuated in Shelley's Hymn of Pan: "I pursued a maiden and clasped a reed:/ Gods and men, we are all deluded thus!" In Magritte's metamorphoses we may discern a similar sense of loss, contending with a denial of it. A related image shows a mountain range in the far distance by night, which assumes the form of a great bird with outstretched wings. On a parapet in the foreground there is a deserted nest with three eggs. The mother bird, become one with nature, broods from afar over her abandoned young (*Le Domaine d'Arnheim*).

An image that greatly pleased Magritte, and which he painted many times, was *L'Empire des Lumières*, a scene in which it is simultaneously night and day. On the earth darkness has fallen, the street lamp glimmers, a few lights show in the windows of the darkened houses, the trees are black silhouettes; but in the sky it is broad midday, a luminous blue with white clouds. We may see in this a reflection of Magritte's childhood memory of coming up out of the darkness of the underground tombs into the sunlight. There seems to be the same fantasied denial and undoing of death that we discerned in the screen memory. Night must not fall. Then the terrible catastrophe that occurred under cover of darkness would not have taken place. One may be reminded of Dylan Thomas' "Rage, rage against the dying of the light." For an artist, light, the necessary condition of vision, is more than for most men life itself. The coexistence of night and day in Magritte's *L'Empire des Lumières*

Figure 3. *L'Empire des Lumières, II* (1950)
Oil on canvas, 31 x 39". Collection, The Museum of Modern
Art, New York. Gift of Dominique and John de Menil

expresses combined acknowledgment and denial of death (Fig. 4).

Another of Magritte's most recurrent images is that of the picture within the picture (*La Condition Humaine*, Fig. 4). He shows the interior of a room with a canvas on an easel placed before the window. The picture on the canvas represents exactly that part of the scene beyond which the canvas blanks out. The part of the

Figure 4. *La Condition Humaine I* (1933)
Oil on canvas, 39½ x 33″. Collection of Claude Spaak

scene on the canvas fits so well into the surrounding view outside that we tend to see it "out there" at the same time that it is located on the easel in the room. As Magritte says, he makes us see the same thing in two places at once. This image, of which Magritte painted many variants, is one of his greatest inventions: a scene painted quite naturalistically, without distortion or dislocation, evokes the greatest uncertainty about what is real. When we see the picture in the room as part of the scene beyond, we have an uneasy sense of having mistaken a picture for something "real." But the room, the easel, the window, the distant landscape are all equally painted canvas. Magritte plays on the counterpoint between illusion and reality with which so many artists and poets have been occupied. "Reality" has many ambiguous connotations. In our way of feeling about it, real and unreal are often associated with the enduring and the ephemeral. "We are such stuff as dreams are made on, and our little life is rounded with a sleep." Artists create illusions, but their works outlast them and will outlast us. This is one of the several paradoxes of Magritte's dual image: he makes us see the picture within the picture as less real than the surrounding scene, but by the criterion of durability it is more real.

Uncertainty about the location of objects in space, the illusion of something far off being very close, is one of Magritte's most pervasive themes. This sense of something being both near and far applies to time past as well as to objects in space. Speaking of the illusion created by the picture within the picture, Magritte (1938) said: "It appears for the spectator at the same time in the interior of the room on the canvas and outside in the real landscape. This existence in two places at once is like the existence of an identical moment both in the past and in the present as it occurs in *'fausse reconnaissance'*" (p. 14). Thus Magritte was himself aware that the strange ambiguity of his pictures was related to a dual feeling about the past, remote and ever-present.

III

I have tried to show in the work of a poet and a painter, each of whom lost his mother in boyhood, some derivatives of the persisting image of the lost parent as both dead and alive. Housman, by identifying the lost mother with the home countryside that he longs for from afar, translated time into space, loss into separation, preserving a hope of return, though he manifestly denied it. Magritte presents an array of images of coexistent life and death, presence and absence, resurrection as possible and absurd, metamorphosis as preservation and loss. Playing with the image of an object which appears both near and far in space, he finds the effect the same as that of experiencing time past in time present. Thus both play with time and space, Housman by translating the past into a distant scene, Magritte by making uncertainties about distance in space stand for the dual sense of the past as remote and near.

Quoting Freud at the beginning of this paper, I stated that the loss of a parent in childhood produces a splitting of the ego as the child both acknowledges and denies the reality of the parent's death. Two opposite views are thus simultaneously maintained, but not mutually confronted; they coexist in isolation. In the images of a poet and a painter we find these opposites fused. The lost parent is both dead and alive, absent but enduring, far and near. This exemplifies the ability of artists generally to dissolve the inner barriers of the mind, to combine the devices of primary and secondary processes, to subject archaic memory to the highest organizing principle. What is otherwise contradiction assumes for the artist the aspect of rich ambiguity. The boundness to an ever-living past, which prevents the neurotic from living in the present, provides the artist with the source and substance of his work, which embodies, in Proust's phrase, "the past recaptured."

BIBLIOGRAPHY

Freud, S. (1917), Mourning and Melancholia. *Standard Edition*, 14:237–260. London: Hogarth Press, 1957.

——— (1927), Fetishism. *Standard Edition*, 21:149–157. London: Hogarth Press, 1961.

Gablik, S. (1970), *Magritte.* Greenwich, Conn.: New York Graphic Society.

Gow, A. S. F. (1936), *A. E. Housman: A Sketch.* Cambridge: University Press.

Housman, A. E. (1896), *A Shropshire Lad.* In: *The Collected Poems of A. E. Housman.* New York: Henry Holt, 1940.

——— (1903), *M. Manilii Astronomicon, Book 1.* Cambridge: University Press, 1937.

—— (1907), Luciliana. *Classical Rev.*, 1:53–74.

—— (1922), *Last Poems.* In: *The Collected Poems of A. E. Housman,* New York: Henry Holt, 1940.

—— (1926), *M. Annei Lucani Belli Civilis.* Oxford: Blackwell, 1950.

—— (1930), *M. Manilii Astronomicon,* Book 5. Cambridge: University Press, 1937.

—— (1936), *More Poems.* In: *The Collected Poems of A. E. Housman.* New York: Henry Holt, 1940.

HOUSMAN, L. (1938), *My Brother: A. E. Housman.* New York: Scribner's.

—— (1967), A. E. Housman's "De Amicitia." *Encounter,* 29:33–41.

MAGRITTE, R. (1938), *La Ligne de Vie.* New York: Photostat of manuscript in Museum of Modern Art.

—— (1954), *Esquisse Auto-biographique.* Brussels: Palais des Beaux-Arts, Editions de la Connaissance.

RICHARDS, G. (1942), *Housman: 1897–1936.* New York: Oxford University Press.

SCUTENAIRE, L. (1945), René Magritte. *La terre n'est pas une valée de larmes.* Brussels: La Boetie, pp. 38–47.

SOBY, J. T. (1965), *René Magritte.* New York: Doubleday.

SYLVESTER, D. (1969), *René Magritte.* New York: Praeger.

SYMONS, K. E. (1937), Boyhood. In: *A. E. Housman: Recollections,* by Katharine E. Symons et al. New York: Henry Holt, pp. 3–38.

WALDBERG, P. (1965), *René Magritte.* Brussels: André de Roche.

WITHERS, P. (1940), *A Buried Life: Personal Recollections of A. E. Housman.* London: Jonathan Cape.

WOLFENSTEIN, M. (1956), Analysis of a Juvenile Poem. *This Annual,* 11:450–470.

—— (1966), How Is Mourning Possible? *This Annual,* 21:93–123.

—— (1969), Loss, Rage, and Repetition. *This Annual,* 24:432–460.

Index

Contents of Volumes 1–27